Kyle's Bed & Breakfast

Kyle's Bed & Breakfast

Greg Fox

KENSINGTON BOOKS
http://www.kensingtonbooks.com

For the readers of Kyle's Bed & Breakfast,
all around the world.
This is for YOU.
And for Jasmine . . . who once told me to not be
afraid to put my heart on the page.

KENSINGTON BOOKS are pubished by

Kensington Publishing Corp.
850 Third Avenue
New York, NY 10022

Copyright © 2004 by Greg Fox

All Kensington titles, imprints and distributed lines are available at special quantity discounts for bulk purchases for sales promotion, premiums, fund-raising, educational or institutional use.

Special book excerpts or customized printings can also be created to fit specific needs. For details, write or phone the office of the Kensington Special Sales Manager: Kensington Publishing Corp., 850 Third Avenue, New York, NY 10022. Attn. Special Sales Department. Phone: 1-800-221-2647.

Kensington and the K logo Reg. U.S. Pat. & TM Off.

ISBN 0-7582-0693-3

First Kensington Trade Paperback Printing: September 2004
10 9 8 7 6 5 4 3 2 1

Printed in the United States of America

Kyle's B & Beginnings

(Or, how this whole thing got off the ground in the first place !!!)*

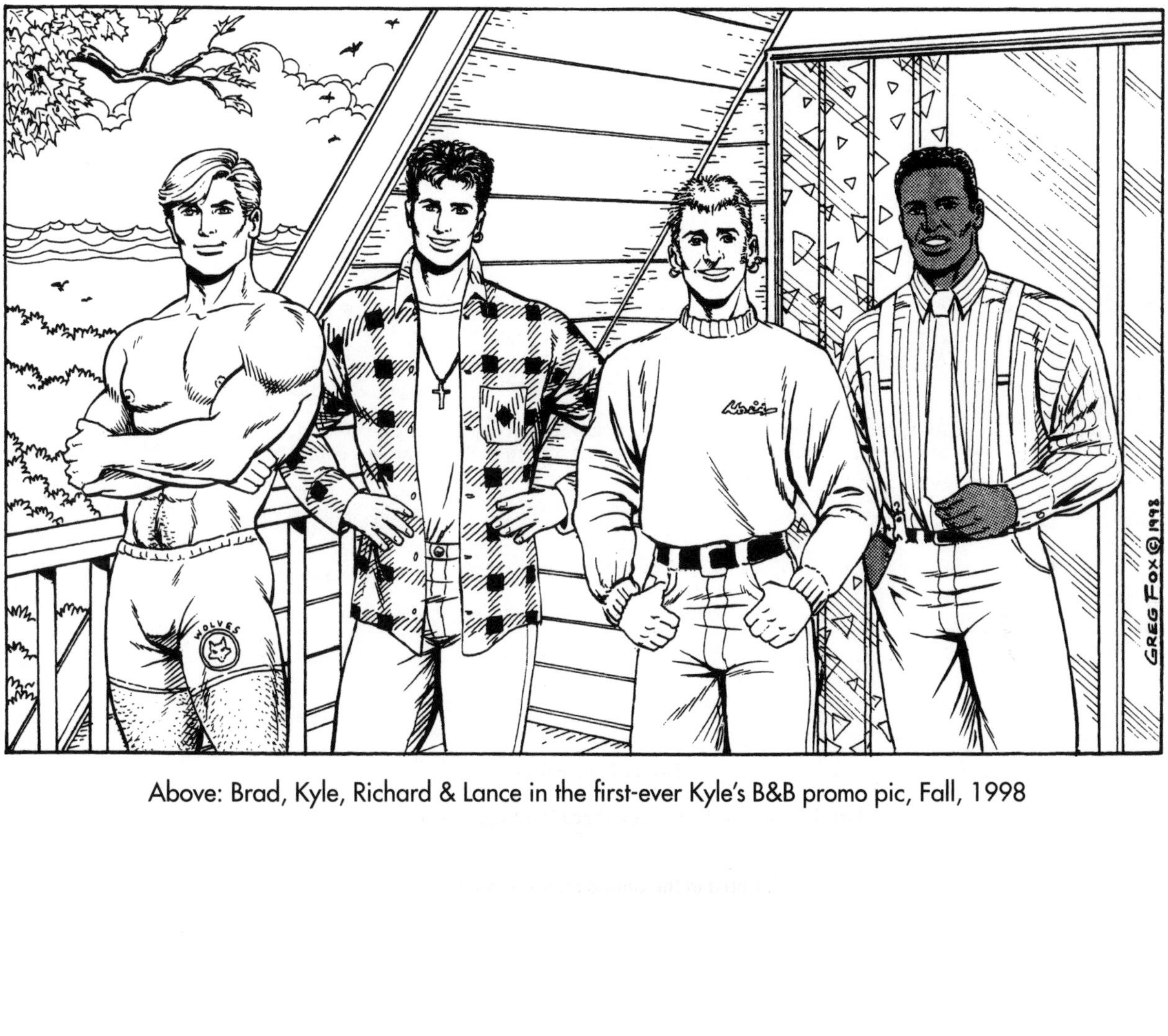
WOLVES
GREG FOX © 1998

Above: Brad, Kyle, Richard & Lance in the first-ever Kyle's B&B promo pic, Fall, 1998

* You might want to skip ahead about 13 pages and go directly to the comic strips themselves, and save this part for **after** you've read through the episodes. Or you can read this first . . . it's up to you! Hey, **you** bought the book . . . you're in charge here! But personally, I like to read these sorts of "behind the scenes" type things **after** I've seen what it's all about. But that's just me!

[illegible]
Marvel, I ended up drawing [illegible] band
biography comics for about a year and
a half. As I like to describe them now,

It all started with those damn baseball players.

Well, sort of.

It was the early 1990s. I was at somewhat of a crossroads, having quit my day job a year earlier to go full-time on the rather roller-coaster-like career path of a comic book artist. This was actually something I'd dreamed about doing since I was 12 years old. And here I was, doing it and getting paid for it, (usually). Granted, I was not exactly drawing the sort of comic books I'd dreamed about when I was 12. I'd wanted to draw **Justice League of America, Green Lantern, Legion of Superheroes.** Instead, there I was, several years after graduating college, drawing a monthly comic book called **Baseball Superstars,** a *baseball player* biography comic. How . . . *exciting.*

In the comic book world, "biography comics" were not exactly considered the most prestigious form of comic book art. When I was first trying to break into the biz, in late 1989, there was a brand new, somewhat radical comic book making a small buzz called **Rock n' Roll Comics.** It featured a different rock band biography in every issue, and got some brief press attention in magazines like **Rolling Stone** and **Spin.** My initial opinion on viewing several issues of it was that, well . . . it was a bit crude and amateurish, and the company that published it, **Revolutionary Comics,** was probably not a company ***I*** would ever want to work for.

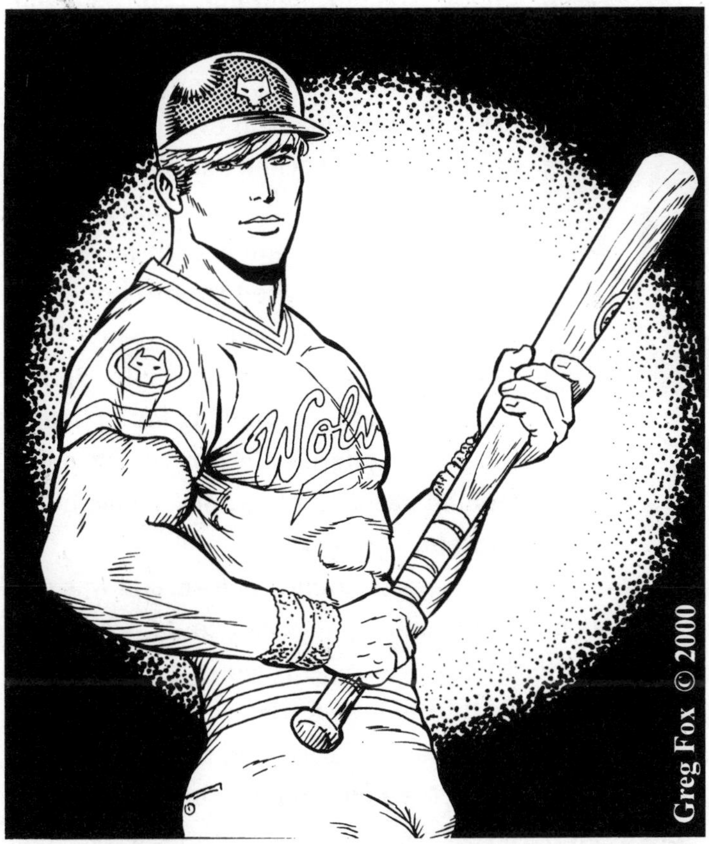
Greg Fox © 2000
Brad Steele, in all of his pec-tacular wonder. The guy around whom the **Kyle's Bed & Breakfast** comic strip was first built.

And then they offered me a job.

Not exactly having bucketfuls of success at breaking into **DC Comics** or **Marvel,** I ended up drawing rock band biography comics for about a year and a half. As I like to describe them now, they were sort of a **VH1 "Behind the Music"** in comic book form. I certainly *was* qualified for it; just prior to getting the **Rock n' Roll Comics** job, I was writing and drawing a comic strip called **Manic Music,** which was running in a national music magazine, about a bunch of rock musicians working in a music

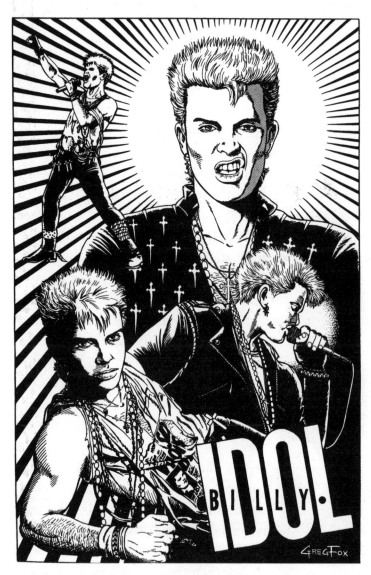
Drawn during my **Rock n' Roll Comics** days, circa 1991

store, (based on my own rock band and music store retail experience . . . yeah, that was the job I quit to draw comic books full time!). I knew how to draw guitars, amps, onstage scenes, rock n' roll people . . . and make it look authentic and believable. Anyway, I figured, if I could do a spectacular job drawing these rock band biography comic books, perhaps **DC** or **Marvel** would take notice, and they'd hire me. That didn't happen, (well, actually it sort of did . . . but more on that later). So I spent a couple of interesting years profiling various famous rock bands and solo artists in comic book style, (including Led Zeppelin, David Bowie, Van Halen, the Cure, KISS, Aerosmith, Poison, Living Color, the Doors, Madonna, and even Vanilla Ice!). But eventually, when I started getting a little antsy that the rock band biography comics were not exactly advancing my career, I switched over to drawing a new title for the same company. They were looking to branch into sports comics, and I was looking for a change, so I was offered the previously mentioned baseball biography comic book, **Baseball Superstars.**

Here, I was charting some new territory. I'd never seen any sports comics before, so I was creating the genre as I went along. I tried to bring in as much dynamic quality as I could, while also retaining true-to-life likenesses of the baseball players I was drawing. Previously, when I was drawing the **Rock n' Roll Comics** biographies, I would tend to immerse myself in the music of whatever band I happened to be drawing, listening to all the music of the band in question during my hours at the drawing board. (Great while I was drawing the **Led Zeppelin** biography; a little tedious when I was drawing the **Whitesnake** one.) To really get a solid feel for the baseball world, I applied this same philosophy; I basically ate, drank, and slept baseball for about a year. So immersed did I become in this baseball world, baseball ideas began making their way into my own comic strip writing. And one idea that particularly struck me was . . . what if there was a *gay*

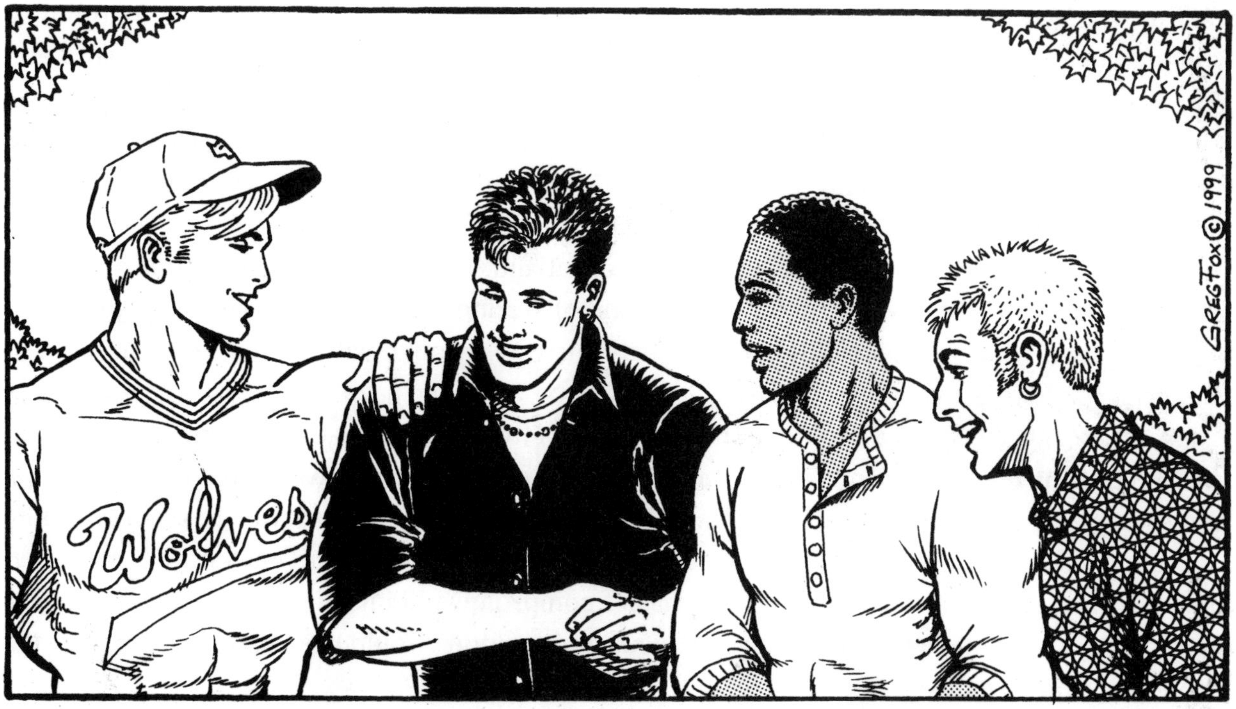
Wolves
GregFox © 1999

Brad, Kyle, Lance and Richard: an early promo pic of the strip, drawn during the first year of its run, 1998-99

professional baseball player? How on earth would he survive in this macho, intolerant, jock-snapping world of pro-baseball?

Of course, this was a full decade before ***Take Me Out***, the Broadway play, would explore this theme. Billy Bean, a major-league baseball player who came out publicly in 1999 after his retirement, was, at that point, still in the closet and playing pro-baseball. Without really thinking about it or having much to base it on, I put pen to paper and started writing some comic strips about a gay baseball player, and his trials & tribulations in the tough world of pro sports. I didn't really plan for it to be an ongoing project. . . . I didn't really have *any* plans for it, actually. I think it was initially more of a joke, a way to relieve the tension of all those hours spent at the drawing board, illustrating the oh-so-reverential biographies of heterosexual baseball players. But before long, I realized that I was suddenly writing the most exciting comic strips I'd ever written, all about a gay baseball player and his gay roommates living in this A-frame house by the harbor.

Though the concept started off as the story of Brad Steele, the aforementioned gay baseball player, it evolved rather quickly into the story of a diverse cast of gay men, with the baseball player being just one of the group. It felt as though I'd found the elusive element I'd been missing in all of my other comic strip writing. To be writing about *gay* characters was liberating, exciting, and overflowing with inspiration. It was *fun.* I *liked* these characters! And, to me, it was an untapped field. This was all *before* ***Will & Grace, Queer As Folk*** or any other gay TV shows had premiered. I hadn't seen all that much gay storytelling in any medium so far, and what little I *had* seen focused on rather narrow-minded, often negatively-portrayed gay stereotyped characters. Where was the diversity of characters, the warmth, the romance? The type of stories that *I* would want to read? I was eager to write about the gay community that *I* knew; the one that featured all kinds of guys . . . some macho, some effeminate, some in between . . . but all equally valid and worthy of respect.

In Brad, the closeted baseball player, I was able to draw upon several closeted, tough-guy jock-types I'd known over the years. . . . nice, but confused and frustrated guys who felt trapped in their circumstances and incapable of expressing their inner feelings.

In Richard, sort of the opposite end of the spectrum, I was able to show a fun and wise-cracking character who also has deep strength and blistering honesty. The type of gay guy who's been out since he was 4 years old and has fought his way through with humor and sheer determination.

For Lance, my original idea was a gay male version of the sort of over-the-top, corporate powerhouse type that Joan Collins on ***Dynasty*** and Heather Locklear on ***Melrose Place*** played so well. And there's certainly some aspects of that in his character, but I was also able to portray in him a proud, level-headed, no-nonsense gay man who's fought his way up the corporate ladder, perhaps not always playing nice, but who also hasn't compromised himself by hiding his sexual orientation. And someone whose brutal assessments and opinions would liven up many a discussion amongst his housemates.

Finally, there was Kyle. Actually, there was Steve . . . a character from my college newspaper comic strip **Wild Time,** who I thought would be the perfect leading man for this gay comic strip, a sort of hunky everyman with a nice sarcastic edge to his personality. However, when I was putting together *another* comic strip, called **An Angel's Story,** in early 1994, Steve *really* seemed like the right guy to play the human-who-becomes-an-angel lead character. (And he *was* the perfect choice for that character). So Steve was out, and I was stuck with casting a character who really had to be the anchoring point of this whole gay comic strip . . . sort of the glue that held the others together.

Instead of creating a clone of Steve, I went with Kyle. There *are* some similarities between the characters; there's a warmth and goodness to them, and a bit of a worldliness that comes from having lived through some wild years. They also both went to Geneseo College, (like me!), and are about the same age. But, where Steve was a rather confident

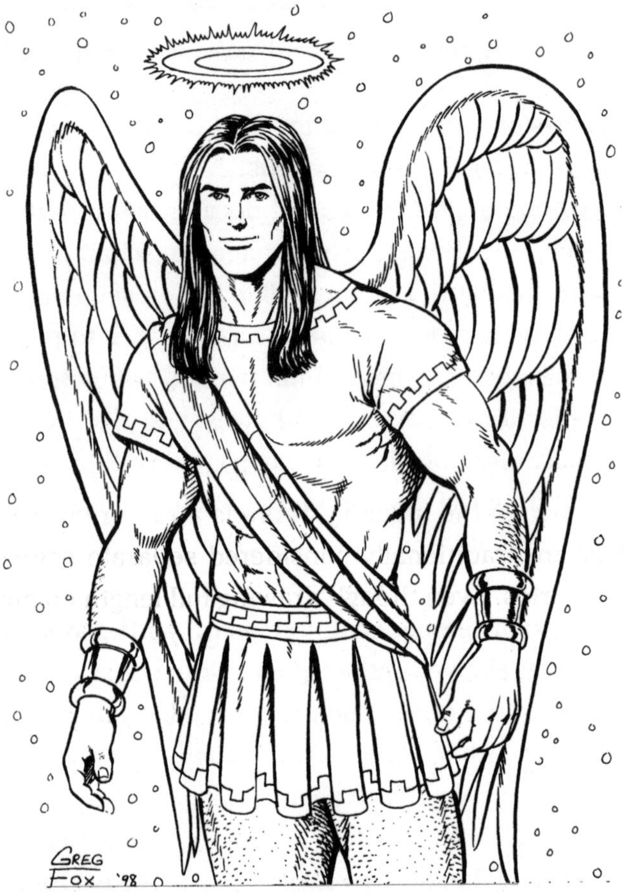
GREG FOX '98
The man who would've been Kyle: Steve Brewer, who instead got his own comic strip, **An Angel's Story**—possibly because he looks better in a skirt than Kyle does!

muscle guy with knockout good looks . . . the kind of guy people crash their shopping carts in supermarkets over, Kyle wasn't quite so confident about his own body. Tall, slim, attractive . . . but not a muscle boy, and more of a quiet, introspective type than Steve. And a few years older than the other guys in the B&B. A guy who's had some quality, (and not-so-quality), relationship experience, and who still believes in romance. What I found in writing Kyle was a way to channel some of the insecurities that many gay men feel, in a world that can be so superficial and judgmental. And also to show a character who rises above all of that and creates a warm, welcoming space for lost souls with his B&B.

And about that B&B . . . that idea came a little later. My original concept was to have these four guys just sharing a house together as housemates. The B&B idea really livened things up a bit and allowed me to bring in new characters on a regular basis. Some would stay, some would go and come back, and some we'd never hear from again. Kind of like real life. Most importantly, though, I wanted the B&B to have a sense of being a warm place, an inviting place. Not some circuit-party crash zone, but a welcoming place for all types of gay men, free of judgment and admission policies.

Finally, I wanted to set the strip in a real place, a real town . . . and what better place than the one I'm most familiar with: Northport, New York, my hometown. Located on the north shore of Long Island, (and part of the larger township of Huntington), Northport is one of those cute little New England-y harbor towns, with lots of boats, docks and seagulls. It was easy to incorporate many of the visuals I see here on a daily basis into the comic strip; the harbor with the tree-covered hills in the distance, often seen through the windows of Kyle's B&B, is the same view I see every day outside my own window. (And for everyone who e-mails me wondering what Northport actually looks like in real life, I suggest renting the movie *In & Out*, starring Kevin Kline and Tom Selleck, which was actually filmed here in Northport. Yes, the **gay** movie. What are the chances of both that movie and *another* gay-themed movie, *L.I.E. and* **Kyle's B&B** coming out of the same town . . . not to mention Walt Whitman? Must be something in the water!).

During the mid-1990s, I fleshed out the concept of the comic strip, put it through various incarnations, (full-length comic book, 4-panel humor strip, and other variations). I ought to say right here, within the industry, there is a rather clear division between comic *books* and comic *strips*. They are traditionally considered separate genres . . . although I always traversed between the two worlds. Even though drawing full length comic books was what I'd originally envisioned back in my 12-year old dreams, along the way I'd always been offered these fun comic strip jobs: in my high school paper, in my college paper, and right after I graduated college, with the **Manic Music** comic strip. So, when I began playing around with this gay B&B comic project, I wasn't sure which way to take it, as a comic strip or a full-length comic book series. For a while, during the development process, I wrote it in both formats to see which I preferred.

But I still wasn't quite sure what to *do* with it. I was trying to get my comic book artist career off the ground, and the idea of shopping around a *gay* comic on the side seemed, well, maybe not a smart thing to do. I have to confess, at the time I wasn't quite sure if I wanted to be so "out there" with my work. Back in 1992, **Marvel Comics** had introduced an "out" gay superhero, Northstar, (with the ensuing media reaction, you would've thought the Pope had come out of the

Wayne, Janine, and Danny, circa 1994: three of the main characters from Manic Music, my comic strip about rock-band and music-store life, which was my first professional comic strip after graduating college. It was also instrumental, (no pun intended), in landing me my first comic book job, with **Rock n' Roll Comics.** The comic strip ran all the while that I worked in the comic book industry, and for a couple of years after, too. In the late 1990s, it was briefly revived as **Rock the House**, with the characters now sharing a house together and making a stab at the big time with their rock band. But **Kyle's B&B** was beginning to take center stage, at that point, in my creative endeavors, and for the time being, for better or for worse, **Rock the House** is now officially . . . un-plugged.

closet.). Personally, I was excited the issue was finally being discussed in mainstream comics. But the overall impression I got, at the time, was that the mainstream comics companies were *very* nervous about tackling gay issues in any depth.

It sounds strange now, considering my current job, that prior to my baseball-comics-inspired gay comic strip, I'd given such little thought to the fact that gay people were practically invisible in most mainstream comic books. It hadn't really bothered me; in fact, it hadn't really *registered* with me. And I'd had little exposure to any gay comics at all; the one local gay magazine here on Long Island, which I saw infrequently, did not even have a comic strip. Luckily, Howard Cruse, the famous, pioneering, hugely-talented gay comics artist, always seemed to pop up at the same comic book conventions I was at. Through meeting him and seeing his work, I began to discover the rich history of gay comics. Over the years he's given me such wonderfully supportive advice, for which I am so very grateful. And then, a divinely-inspired meeting with Ivan Velez, Jr., creator of the spectacular gay comic book series **Tales From the Closet,** right around the time I was struggling with what to do with **Kyle's B&B,** gave me some much-needed encouragement to go forward with the comic strip.

After my tenure drawing **Baseball Superstars**, (and a brief return to **Rock n' Roll Comics**), I eventually moved up from drawing biography comics and had a fun year drawing an outer-space, mystical, other-universe book called **Doctor Chaos** for **Triumphant Comics.** I even got hired by **Marvel Comics** for a quickie eight-page story called **NFL Quarterback Club,** (yes, it was as ridiculously absurd as it sounds), a job I got largely due to my experience drawing sports biography comics, (it finally paid off). But at that point, I could not ignore this gay comic strip any longer. I kept coming back to the fact that I had *never* felt so strongly about any project I'd ever worked on before. It felt important . . . it felt vital . . . it felt fun . . . and it felt like where I needed to be.

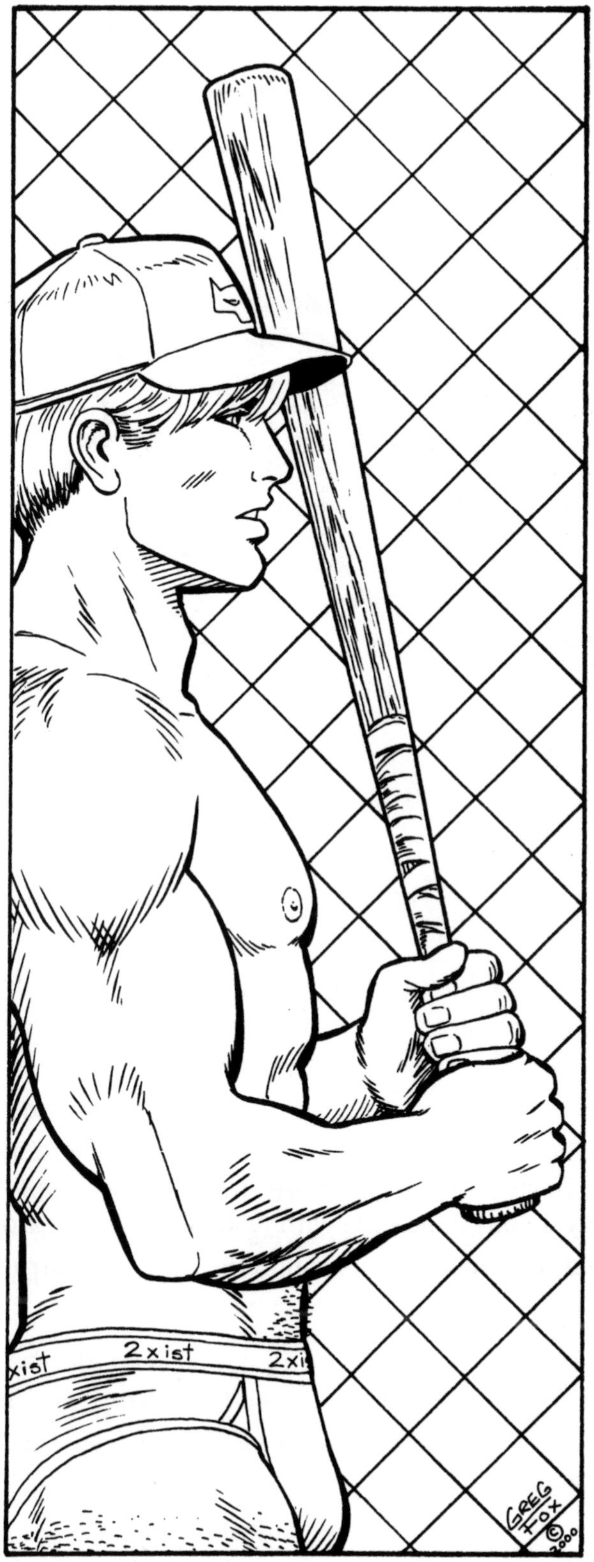
2xist
2xist
2xi
GREG FOX
©2000

Brad Steele of **Kyle's B&B**: he may be shy about coming out of the closet, but he doesn't seem to have any shyness about showing off his body!

I left the comic book industry around this time to focus on developing the as yet unnamed strip, (the working title was **"Housemates"**). Though I did continue writing and drawing the two comic strips that I had running in other magazines at the time.... the aforementioned **Manic Music** and **An Angel's Story,** about that hunky, gay-friendly angel named Steve, (which also happened to be my first published work to ever explore gay issues).

Kyle's Bed & Breakfast really "gelled" as a concept around mid-1996. I finally settled on the current nine to ten panel format, which really clicked with my writing style. But at that point, (1996-97), I was also thoroughly wrapped up in the **An Angel's Story** comic strip and the launch of **Manic Music's** "sequel" comic strip, **Rock the House.** Once again, I found myself in a situation where I had other comics keeping me from going forward with **Kyle's B&B.** Which is why it took until the Spring of 1998 to finally get the first five episodes of **Kyle's B&B** drawn up and ready to submit.

Summer of 1998 was all about sending the comic strip to every regional gay magazine I could find a listing for. I was hoping to self-syndicate it to some local gay publications around the country and see what happened. Unexpectedly, ***Genre*** magazine, (a national gay publication), called me and said, even though they didn't normally run comic strips, they'd like to run a few episodes. The strip premiered in **Genre** in their November, 1998 issue, (released right around Halloween). The following winter, 1999, the **Kyle's B&B** website premiered and immediately began drawing a rather devoted following around the world. And that spring, the strip was picked up by two great regional gay mags, on opposite coasts: ***Outlook-Long Island*** in New York, and ***The Orange County Blade*** in California. By the end of 1999, after several more

I LEAVE YOU NOW, CHAOS... BUT MARK MY WORDS...
...FOR PATHOS TO SURVIVE...THE CHILD MUST DIE!
NO...NO!!!
THERE MUST BE SOME OTHER WAY!!!

Two previously unpublished panels from **Doctor Chaos**, the grandly heroic, other-dimensional sci-fi comic book I drew for **Triumphant Comics** for a year (1993-94). At the time, I was itching to get started on **Kyle's B&B**, but now, I'm thankful for the year I spent doing **Doctor Chaos**, as it got the "super-hero bug" out of my system. Well, not completely . . . I'm still a big comic book freak.

magazines had picked up the strip, I made the bold leap to go from doing one new episode a month to doing the strip biweekly, (every other week).

I think I was unprepared, though wonderfully surprised, by how many people took this comic strip into their hearts. From the beginning, I was blessed to receive the most passionate e-mails from readers who really cared deeply about these characters. Surprisingly, not just from gay people, either. And more surprisingly, from all around the globe, not just in the USA and Canada. Sweden, Norway, Australia, Italy, France, Great Britain, Ireland, Germany, Belgium, the Netherlands, Iceland, Switzerland, the Czech Republic, Israel, South Africa, Peru, New Zealand, Singapore, Russia, Brazil, Japan, Mexico. . . . these are just some of the countries that have devoted readers of the strip who write me regularly to share their opinions on the storylines, the characters, or just to say "hi."

Interestingly, I get more than a few e-mails from people who somehow think this is a *real* B&B, and they'd like to make reservations, and to meet the characters in person. Well, who am I to argue? It's as "real" as you want it to be! (Afraid I cannot take your reservations, though . . . but I *can* suggest some nice alternate locations in the Northport area.)

Which brings us to this, the first collected edition of **Kyle's Bed & Breakfast.** One of the most often-asked questions I get from readers of the strip is, "Where can I see the early episodes, to see how this all started?" Or, "When is a book coming out, with all the strips in one volume?" Well, I'm happy, (and relieved!), that I'll be able to answer those questions now by directing them to this book! Contained within this volume are the first five years of **Kyle's B&B** episodes, starting in October 1998 through October 2003, (look for the © symbol within each episode to determine what year any particular episode is from. You may notice the website address at the bottom of each episode changes about halfway through the book—that's when I got what is the current website address, **www.kylecomics.com**). Also in this book is a little added extras: a brand new, never-before-published two-page mini story; some other **Kyle's B&B** artwork from over the years; as well as the often asked for, never-before-seen, blueprints of the actual floor plan of the **Kyle's B&B** house! So now, you can *finally* see how all those rooms are laid out, and just what lays down that hallway or up those stairs!

People often ask what the future holds in store for these characters . . . whether I'm ever going to end the strip, how I feel about new stories and such. Well, folks, it feels to me like I'm just getting started here. I have *plenty* of stories to tell with these characters, and some rather interesting new characters to introduce into the mix, waiting in the wings. God willing, I hope to be doing this for many, many years to come. No, I'm not itching to move on to some other project. Are you kidding me? This is the best job in the world. Thank you for being a part of it, and for helping to make it happen!

Excelsior!!!

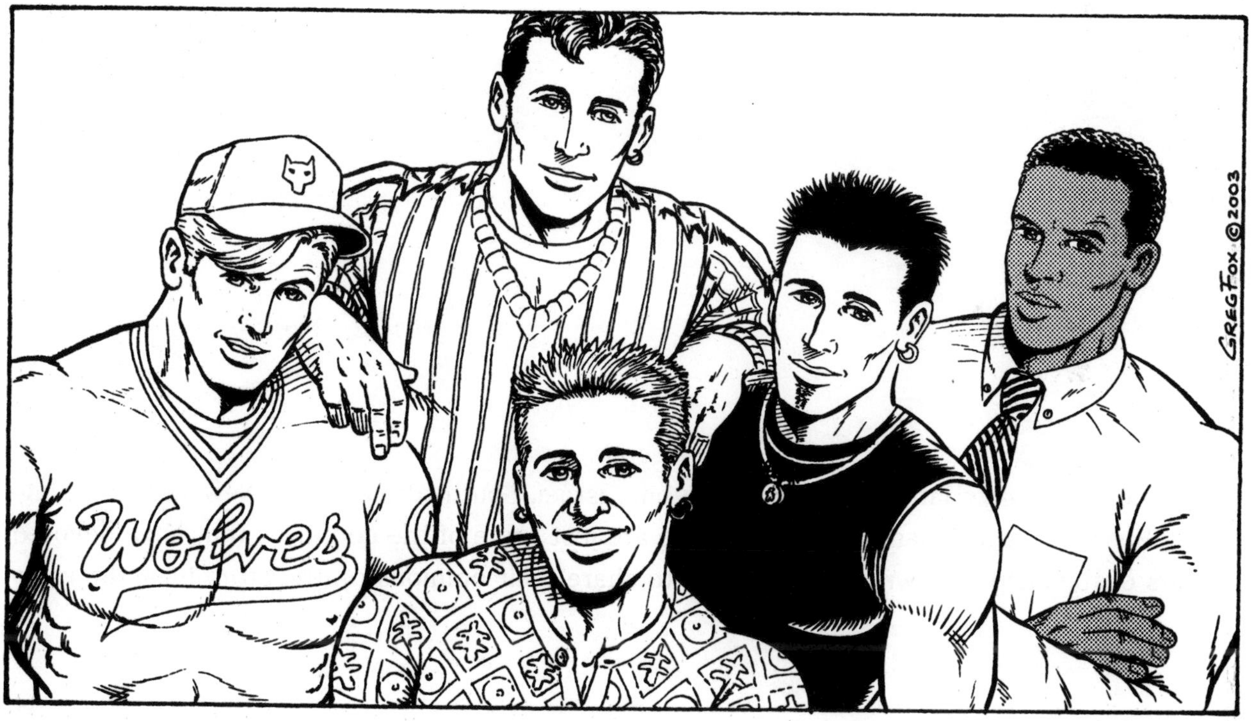
Wolves
GREGFOX ©2003

The Episodes

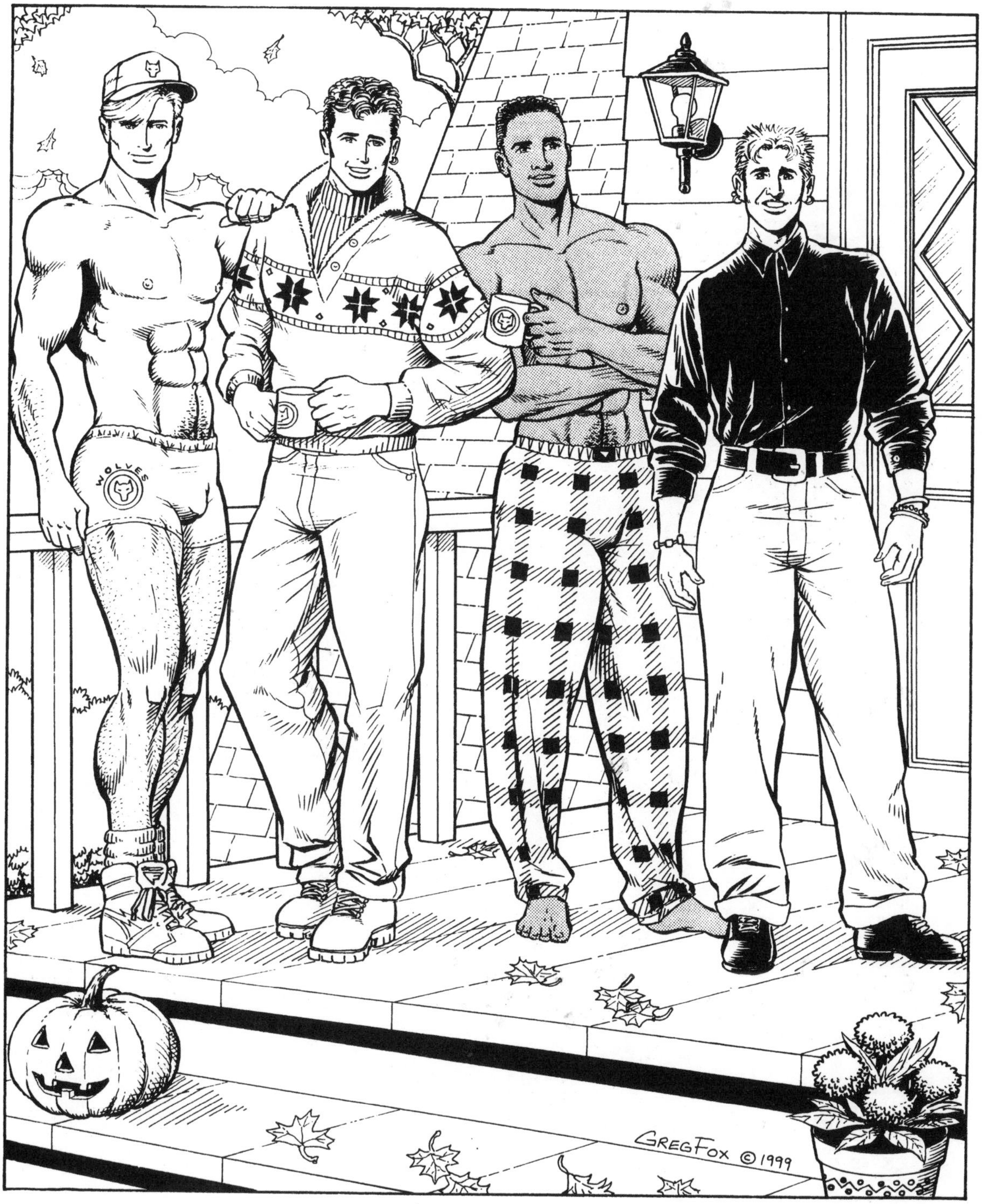
WOLVES
GREGFOX ©1999

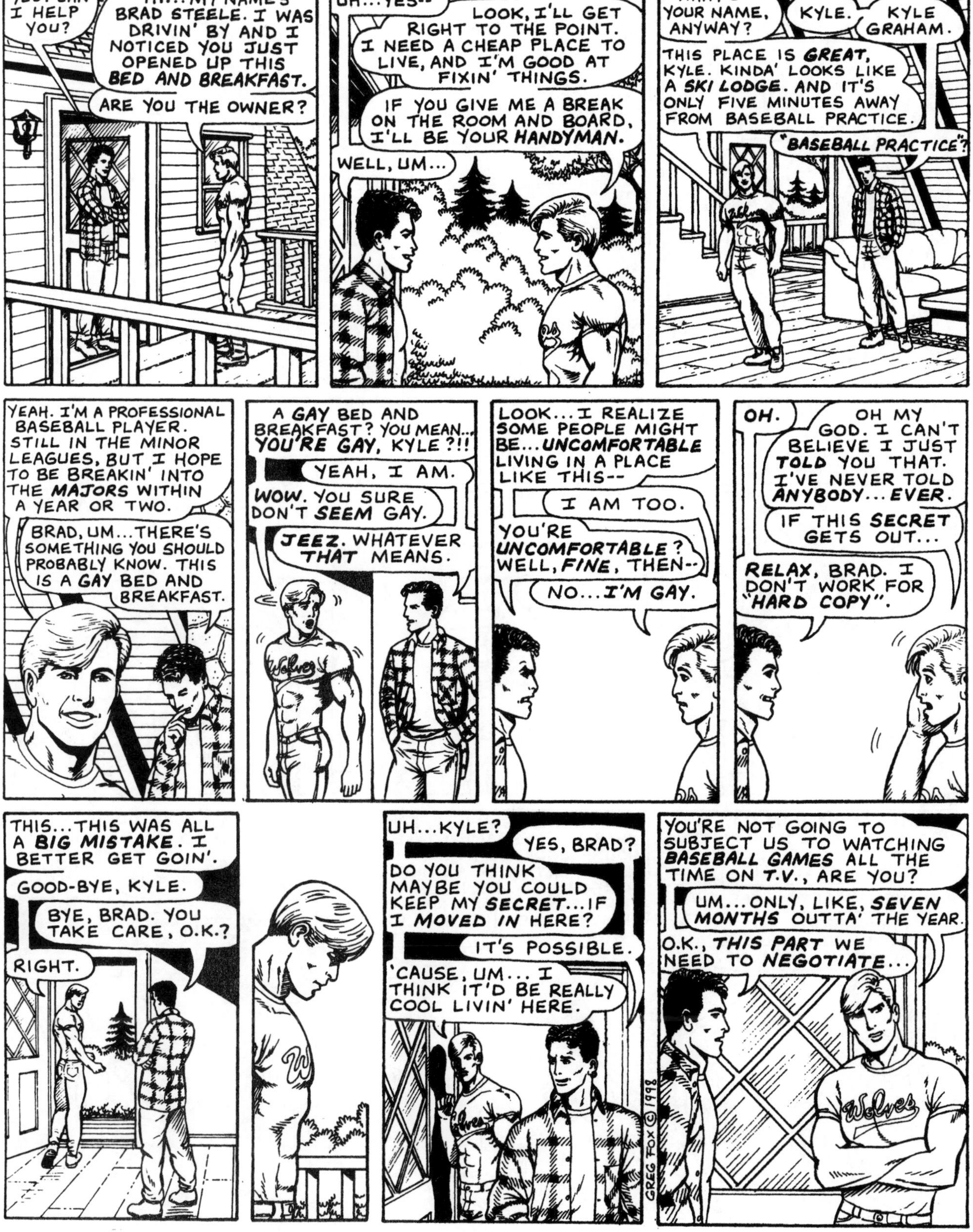
YES? CAN I HELP YOU?
HI... MY NAME'S BRAD STEELE. I WAS DRIVIN' BY AND I NOTICED YOU JUST OPENED UP THIS BED AND BREAKFAST.
ARE YOU THE OWNER?
UH... YES--
LOOK, I'LL GET RIGHT TO THE POINT. I NEED A CHEAP PLACE TO LIVE, AND I'M GOOD AT FIXIN' THINGS.
IF YOU GIVE ME A BREAK ON THE ROOM AND BOARD, I'LL BE YOUR HANDYMAN.
WELL, UM...
WHAT'S YOUR NAME, ANYWAY?
KYLE.
KYLE GRAHAM.
THIS PLACE IS GREAT, KYLE. KINDA' LOOKS LIKE A SKI LODGE. AND IT'S ONLY FIVE MINUTES AWAY FROM BASEBALL PRACTICE.
"BASEBALL PRACTICE"?
YEAH. I'M A PROFESSIONAL BASEBALL PLAYER. STILL IN THE MINOR LEAGUES, BUT I HOPE TO BE BREAKIN' INTO THE MAJORS WITHIN A YEAR OR TWO.
BRAD, UM... THERE'S SOMETHING YOU SHOULD PROBABLY KNOW. THIS IS A GAY BED AND BREAKFAST.
A GAY BED AND BREAKFAST? YOU MEAN... YOU'RE GAY, KYLE?!!
YEAH, I AM.
WOW. YOU SURE DON'T SEEM GAY.
JEEZ. WHATEVER THAT MEANS.
LOOK... I REALIZE SOME PEOPLE MIGHT BE... UNCOMFORTABLE LIVING IN A PLACE LIKE THIS--
I AM TOO.
YOU'RE UNCOMFORTABLE? WELL, FINE, THEN--
NO... I'M GAY.
OH.
OH MY GOD. I CAN'T BELIEVE I JUST TOLD YOU THAT. I'VE NEVER TOLD ANYBODY... EVER.
IF THIS SECRET GETS OUT...
RELAX, BRAD. I DON'T WORK FOR "HARD COPY".
THIS... THIS WAS ALL A BIG MISTAKE. I BETTER GET GOIN'.
GOOD-BYE, KYLE.
BYE, BRAD. YOU TAKE CARE, O.K.?
RIGHT.
UH... KYLE?
YES, BRAD?
DO YOU THINK MAYBE YOU COULD KEEP MY SECRET... IF I MOVED IN HERE?
IT'S POSSIBLE.
'CAUSE, UM... I THINK IT'D BE REALLY COOL LIVIN' HERE.
GREG FOX © 1998
YOU'RE NOT GOING TO SUBJECT US TO WATCHING BASEBALL GAMES ALL THE TIME ON T.V., ARE YOU?
UM... ONLY, LIKE, SEVEN MONTHS OUTTA' THE YEAR.
O.K., THIS PART WE NEED TO NEGOTIATE...

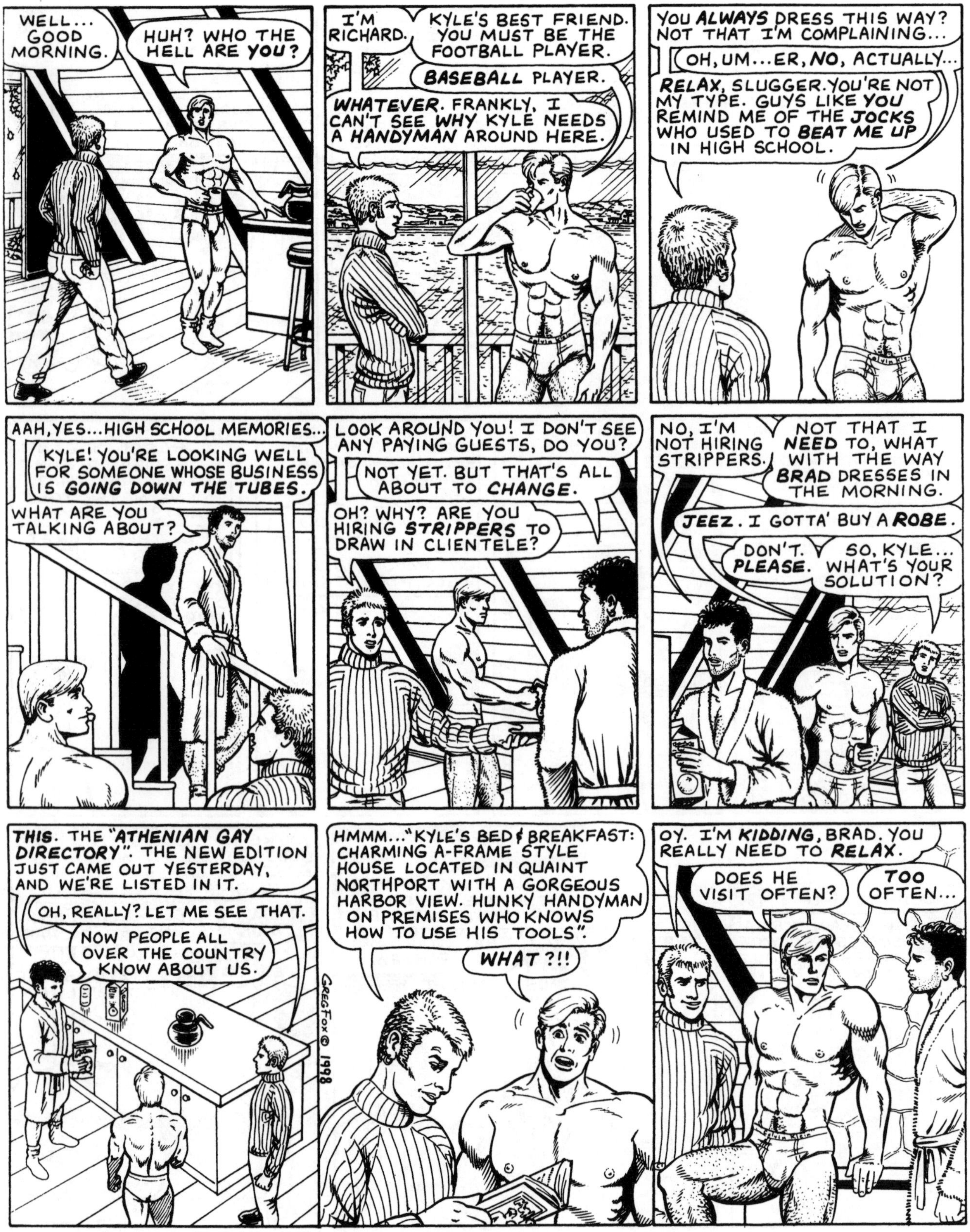
WELL... GOOD MORNING.
HUH? WHO THE HELL ARE YOU?
I'M RICHARD.
KYLE'S BEST FRIEND. YOU MUST BE THE FOOTBALL PLAYER.
BASEBALL PLAYER.
WHATEVER. FRANKLY, I CAN'T SEE WHY KYLE NEEDS A HANDYMAN AROUND HERE.
YOU ALWAYS DRESS THIS WAY? NOT THAT I'M COMPLAINING...
OH, UM...ER, NO, ACTUALLY...
RELAX, SLUGGER. YOU'RE NOT MY TYPE. GUYS LIKE YOU REMIND ME OF THE JOCKS WHO USED TO BEAT ME UP IN HIGH SCHOOL.
AAH, YES...HIGH SCHOOL MEMORIES...
KYLE! YOU'RE LOOKING WELL FOR SOMEONE WHOSE BUSINESS IS GOING DOWN THE TUBES.
WHAT ARE YOU TALKING ABOUT?
LOOK AROUND YOU! I DON'T SEE ANY PAYING GUESTS, DO YOU?
NOT YET. BUT THAT'S ALL ABOUT TO CHANGE.
OH? WHY? ARE YOU HIRING STRIPPERS TO DRAW IN CLIENTELE?
NO, I'M NOT HIRING STRIPPERS.
NOT THAT I NEED TO, WHAT WITH THE WAY BRAD DRESSES IN THE MORNING.
JEEZ. I GOTTA' BUY A ROBE.
DON'T. PLEASE.
SO, KYLE... WHAT'S YOUR SOLUTION?
THIS. THE "ATHENIAN GAY DIRECTORY". THE NEW EDITION JUST CAME OUT YESTERDAY, AND WE'RE LISTED IN IT.
OH, REALLY? LET ME SEE THAT.
NOW PEOPLE ALL OVER THE COUNTRY KNOW ABOUT US.
GREGFOX © 1998
HMMM..."KYLE'S BED & BREAKFAST: CHARMING A-FRAME STYLE HOUSE LOCATED IN QUAINT NORTHPORT WITH A GORGEOUS HARBOR VIEW. HUNKY HANDYMAN ON PREMISES WHO KNOWS HOW TO USE HIS TOOLS".
WHAT?!!
OY. I'M KIDDING, BRAD. YOU REALLY NEED TO RELAX.
DOES HE VISIT OFTEN?
TOO OFTEN...

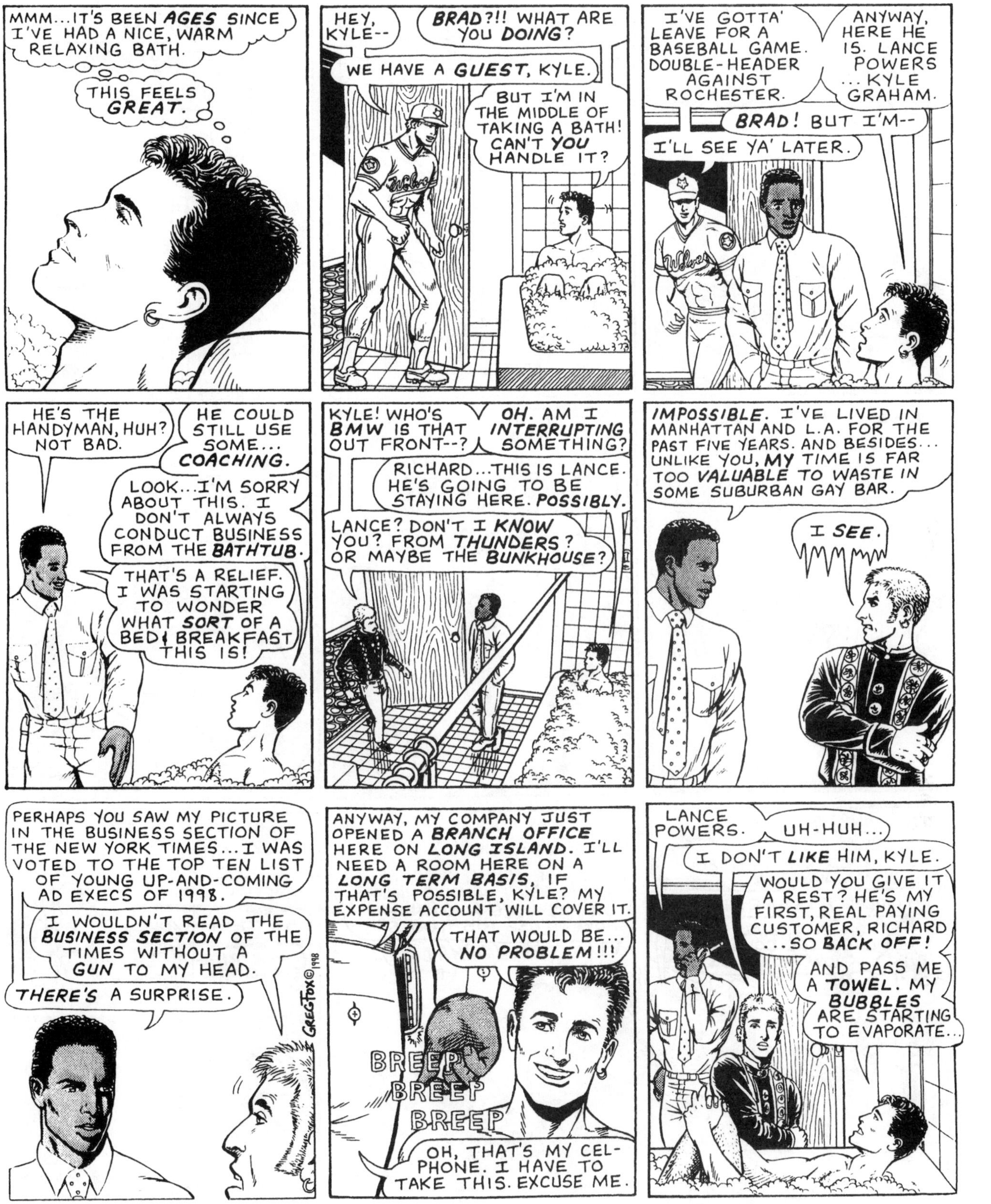
MMM...IT'S BEEN AGES SINCE I'VE HAD A NICE, WARM RELAXING BATH.
THIS FEELS GREAT.
HEY, KYLE--
BRAD?!! WHAT ARE YOU DOING?
WE HAVE A GUEST, KYLE.
BUT I'M IN THE MIDDLE OF TAKING A BATH! CAN'T YOU HANDLE IT?
I'VE GOTTA' LEAVE FOR A BASEBALL GAME. DOUBLE-HEADER AGAINST ROCHESTER.
ANYWAY, HERE HE IS. LANCE POWERS ...KYLE GRAHAM.
BRAD! BUT I'M--
I'LL SEE YA' LATER.
HE'S THE HANDYMAN, HUH? NOT BAD.
HE COULD STILL USE SOME... COACHING.
LOOK...I'M SORRY ABOUT THIS. I DON'T ALWAYS CONDUCT BUSINESS FROM THE BATHTUB.
THAT'S A RELIEF. I WAS STARTING TO WONDER WHAT SORT OF A BED & BREAKFAST THIS IS!
KYLE! WHO'S BMW IS THAT OUT FRONT--?
OH. AM I INTERRUPTING SOMETHING?
RICHARD...THIS IS LANCE. HE'S GOING TO BE STAYING HERE. POSSIBLY.
LANCE? DON'T I KNOW YOU? FROM THUNDERS? OR MAYBE THE BUNKHOUSE?
IMPOSSIBLE. I'VE LIVED IN MANHATTAN AND L.A. FOR THE PAST FIVE YEARS. AND BESIDES... UNLIKE YOU, MY TIME IS FAR TOO VALUABLE TO WASTE IN SOME SUBURBAN GAY BAR.
I SEE.
PERHAPS YOU SAW MY PICTURE IN THE BUSINESS SECTION OF THE NEW YORK TIMES...I WAS VOTED TO THE TOP TEN LIST OF YOUNG UP-AND-COMING AD EXECS OF 1998.
I WOULDN'T READ THE BUSINESS SECTION OF THE TIMES WITHOUT A GUN TO MY HEAD.
THERE'S A SURPRISE.
GREG FOX © 1998
ANYWAY, MY COMPANY JUST OPENED A BRANCH OFFICE HERE ON LONG ISLAND. I'LL NEED A ROOM HERE ON A LONG TERM BASIS, IF THAT'S POSSIBLE, KYLE? MY EXPENSE ACCOUNT WILL COVER IT.
THAT WOULD BE... NO PROBLEM!!!
BREEP
BREEP
BREEP
OH, THAT'S MY CEL-PHONE. I HAVE TO TAKE THIS. EXCUSE ME.
LANCE POWERS.
UH-HUH...
I DON'T LIKE HIM, KYLE.
WOULD YOU GIVE IT A REST? HE'S MY FIRST, REAL PAYING CUSTOMER, RICHARD ...SO BACK OFF!
AND PASS ME A TOWEL. MY BUBBLES ARE STARTING TO EVAPORATE...

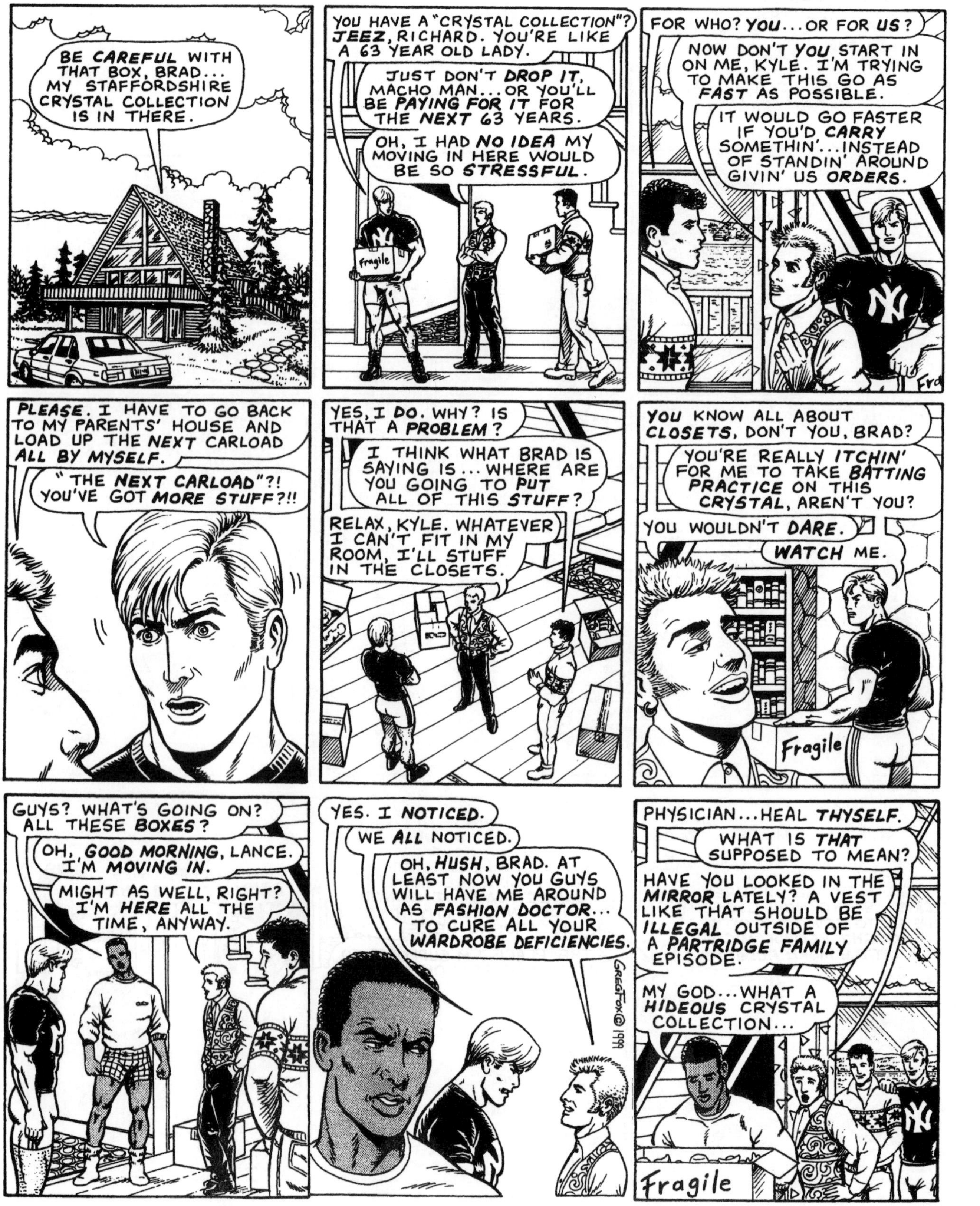
BE CAREFUL WITH THAT BOX, BRAD... MY STAFFORDSHIRE CRYSTAL COLLECTION IS IN THERE.
YOU HAVE A "CRYSTAL COLLECTION"? JEEZ, RICHARD. YOU'RE LIKE A 63 YEAR OLD LADY.
JUST DON'T DROP IT, MACHO MAN... OR YOU'LL BE PAYING FOR IT FOR THE NEXT 63 YEARS.
OH, I HAD NO IDEA MY MOVING IN HERE WOULD BE SO STRESSFUL.
Fragile
FOR WHO? YOU... OR FOR US?
NOW DON'T YOU START IN ON ME, KYLE. I'M TRYING TO MAKE THIS GO AS FAST AS POSSIBLE.
IT WOULD GO FASTER IF YOU'D CARRY SOMETHIN'... INSTEAD OF STANDIN' AROUND GIVIN' US ORDERS.
PLEASE. I HAVE TO GO BACK TO MY PARENTS' HOUSE AND LOAD UP THE NEXT CARLOAD ALL BY MYSELF.
"THE NEXT CARLOAD"?! YOU'VE GOT MORE STUFF?!!
YES, I DO. WHY? IS THAT A PROBLEM?
I THINK WHAT BRAD IS SAYING IS... WHERE ARE YOU GOING TO PUT ALL OF THIS STUFF?
RELAX, KYLE. WHATEVER I CAN'T FIT IN MY ROOM, I'LL STUFF IN THE CLOSETS.
YOU KNOW ALL ABOUT CLOSETS, DON'T YOU, BRAD?
YOU'RE REALLY ITCHIN' FOR ME TO TAKE BATTING PRACTICE ON THIS CRYSTAL, AREN'T YOU?
YOU WOULDN'T DARE.
WATCH ME.
Fragile
GUYS? WHAT'S GOING ON? ALL THESE BOXES?
OH, GOOD MORNING, LANCE. I'M MOVING IN.
MIGHT AS WELL, RIGHT? I'M HERE ALL THE TIME, ANYWAY.
YES. I NOTICED.
WE ALL NOTICED.
OH, HUSH, BRAD. AT LEAST NOW YOU GUYS WILL HAVE ME AROUND AS FASHION DOCTOR... TO CURE ALL YOUR WARDROBE DEFICIENCIES.
GREGFOX © 1999
PHYSICIAN... HEAL THYSELF.
WHAT IS THAT SUPPOSED TO MEAN?
HAVE YOU LOOKED IN THE MIRROR LATELY? A VEST LIKE THAT SHOULD BE ILLEGAL OUTSIDE OF A PARTRIDGE FAMILY EPISODE.
MY GOD... WHAT A HIDEOUS CRYSTAL COLLECTION...
Fragile

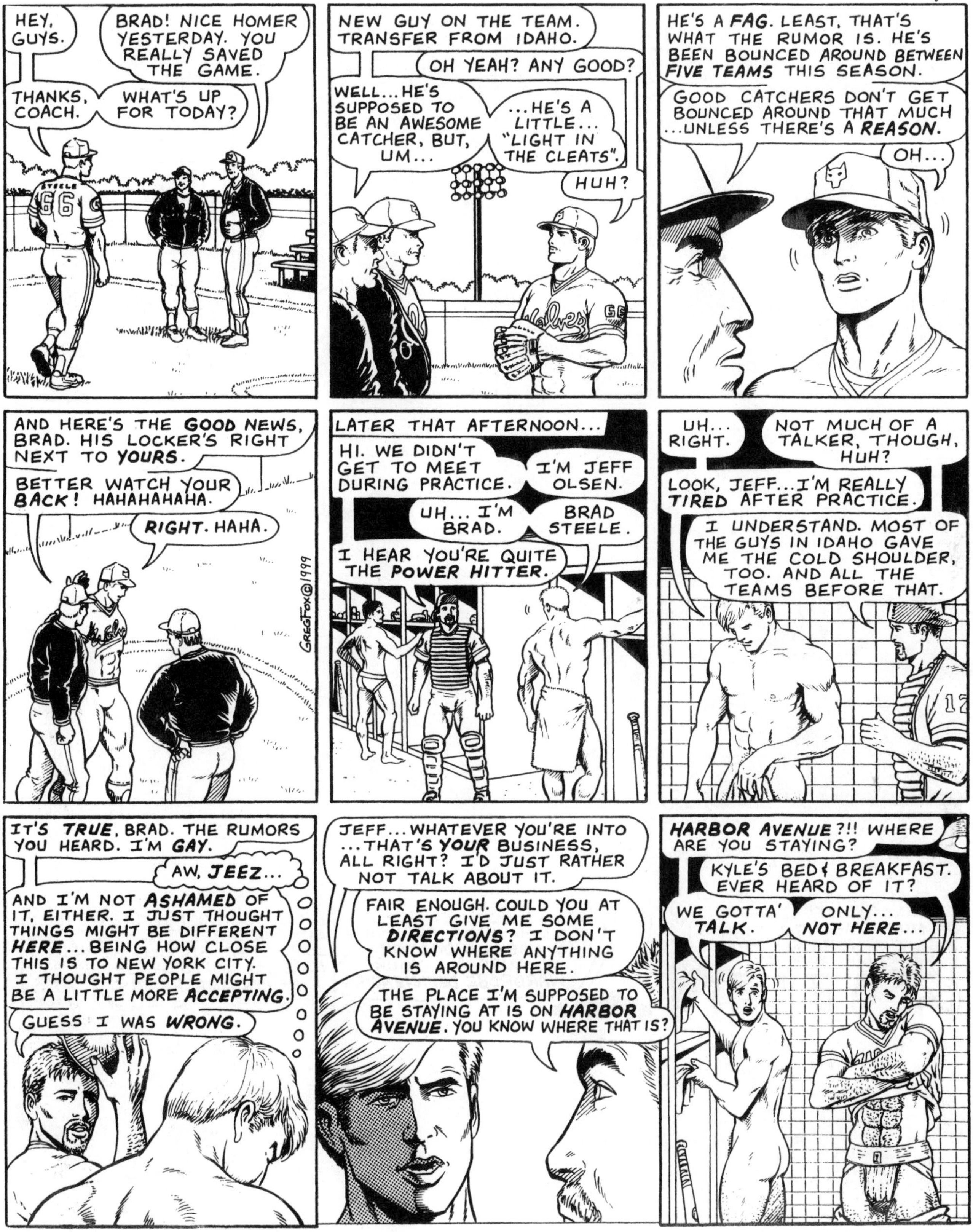
HEY, GUYS.
BRAD! NICE HOMER YESTERDAY. YOU REALLY SAVED THE GAME.
THANKS, COACH.
WHAT'S UP FOR TODAY?
NEW GUY ON THE TEAM. TRANSFER FROM IDAHO.
OH YEAH? ANY GOOD?
WELL... HE'S SUPPOSED TO BE AN AWESOME CATCHER, BUT, UM...
...HE'S A LITTLE... "LIGHT IN THE CLEATS".
HUH?
HE'S A FAG. LEAST, THAT'S WHAT THE RUMOR IS. HE'S BEEN BOUNCED AROUND BETWEEN FIVE TEAMS THIS SEASON.
GOOD CATCHERS DON'T GET BOUNCED AROUND THAT MUCH ...UNLESS THERE'S A REASON.
OH...
AND HERE'S THE GOOD NEWS, BRAD. HIS LOCKER'S RIGHT NEXT TO YOURS.
BETTER WATCH YOUR BACK! HAHAHAHAHA.
RIGHT. HAHA.
GREGFOX©1999
LATER THAT AFTERNOON...
HI. WE DIDN'T GET TO MEET DURING PRACTICE.
I'M JEFF OLSEN.
UH... I'M BRAD.
BRAD STEELE.
I HEAR YOU'RE QUITE THE POWER HITTER.
UH... RIGHT.
NOT MUCH OF A TALKER, THOUGH, HUH?
LOOK, JEFF... I'M REALLY TIRED AFTER PRACTICE.
I UNDERSTAND. MOST OF THE GUYS IN IDAHO GAVE ME THE COLD SHOULDER, TOO. AND ALL THE TEAMS BEFORE THAT.
IT'S TRUE, BRAD. THE RUMORS YOU HEARD. I'M GAY.
AW, JEEZ...
AND I'M NOT ASHAMED OF IT, EITHER. I JUST THOUGHT THINGS MIGHT BE DIFFERENT HERE... BEING HOW CLOSE THIS IS TO NEW YORK CITY. I THOUGHT PEOPLE MIGHT BE A LITTLE MORE ACCEPTING.
GUESS I WAS WRONG.
JEFF... WHATEVER YOU'RE INTO ...THAT'S YOUR BUSINESS, ALL RIGHT? I'D JUST RATHER NOT TALK ABOUT IT.
FAIR ENOUGH. COULD YOU AT LEAST GIVE ME SOME DIRECTIONS? I DON'T KNOW WHERE ANYTHING IS AROUND HERE.
THE PLACE I'M SUPPOSED TO BE STAYING AT IS ON HARBOR AVENUE. YOU KNOW WHERE THAT IS?
HARBOR AVENUE?!! WHERE ARE YOU STAYING?
KYLE'S BED & BREAKFAST. EVER HEARD OF IT?
WE GOTTA' TALK.
ONLY... NOT HERE...

...AND BREAKFAST IS SERVED BETWEEN 7 AND 9 EVERY MORNING.

SOUNDS GOOD, KYLE.

HEY, BRAD.

OH, UH... HI, KYLE.

I ASSUME YOU TWO HAVE ALREADY MET?

YEAH. WE MET.

KYLE WAS JUST SHOWING ME AROUND, BRAD. IT'S A NICE HOUSE.

YEAH, IT'S GREAT.

UH, LOOK... I GOTTA' RUN. I GOT SOME... LAUNDRY TO DO.

BRAD, YOU CAN RELAX. I'M NOT GOING TO TELL ANYONE ON THE TEAM THAT YOU'RE GAY.

JUST BECAUSE I'M OUT, I DON'T EXPECT THAT OF EVERYONE ELSE.

YOU'RE A REAL HERO, JEFF. CONGRATULATIONS.

WHAT'S WITH THE ATTITUDE?

UM... MAYBE I'D BETTER LEAVE YOU TWO ALONE...

NO, KYLE. I WANT YOU TO BACK ME UP ON THIS.

BACK YOU UP? ON WHAT? YOU'RE STARTING TO SOUND LIKE A REAL JERK, BRAD.

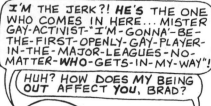

I'M THE JERK?! HE'S THE ONE WHO COMES IN HERE... MISTER GAY-ACTIVIST-"I'M-GONNA'-BE-THE-FIRST-OPENLY-GAY-PLAYER-IN-THE-MAJOR-LEAGUES-NO-MATTER-WHO-GETS-IN-MY-WAY"!

HUH? HOW DOES MY BEING OUT AFFECT YOU, BRAD?

LOOK...IT'S HARD ENOUGH FOR ME BEING IN THE CLOSET ON A MINOR LEAGUE BASEBALL TEAM.

NOW YOU SHOW UP AND EVERYBODY ON THE TEAM IS TALKIN' ABOUT GAY THIS AND GAY THAT 'CAUSE YOU'RE SHOVIN' IT IN EVERYONE'S FACES.

YOU HAVE ANY IDEA WHAT IT'S LIKE FOR ME?!

BRAD, FIRST OF ALL, I'M NOT "SHOVING IT IN EVERYONE'S FACES". I DON'T HIDE THAT I'M GAY, BUT I DON'T MAKE AN ISSUE OUT OF IT, EITHER. IT'S EVERYONE ELSE WHO DOES THAT.

AND SECOND OF ALL, IF MY BEING OUT MAKES IT A LITTLE LESS COMFORTABLE FOR YOU TO BE IN THE CLOSET, WELL... TOUGH. THAT'S THE PRICE YOU PAY FOR BEING A CLOSET CASE.

WHO ARE YOU CALLIN' A CLOSET CASE?!!

GUYS!!! THAT'S ENOUGH!

FINE. I HAVE TO GO, ANYWAY.

JUST STAY OUTTA' MY WAY, OLSEN.

NO PROBLEM.

SLAM

SO, UH...I GUESS THE TWO OF YOU WON'T BE CARPOOLING TO BASEBALL PRACTICE?

NOT LIKELY...

© GREG FOX 1999

HEY, BRAD...THE YANKEE GAME'S ABOUT TO START. WANT TO WATCH?

NO THANKS. I'M GOIN' FOR A JOG AT SUNKEN MEADOW.

AND BY THE WAY... QUIT ACTIN' LIKE WE'RE BUDDIES, OLSEN. 'CAUSE WE AIN'T!

NICE TRY.

OH...HEY, KYLE. YOU OVERHEARD, HUH?

HOW ABOUT YOU? CARE TO JOIN ME?

I'LL WATCH A FEW INNINGS. BUT I'M SURE BRAD WOULD ENJOY THIS MORE THAN I WILL.

WITH ME HERE? I DON'T THINK SO. I'M NOT SURPRISED HE DUCKED OUT.

I DON'T GET IT, JEFF. IT SEEMS LIKE YOU TWO SHOULD REALLY HIT IT OFF.

WHY? BECAUSE WE'RE BOTH GAY AND WE'RE BOTH PROFESSIONAL BASEBALL PLAYERS?

WELL...YEAH. I MEAN...HOW OFTEN DO YOU GET A CHANCE TO MEET OTHER GAY PLAYERS?

NOT OFTEN. BUT THE FACT THAT I'M OUT OF THE CLOSET AND BRAD'S NOT, WELL... IT'S NOT A GOOD MIX.

BESIDES...I'VE TRIED TO BE FRIENDS WITH HIM. HE'S THE ONE WITH THE PROBLEM.

I SUPPOSE. STILL--

KYLE...I DON'T WANT TO TALK ABOUT BRAD AND ME. I WANT TO TALK ABOUT US.

"US"? WHAT ABOUT "US"?

EXACTLY. WHAT ABOUT US?

GREGFOX©1999

JEFF... UM...

YOU KNOW I'VE BEEN ATTRACTED TO YOU SINCE THE DAY I MOVED IN HERE. AND I THINK MAYBE YOU LIKE ME, TOO.

JEFF...HOW OLD ARE YOU? 22? 23?

21.

JEEZ. MAYBE IF I WAS FIVE...OR TEN YEARS YOUNGER...

WHAT'S THE BIG DEAL? YOU CAN'T BE OLDER THAN 28 OR 29.

BOY, ALL THAT SUN-BLOCK ACTUALLY PAID OFF.

JEFF, REALLY...I JUST DON'T THINK--

KYLE...

HEY, OLSEN...ANYBODY SCORE YET? I CHANGED MY MIND ABOUT GOIN'...

...JOGGING...

OH.

SORRY TO INTERRUPT. BRAD...WAIT!

HE HAD TO PICK NOW TO GET FRIENDLY WITH ME?

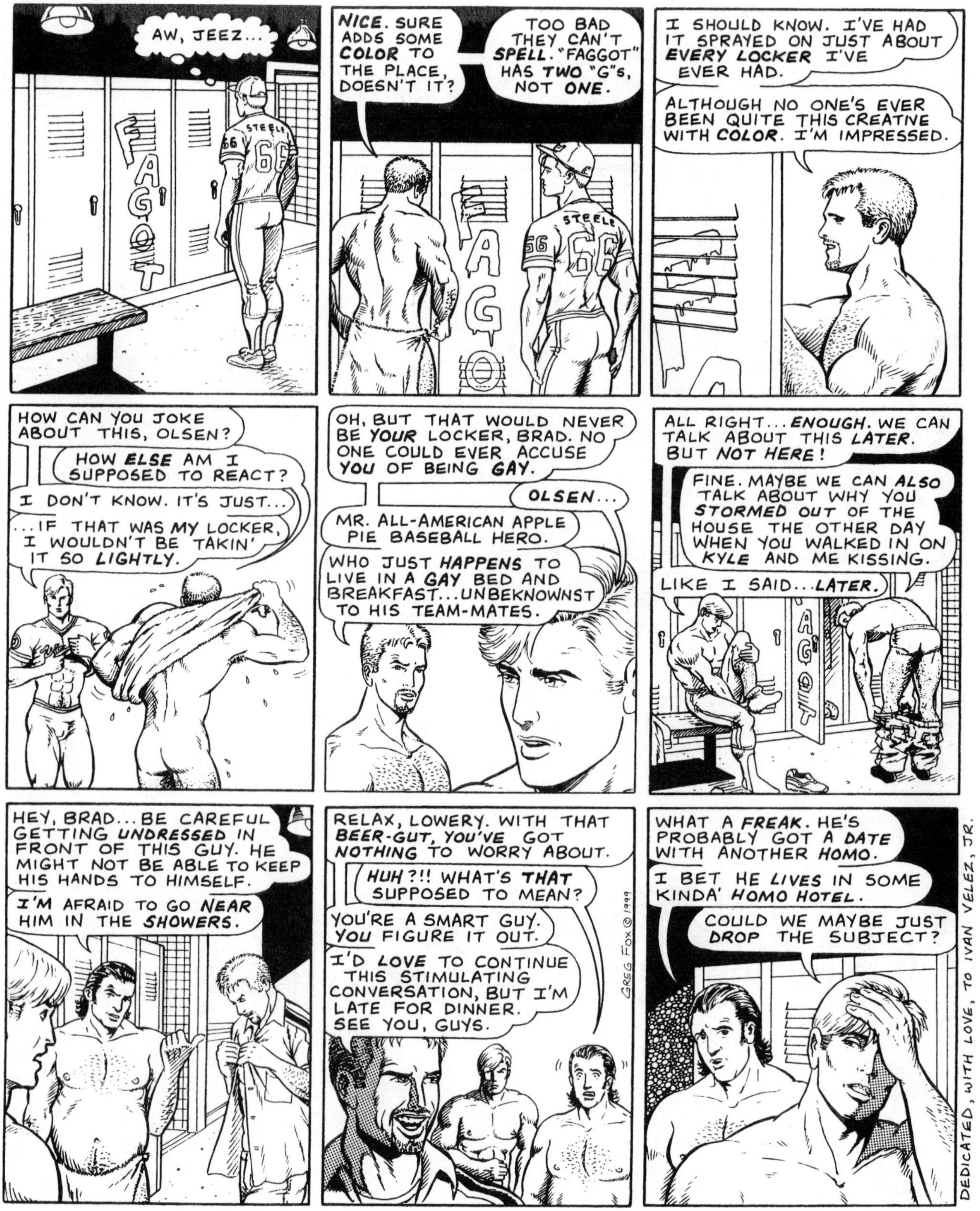
AW, JEEZ...
STEELE 66
FAGOT
NICE. SURE ADDS SOME COLOR TO THE PLACE, DOESN'T IT?
TOO BAD THEY CAN'T SPELL. "FAGGOT" HAS TWO "G"s, NOT ONE.
I SHOULD KNOW. I'VE HAD IT SPRAYED ON JUST ABOUT EVERY LOCKER I'VE EVER HAD.
ALTHOUGH NO ONE'S EVER BEEN QUITE THIS CREATIVE WITH COLOR. I'M IMPRESSED.
HOW CAN YOU JOKE ABOUT THIS, OLSEN?
HOW ELSE AM I SUPPOSED TO REACT?
I DON'T KNOW. IT'S JUST...
...IF THAT WAS MY LOCKER, I WOULDN'T BE TAKIN' IT SO LIGHTLY.
OH, BUT THAT WOULD NEVER BE YOUR LOCKER, BRAD. NO ONE COULD EVER ACCUSE YOU OF BEING GAY.
OLSEN...
MR. ALL-AMERICAN APPLE PIE BASEBALL HERO.
WHO JUST HAPPENS TO LIVE IN A GAY BED AND BREAKFAST...UNBEKNOWNST TO HIS TEAM-MATES.
ALL RIGHT... ENOUGH. WE CAN TALK ABOUT THIS LATER. BUT NOT HERE!
FINE. MAYBE WE CAN ALSO TALK ABOUT WHY YOU STORMED OUT OF THE HOUSE THE OTHER DAY WHEN YOU WALKED IN ON KYLE AND ME KISSING.
LIKE I SAID... LATER.
HEY, BRAD... BE CAREFUL GETTING UNDRESSED IN FRONT OF THIS GUY. HE MIGHT NOT BE ABLE TO KEEP HIS HANDS TO HIMSELF.
I'M AFRAID TO GO NEAR HIM IN THE SHOWERS.
RELAX, LOWERY. WITH THAT BEER-GUT, YOU'VE GOT NOTHING TO WORRY ABOUT.
HUH?!! WHAT'S THAT SUPPOSED TO MEAN?
YOU'RE A SMART GUY. YOU FIGURE IT OUT.
I'D LOVE TO CONTINUE THIS STIMULATING CONVERSATION, BUT I'M LATE FOR DINNER. SEE YOU, GUYS.
GREG FOX © 1999
WHAT A FREAK. HE'S PROBABLY GOT A DATE WITH ANOTHER HOMO.
I BET HE LIVES IN SOME KINDA' HOMO HOTEL.
COULD WE MAYBE JUST DROP THE SUBJECT?
DEDICATED, WITH LOVE, TO IVAN VELEZ, JR.

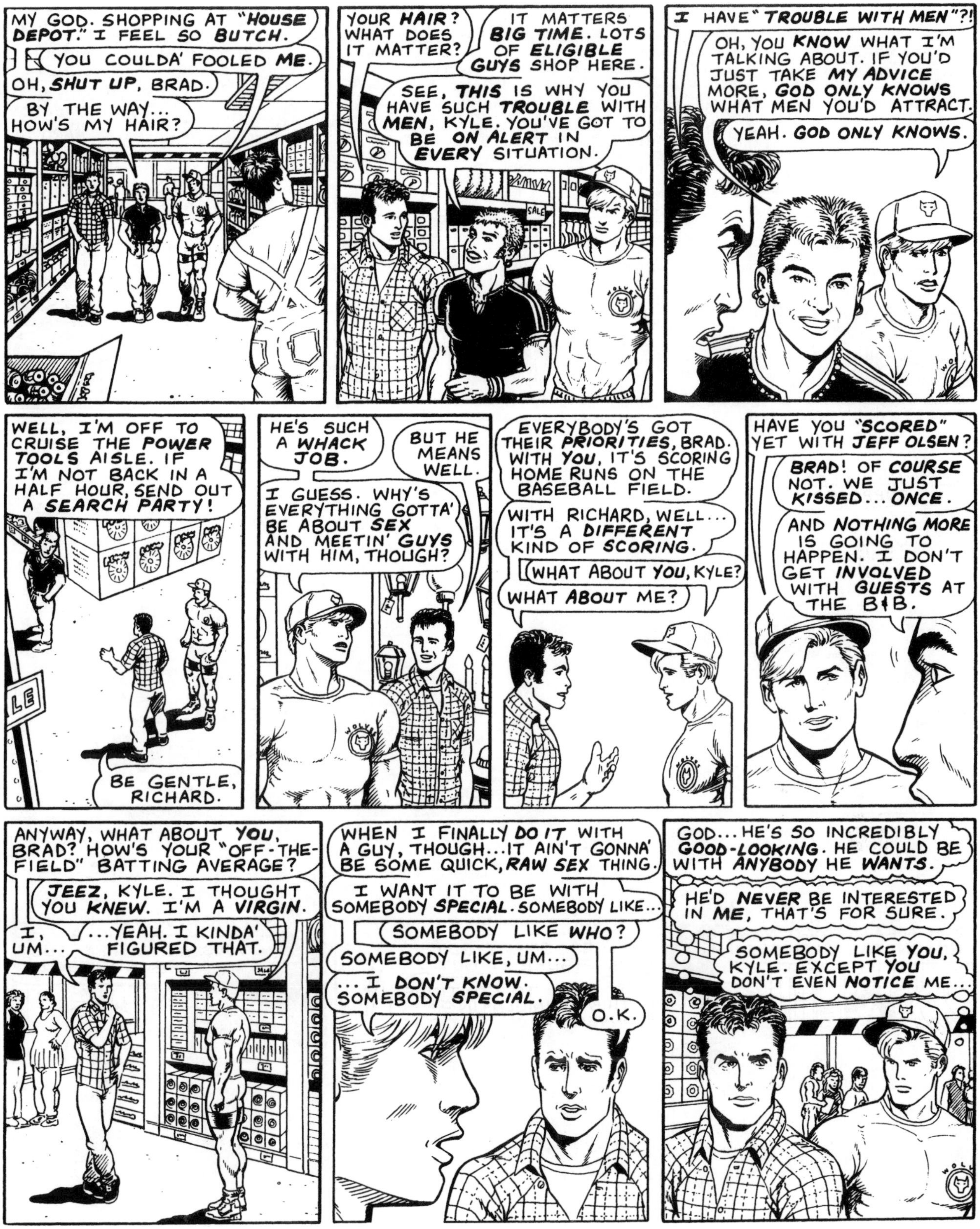
MY GOD. SHOPPING AT "HOUSE DEPOT." I FEEL SO BUTCH.
YOU COULDA' FOOLED ME.
OH, SHUT UP, BRAD.
BY THE WAY... HOW'S MY HAIR?
YOUR HAIR? WHAT DOES IT MATTER?
IT MATTERS BIG TIME. LOTS OF ELIGIBLE GUYS SHOP HERE.
SEE, THIS IS WHY YOU HAVE SUCH TROUBLE WITH MEN, KYLE. YOU'VE GOT TO BE ON ALERT IN EVERY SITUATION.
SALE
I HAVE "TROUBLE WITH MEN"?!
OH, YOU KNOW WHAT I'M TALKING ABOUT. IF YOU'D JUST TAKE MY ADVICE MORE, GOD ONLY KNOWS WHAT MEN YOU'D ATTRACT.
YEAH. GOD ONLY KNOWS.
WELL, I'M OFF TO CRUISE THE POWER TOOLS AISLE. IF I'M NOT BACK IN A HALF HOUR, SEND OUT A SEARCH PARTY!
BE GENTLE, RICHARD.
HE'S SUCH A WHACK JOB.
BUT HE MEANS WELL.
I GUESS. WHY'S EVERYTHING GOTTA' BE ABOUT SEX AND MEETIN' GUYS WITH HIM, THOUGH?
EVERYBODY'S GOT THEIR PRIORITIES, BRAD. WITH YOU, IT'S SCORING HOME RUNS ON THE BASEBALL FIELD.
WITH RICHARD, WELL... IT'S A DIFFERENT KIND OF SCORING.
WHAT ABOUT YOU, KYLE?
WHAT ABOUT ME?
HAVE YOU "SCORED" YET WITH JEFF OLSEN?
BRAD! OF COURSE NOT. WE JUST KISSED... ONCE.
AND NOTHING MORE IS GOING TO HAPPEN. I DON'T GET INVOLVED WITH GUESTS AT THE B&B.
ANYWAY, WHAT ABOUT YOU, BRAD? HOW'S YOUR "OFF-THE-FIELD" BATTING AVERAGE?
JEEZ, KYLE. I THOUGHT YOU KNEW. I'M A VIRGIN.
I, UM...
...YEAH. I KINDA' FIGURED THAT.
WHEN I FINALLY DO IT WITH A GUY, THOUGH... IT AIN'T GONNA' BE SOME QUICK, RAW SEX THING.
I WANT IT TO BE WITH SOMEBODY SPECIAL. SOMEBODY LIKE...
SOMEBODY LIKE WHO?
SOMEBODY LIKE, UM...
... I DON'T KNOW. SOMEBODY SPECIAL.
O.K.
GOD... HE'S SO INCREDIBLY GOOD-LOOKING. HE COULD BE WITH ANYBODY HE WANTS.
HE'D NEVER BE INTERESTED IN ME, THAT'S FOR SURE.
SOMEBODY LIKE YOU, KYLE. EXCEPT YOU DON'T EVEN NOTICE ME...

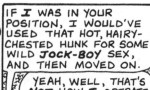

SO LET ME GET THIS STRAIGHT, KYLE. YOU *TURNED DOWN* JEFF OLSEN?

THAT'S RIGHT.

UN-*BELIEVABLE*.

IF *I* WAS IN YOUR POSITION, I WOULD'VE USED THAT HOT, HAIRY-CHESTED HUNK FOR SOME WILD *JOCK-BOY* SEX, AND THEN MOVED ON.

YEAH, WELL, THAT'S *NOT HOW I* OPERATE.

AND BESIDES...IT'S PROBABLY NOT A GOOD IDEA FOR ME TO GET INVOLVED WITH *ANY* GUESTS HERE AT THE B&B.

IF I SPENT TIME WORRYING ABOUT STUFF LIKE *THAT*, I'D NEVER HAVE *ANY* SEX.

I DON'T THINK THE *CONDOM INDUSTRY* COULD *WITHSTAND* SUCH A LOSS OF *REVENUE*.

LANCE. THIS IS A *PRIVATE* CONVERSATION.

RELAX, RICHARD... LANCE KNOWS ALL ABOUT THIS ALREADY.

OH, HE *DOES*, DOES HE?

I THOUGHT I HAD AN *EXCLUSIVE* ON THIS.

WHO *ARE* YOU? *LIZ SMITH*?

WELL, IF YOU WANT *MY* OPINION, KYLE, I THINK YOU DID THE *RIGHT THING*. FROM A BUSINESS STANDPOINT.

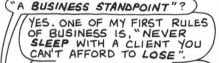

"A *BUSINESS STANDPOINT*"?

YES. ONE OF MY FIRST RULES OF BUSINESS IS, "*NEVER SLEEP* WITH A CLIENT YOU CAN'T AFFORD TO *LOSE*".

AND KYLE CAN'T AFFORD TO LOSE *ANY GUESTS* RIGHT NOW, WHILE HE'S TRYING TO BUILD HIS BUSINESS. THE FINANCIAL RISK IS TOO GREAT.

UGH. YOU'RE SUCH A *ROMANTIC*, LANCE. I CAN JUST *IMAGINE* WHAT YOU'RE LIKE IN *BED*.

TRUST ME...THAT IS *ONE* THING THAT WILL *ALWAYS* REMAIN IN YOUR *IMAGINATION*.

THAT'S *FINE* WITH ME.

GUYS...

MEANWHILE...

OLSEN? HOW COME YOU'RE CLEANIN' OUT YOUR LOCKER?

I'VE BEEN TRADED, BRAD. TO ALABAMA.

GET OUTTA' HERE! I MEAN... AS MUCH AS I DON'T LIKE YOU, YOU'RE THE *BEST CATCHER* THIS TEAM'S EVER HAD. THERE'S GOTTA' BE SOME MISTAKE!

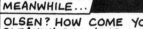

IT'S NO MISTAKE, BRAD.

WHO KNOWS...MAYBE *SOMEDAY* I'LL FIND A TEAM THAT PLACES A HIGHER VALUE ON *PLAYING ABILITY* THAN ON *SEXUAL ORIENTATION*.

HEY...AT LEAST NOW YOU'LL HAVE *KYLE* ALL TO YOURSELF.

KYLE?! WHA-WHAT MAKES YOU THINK I'M INTERESTED IN *KYLE*?!

PLEASE. WHY *ELSE* WERE YOU READY TO TAKE MY *HEAD OFF* WHEN YOU WALKED IN ON US *KISSING*?

UM...'CAUSE YOU WERE DOIN' IT DURING A *YANKEE GAME*?

NICE TRY...

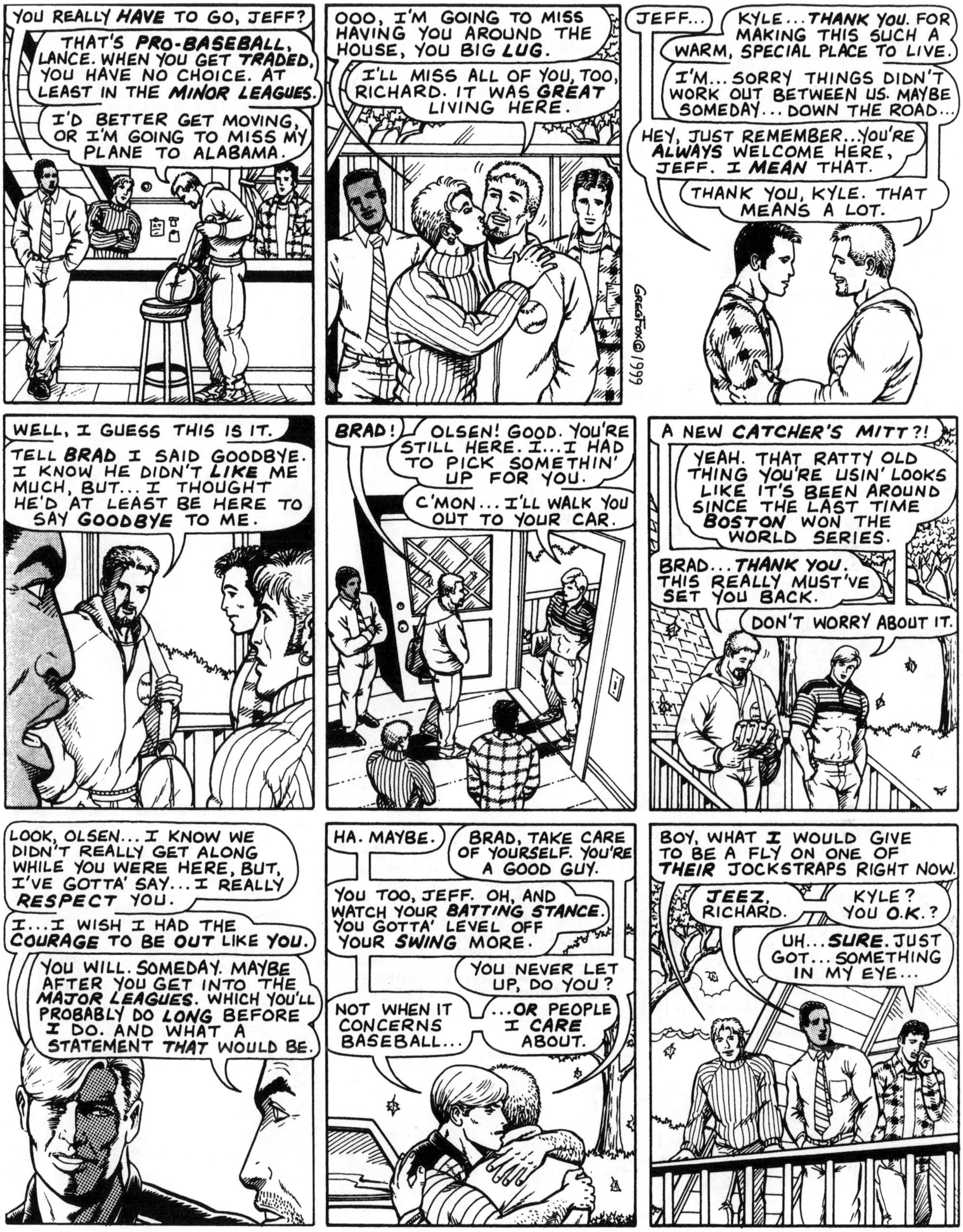
YOU REALLY HAVE TO GO, JEFF?
THAT'S PRO-BASEBALL, LANCE. WHEN YOU GET TRADED, YOU HAVE NO CHOICE. AT LEAST IN THE MINOR LEAGUES.
I'D BETTER GET MOVING, OR I'M GOING TO MISS MY PLANE TO ALABAMA.
OOO, I'M GOING TO MISS HAVING YOU AROUND THE HOUSE, YOU BIG LUG.
I'LL MISS ALL OF YOU, TOO, RICHARD. IT WAS GREAT LIVING HERE.
GREG FOX © 1999
JEFF...
KYLE... THANK YOU. FOR MAKING THIS SUCH A WARM, SPECIAL PLACE TO LIVE.
I'M... SORRY THINGS DIDN'T WORK OUT BETWEEN US. MAYBE SOMEDAY... DOWN THE ROAD...
HEY, JUST REMEMBER... YOU'RE ALWAYS WELCOME HERE, JEFF. I MEAN THAT.
THANK YOU, KYLE. THAT MEANS A LOT.
WELL, I GUESS THIS IS IT.
TELL BRAD I SAID GOODBYE. I KNOW HE DIDN'T LIKE ME MUCH, BUT... I THOUGHT HE'D AT LEAST BE HERE TO SAY GOODBYE TO ME.
BRAD!
OLSEN! GOOD. YOU'RE STILL HERE. I... I HAD TO PICK SOMETHIN' UP FOR YOU.
C'MON... I'LL WALK YOU OUT TO YOUR CAR.
A NEW CATCHER'S MITT?!
YEAH. THAT RATTY OLD THING YOU'RE USIN' LOOKS LIKE IT'S BEEN AROUND SINCE THE LAST TIME BOSTON WON THE WORLD SERIES.
BRAD... THANK YOU. THIS REALLY MUST'VE SET YOU BACK.
DON'T WORRY ABOUT IT.
LOOK, OLSEN... I KNOW WE DIDN'T REALLY GET ALONG WHILE YOU WERE HERE, BUT, I'VE GOTTA' SAY... I REALLY RESPECT YOU.
I... I WISH I HAD THE COURAGE TO BE OUT LIKE YOU.
YOU WILL. SOMEDAY. MAYBE AFTER YOU GET INTO THE MAJOR LEAGUES. WHICH YOU'LL PROBABLY DO LONG BEFORE I DO. AND WHAT A STATEMENT THAT WOULD BE.
HA. MAYBE.
BRAD, TAKE CARE OF YOURSELF. YOU'RE A GOOD GUY.
YOU TOO, JEFF. OH, AND WATCH YOUR BATTING STANCE. YOU GOTTA' LEVEL OFF YOUR SWING MORE.
YOU NEVER LET UP, DO YOU?
NOT WHEN IT CONCERNS BASEBALL...
...OR PEOPLE I CARE ABOUT.
BOY, WHAT I WOULD GIVE TO BE A FLY ON ONE OF THEIR JOCKSTRAPS RIGHT NOW.
JEEZ, RICHARD.
KYLE? YOU O.K.?
UH... SURE. JUST GOT... SOMETHING IN MY EYE...

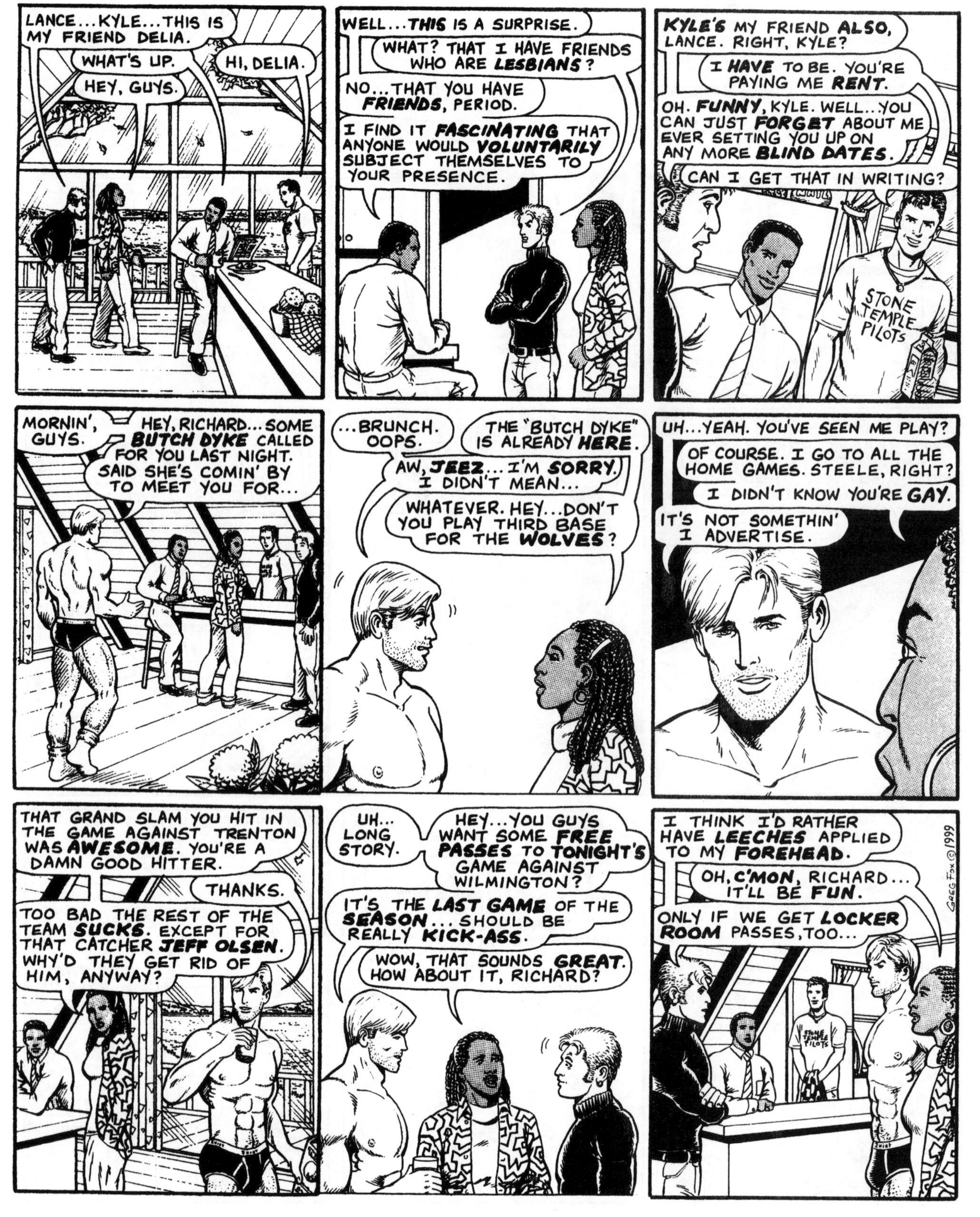
LANCE...KYLE...THIS IS MY FRIEND DELIA.
WHAT'S UP.
HI, DELIA.
HEY, GUYS.
WELL...THIS IS A SURPRISE.
WHAT? THAT I HAVE FRIENDS WHO ARE LESBIANS?
NO...THAT YOU HAVE FRIENDS, PERIOD.
I FIND IT FASCINATING THAT ANYONE WOULD VOLUNTARILY SUBJECT THEMSELVES TO YOUR PRESENCE.
KYLE'S MY FRIEND ALSO, LANCE. RIGHT, KYLE?
I HAVE TO BE. YOU'RE PAYING ME RENT.
OH. FUNNY, KYLE. WELL...YOU CAN JUST FORGET ABOUT ME EVER SETTING YOU UP ON ANY MORE BLIND DATES.
CAN I GET THAT IN WRITING?
STONE TEMPLE PILOTS
MORNIN', GUYS.
HEY, RICHARD...SOME BUTCH DYKE CALLED FOR YOU LAST NIGHT. SAID SHE'S COMIN' BY TO MEET YOU FOR...
...BRUNCH. OOPS.
THE "BUTCH DYKE" IS ALREADY HERE.
AW, JEEZ...I'M SORRY. I DIDN'T MEAN...
WHATEVER. HEY...DON'T YOU PLAY THIRD BASE FOR THE WOLVES?
UH...YEAH. YOU'VE SEEN ME PLAY?
OF COURSE. I GO TO ALL THE HOME GAMES. STEELE, RIGHT?
I DIDN'T KNOW YOU'RE GAY.
IT'S NOT SOMETHIN' I ADVERTISE.
THAT GRAND SLAM YOU HIT IN THE GAME AGAINST TRENTON WAS AWESOME. YOU'RE A DAMN GOOD HITTER.
THANKS.
TOO BAD THE REST OF THE TEAM SUCKS. EXCEPT FOR THAT CATCHER JEFF OLSEN. WHY'D THEY GET RID OF HIM, ANYWAY?
UH... LONG STORY.
HEY...YOU GUYS WANT SOME FREE PASSES TO TONIGHT'S GAME AGAINST WILMINGTON?
IT'S THE LAST GAME OF THE SEASON...SHOULD BE REALLY KICK-ASS.
WOW, THAT SOUNDS GREAT. HOW ABOUT IT, RICHARD?
I THINK I'D RATHER HAVE LEECHES APPLIED TO MY FOREHEAD.
OH, C'MON, RICHARD... IT'LL BE FUN.
ONLY IF WE GET LOCKER ROOM PASSES, TOO...
STONE TEMPLE PILOTS
GREG FOX © 1999

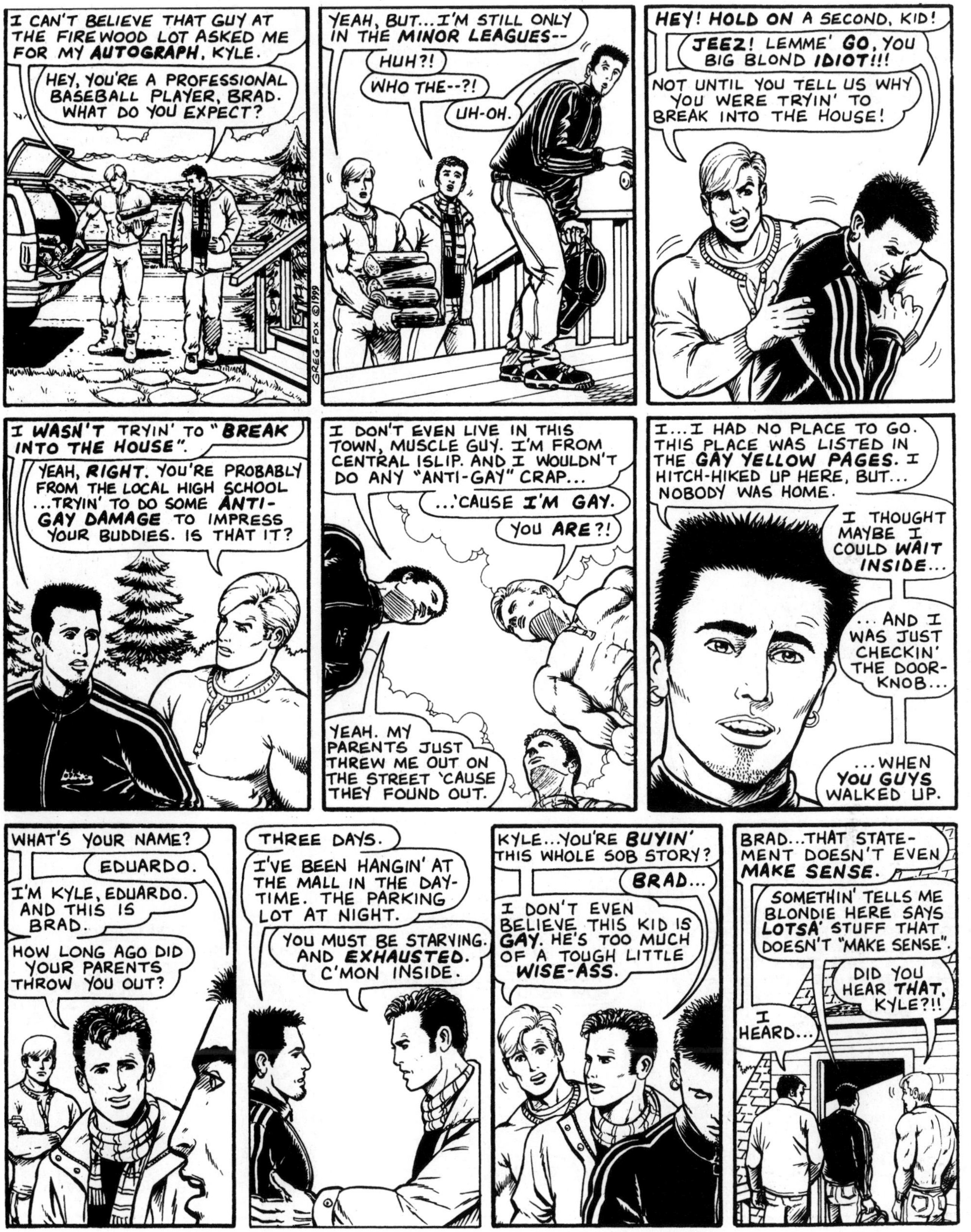
I CAN'T BELIEVE THAT GUY AT THE FIREWOOD LOT ASKED ME FOR MY AUTOGRAPH, KYLE.
HEY, YOU'RE A PROFESSIONAL BASEBALL PLAYER, BRAD. WHAT DO YOU EXPECT?
GREG FOX ©1999
YEAH, BUT...I'M STILL ONLY IN THE MINOR LEAGUES--
HUH?!
WHO THE--?!
UH-OH.
HEY! HOLD ON A SECOND, KID!
JEEZ! LEMME' GO, YOU BIG BLOND IDIOT!!!
NOT UNTIL YOU TELL US WHY YOU WERE TRYIN' TO BREAK INTO THE HOUSE!
I WASN'T TRYIN' TO "BREAK INTO THE HOUSE".
YEAH, RIGHT. YOU'RE PROBABLY FROM THE LOCAL HIGH SCHOOL ...TRYIN' TO DO SOME ANTI-GAY DAMAGE TO IMPRESS YOUR BUDDIES. IS THAT IT?
I DON'T EVEN LIVE IN THIS TOWN, MUSCLE GUY. I'M FROM CENTRAL ISLIP. AND I WOULDN'T DO ANY "ANTI-GAY" CRAP...
...'CAUSE I'M GAY.
YOU ARE?!
YEAH. MY PARENTS JUST THREW ME OUT ON THE STREET 'CAUSE THEY FOUND OUT.
I...I HAD NO PLACE TO GO. THIS PLACE WAS LISTED IN THE GAY YELLOW PAGES. I HITCH-HIKED UP HERE, BUT... NOBODY WAS HOME.
I THOUGHT MAYBE I COULD WAIT INSIDE...
...AND I WAS JUST CHECKIN' THE DOOR-KNOB...
...WHEN YOU GUYS WALKED UP.
WHAT'S YOUR NAME?
EDUARDO.
I'M KYLE, EDUARDO. AND THIS IS BRAD.
HOW LONG AGO DID YOUR PARENTS THROW YOU OUT?
THREE DAYS.
I'VE BEEN HANGIN' AT THE MALL IN THE DAY-TIME. THE PARKING LOT AT NIGHT.
YOU MUST BE STARVING. AND EXHAUSTED. C'MON INSIDE.
KYLE...YOU'RE BUYIN' THIS WHOLE SOB STORY?
BRAD...
I DON'T EVEN BELIEVE THIS KID IS GAY. HE'S TOO MUCH OF A TOUGH LITTLE WISE-ASS.
BRAD...THAT STATE-MENT DOESN'T EVEN MAKE SENSE.
SOMETHIN' TELLS ME BLONDIE HERE SAYS LOTSA' STUFF THAT DOESN'T "MAKE SENSE".
DID YOU HEAR THAT, KYLE?!!
I HEARD...

IS THAT KID STILL SLEEPIN', KYLE?

HE HAS A *NAME*, BRAD. *EDUARDO*.

WHATEVER. I JUST THINK YOU'RE GETTIN' IN *OVER* YOUR *HEAD* LETTIN' HIM STAY HERE.

HE'S STILL IN *HIGH SCHOOL*. SHOULDN'T YOU CONTACT HIS *PARENTS*? AREN'T THERE *LAWS* ABOUT THIS?

I TURNED *EIGHTEEN* TWO WEEKS AGO, BIG GUY. I CAN DO WHAT I *WANT*.

AND AS FOR MY PARENTS... THEY DON'T GIVE A CRAP *WHAT I DO*.

THEY TOLD ME THEY'D RATHER HAVE A *DEAD* SON THAN A *GAY* SON WHEN THEY THREW ME OUT ON THE STREET LAST WEEK.

I DON'T BELIEVE THAT.

BELIEVE WHATEVER THE HELL YOU *WANT*, MUSCLE-HEAD.

WHAT ABOUT HIGH SCHOOL, EDUARDO?

I HAD ONE SEMESTER LEFT 'TIL GRADUATION, KYLE.

BUT I AIN'T GOIN' BACK THERE, EITHER.

EVER SINCE WORD GOT OUT THAT I'M *GAY*, I'VE BEEN A *TARGET*.

JEEZ. ALL THIS *DRAMA*. THE KID'S A GODDAMN WALKIN' "PARTY OF FIVE" EPISODE.

HEY, I DIDN'T ASK FOR YOUR *PITY*, MAN.

I JUST NEEDED A PLACE TO *CRASH*.

SO... WHAT NOW?

I'M GONNA GO OUT AND GET A *JOB*, KYLE. SO I CAN PAY YOU TO LET ME STAY HERE...IF THAT'S O.K. WITH YOU.

A JOB?!! WHAT'S A *HIGH-SCHOOL DROP-OUT* QUALIFIED TO DO... 'SIDES FLIPPIN' BURGERS AT McDONALDS?

SO THEN I'LL FLIP BURGERS AT McDONALDS.

NOT *EVERYBODY* CAN BE A WHITE-BREAD ALL-AMERICAN CLOSET-CASE MINOR-LEAGUE BASEBALL STAR LIKE *YOU*, JOCK-FACE.

YA' KNOW, YOU'RE *REALLY* STARTIN' TO GET ON MY NERVES, PUNK.

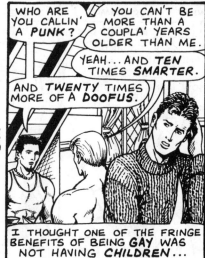

WHO ARE YOU CALLIN' A *PUNK*?

YOU CAN'T BE MORE THAN A COUPLA' YEARS OLDER THAN ME.

YEAH...AND *TEN* TIMES *SMARTER*.

AND *TWENTY* TIMES MORE OF A *DOOFUS*.

I THOUGHT ONE OF THE FRINGE BENEFITS OF BEING *GAY* WAS NOT HAVING *CHILDREN*...

I'LL BE OUT OF HERE IN A SEC, KYLE.

OH, UH... I DIDN'T REALIZE YOU WERE STILL IN HERE, EDUARDO.

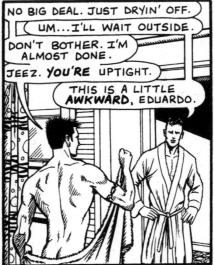

NO BIG DEAL. JUST DRYIN' OFF.

UM... I'LL WAIT OUTSIDE.

DON'T BOTHER. I'M ALMOST DONE.

JEEZ. YOU'RE UPTIGHT.

THIS IS A LITTLE AWKWARD, EDUARDO.

WHY? BRAD'S ALWAYS STRUTTIN' AROUND THE HOUSE IN HIS C.K. BRIEFS.

HE DOESN'T STRUT AROUND NUDE.

CLOSE ENOUGH. YOU THINK I GOT A GOOD BODY, KYLE?

EDUARDO...

I MEAN, I KNOW I AIN'T A BIG MUSCLE GUY LIKE BRAD, BUT ...I THINK I'M PRETTY DECENT.

WHAT DO YOU THINK?

I THINK I'VE HAD ENOUGH OF THIS CONVERSATION.

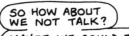

SO HOW ABOUT WE NOT TALK?

MAYBE WE COULD TAKE A SHOWER TOGETHER?

YOU ALREADY TOOK A SHOWER.

I'M UP FOR ANOTHER ONE.

EDUARDO...

C'MON, KYLE...YOU'RE A HOT GUY. I REALLY LIKE YOU. AND I'M OVER EIGHTEEN, IF THAT'S WHAT YOU'RE WORRIED ABOUT.

LET ME PAY YOU BACK FOR ALL YOU'VE DONE FOR ME...LETTIN' ME STAY HERE N' ALL.

THAT'S WHAT THIS IS? PAYBACK?

WELL... SORT OF.

I MEAN...AREN'T YOU EXPECTING THIS? WHY ELSE WOULD YOU LET ME STAY HERE WITHOUT PAYIN' RENT?

BECAUSE YOU WERE IN TROUBLE...AND YOU NEEDED A PLACE TO STAY. I NEVER EXPECTED ANY SEXUAL PAYBACK.

OH. WOW. NOW I FEEL REALLY STUPID.

FORGET ABOUT IT. YOU WANNA' GET OUTTA' HERE NOW? SO I CAN TAKE MY SHOWER?

SURE, KYLE.

KYLE?

YEAH?

THANKS, MAN. NO ONE'S EVER TREATED ME THIS WAY BEFORE. I'M SO USED TO...

...BEIN' USED.

GregFox©2000

"USED TO BEIN' USED". THAT SOUNDS LIKE...

...A REALLY BAD EAGLES SONG OR SOMETHING.

HEY, KYLE...I'D SLEEP WITH YOU ANYWAY. NEVER MIND THE "PAYBACK" STUFF.

JUST THOUGHT YOU SHOULD KNOW THAT.

GOODBYE, EDUARDO...

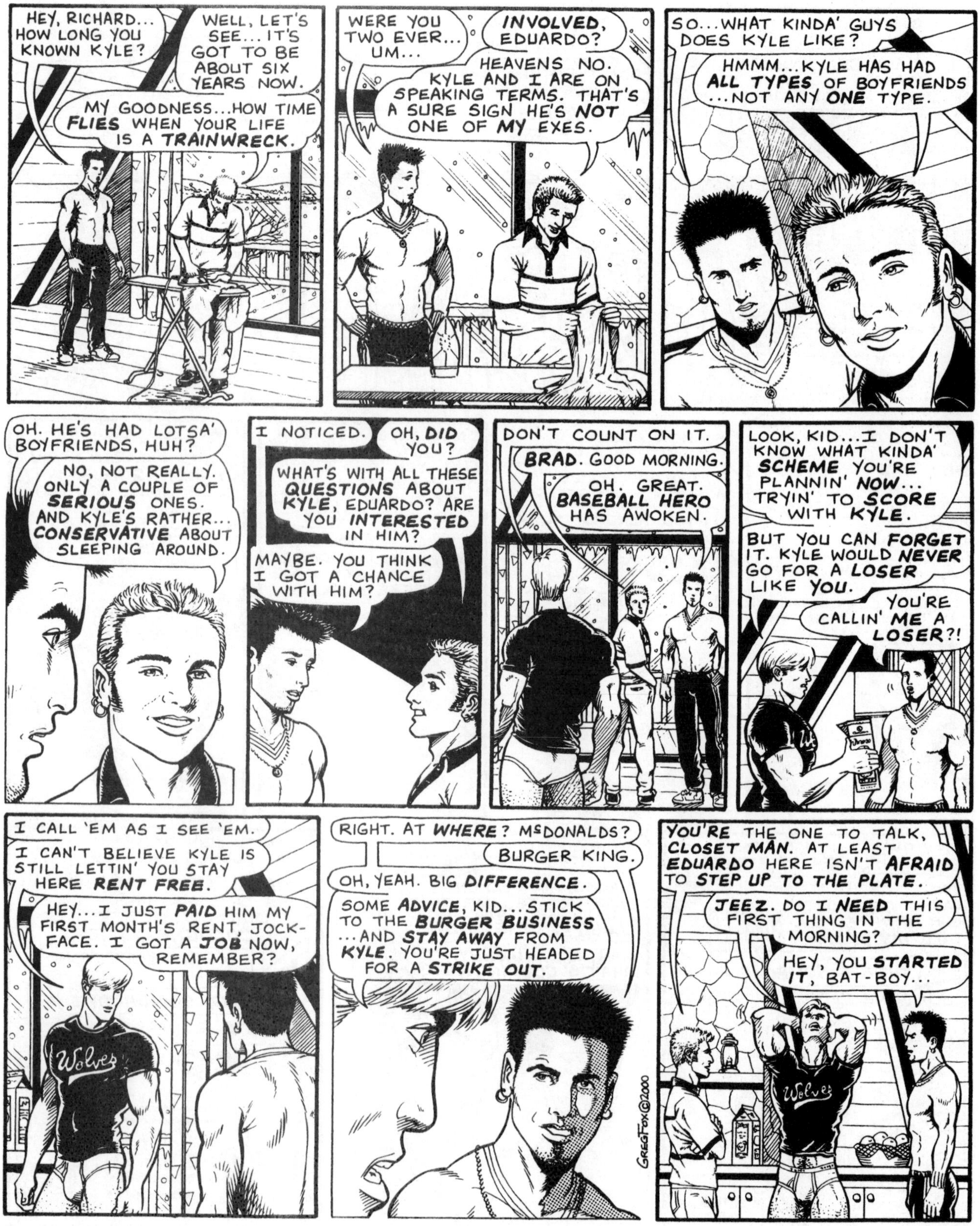
HEY, RICHARD... HOW LONG YOU KNOWN KYLE?
WELL, LET'S SEE... IT'S GOT TO BE ABOUT SIX YEARS NOW.
MY GOODNESS...HOW TIME FLIES WHEN YOUR LIFE IS A TRAINWRECK.
WERE YOU TWO EVER... UM...
INVOLVED, EDUARDO?
HEAVENS NO. KYLE AND I ARE ON SPEAKING TERMS. THAT'S A SURE SIGN HE'S NOT ONE OF MY EXES.
SO...WHAT KINDA' GUYS DOES KYLE LIKE?
HMMM...KYLE HAS HAD ALL TYPES OF BOYFRIENDS ...NOT ANY ONE TYPE.
OH. HE'S HAD LOTSA' BOYFRIENDS, HUH?
NO, NOT REALLY. ONLY A COUPLE OF SERIOUS ONES. AND KYLE'S RATHER... CONSERVATIVE ABOUT SLEEPING AROUND.
I NOTICED.
OH, DID YOU?
WHAT'S WITH ALL THESE QUESTIONS ABOUT KYLE, EDUARDO? ARE YOU INTERESTED IN HIM?
MAYBE. YOU THINK I GOT A CHANCE WITH HIM?
DON'T COUNT ON IT.
BRAD. GOOD MORNING.
OH. GREAT. BASEBALL HERO HAS AWOKEN.
LOOK, KID...I DON'T KNOW WHAT KINDA' SCHEME YOU'RE PLANNIN' NOW... TRYIN' TO SCORE WITH KYLE.
BUT YOU CAN FORGET IT. KYLE WOULD NEVER GO FOR A LOSER LIKE YOU.
YOU'RE CALLIN' ME A LOSER?!
I CALL 'EM AS I SEE 'EM.
I CAN'T BELIEVE KYLE IS STILL LETTIN' YOU STAY HERE RENT FREE.
HEY... I JUST PAID HIM MY FIRST MONTH'S RENT, JOCK-FACE. I GOT A JOB NOW, REMEMBER?
RIGHT. AT WHERE? McDONALDS?
BURGER KING.
OH, YEAH. BIG DIFFERENCE.
SOME ADVICE, KID... STICK TO THE BURGER BUSINESS ...AND STAY AWAY FROM KYLE. YOU'RE JUST HEADED FOR A STRIKE OUT.
GREGFOX©2000
YOU'RE THE ONE TO TALK, CLOSET MAN. AT LEAST EDUARDO HERE ISN'T AFRAID TO STEP UP TO THE PLATE.
JEEZ. DO I NEED THIS FIRST THING IN THE MORNING?
HEY, YOU STARTED IT, BAT-BOY...

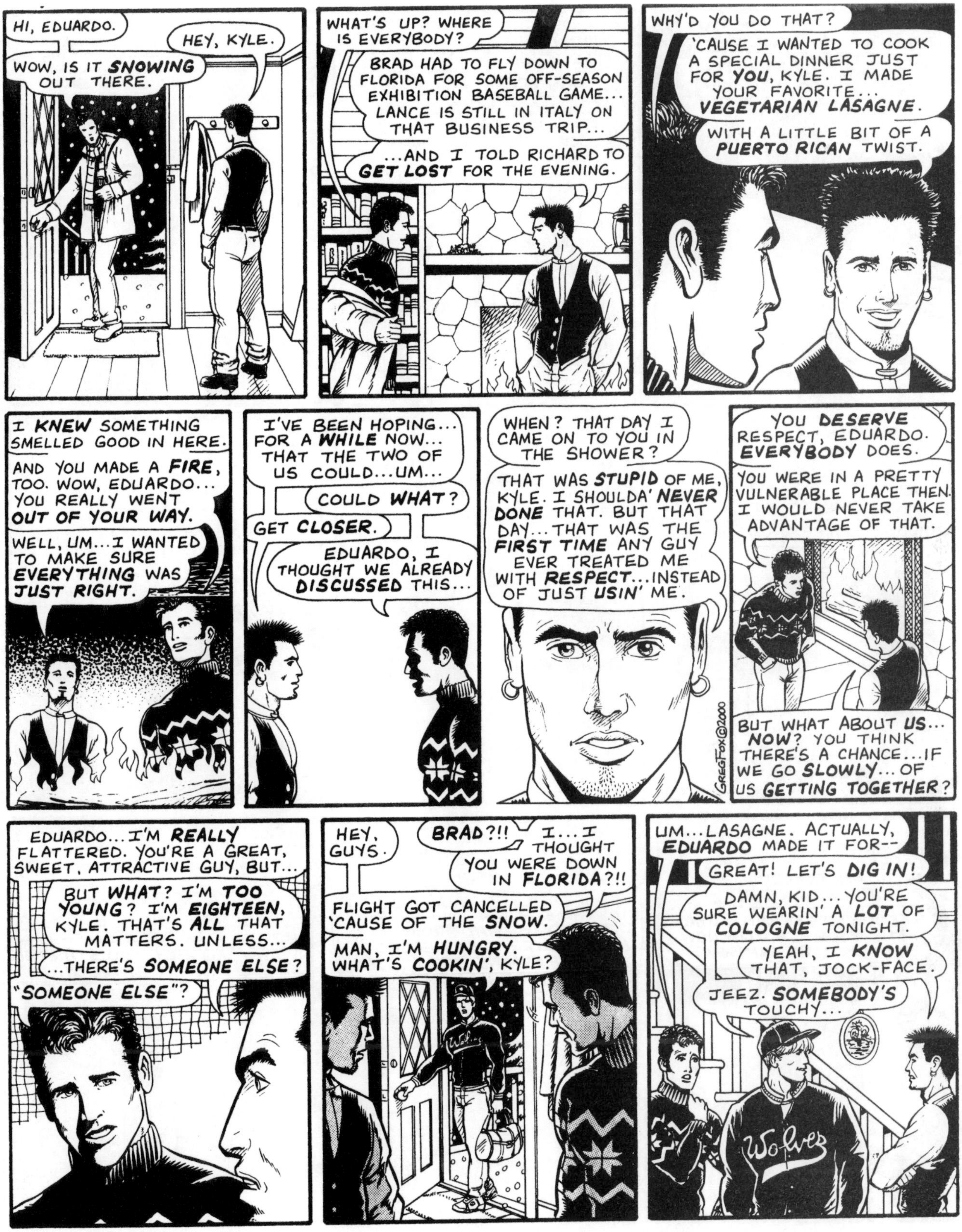
HI, EDUARDO.
HEY, KYLE.
WOW, IS IT SNOWING OUT THERE.
WHAT'S UP? WHERE IS EVERYBODY?
BRAD HAD TO FLY DOWN TO FLORIDA FOR SOME OFF-SEASON EXHIBITION BASEBALL GAME... LANCE IS STILL IN ITALY ON THAT BUSINESS TRIP...
...AND I TOLD RICHARD TO GET LOST FOR THE EVENING.
WHY'D YOU DO THAT?
'CAUSE I WANTED TO COOK A SPECIAL DINNER JUST FOR YOU, KYLE. I MADE YOUR FAVORITE... VEGETARIAN LASAGNE.
WITH A LITTLE BIT OF A PUERTO RICAN TWIST.
I KNEW SOMETHING SMELLED GOOD IN HERE.
AND YOU MADE A FIRE, TOO. WOW, EDUARDO... YOU REALLY WENT OUT OF YOUR WAY.
WELL, UM... I WANTED TO MAKE SURE EVERYTHING WAS JUST RIGHT.
I'VE BEEN HOPING... FOR A WHILE NOW... THAT THE TWO OF US COULD... UM...
COULD WHAT?
GET CLOSER.
EDUARDO, I THOUGHT WE ALREADY DISCUSSED THIS...
WHEN? THAT DAY I CAME ON TO YOU IN THE SHOWER?
THAT WAS STUPID OF ME, KYLE. I SHOULDA' NEVER DONE THAT. BUT THAT DAY... THAT WAS THE FIRST TIME ANY GUY EVER TREATED ME WITH RESPECT... INSTEAD OF JUST USIN' ME.
GREG FOX ©2000
YOU DESERVE RESPECT, EDUARDO. EVERYBODY DOES.
YOU WERE IN A PRETTY VULNERABLE PLACE THEN. I WOULD NEVER TAKE ADVANTAGE OF THAT.
BUT WHAT ABOUT US... NOW? YOU THINK THERE'S A CHANCE... IF WE GO SLOWLY... OF US GETTING TOGETHER?
EDUARDO... I'M REALLY FLATTERED. YOU'RE A GREAT, SWEET, ATTRACTIVE GUY, BUT...
BUT WHAT? I'M TOO YOUNG? I'M EIGHTEEN, KYLE. THAT'S ALL THAT MATTERS. UNLESS...
...THERE'S SOMEONE ELSE?
"SOMEONE ELSE"?
HEY, GUYS.
BRAD?!!
I... I THOUGHT YOU WERE DOWN IN FLORIDA?!!
FLIGHT GOT CANCELLED 'CAUSE OF THE SNOW.
MAN, I'M HUNGRY. WHAT'S COOKIN', KYLE?
UM... LASAGNE. ACTUALLY, EDUARDO MADE IT FOR--
GREAT! LET'S DIG IN!
DAMN, KID... YOU'RE SURE WEARIN' A LOT OF COLOGNE TONIGHT.
YEAH, I KNOW THAT, JOCK-FACE.
JEEZ. SOMEBODY'S TOUCHY...
Wolves

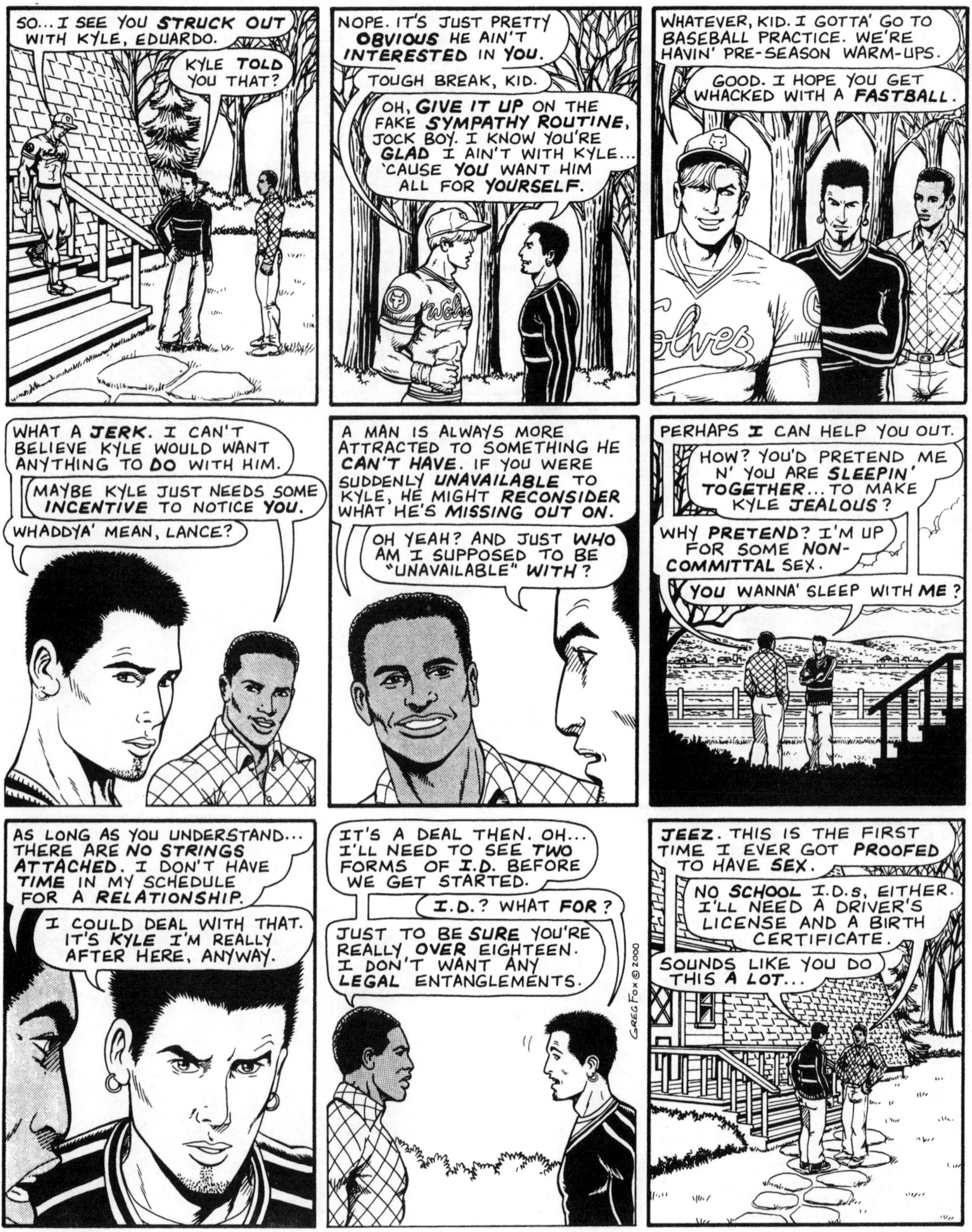

SO... I SEE YOU STRUCK OUT WITH KYLE, EDUARDO.
KYLE TOLD YOU THAT?
NOPE. IT'S JUST PRETTY OBVIOUS HE AIN'T INTERESTED IN YOU.
TOUGH BREAK, KID.
OH, GIVE IT UP ON THE FAKE SYMPATHY ROUTINE, JOCK BOY. I KNOW YOU'RE GLAD I AIN'T WITH KYLE... 'CAUSE YOU WANT HIM ALL FOR YOURSELF.
WHATEVER, KID. I GOTTA' GO TO BASEBALL PRACTICE. WE'RE HAVIN' PRE-SEASON WARM-UPS.
GOOD. I HOPE YOU GET WHACKED WITH A FASTBALL.
WHAT A JERK. I CAN'T BELIEVE KYLE WOULD WANT ANYTHING TO DO WITH HIM.
MAYBE KYLE JUST NEEDS SOME INCENTIVE TO NOTICE YOU.
WHADDYA' MEAN, LANCE?
A MAN IS ALWAYS MORE ATTRACTED TO SOMETHING HE CAN'T HAVE. IF YOU WERE SUDDENLY UNAVAILABLE TO KYLE, HE MIGHT RECONSIDER WHAT HE'S MISSING OUT ON.
OH YEAH? AND JUST WHO AM I SUPPOSED TO BE "UNAVAILABLE" WITH?
PERHAPS I CAN HELP YOU OUT.
HOW? YOU'D PRETEND ME N' YOU ARE SLEEPIN' TOGETHER... TO MAKE KYLE JEALOUS?
WHY PRETEND? I'M UP FOR SOME NON-COMMITTAL SEX.
YOU WANNA' SLEEP WITH ME?
AS LONG AS YOU UNDERSTAND... THERE ARE NO STRINGS ATTACHED. I DON'T HAVE TIME IN MY SCHEDULE FOR A RELATIONSHIP.
I COULD DEAL WITH THAT. IT'S KYLE I'M REALLY AFTER HERE, ANYWAY.
IT'S A DEAL THEN. OH... I'LL NEED TO SEE TWO FORMS OF I.D. BEFORE WE GET STARTED.
I.D.? WHAT FOR?
JUST TO BE SURE YOU'RE REALLY OVER EIGHTEEN. I DON'T WANT ANY LEGAL ENTANGLEMENTS.
GREG FOX © 2000
JEEZ. THIS IS THE FIRST TIME I EVER GOT PROOFED TO HAVE SEX.
NO SCHOOL I.D.s, EITHER. I'LL NEED A DRIVER'S LICENSE AND A BIRTH CERTIFICATE.
SOUNDS LIKE YOU DO THIS A LOT...

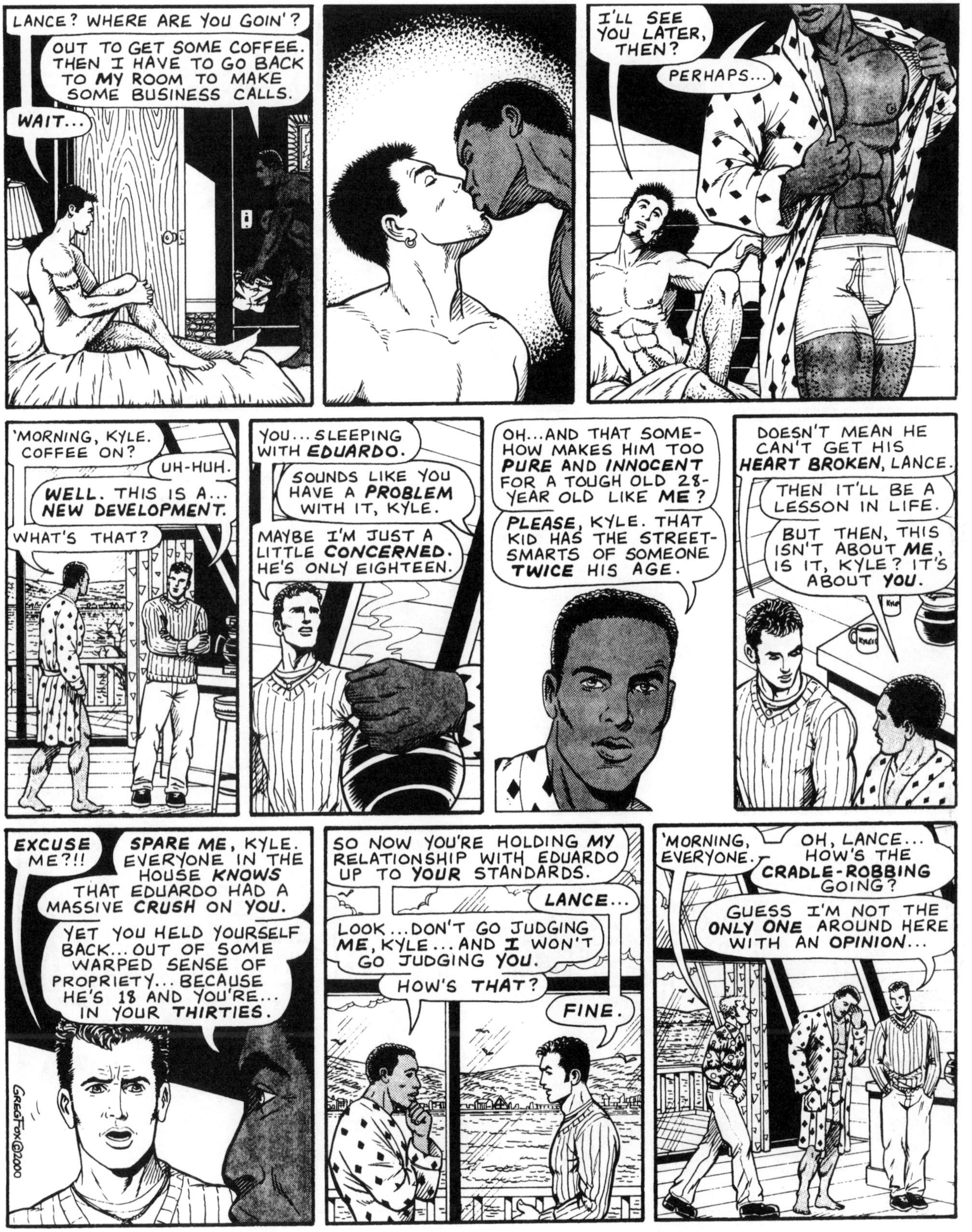
LANCE? WHERE ARE YOU GOIN'?
OUT TO GET SOME COFFEE. THEN I HAVE TO GO BACK TO MY ROOM TO MAKE SOME BUSINESS CALLS.
WAIT...
I'LL SEE YOU LATER, THEN?
PERHAPS...
'MORNING, KYLE. COFFEE ON?
UH-HUH.
WELL. THIS IS A... NEW DEVELOPMENT.
WHAT'S THAT?
YOU... SLEEPING WITH EDUARDO.
SOUNDS LIKE YOU HAVE A PROBLEM WITH IT, KYLE.
MAYBE I'M JUST A LITTLE CONCERNED. HE'S ONLY EIGHTEEN.
OH...AND THAT SOME-HOW MAKES HIM TOO PURE AND INNOCENT FOR A TOUGH OLD 28-YEAR OLD LIKE ME?
PLEASE, KYLE. THAT KID HAS THE STREET-SMARTS OF SOMEONE TWICE HIS AGE.
DOESN'T MEAN HE CAN'T GET HIS HEART BROKEN, LANCE.
THEN IT'LL BE A LESSON IN LIFE.
BUT THEN, THIS ISN'T ABOUT ME, IS IT, KYLE? IT'S ABOUT YOU.
EXCUSE ME?!!
SPARE ME, KYLE. EVERYONE IN THE HOUSE KNOWS THAT EDUARDO HAD A MASSIVE CRUSH ON YOU.
YET YOU HELD YOURSELF BACK... OUT OF SOME WARPED SENSE OF PROPRIETY... BECAUSE HE'S 18 AND YOU'RE... IN YOUR THIRTIES.
GREGFOX©2000
SO NOW YOU'RE HOLDING MY RELATIONSHIP WITH EDUARDO UP TO YOUR STANDARDS.
LANCE...
LOOK... DON'T GO JUDGING ME, KYLE... AND I WON'T GO JUDGING YOU.
HOW'S THAT?
FINE.
'MORNING, EVERYONE.
OH, LANCE... HOW'S THE CRADLE-ROBBING GOING?
GUESS I'M NOT THE ONLY ONE AROUND HERE WITH AN OPINION...

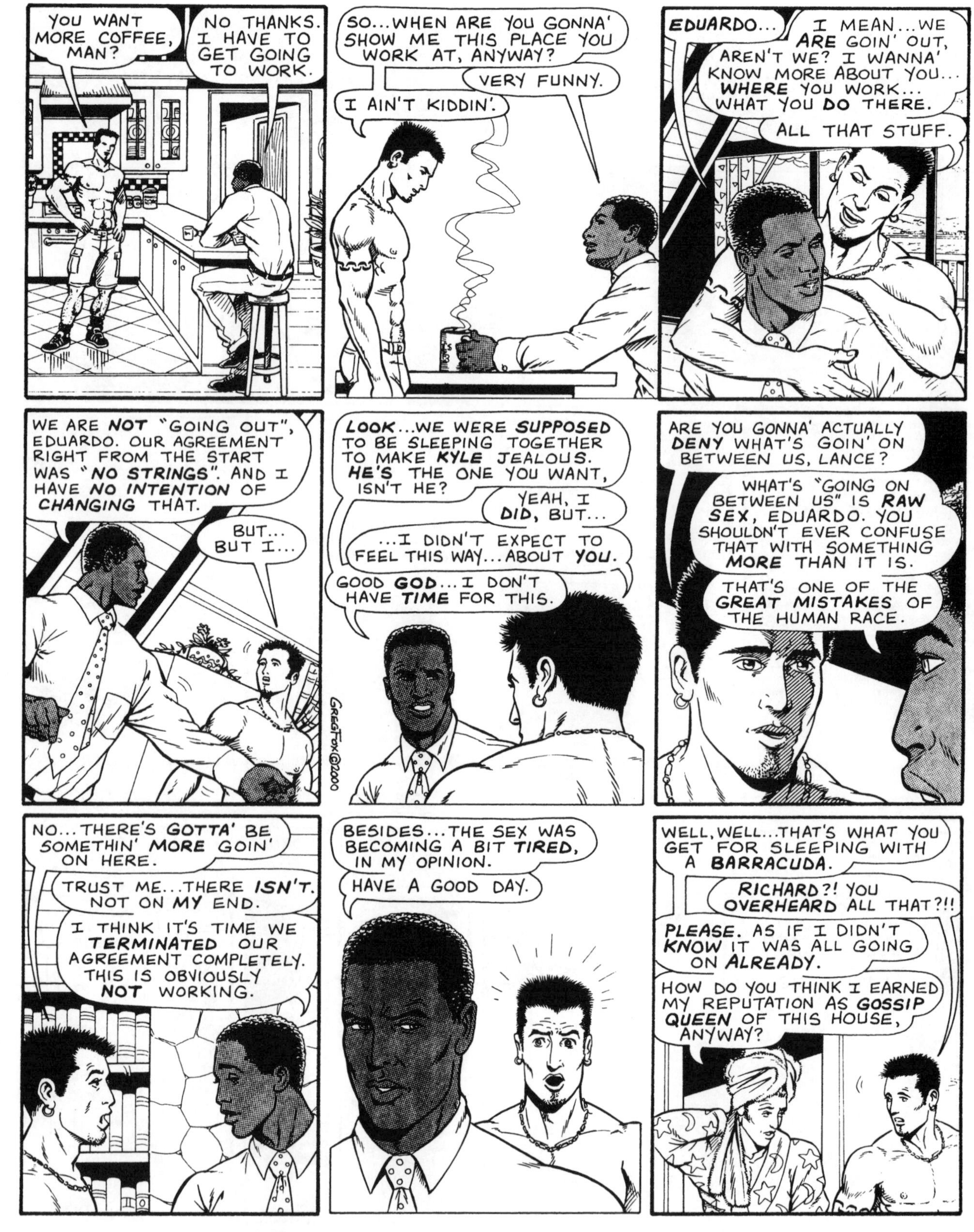

YOU WANT MORE COFFEE, MAN?
NO THANKS. I HAVE TO GET GOING TO WORK.
SO...WHEN ARE YOU GONNA' SHOW ME THIS PLACE YOU WORK AT, ANYWAY?
VERY FUNNY.
I AIN'T KIDDIN'.
EDUARDO...
I MEAN...WE ARE GOIN' OUT, AREN'T WE? I WANNA' KNOW MORE ABOUT YOU... WHERE YOU WORK... WHAT YOU DO THERE.
ALL THAT STUFF.
WE ARE NOT "GOING OUT", EDUARDO. OUR AGREEMENT RIGHT FROM THE START WAS "NO STRINGS". AND I HAVE NO INTENTION OF CHANGING THAT.
BUT... BUT I...
LOOK...WE WERE SUPPOSED TO BE SLEEPING TOGETHER TO MAKE KYLE JEALOUS. HE'S THE ONE YOU WANT, ISN'T HE?
YEAH, I DID, BUT...
...I DIDN'T EXPECT TO FEEL THIS WAY...ABOUT YOU.
GOOD GOD...I DON'T HAVE TIME FOR THIS.
GREGFOX©2000
ARE YOU GONNA' ACTUALLY DENY WHAT'S GOIN' ON BETWEEN US, LANCE?
WHAT'S "GOING ON BETWEEN US" IS RAW SEX, EDUARDO. YOU SHOULDN'T EVER CONFUSE THAT WITH SOMETHING MORE THAN IT IS.
THAT'S ONE OF THE GREAT MISTAKES OF THE HUMAN RACE.
NO...THERE'S GOTTA' BE SOMETHIN' MORE GOIN' ON HERE.
TRUST ME...THERE ISN'T. NOT ON MY END.
I THINK IT'S TIME WE TERMINATED OUR AGREEMENT COMPLETELY. THIS IS OBVIOUSLY NOT WORKING.
BESIDES...THE SEX WAS BECOMING A BIT TIRED, IN MY OPINION.
HAVE A GOOD DAY.
WELL, WELL...THAT'S WHAT YOU GET FOR SLEEPING WITH A BARRACUDA.
RICHARD?! YOU OVERHEARD ALL THAT?!!
PLEASE. AS IF I DIDN'T KNOW IT WAS ALL GOING ON ALREADY.
HOW DO YOU THINK I EARNED MY REPUTATION AS GOSSIP QUEEN OF THIS HOUSE, ANYWAY?

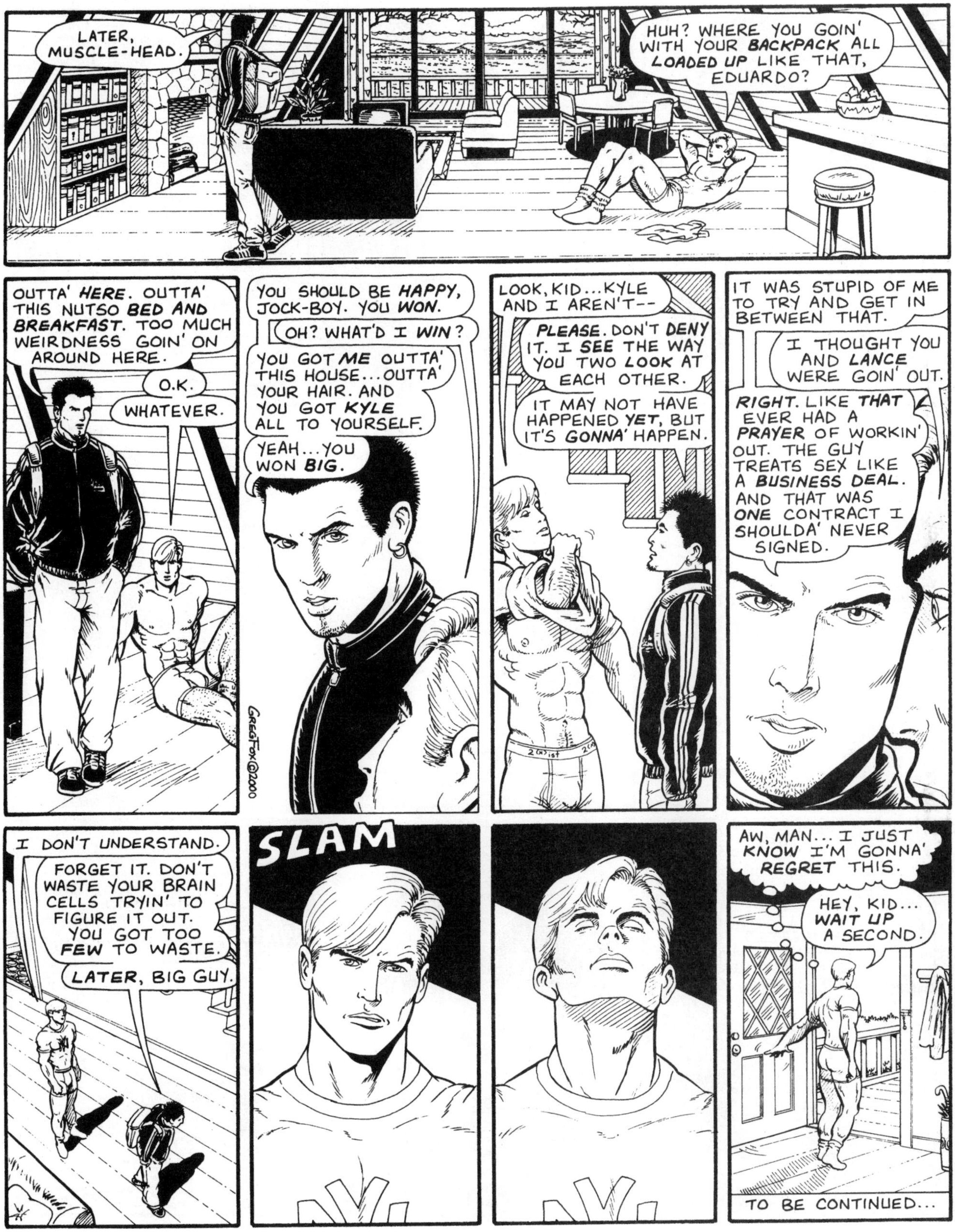

LATER, MUSCLE-HEAD.
HUH? WHERE YOU GOIN' WITH YOUR BACKPACK ALL LOADED UP LIKE THAT, EDUARDO?
OUTTA' HERE. OUTTA' THIS NUTSO BED AND BREAKFAST. TOO MUCH WEIRDNESS GOIN' ON AROUND HERE.
O.K.
WHATEVER.
GREG FOX ©2000
YOU SHOULD BE HAPPY, JOCK-BOY. YOU WON.
OH? WHAT'D I WIN?
YOU GOT ME OUTTA' THIS HOUSE...OUTTA' YOUR HAIR. AND YOU GOT KYLE ALL TO YOURSELF.
YEAH...YOU WON BIG.
LOOK, KID...KYLE AND I AREN'T--
PLEASE. DON'T DENY IT. I SEE THE WAY YOU TWO LOOK AT EACH OTHER.
IT MAY NOT HAVE HAPPENED YET, BUT IT'S GONNA' HAPPEN.
IT WAS STUPID OF ME TO TRY AND GET IN BETWEEN THAT.
I THOUGHT YOU AND LANCE WERE GOIN' OUT.
RIGHT. LIKE THAT EVER HAD A PRAYER OF WORKIN' OUT. THE GUY TREATS SEX LIKE A BUSINESS DEAL. AND THAT WAS ONE CONTRACT I SHOULDA' NEVER SIGNED.
I DON'T UNDERSTAND.
FORGET IT. DON'T WASTE YOUR BRAIN CELLS TRYIN' TO FIGURE IT OUT. YOU GOT TOO FEW TO WASTE.
LATER, BIG GUY.
SLAM
AW, MAN... I JUST KNOW I'M GONNA' REGRET THIS.
HEY, KID... WAIT UP A SECOND.
TO BE CONTINUED...

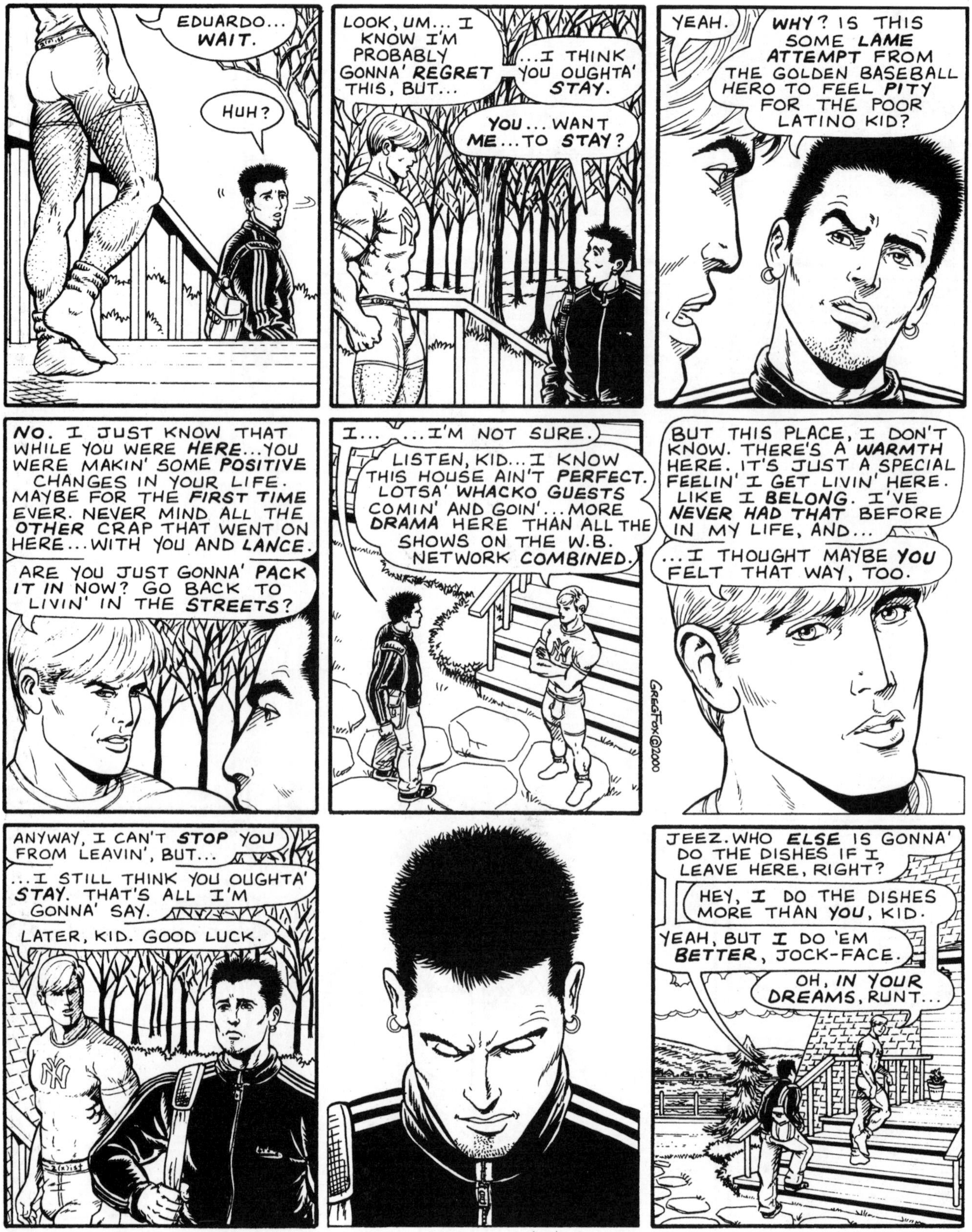
EDUARDO... WAIT.
HUH?
LOOK, UM... I KNOW I'M PROBABLY GONNA' REGRET THIS, BUT...
...I THINK YOU OUGHTA' STAY.
YOU... WANT ME... TO STAY?
YEAH.
WHY? IS THIS SOME LAME ATTEMPT FROM THE GOLDEN BASEBALL HERO TO FEEL PITY FOR THE POOR LATINO KID?
NO. I JUST KNOW THAT WHILE YOU WERE HERE...YOU WERE MAKIN' SOME POSITIVE CHANGES IN YOUR LIFE. MAYBE FOR THE FIRST TIME EVER. NEVER MIND ALL THE OTHER CRAP THAT WENT ON HERE... WITH YOU AND LANCE.
ARE YOU JUST GONNA' PACK IT IN NOW? GO BACK TO LIVIN' IN THE STREETS?
I...
...I'M NOT SURE.
LISTEN, KID... I KNOW THIS HOUSE AIN'T PERFECT. LOTSA' WHACKO GUESTS COMIN' AND GOIN'... MORE DRAMA HERE THAN ALL THE SHOWS ON THE W.B. NETWORK COMBINED.
GREG FOX © 2000
BUT THIS PLACE, I DON'T KNOW. THERE'S A WARMTH HERE. IT'S JUST A SPECIAL FEELIN' I GET LIVIN' HERE. LIKE I BELONG. I'VE NEVER HAD THAT BEFORE IN MY LIFE, AND...
...I THOUGHT MAYBE YOU FELT THAT WAY, TOO.
ANYWAY, I CAN'T STOP YOU FROM LEAVIN', BUT...
...I STILL THINK YOU OUGHTA' STAY. THAT'S ALL I'M GONNA' SAY.
LATER, KID. GOOD LUCK.
JEEZ. WHO ELSE IS GONNA' DO THE DISHES IF I LEAVE HERE, RIGHT?
HEY, I DO THE DISHES MORE THAN YOU, KID.
YEAH, BUT I DO 'EM BETTER, JOCK-FACE.
OH, IN YOUR DREAMS, RUNT...

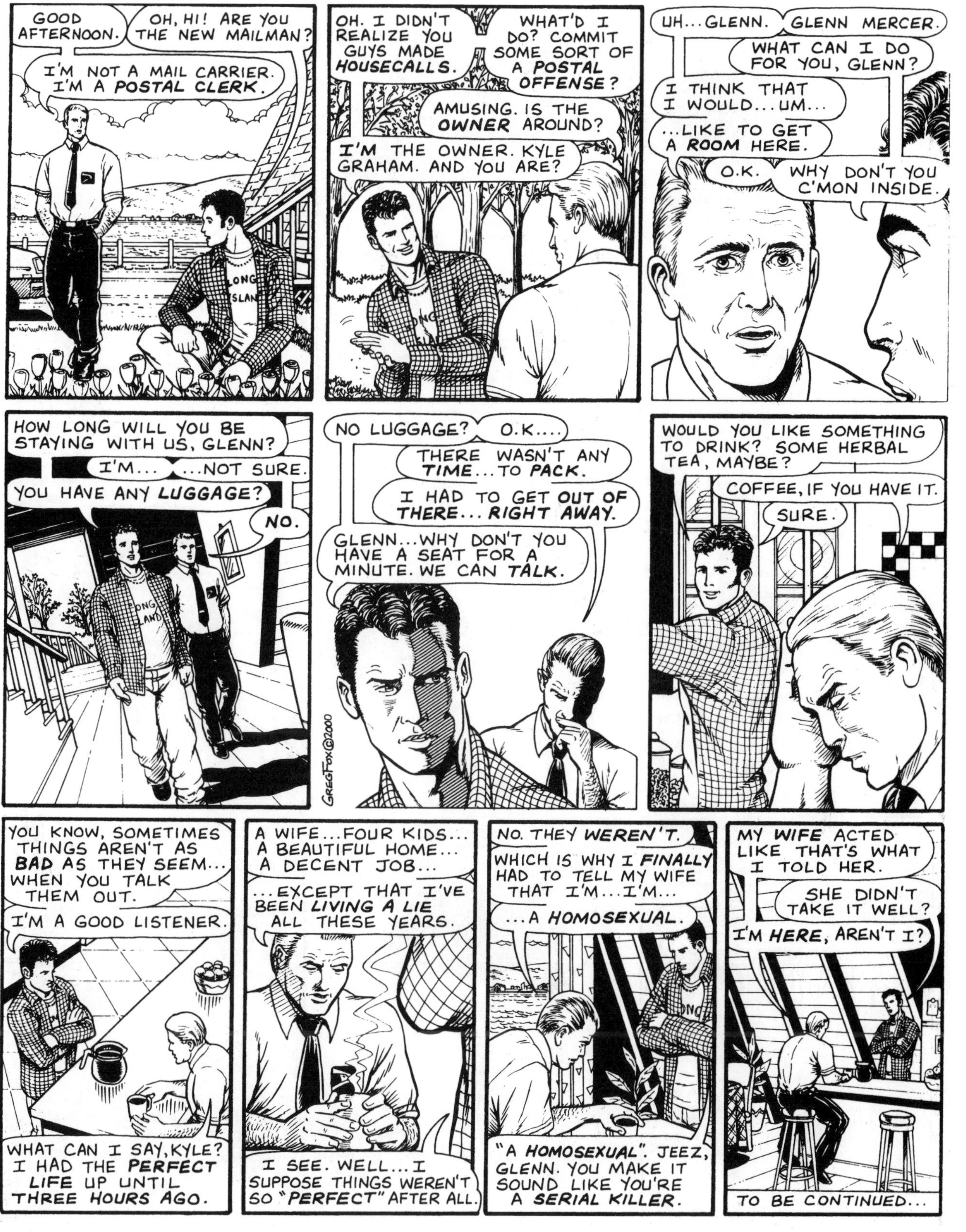
GOOD AFTERNOON.
OH, HI! ARE YOU THE NEW MAILMAN?
I'M NOT A MAIL CARRIER. I'M A POSTAL CLERK.
OH. I DIDN'T REALIZE YOU GUYS MADE HOUSECALLS.
WHAT'D I DO? COMMIT SOME SORT OF A POSTAL OFFENSE?
AMUSING. IS THE OWNER AROUND?
I'M THE OWNER. KYLE GRAHAM. AND YOU ARE?
UH...GLENN.
GLENN MERCER.
WHAT CAN I DO FOR YOU, GLENN?
I THINK THAT I WOULD...UM...
...LIKE TO GET A ROOM HERE.
O.K.
WHY DON'T YOU C'MON INSIDE.
HOW LONG WILL YOU BE STAYING WITH US, GLENN?
I'M...
...NOT SURE.
YOU HAVE ANY LUGGAGE?
NO.
NO LUGGAGE?
O.K....
THERE WASN'T ANY TIME...TO PACK.
I HAD TO GET OUT OF THERE...RIGHT AWAY.
GLENN...WHY DON'T YOU HAVE A SEAT FOR A MINUTE. WE CAN TALK.
GREG FOX ©2000
WOULD YOU LIKE SOMETHING TO DRINK? SOME HERBAL TEA, MAYBE?
COFFEE, IF YOU HAVE IT.
SURE.
YOU KNOW, SOMETIMES THINGS AREN'T AS BAD AS THEY SEEM... WHEN YOU TALK THEM OUT.
I'M A GOOD LISTENER.
WHAT CAN I SAY, KYLE? I HAD THE PERFECT LIFE UP UNTIL THREE HOURS AGO.
A WIFE...FOUR KIDS... A BEAUTIFUL HOME... A DECENT JOB...
...EXCEPT THAT I'VE BEEN LIVING A LIE ALL THESE YEARS.
I SEE. WELL...I SUPPOSE THINGS WEREN'T SO "PERFECT" AFTER ALL.
NO. THEY WEREN'T.
WHICH IS WHY I FINALLY HAD TO TELL MY WIFE THAT I'M...I'M...
...A HOMOSEXUAL.
"A HOMOSEXUAL". JEEZ, GLENN. YOU MAKE IT SOUND LIKE YOU'RE A SERIAL KILLER.
MY WIFE ACTED LIKE THAT'S WHAT I TOLD HER.
SHE DIDN'T TAKE IT WELL?
I'M HERE, AREN'T I?
TO BE CONTINUED...

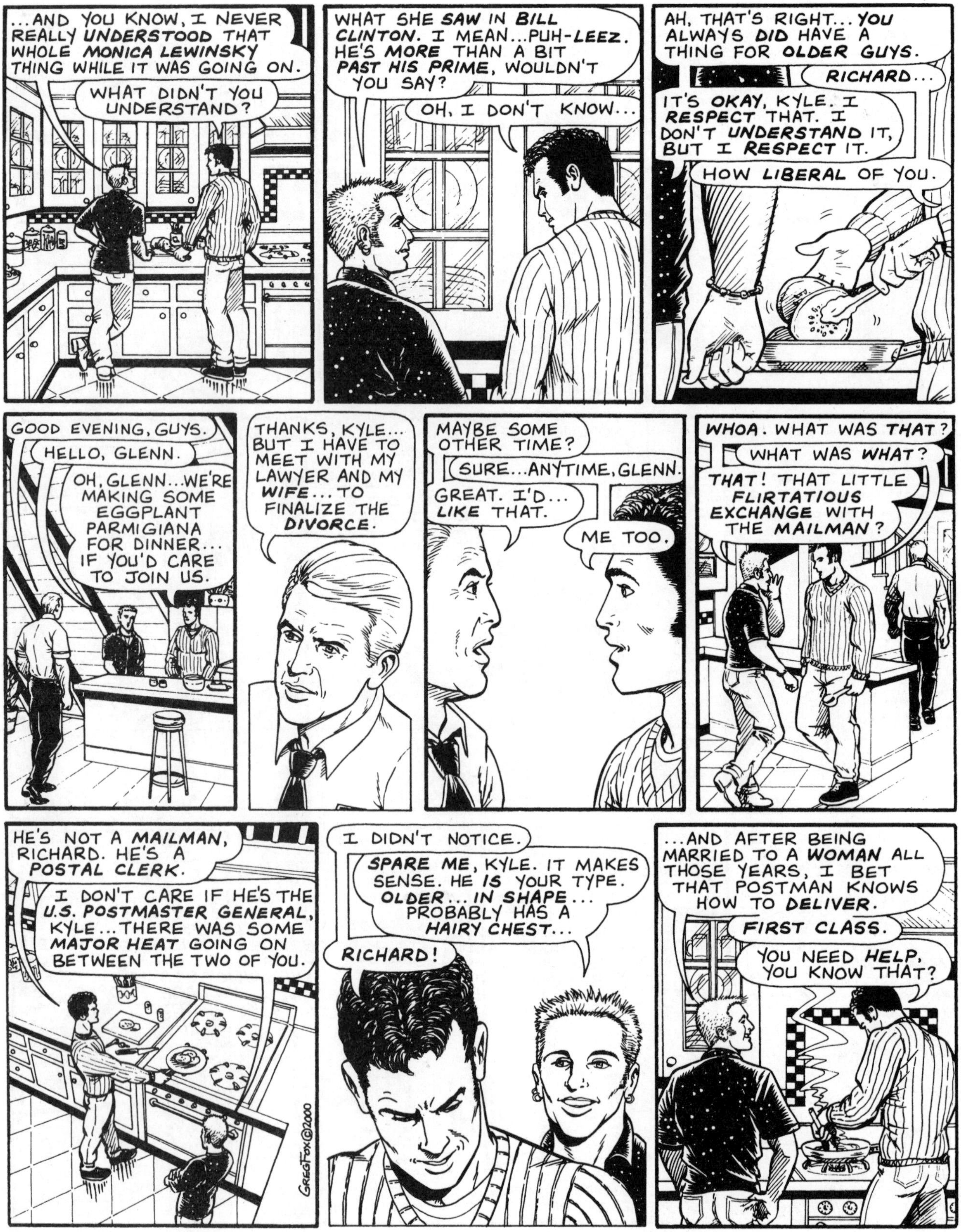
...AND YOU KNOW, I NEVER REALLY UNDERSTOOD THAT WHOLE MONICA LEWINSKY THING WHILE IT WAS GOING ON.
WHAT DIDN'T YOU UNDERSTAND?
WHAT SHE SAW IN BILL CLINTON. I MEAN...PUH-LEEZ. HE'S MORE THAN A BIT PAST HIS PRIME, WOULDN'T YOU SAY?
OH, I DON'T KNOW...
AH, THAT'S RIGHT... YOU ALWAYS DID HAVE A THING FOR OLDER GUYS.
RICHARD...
IT'S OKAY, KYLE. I RESPECT THAT. I DON'T UNDERSTAND IT, BUT I RESPECT IT.
HOW LIBERAL OF YOU.
GOOD EVENING, GUYS.
HELLO, GLENN.
OH, GLENN...WE'RE MAKING SOME EGGPLANT PARMIGIANA FOR DINNER... IF YOU'D CARE TO JOIN US.
THANKS, KYLE... BUT I HAVE TO MEET WITH MY LAWYER AND MY WIFE... TO FINALIZE THE DIVORCE.
MAYBE SOME OTHER TIME?
SURE...ANYTIME, GLENN.
GREAT. I'D... LIKE THAT.
ME TOO.
WHOA. WHAT WAS THAT?
WHAT WAS WHAT?
THAT! THAT LITTLE FLIRTATIOUS EXCHANGE WITH THE MAILMAN?
HE'S NOT A MAILMAN, RICHARD. HE'S A POSTAL CLERK.
I DON'T CARE IF HE'S THE U.S. POSTMASTER GENERAL, KYLE...THERE WAS SOME MAJOR HEAT GOING ON BETWEEN THE TWO OF YOU.
GREGFOX©2000
I DIDN'T NOTICE.
SPARE ME, KYLE. IT MAKES SENSE. HE IS YOUR TYPE. OLDER... IN SHAPE... PROBABLY HAS A HAIRY CHEST...
RICHARD!
...AND AFTER BEING MARRIED TO A WOMAN ALL THOSE YEARS, I BET THAT POSTMAN KNOWS HOW TO DELIVER.
FIRST CLASS.
YOU NEED HELP, YOU KNOW THAT?

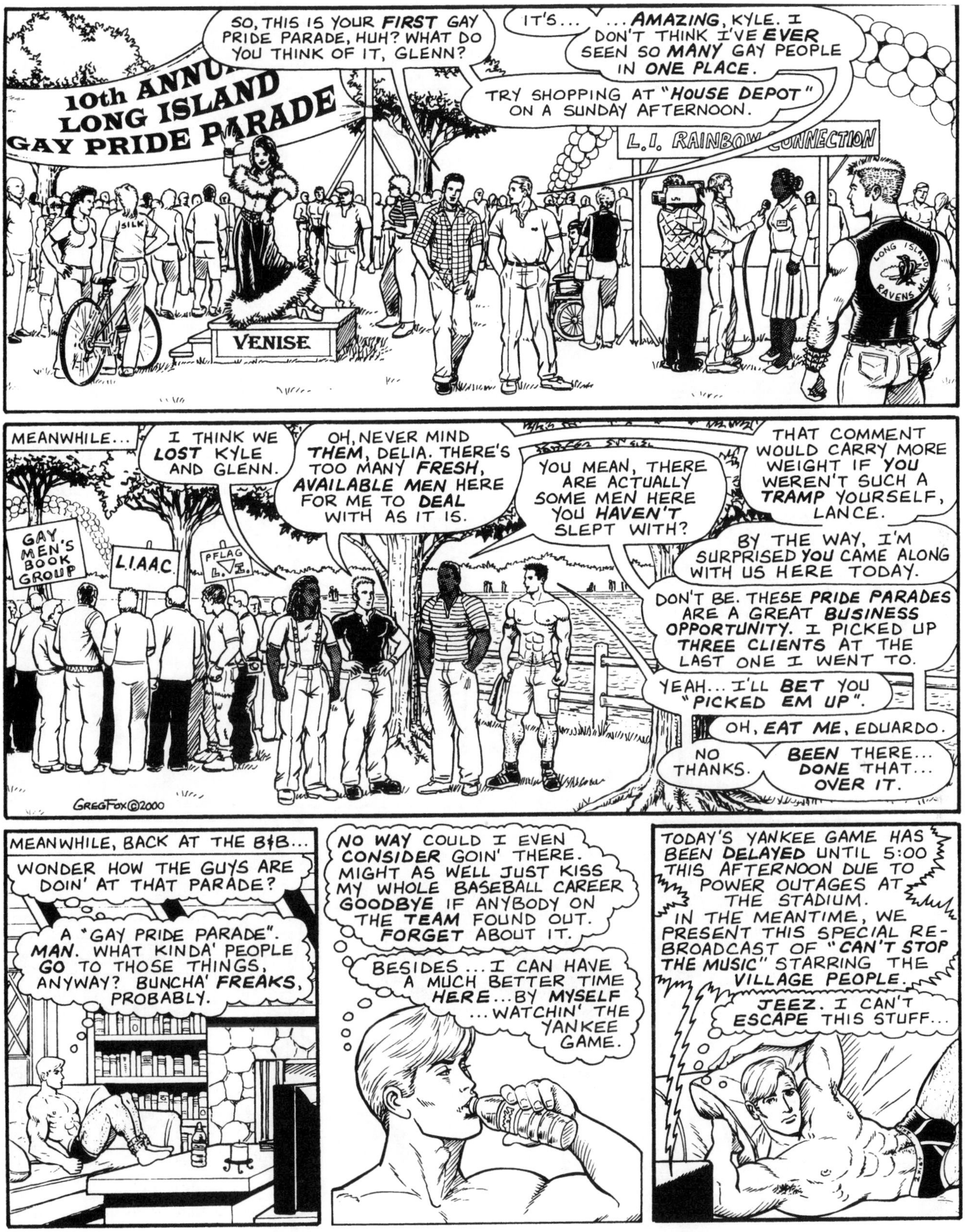

SO, THIS IS YOUR FIRST GAY PRIDE PARADE, HUH? WHAT DO YOU THINK OF IT, GLENN?
IT'S...
...AMAZING, KYLE. I DON'T THINK I'VE EVER SEEN SO MANY GAY PEOPLE IN ONE PLACE.
TRY SHOPPING AT "HOUSE DEPOT" ON A SUNDAY AFTERNOON.
10th ANNU
LONG ISLAND
GAY PRIDE PARADE
VENISE
L.I. RAINBOW
MEANWHILE...
I THINK WE LOST KYLE AND GLENN.
OH, NEVER MIND THEM, DELIA. THERE'S TOO MANY FRESH, AVAILABLE MEN HERE FOR ME TO DEAL WITH AS IT IS.
YOU MEAN, THERE ARE ACTUALLY SOME MEN HERE YOU HAVEN'T SLEPT WITH?
THAT COMMENT WOULD CARRY MORE WEIGHT IF YOU WEREN'T SUCH A TRAMP YOURSELF, LANCE.
BY THE WAY, I'M SURPRISED YOU CAME ALONG WITH US HERE TODAY.
DON'T BE. THESE PRIDE PARADES ARE A GREAT BUSINESS OPPORTUNITY. I PICKED UP THREE CLIENTS AT THE LAST ONE I WENT TO.
YEAH... I'LL BET YOU "PICKED EM UP".
OH, EAT ME, EDUARDO.
NO THANKS.
BEEN THERE... DONE THAT... OVER IT.
GAY MEN'S BOOK GROUP
L.I.A.A.C.
PFLAG L.I.
GREGFOX©2000
MEANWHILE, BACK AT THE B&B...
WONDER HOW THE GUYS ARE DOIN' AT THAT PARADE?
A "GAY PRIDE PARADE". MAN. WHAT KINDA' PEOPLE GO TO THOSE THINGS, ANYWAY? BUNCHA' FREAKS, PROBABLY.
NO WAY COULD I EVEN CONSIDER GOIN' THERE. MIGHT AS WELL JUST KISS MY WHOLE BASEBALL CAREER GOODBYE IF ANYBODY ON THE TEAM FOUND OUT. FORGET ABOUT IT.
BESIDES... I CAN HAVE A MUCH BETTER TIME HERE...BY MYSELF ...WATCHIN' THE YANKEE GAME.
TODAY'S YANKEE GAME HAS BEEN DELAYED UNTIL 5:00 THIS AFTERNOON DUE TO POWER OUTAGES AT THE STADIUM. IN THE MEANTIME, WE PRESENT THIS SPECIAL RE-BROADCAST OF "CAN'T STOP THE MUSIC" STARRING THE VILLAGE PEOPLE.
JEEZ. I CAN'T ESCAPE THIS STUFF...

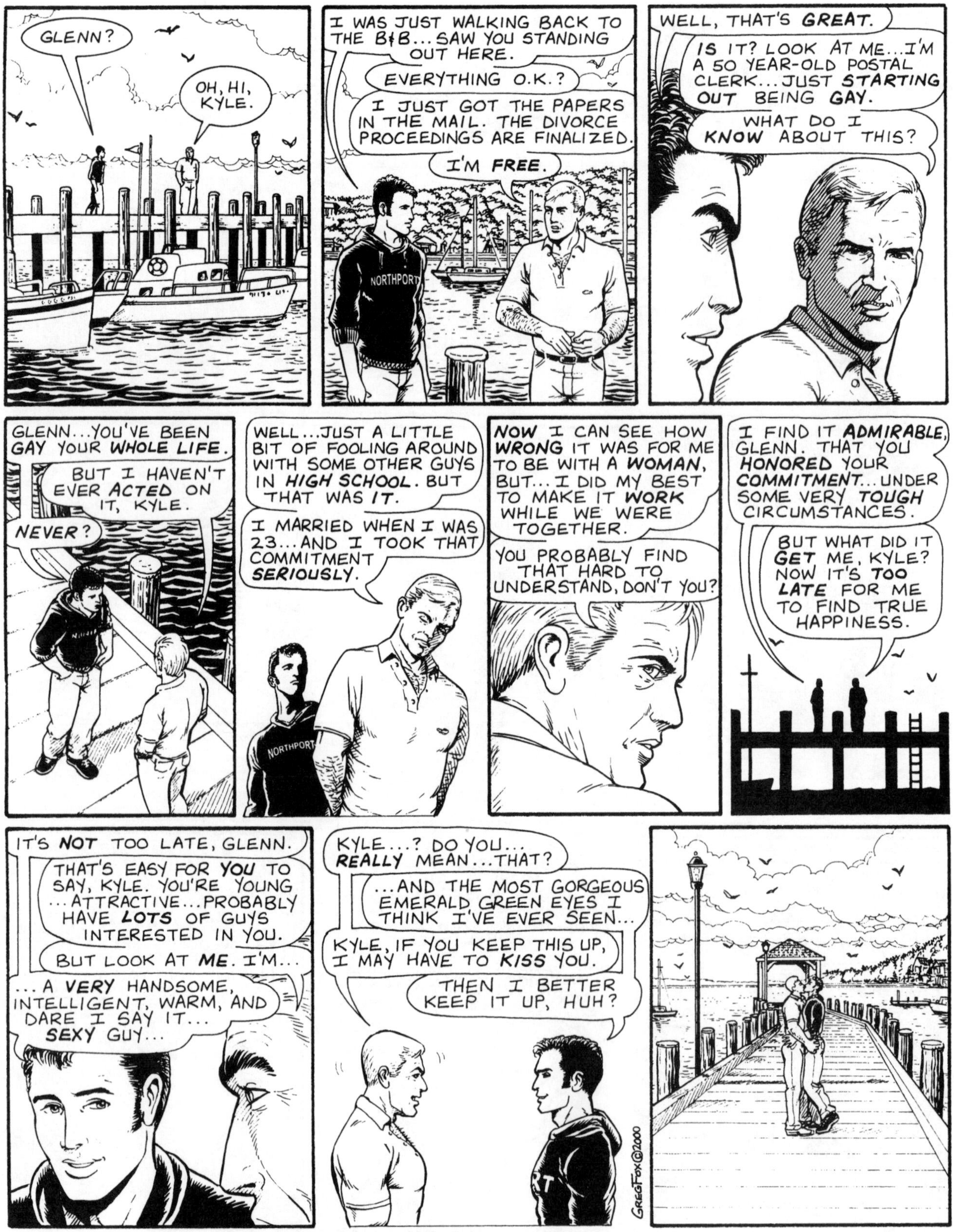
GLENN?
OH, HI, KYLE.
I WAS JUST WALKING BACK TO THE B&B... SAW YOU STANDING OUT HERE.
EVERYTHING O.K.?
I JUST GOT THE PAPERS IN THE MAIL. THE DIVORCE PROCEEDINGS ARE FINALIZED.
I'M FREE.
NORTHPORT
WELL, THAT'S GREAT.
IS IT? LOOK AT ME... I'M A 50 YEAR-OLD POSTAL CLERK... JUST STARTING OUT BEING GAY.
WHAT DO I KNOW ABOUT THIS?
GLENN... YOU'VE BEEN GAY YOUR WHOLE LIFE.
BUT I HAVEN'T EVER ACTED ON IT, KYLE.
NEVER?
WELL... JUST A LITTLE BIT OF FOOLING AROUND WITH SOME OTHER GUYS IN HIGH SCHOOL. BUT THAT WAS IT.
I MARRIED WHEN I WAS 23... AND I TOOK THAT COMMITMENT SERIOUSLY.
NORTHPORT
NOW I CAN SEE HOW WRONG IT WAS FOR ME TO BE WITH A WOMAN, BUT... I DID MY BEST TO MAKE IT WORK WHILE WE WERE TOGETHER.
YOU PROBABLY FIND THAT HARD TO UNDERSTAND, DON'T YOU?
I FIND IT ADMIRABLE, GLENN. THAT YOU HONORED YOUR COMMITMENT... UNDER SOME VERY TOUGH CIRCUMSTANCES.
BUT WHAT DID IT GET ME, KYLE? NOW IT'S TOO LATE FOR ME TO FIND TRUE HAPPINESS.
IT'S NOT TOO LATE, GLENN.
THAT'S EASY FOR YOU TO SAY, KYLE. YOU'RE YOUNG ... ATTRACTIVE... PROBABLY HAVE LOTS OF GUYS INTERESTED IN YOU.
BUT LOOK AT ME. I'M...
... A VERY HANDSOME, INTELLIGENT, WARM, AND DARE I SAY IT... SEXY GUY...
KYLE...? DO YOU... REALLY MEAN... THAT?
...AND THE MOST GORGEOUS EMERALD GREEN EYES I THINK I'VE EVER SEEN...
KYLE, IF YOU KEEP THIS UP, I MAY HAVE TO KISS YOU.
THEN I BETTER KEEP IT UP, HUH?
GREGFOX©2000

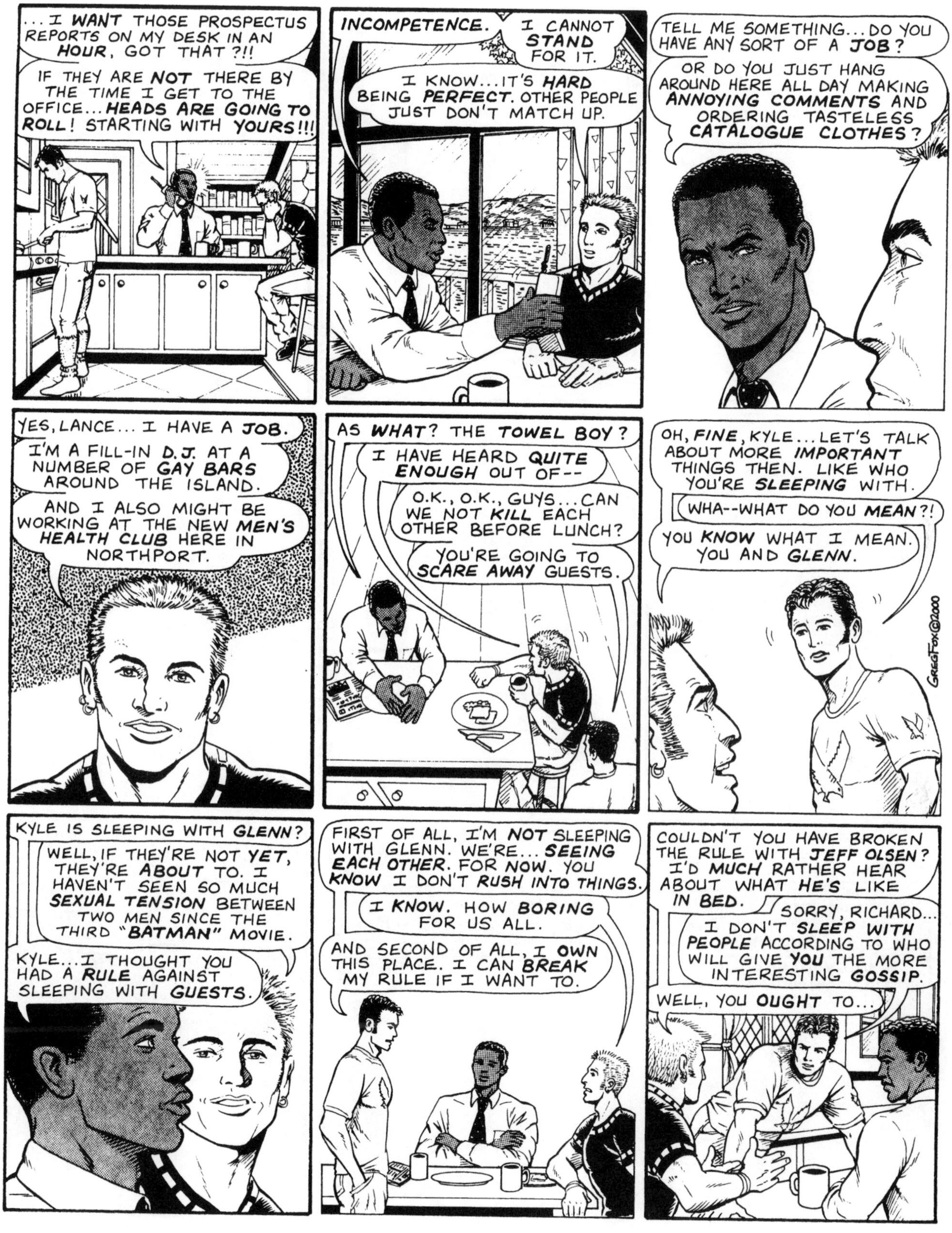
...I WANT THOSE PROSPECTUS REPORTS ON MY DESK IN AN HOUR, GOT THAT?!!
IF THEY ARE NOT THERE BY THE TIME I GET TO THE OFFICE... HEADS ARE GOING TO ROLL! STARTING WITH YOURS!!!
INCOMPETENCE.
I CANNOT STAND FOR IT.
I KNOW... IT'S HARD BEING PERFECT. OTHER PEOPLE JUST DON'T MATCH UP.
TELL ME SOMETHING... DO YOU HAVE ANY SORT OF A JOB?
OR DO YOU JUST HANG AROUND HERE ALL DAY MAKING ANNOYING COMMENTS AND ORDERING TASTELESS CATALOGUE CLOTHES?
YES, LANCE... I HAVE A JOB.
I'M A FILL-IN D.J. AT A NUMBER OF GAY BARS AROUND THE ISLAND.
AND I ALSO MIGHT BE WORKING AT THE NEW MEN'S HEALTH CLUB HERE IN NORTHPORT.
AS WHAT? THE TOWEL BOY?
I HAVE HEARD QUITE ENOUGH OUT OF--
O.K., O.K., GUYS... CAN WE NOT KILL EACH OTHER BEFORE LUNCH?
YOU'RE GOING TO SCARE AWAY GUESTS.
OH, FINE, KYLE... LET'S TALK ABOUT MORE IMPORTANT THINGS THEN. LIKE WHO YOU'RE SLEEPING WITH.
WHA--WHAT DO YOU MEAN?!
YOU KNOW WHAT I MEAN. YOU AND GLENN.
GREGFOX©2000
KYLE IS SLEEPING WITH GLENN?
WELL, IF THEY'RE NOT YET, THEY'RE ABOUT TO. I HAVEN'T SEEN SO MUCH SEXUAL TENSION BETWEEN TWO MEN SINCE THE THIRD "BATMAN" MOVIE.
KYLE... I THOUGHT YOU HAD A RULE AGAINST SLEEPING WITH GUESTS.
FIRST OF ALL, I'M NOT SLEEPING WITH GLENN. WE'RE... SEEING EACH OTHER. FOR NOW. YOU KNOW I DON'T RUSH INTO THINGS.
I KNOW. HOW BORING FOR US ALL.
AND SECOND OF ALL, I OWN THIS PLACE. I CAN BREAK MY RULE IF I WANT TO.
COULDN'T YOU HAVE BROKEN THE RULE WITH JEFF OLSEN? I'D MUCH RATHER HEAR ABOUT WHAT HE'S LIKE IN BED.
SORRY, RICHARD... I DON'T SLEEP WITH PEOPLE ACCORDING TO WHO WILL GIVE YOU THE MORE INTERESTING GOSSIP.
WELL, YOU OUGHT TO...

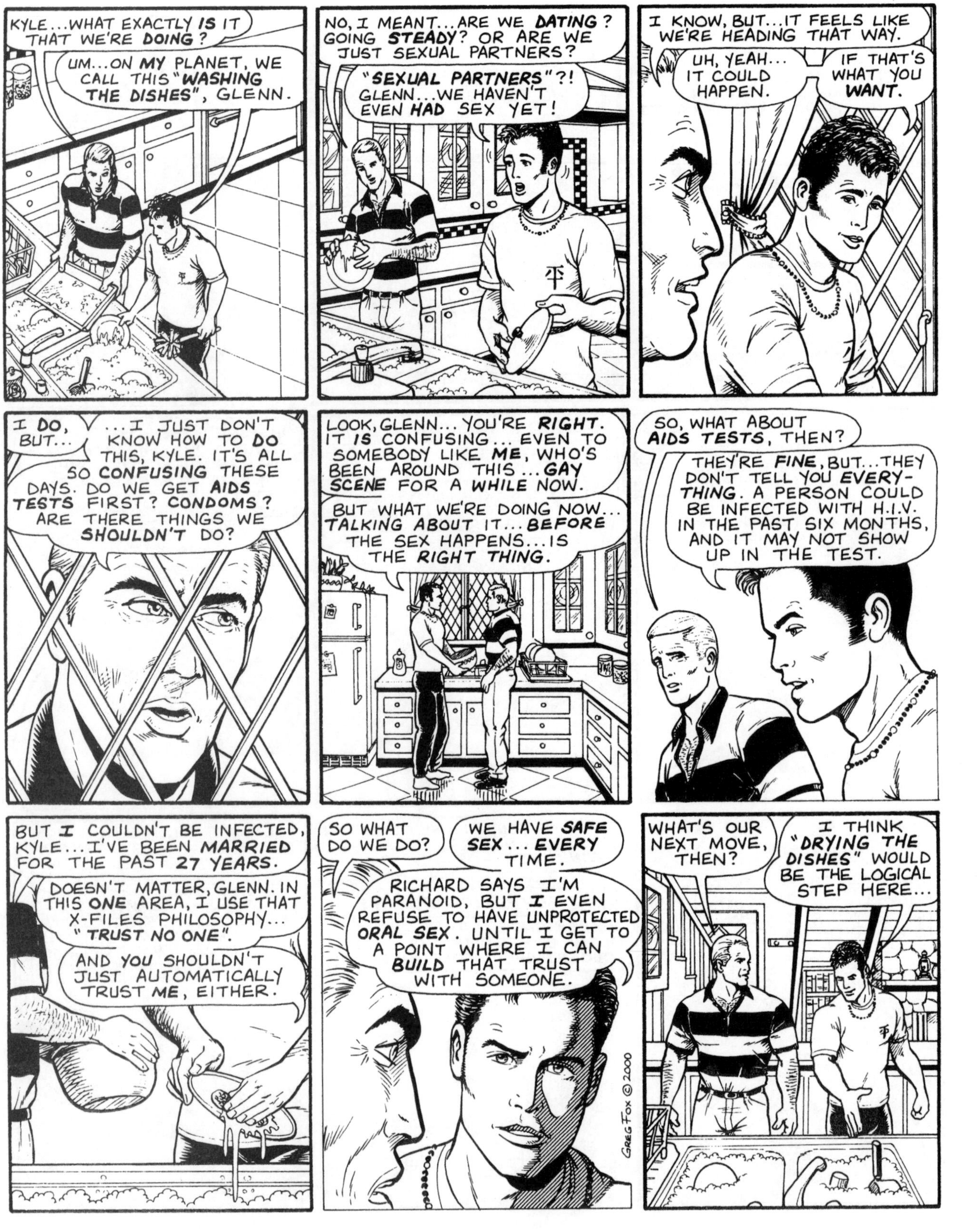
KYLE...WHAT EXACTLY IS IT THAT WE'RE DOING?
UM...ON MY PLANET, WE CALL THIS "WASHING THE DISHES", GLENN.
NO, I MEANT...ARE WE DATING? GOING STEADY? OR ARE WE JUST SEXUAL PARTNERS?
"SEXUAL PARTNERS"?! GLENN...WE HAVEN'T EVEN HAD SEX YET!
I KNOW, BUT...IT FEELS LIKE WE'RE HEADING THAT WAY.
UH, YEAH... IT COULD HAPPEN.
IF THAT'S WHAT YOU WANT.
I DO, BUT...
...I JUST DON'T KNOW HOW TO DO THIS, KYLE. IT'S ALL SO CONFUSING THESE DAYS. DO WE GET AIDS TESTS FIRST? CONDOMS? ARE THERE THINGS WE SHOULDN'T DO?
LOOK, GLENN... YOU'RE RIGHT. IT IS CONFUSING... EVEN TO SOMEBODY LIKE ME, WHO'S BEEN AROUND THIS...GAY SCENE FOR A WHILE NOW.
BUT WHAT WE'RE DOING NOW... TALKING ABOUT IT... BEFORE THE SEX HAPPENS...IS THE RIGHT THING.
SO, WHAT ABOUT AIDS TESTS, THEN?
THEY'RE FINE, BUT...THEY DON'T TELL YOU EVERYTHING. A PERSON COULD BE INFECTED WITH H.I.V. IN THE PAST SIX MONTHS, AND IT MAY NOT SHOW UP IN THE TEST.
BUT I COULDN'T BE INFECTED, KYLE...I'VE BEEN MARRIED FOR THE PAST 27 YEARS.
DOESN'T MATTER, GLENN. IN THIS ONE AREA, I USE THAT X-FILES PHILOSOPHY... "TRUST NO ONE".
AND YOU SHOULDN'T JUST AUTOMATICALLY TRUST ME, EITHER.
SO WHAT DO WE DO?
WE HAVE SAFE SEX... EVERY TIME.
RICHARD SAYS I'M PARANOID, BUT I EVEN REFUSE TO HAVE UNPROTECTED ORAL SEX. UNTIL I GET TO A POINT WHERE I CAN BUILD THAT TRUST WITH SOMEONE.
GREG FOX © 2000
WHAT'S OUR NEXT MOVE, THEN?
I THINK "DRYING THE DISHES" WOULD BE THE LOGICAL STEP HERE...

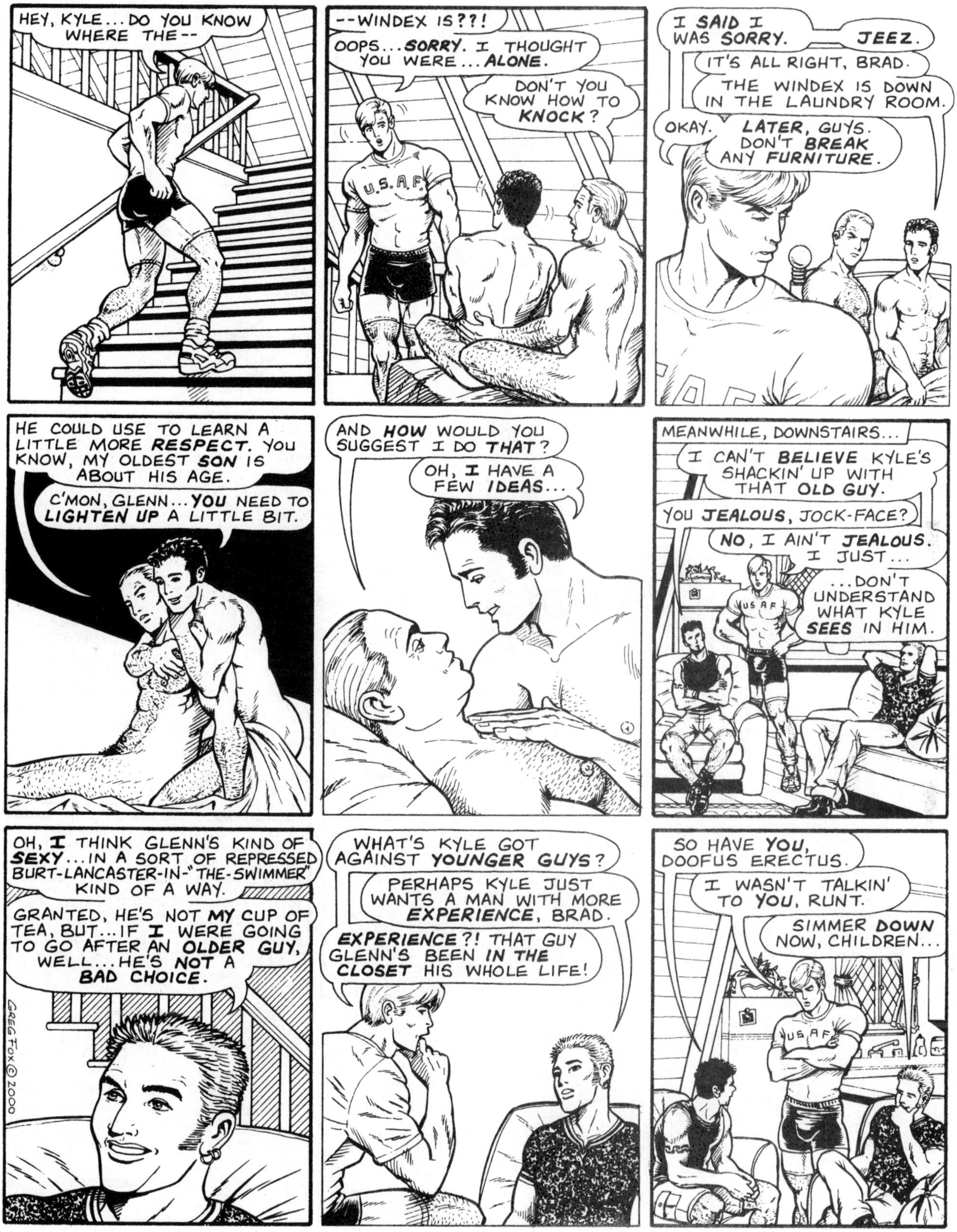
HEY, KYLE... DO YOU KNOW WHERE THE--
--WINDEX IS???!
OOPS... SORRY. I THOUGHT YOU WERE... ALONE.
DON'T YOU KNOW HOW TO KNOCK?
I SAID I WAS SORRY.
JEEZ.
IT'S ALL RIGHT, BRAD.
THE WINDEX IS DOWN IN THE LAUNDRY ROOM.
OKAY.
LATER, GUYS. DON'T BREAK ANY FURNITURE.
HE COULD USE TO LEARN A LITTLE MORE RESPECT. YOU KNOW, MY OLDEST SON IS ABOUT HIS AGE.
C'MON, GLENN... YOU NEED TO LIGHTEN UP A LITTLE BIT.
AND HOW WOULD YOU SUGGEST I DO THAT?
OH, I HAVE A FEW IDEAS...
MEANWHILE, DOWNSTAIRS...
I CAN'T BELIEVE KYLE'S SHACKIN' UP WITH THAT OLD GUY.
YOU JEALOUS, JOCK-FACE?
NO, I AIN'T JEALOUS. I JUST...
...DON'T UNDERSTAND WHAT KYLE SEES IN HIM.
OH, I THINK GLENN'S KIND OF SEXY... IN A SORT OF REPRESSED BURT-LANCASTER-IN-"THE-SWIMMER" KIND OF A WAY.
GRANTED, HE'S NOT MY CUP OF TEA, BUT... IF I WERE GOING TO GO AFTER AN OLDER GUY, WELL... HE'S NOT A BAD CHOICE.
GREG FOX © 2000
WHAT'S KYLE GOT AGAINST YOUNGER GUYS?
PERHAPS KYLE JUST WANTS A MAN WITH MORE EXPERIENCE, BRAD.
EXPERIENCE?! THAT GUY GLENN'S BEEN IN THE CLOSET HIS WHOLE LIFE!
SO HAVE YOU, DOOFUS ERECTUS.
I WASN'T TALKIN' TO YOU, RUNT.
SIMMER DOWN NOW, CHILDREN...

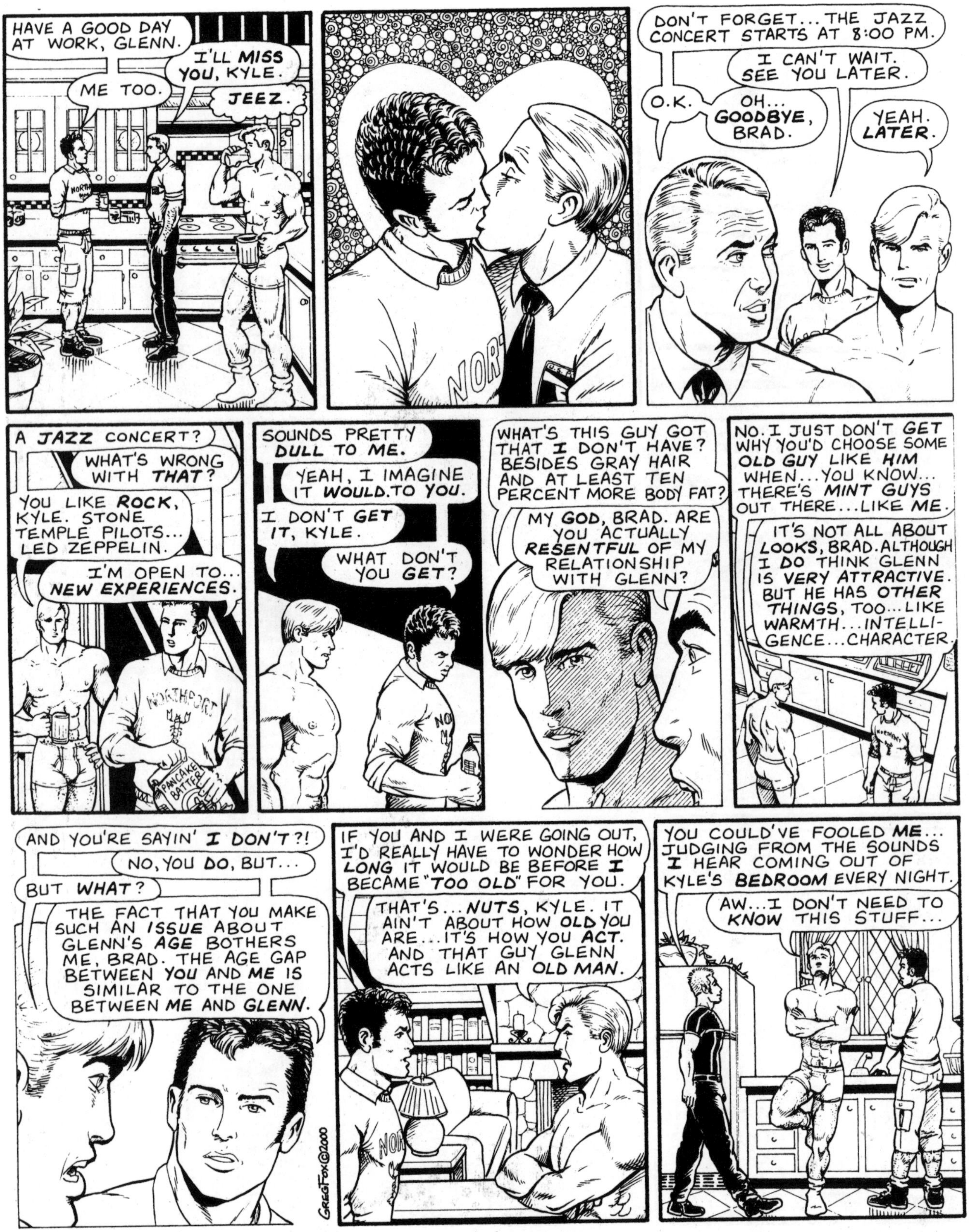

HAVE A GOOD DAY AT WORK, GLENN.
I'LL MISS YOU, KYLE.
ME TOO.
JEEZ.
DON'T FORGET... THE JAZZ CONCERT STARTS AT 8:00 PM.
I CAN'T WAIT. SEE YOU LATER.
O.K.
OH... GOODBYE, BRAD.
YEAH. LATER.
A JAZZ CONCERT?
WHAT'S WRONG WITH THAT?
YOU LIKE ROCK, KYLE. STONE TEMPLE PILOTS... LED ZEPPELIN.
I'M OPEN TO... NEW EXPERIENCES.
PANCAKE BATTER
SOUNDS PRETTY DULL TO ME.
YEAH, I IMAGINE IT WOULD. TO YOU.
I DON'T GET IT, KYLE.
WHAT DON'T YOU GET?
WHAT'S THIS GUY GOT THAT I DON'T HAVE? BESIDES GRAY HAIR AND AT LEAST TEN PERCENT MORE BODY FAT?
MY GOD, BRAD. ARE YOU ACTUALLY RESENTFUL OF MY RELATIONSHIP WITH GLENN?
NO. I JUST DON'T GET WHY YOU'D CHOOSE SOME OLD GUY LIKE HIM WHEN... YOU KNOW... THERE'S MINT GUYS OUT THERE... LIKE ME.
IT'S NOT ALL ABOUT LOOKS, BRAD. ALTHOUGH I DO THINK GLENN IS VERY ATTRACTIVE. BUT HE HAS OTHER THINGS, TOO... LIKE WARMTH... INTELLI-GENCE... CHARACTER.
AND YOU'RE SAYIN' I DON'T?!
NO, YOU DO, BUT...
BUT WHAT?
THE FACT THAT YOU MAKE SUCH AN ISSUE ABOUT GLENN'S AGE BOTHERS ME, BRAD. THE AGE GAP BETWEEN YOU AND ME IS SIMILAR TO THE ONE BETWEEN ME AND GLENN.
IF YOU AND I WERE GOING OUT, I'D REALLY HAVE TO WONDER HOW LONG IT WOULD BE BEFORE I BECAME "TOO OLD" FOR YOU.
THAT'S... NUTS, KYLE. IT AIN'T ABOUT HOW OLD YOU ARE... IT'S HOW YOU ACT. AND THAT GUY GLENN ACTS LIKE AN OLD MAN.
GREGFOX©2000
YOU COULD'VE FOOLED ME... JUDGING FROM THE SOUNDS I HEAR COMING OUT OF KYLE'S BEDROOM EVERY NIGHT.
AW... I DON'T NEED TO KNOW THIS STUFF...

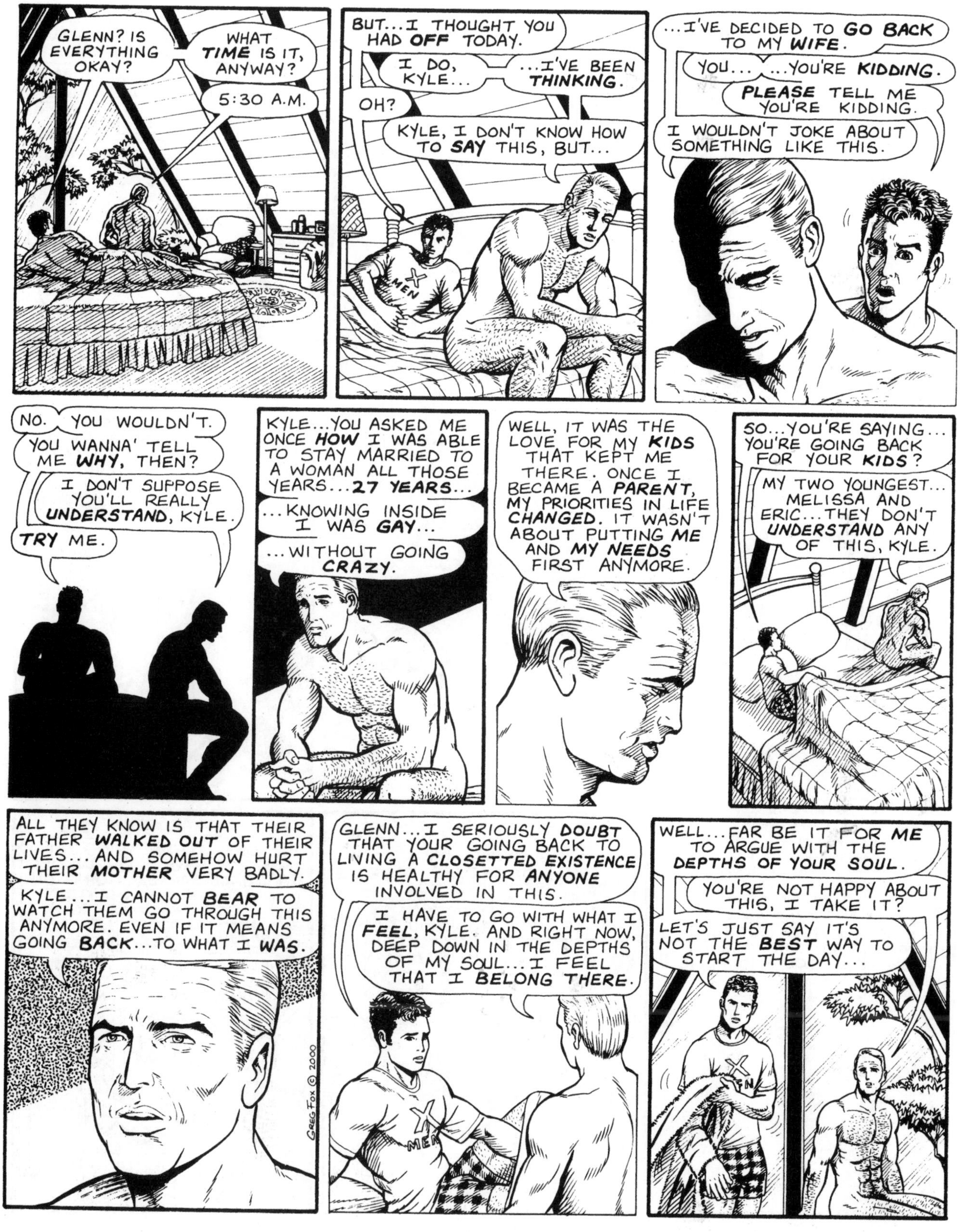

GLENN? IS EVERYTHING OKAY?
WHAT TIME IS IT, ANYWAY?
5:30 A.M.
BUT... I THOUGHT YOU HAD OFF TODAY.
I DO, KYLE...
...I'VE BEEN THINKING.
OH?
KYLE, I DON'T KNOW HOW TO SAY THIS, BUT...
...I'VE DECIDED TO GO BACK TO MY WIFE.
YOU...
...YOU'RE KIDDING.
PLEASE TELL ME YOU'RE KIDDING.
I WOULDN'T JOKE ABOUT SOMETHING LIKE THIS.
NO.
YOU WOULDN'T.
YOU WANNA' TELL ME WHY, THEN?
I DON'T SUPPOSE YOU'LL REALLY UNDERSTAND, KYLE.
TRY ME.
KYLE... YOU ASKED ME ONCE HOW I WAS ABLE TO STAY MARRIED TO A WOMAN ALL THOSE YEARS... 27 YEARS...
...KNOWING INSIDE I WAS GAY...
...WITHOUT GOING CRAZY.
WELL, IT WAS THE LOVE FOR MY KIDS THAT KEPT ME THERE. ONCE I BECAME A PARENT, MY PRIORITIES IN LIFE CHANGED. IT WASN'T ABOUT PUTTING ME AND MY NEEDS FIRST ANYMORE.
SO... YOU'RE SAYING... YOU'RE GOING BACK FOR YOUR KIDS?
MY TWO YOUNGEST... MELISSA AND ERIC... THEY DON'T UNDERSTAND ANY OF THIS, KYLE.
ALL THEY KNOW IS THAT THEIR FATHER WALKED OUT OF THEIR LIVES... AND SOMEHOW HURT THEIR MOTHER VERY BADLY.
KYLE... I CANNOT BEAR TO WATCH THEM GO THROUGH THIS ANYMORE. EVEN IF IT MEANS GOING BACK... TO WHAT I WAS.
GREG FOX © 2000
GLENN... I SERIOUSLY DOUBT THAT YOUR GOING BACK TO LIVING A CLOSETTED EXISTENCE IS HEALTHY FOR ANYONE INVOLVED IN THIS.
I HAVE TO GO WITH WHAT I FEEL, KYLE. AND RIGHT NOW, DEEP DOWN IN THE DEPTHS OF MY SOUL... I FEEL THAT I BELONG THERE.
WELL... FAR BE IT FOR ME TO ARGUE WITH THE DEPTHS OF YOUR SOUL.
YOU'RE NOT HAPPY ABOUT THIS, I TAKE IT?
LET'S JUST SAY IT'S NOT THE BEST WAY TO START THE DAY...

Panel 1:
ALL DONE PACKIN', I SEE?

HUH?

OH...YES, BRAD. I WAS JUST STRAIGHTENING UP THE ROOM BEFORE I LEAVE.

Panel 2:

NICE. SLIP OUTTA' HERE BEFORE KYLE GETS BACK FROM THE SUPERMARKET, HUH?

THAT WAY YOU DON'T GOTTA' *FACE* HIM... LIKE A *MAN*.

Panel 3:

NOT THAT THIS IS *ANY* OF *YOUR* BUSINESS, BRAD...BUT I *AM* WAITING FOR KYLE TO GET BACK.

I WOULDN'T JUST *LEAVE*, AFTER...

Panel 4:

AFTER *WHAT*? AFTER ALL YOU TWO HAVE BEEN THROUGH?

PLEASE. I'M *GLAD* YOU'RE RUNNIN' BACK TO YOUR LITTLE *WIFE*, MERCER. KYLE DESERVES A LOT *BETTER* THAN YOU.

Panel 5:
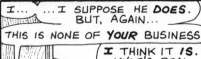

I... ...I SUPPOSE HE *DOES.* BUT, AGAIN...

THIS IS NONE OF *YOUR* BUSINESS.

I THINK IT *IS.* KYLE'S REAL *IMPORTANT* TO ME, MERCER... PROBABLY THE *BEST FRIEND* I EVER HAD.

AND I DON'T LIKE SEEIN' HIM GET *HURT*...BY A *LOSER* LIKE YOU.

Panel 6:

YOU THINK I *ENJOY* DOING THIS, BRAD?! WALKING OUT ON THE *ONLY* RELATIONSHIP IN MY *LIFE* WHERE I'VE EVER LOVED *COMPLETELY*... *FULLY*...*NATURALLY*?!!

THIS IS *TEARING ME APART.*

OH...AM I SUPPOSED TO FEEL *SORRY* FOR YOU NOW?

GREG FOX © 2000

Panel 7:
YOU CAN FEEL WHATEVER YOU *WANT.* BUT DON'T *EVER* BELIEVE THAT I DON'T *LOVE* KYLE, *DEEPLY.* BECAUSE I DO.

THIS JUST WASN'T... *MEANT* TO *BE.*

YEAH. WHATEVER.

Panel 8:

BRAD...YOU *CAN* DO ME ONE *FAVOR.*

A *FAVOR*? FOR *YOU*? WHY *SHOULD* I?

BECAUSE IT'S REALLY FOR *KYLE.*

I'VE SEEN HOW MUCH YOU *CARE* FOR HIM. I THINK MAYBE YOU...CARE FOR HIM AS *MORE* THAN A FRIEND?

Panel 9:

YOU'RE A GOOD MAN, BRAD. BE *WITH* HIM. HE *DESERVES* SOMEONE LIKE YOU.

YEAH. MAYBE.

WELL...I GUESS THAT'S UP TO *KYLE*, ISN'T IT?

Panel 10:

YES...I IMAGINE IT *IS.*

AND ONE *OTHER* THING...I KNOW YOU HAVE YOUR WHOLE *BASEBALL CAREER* GOING ON. DON'T EVER DO WHAT *I* DID...GET *MARRIED* TO A *WOMAN* TO KEEP UP *APPEARANCES.*

ALL RIGHT, LET'S NOT TURN THIS INTO A *CLOSET-CASE CONVENTION* HERE, MERCER...

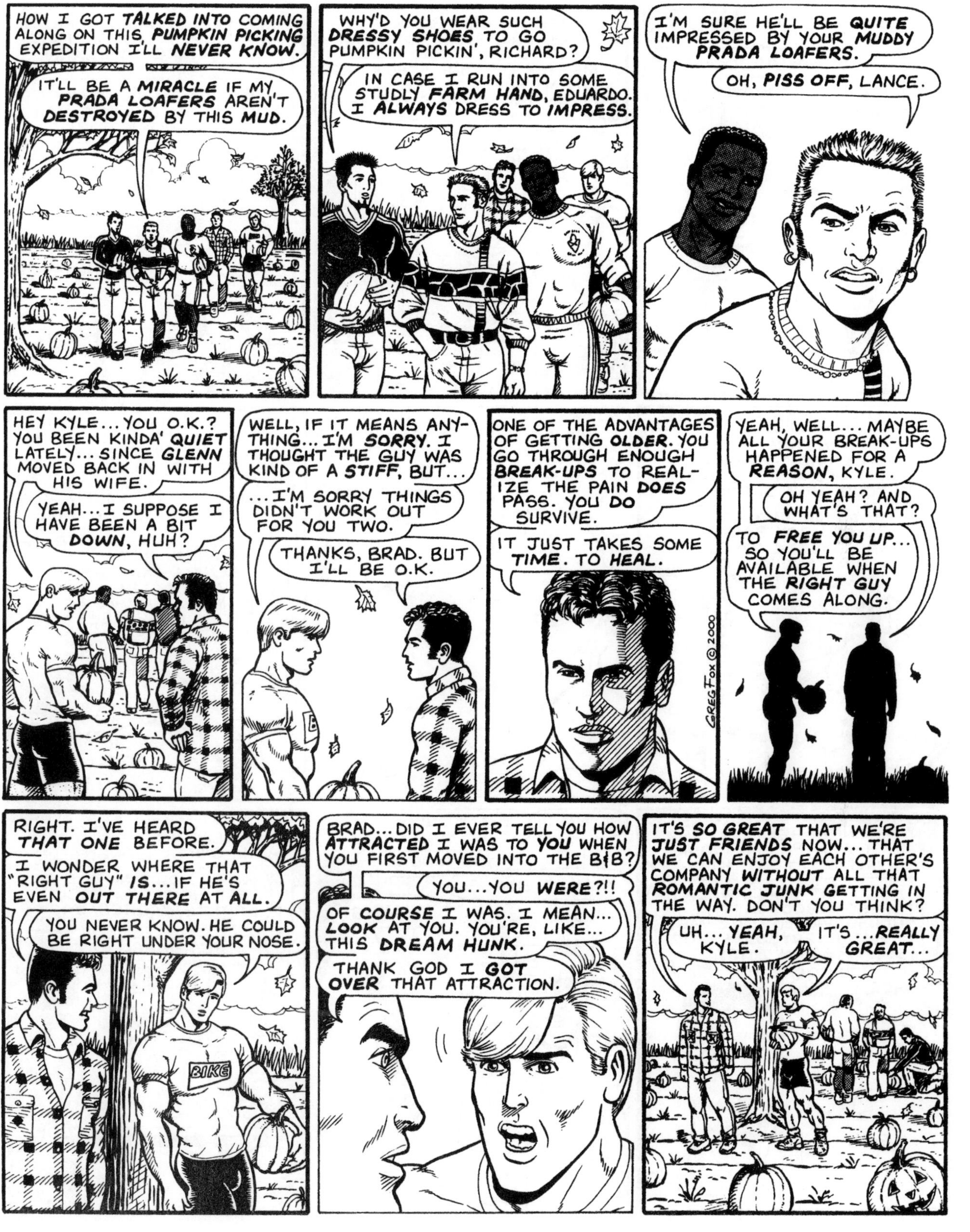

HOW I GOT TALKED INTO COMING ALONG ON THIS PUMPKIN PICKING EXPEDITION I'LL NEVER KNOW.
IT'LL BE A MIRACLE IF MY PRADA LOAFERS AREN'T DESTROYED BY THIS MUD.
WHY'D YOU WEAR SUCH DRESSY SHOES TO GO PUMPKIN PICKIN', RICHARD?
IN CASE I RUN INTO SOME STUDLY FARM HAND, EDUARDO. I ALWAYS DRESS TO IMPRESS.
I'M SURE HE'LL BE QUITE IMPRESSED BY YOUR MUDDY PRADA LOAFERS.
OH, PISS OFF, LANCE.
HEY KYLE... YOU O.K.? YOU BEEN KINDA' QUIET LATELY... SINCE GLENN MOVED BACK IN WITH HIS WIFE.
YEAH... I SUPPOSE I HAVE BEEN A BIT DOWN, HUH?
WELL, IF IT MEANS ANYTHING... I'M SORRY. I THOUGHT THE GUY WAS KIND OF A STIFF, BUT...
... I'M SORRY THINGS DIDN'T WORK OUT FOR YOU TWO.
THANKS, BRAD. BUT I'LL BE O.K.
ONE OF THE ADVANTAGES OF GETTING OLDER. YOU GO THROUGH ENOUGH BREAK-UPS TO REALIZE THE PAIN DOES PASS. YOU DO SURVIVE.
IT JUST TAKES SOME TIME. TO HEAL.
GREG FOX © 2000
YEAH, WELL... MAYBE ALL YOUR BREAK-UPS HAPPENED FOR A REASON, KYLE.
OH YEAH? AND WHAT'S THAT?
TO FREE YOU UP... SO YOU'LL BE AVAILABLE WHEN THE RIGHT GUY COMES ALONG.
RIGHT. I'VE HEARD THAT ONE BEFORE.
I WONDER WHERE THAT "RIGHT GUY" IS... IF HE'S EVEN OUT THERE AT ALL.
YOU NEVER KNOW. HE COULD BE RIGHT UNDER YOUR NOSE.
BIKE
BRAD... DID I EVER TELL YOU HOW ATTRACTED I WAS TO YOU WHEN YOU FIRST MOVED INTO THE B&B?
YOU... YOU WERE?!!
OF COURSE I WAS. I MEAN... LOOK AT YOU. YOU'RE, LIKE... THIS DREAM HUNK.
THANK GOD I GOT OVER THAT ATTRACTION.
IT'S SO GREAT THAT WE'RE JUST FRIENDS NOW... THAT WE CAN ENJOY EACH OTHER'S COMPANY WITHOUT ALL THAT ROMANTIC JUNK GETTING IN THE WAY. DON'T YOU THINK?
UH... YEAH, KYLE.
IT'S ...REALLY GREAT...

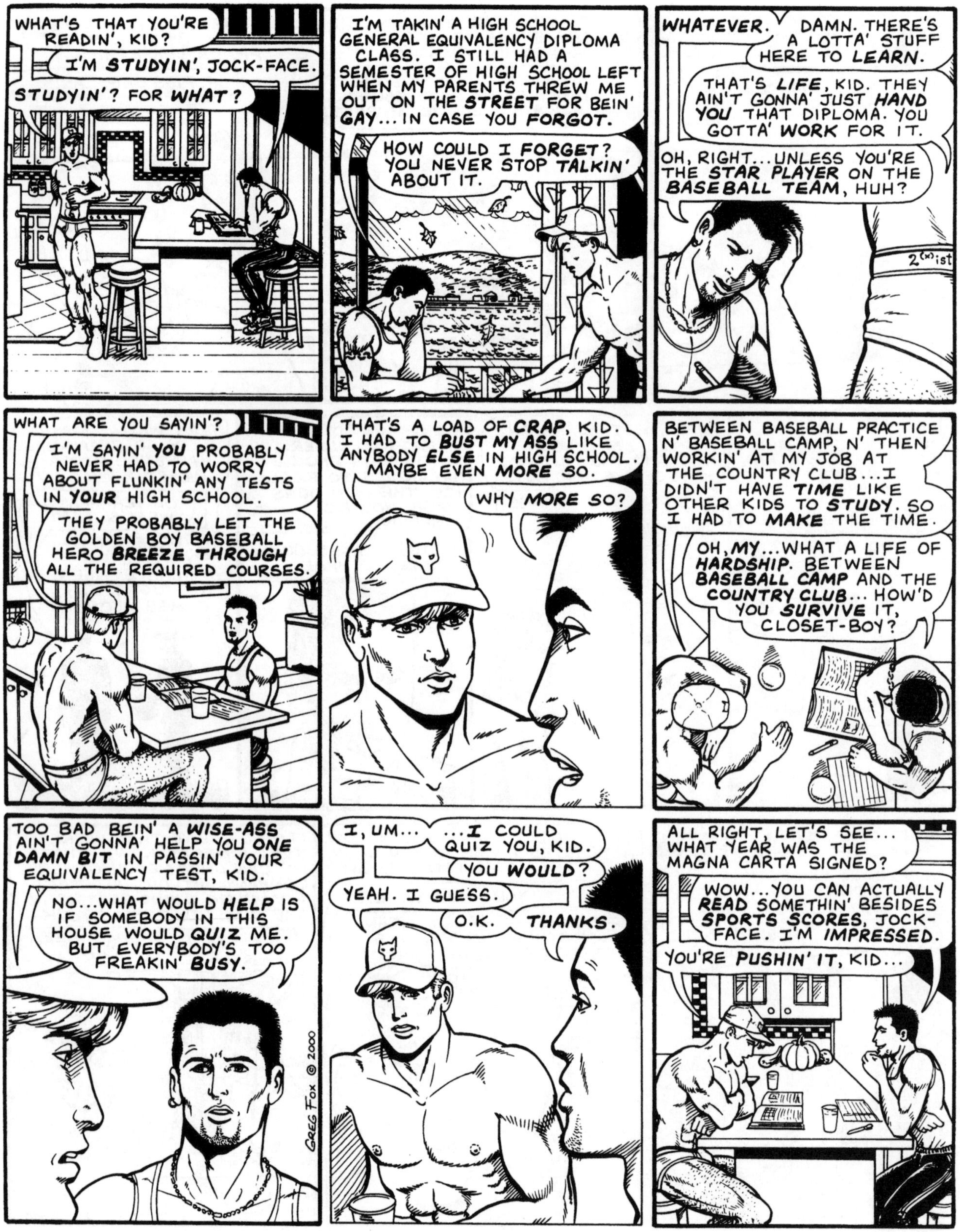
WHAT'S THAT YOU'RE READIN', KID?
I'M STUDYIN', JOCK-FACE.
STUDYIN'? FOR WHAT?
I'M TAKIN' A HIGH SCHOOL GENERAL EQUIVALENCY DIPLOMA CLASS. I STILL HAD A SEMESTER OF HIGH SCHOOL LEFT WHEN MY PARENTS THREW ME OUT ON THE STREET FOR BEIN' GAY... IN CASE YOU FORGOT.
HOW COULD I FORGET? YOU NEVER STOP TALKIN' ABOUT IT.
WHATEVER.
DAMN. THERE'S A LOTTA' STUFF HERE TO LEARN.
THAT'S LIFE, KID. THEY AIN'T GONNA' JUST HAND YOU THAT DIPLOMA. YOU GOTTA' WORK FOR IT.
OH, RIGHT... UNLESS YOU'RE THE STAR PLAYER ON THE BASEBALL TEAM, HUH?
WHAT ARE YOU SAYIN'?
I'M SAYIN' YOU PROBABLY NEVER HAD TO WORRY ABOUT FLUNKIN' ANY TESTS IN YOUR HIGH SCHOOL.
THEY PROBABLY LET THE GOLDEN BOY BASEBALL HERO BREEZE THROUGH ALL THE REQUIRED COURSES.
THAT'S A LOAD OF CRAP, KID. I HAD TO BUST MY ASS LIKE ANYBODY ELSE IN HIGH SCHOOL. MAYBE EVEN MORE SO.
WHY MORE SO?
BETWEEN BASEBALL PRACTICE N' BASEBALL CAMP, N' THEN WORKIN' AT MY JOB AT THE COUNTRY CLUB... I DIDN'T HAVE TIME LIKE OTHER KIDS TO STUDY. SO I HAD TO MAKE THE TIME.
OH, MY... WHAT A LIFE OF HARDSHIP. BETWEEN BASEBALL CAMP AND THE COUNTRY CLUB... HOW'D YOU SURVIVE IT, CLOSET-BOY?
TOO BAD BEIN' A WISE-ASS AIN'T GONNA' HELP YOU ONE DAMN BIT IN PASSIN' YOUR EQUIVALENCY TEST, KID.
NO... WHAT WOULD HELP IS IF SOMEBODY IN THIS HOUSE WOULD QUIZ ME. BUT EVERYBODY'S TOO FREAKIN' BUSY.
GREG FOX © 2000
I, UM...
...I COULD QUIZ YOU, KID.
YOU WOULD?
YEAH. I GUESS.
O.K.
THANKS.
ALL RIGHT, LET'S SEE... WHAT YEAR WAS THE MAGNA CARTA SIGNED?
WOW... YOU CAN ACTUALLY READ SOMETHIN' BESIDES SPORTS SCORES, JOCK-FACE. I'M IMPRESSED.
YOU'RE PUSHIN' IT, KID...

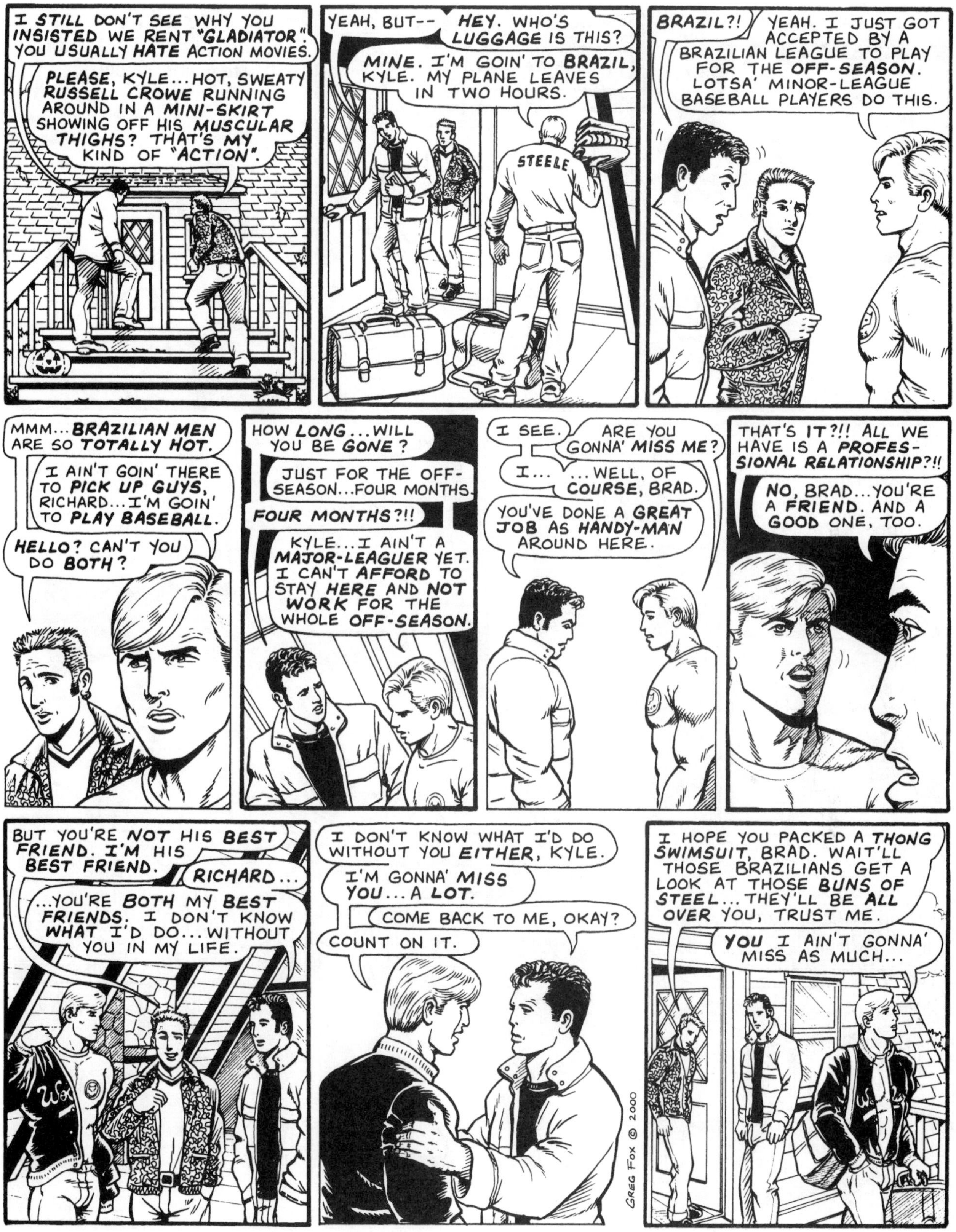
I STILL DON'T SEE WHY YOU INSISTED WE RENT "GLADIATOR". YOU USUALLY HATE ACTION MOVIES.
PLEASE, KYLE... HOT, SWEATY RUSSELL CROWE RUNNING AROUND IN A MINI-SKIRT SHOWING OFF HIS MUSCULAR THIGHS? THAT'S MY KIND OF "ACTION".
YEAH, BUT--
HEY. WHO'S LUGGAGE IS THIS?
MINE. I'M GOIN' TO BRAZIL, KYLE. MY PLANE LEAVES IN TWO HOURS.
STEELE
BRAZIL?!
YEAH. I JUST GOT ACCEPTED BY A BRAZILIAN LEAGUE TO PLAY FOR THE OFF-SEASON. LOTSA' MINOR-LEAGUE BASEBALL PLAYERS DO THIS.
MMM... BRAZILIAN MEN ARE SO TOTALLY HOT.
I AIN'T GOIN' THERE TO PICK UP GUYS, RICHARD... I'M GOIN' TO PLAY BASEBALL.
HELLO? CAN'T YOU DO BOTH?
HOW LONG... WILL YOU BE GONE?
JUST FOR THE OFF-SEASON... FOUR MONTHS.
FOUR MONTHS?!!
KYLE... I AIN'T A MAJOR-LEAGUER YET. I CAN'T AFFORD TO STAY HERE AND NOT WORK FOR THE WHOLE OFF-SEASON.
I SEE.
ARE YOU GONNA' MISS ME?
I...
...WELL, OF COURSE, BRAD.
YOU'VE DONE A GREAT JOB AS HANDY-MAN AROUND HERE.
THAT'S IT?!! ALL WE HAVE IS A PROFESSIONAL RELATIONSHIP?!!
NO, BRAD... YOU'RE A FRIEND. AND A GOOD ONE, TOO.
BUT YOU'RE NOT HIS BEST FRIEND. I'M HIS BEST FRIEND.
RICHARD...
...YOU'RE BOTH MY BEST FRIENDS. I DON'T KNOW WHAT I'D DO... WITHOUT YOU IN MY LIFE.
I DON'T KNOW WHAT I'D DO WITHOUT YOU EITHER, KYLE.
I'M GONNA' MISS YOU... A LOT.
COME BACK TO ME, OKAY?
COUNT ON IT.
GREG FOX © 2000
I HOPE YOU PACKED A THONG SWIMSUIT, BRAD. WAIT'LL THOSE BRAZILIANS GET A LOOK AT THOSE BUNS OF STEEL... THEY'LL BE ALL OVER YOU, TRUST ME.
YOU I AIN'T GONNA' MISS AS MUCH...

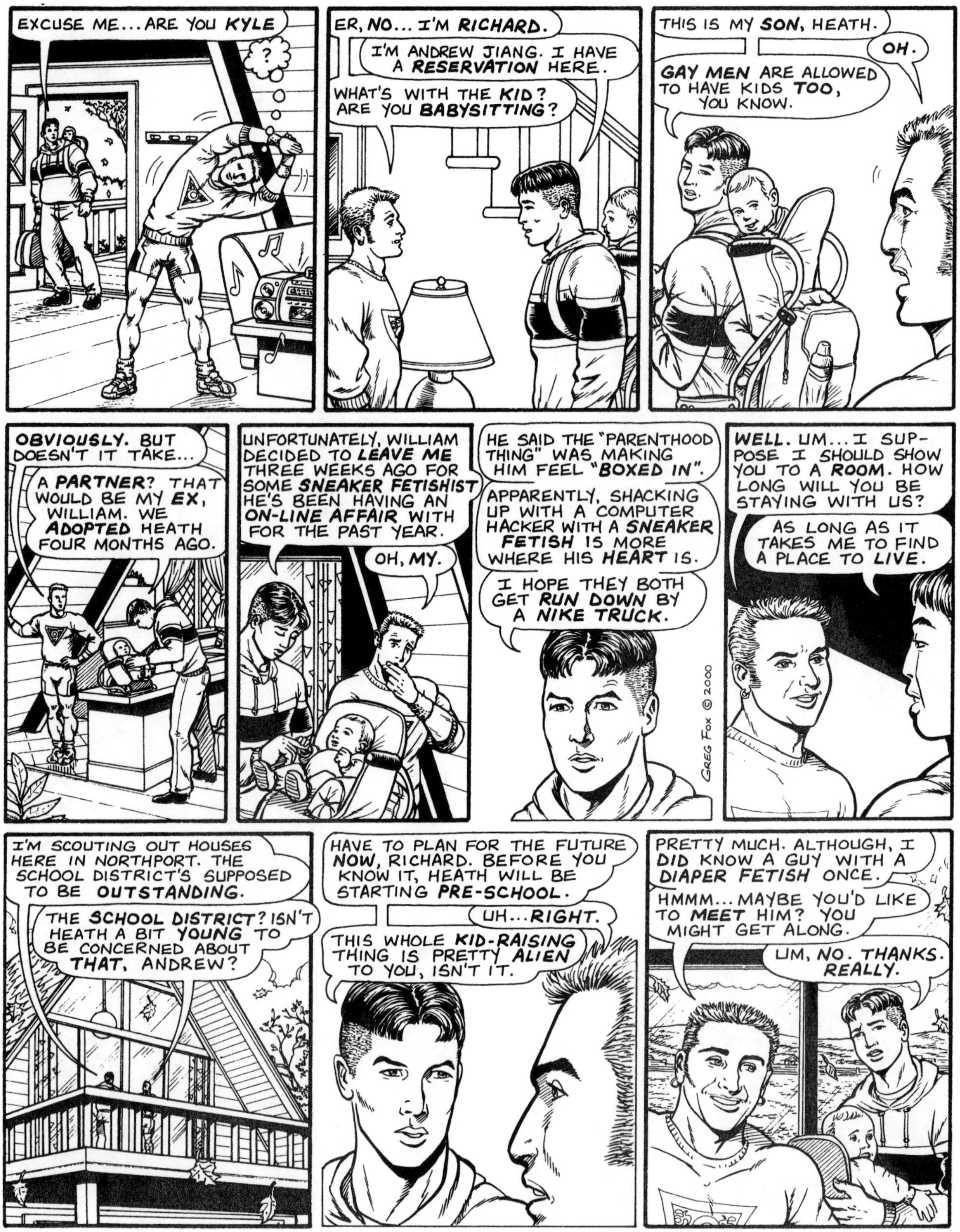

EXCUSE ME... ARE YOU KYLE
?
ER, NO... I'M RICHARD.
I'M ANDREW JIANG. I HAVE A RESERVATION HERE.
WHAT'S WITH THE KID? ARE YOU BABYSITTING?
THIS IS MY SON, HEATH.
OH.
GAY MEN ARE ALLOWED TO HAVE KIDS TOO, YOU KNOW.
OBVIOUSLY. BUT DOESN'T IT TAKE...
A PARTNER? THAT WOULD BE MY EX, WILLIAM. WE ADOPTED HEATH FOUR MONTHS AGO.
UNFORTUNATELY, WILLIAM DECIDED TO LEAVE ME THREE WEEKS AGO FOR SOME SNEAKER FETISHIST HE'S BEEN HAVING AN ON-LINE AFFAIR WITH FOR THE PAST YEAR.
OH, MY.
HE SAID THE "PARENTHOOD THING" WAS MAKING HIM FEEL "BOXED IN".
APPARENTLY, SHACKING UP WITH A COMPUTER HACKER WITH A SNEAKER FETISH IS MORE WHERE HIS HEART IS.
I HOPE THEY BOTH GET RUN DOWN BY A NIKE TRUCK.
GREG FOX © 2000
WELL. UM... I SUPPOSE I SHOULD SHOW YOU TO A ROOM. HOW LONG WILL YOU BE STAYING WITH US?
AS LONG AS IT TAKES ME TO FIND A PLACE TO LIVE.
I'M SCOUTING OUT HOUSES HERE IN NORTHPORT. THE SCHOOL DISTRICT'S SUPPOSED TO BE OUTSTANDING.
THE SCHOOL DISTRICT? ISN'T HEATH A BIT YOUNG TO BE CONCERNED ABOUT THAT, ANDREW?
HAVE TO PLAN FOR THE FUTURE NOW, RICHARD. BEFORE YOU KNOW IT, HEATH WILL BE STARTING PRE-SCHOOL.
UH... RIGHT.
THIS WHOLE KID-RAISING THING IS PRETTY ALIEN TO YOU, ISN'T IT.
PRETTY MUCH. ALTHOUGH, I DID KNOW A GUY WITH A DIAPER FETISH ONCE.
HMMM... MAYBE YOU'D LIKE TO MEET HIM? YOU MIGHT GET ALONG.
UM, NO. THANKS. REALLY.

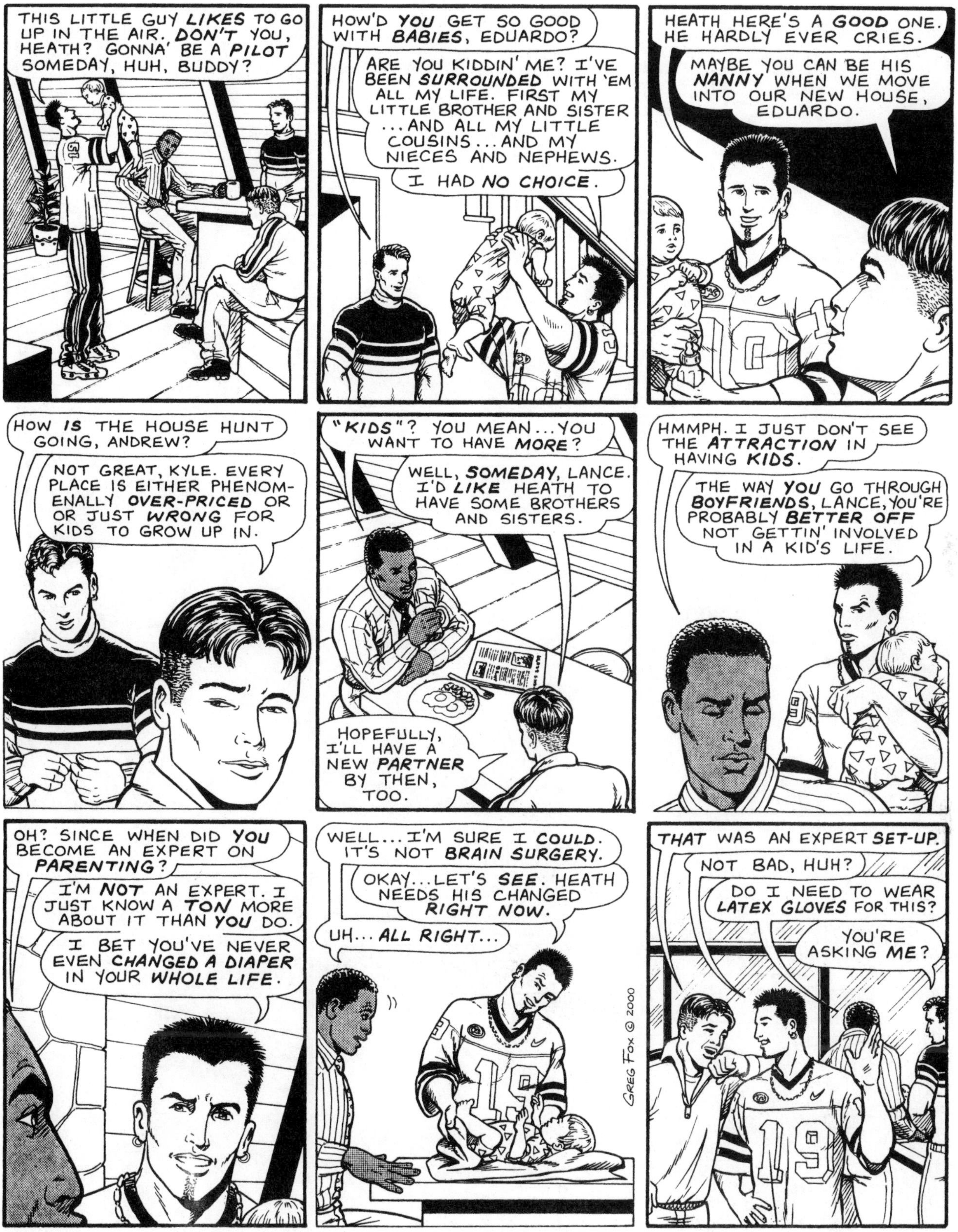

THIS LITTLE GUY LIKES TO GO UP IN THE AIR. DON'T YOU, HEATH? GONNA' BE A PILOT SOMEDAY, HUH, BUDDY?
HOW'D YOU GET SO GOOD WITH BABIES, EDUARDO?
ARE YOU KIDDIN' ME? I'VE BEEN SURROUNDED WITH 'EM ALL MY LIFE. FIRST MY LITTLE BROTHER AND SISTER ...AND ALL MY LITTLE COUSINS... AND MY NIECES AND NEPHEWS.
I HAD NO CHOICE.
HEATH HERE'S A GOOD ONE. HE HARDLY EVER CRIES.
MAYBE YOU CAN BE HIS NANNY WHEN WE MOVE INTO OUR NEW HOUSE, EDUARDO.
HOW IS THE HOUSE HUNT GOING, ANDREW?
NOT GREAT, KYLE. EVERY PLACE IS EITHER PHENOMENALLY OVER-PRICED OR OR JUST WRONG FOR KIDS TO GROW UP IN.
"KIDS"? YOU MEAN...YOU WANT TO HAVE MORE?
WELL, SOMEDAY, LANCE. I'D LIKE HEATH TO HAVE SOME BROTHERS AND SISTERS.
HOPEFULLY, I'LL HAVE A NEW PARTNER BY THEN, TOO.
HMMPH. I JUST DON'T SEE THE ATTRACTION IN HAVING KIDS.
THE WAY YOU GO THROUGH BOYFRIENDS, LANCE, YOU'RE PROBABLY BETTER OFF NOT GETTIN' INVOLVED IN A KID'S LIFE.
OH? SINCE WHEN DID YOU BECOME AN EXPERT ON PARENTING?
I'M NOT AN EXPERT. I JUST KNOW A TON MORE ABOUT IT THAN YOU DO.
I BET YOU'VE NEVER EVEN CHANGED A DIAPER IN YOUR WHOLE LIFE.
WELL... I'M SURE I COULD. IT'S NOT BRAIN SURGERY.
OKAY...LET'S SEE. HEATH NEEDS HIS CHANGED RIGHT NOW.
UH... ALL RIGHT...
GREG FOX © 2000
THAT WAS AN EXPERT SET-UP.
NOT BAD, HUH?
DO I NEED TO WEAR LATEX GLOVES FOR THIS?
YOU'RE ASKING ME?

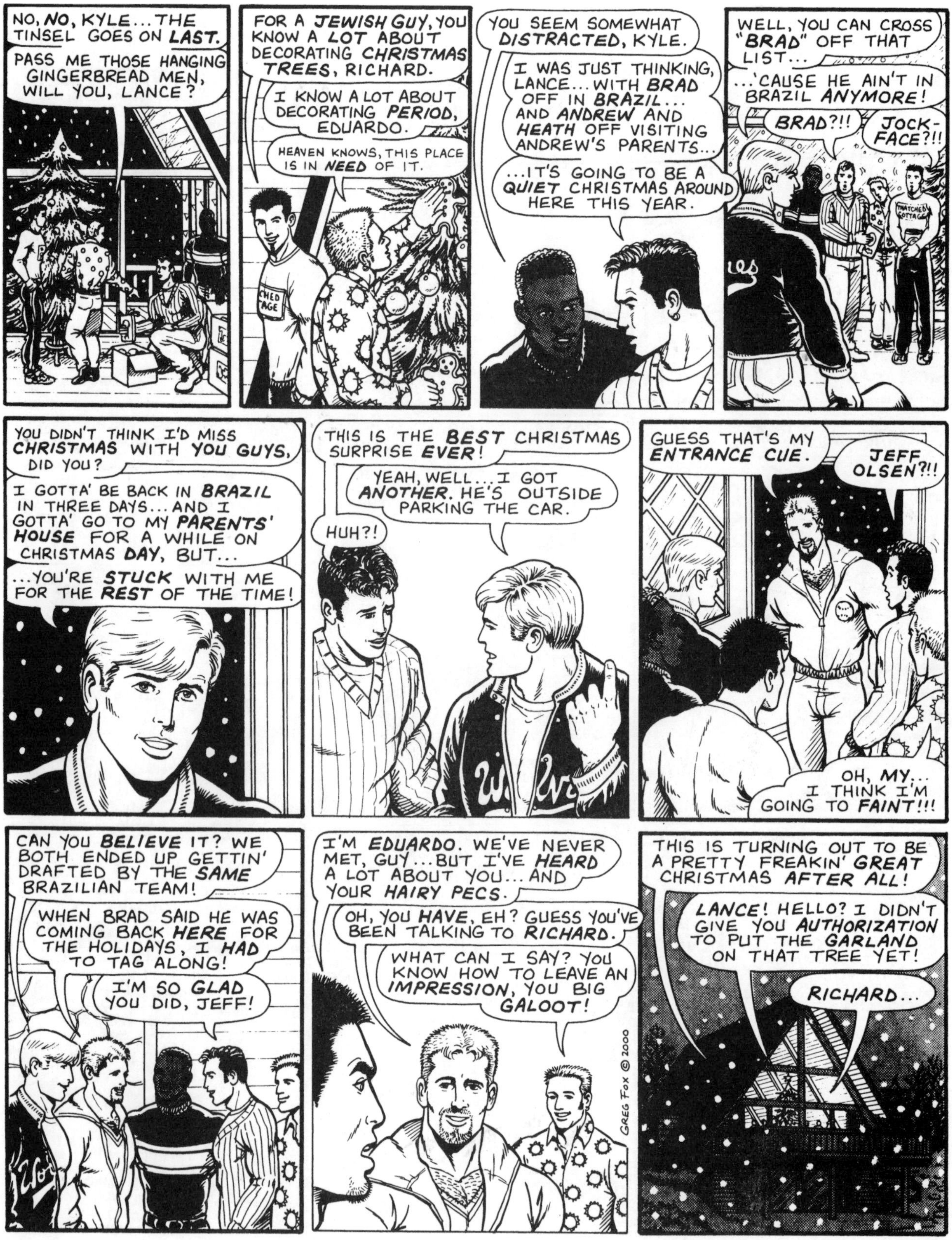
NO, NO, KYLE... THE TINSEL GOES ON LAST.
PASS ME THOSE HANGING GINGERBREAD MEN, WILL YOU, LANCE?
FOR A JEWISH GUY, YOU KNOW A LOT ABOUT DECORATING CHRISTMAS TREES, RICHARD.
I KNOW A LOT ABOUT DECORATING PERIOD, EDUARDO.
HEAVEN KNOWS, THIS PLACE IS IN NEED OF IT.
YOU SEEM SOMEWHAT DISTRACTED, KYLE.
I WAS JUST THINKING, LANCE... WITH BRAD OFF IN BRAZIL... AND ANDREW AND HEATH OFF VISITING ANDREW'S PARENTS...
...IT'S GOING TO BE A QUIET CHRISTMAS AROUND HERE THIS YEAR.
WELL, YOU CAN CROSS "BRAD" OFF THAT LIST...
...'CAUSE HE AIN'T IN BRAZIL ANYMORE!
BRAD?!!
JOCK-FACE?!!
THATCHED COTTAGE
YOU DIDN'T THINK I'D MISS CHRISTMAS WITH YOU GUYS, DID YOU?
I GOTTA' BE BACK IN BRAZIL IN THREE DAYS... AND I GOTTA' GO TO MY PARENTS' HOUSE FOR A WHILE ON CHRISTMAS DAY, BUT...
...YOU'RE STUCK WITH ME FOR THE REST OF THE TIME!
THIS IS THE BEST CHRISTMAS SURPRISE EVER!
YEAH, WELL... I GOT ANOTHER. HE'S OUTSIDE PARKING THE CAR.
HUH?!
GUESS THAT'S MY ENTRANCE CUE.
JEFF OLSEN?!!
OH, MY... I THINK I'M GOING TO FAINT!!!
CAN YOU BELIEVE IT? WE BOTH ENDED UP GETTIN' DRAFTED BY THE SAME BRAZILIAN TEAM!
WHEN BRAD SAID HE WAS COMING BACK HERE FOR THE HOLIDAYS, I HAD TO TAG ALONG!
I'M SO GLAD YOU DID, JEFF!
I'M EDUARDO. WE'VE NEVER MET, GUY... BUT I'VE HEARD A LOT ABOUT YOU... AND YOUR HAIRY PECS.
OH, YOU HAVE, EH? GUESS YOU'VE BEEN TALKING TO RICHARD.
WHAT CAN I SAY? YOU KNOW HOW TO LEAVE AN IMPRESSION, YOU BIG GALOOT!
GREG FOX © 2000
THIS IS TURNING OUT TO BE A PRETTY FREAKIN' GREAT CHRISTMAS AFTER ALL!
LANCE! HELLO? I DIDN'T GIVE YOU AUTHORIZATION TO PUT THE GARLAND ON THAT TREE YET!
RICHARD...

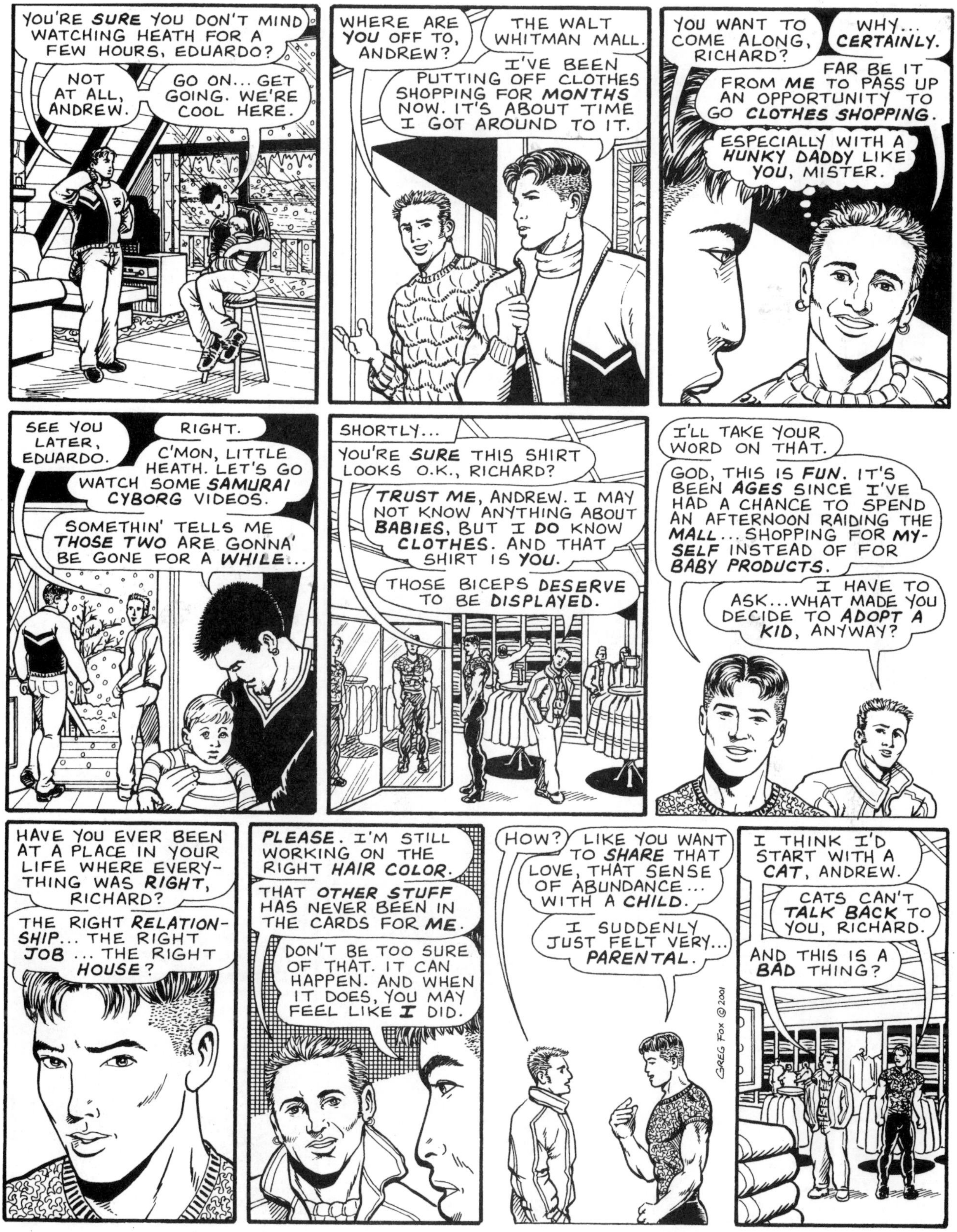
YOU'RE SURE YOU DON'T MIND WATCHING HEATH FOR A FEW HOURS, EDUARDO?
NOT AT ALL, ANDREW.
GO ON... GET GOING. WE'RE COOL HERE.
WHERE ARE YOU OFF TO, ANDREW?
THE WALT WHITMAN MALL.
I'VE BEEN PUTTING OFF CLOTHES SHOPPING FOR MONTHS NOW. IT'S ABOUT TIME I GOT AROUND TO IT.
YOU WANT TO COME ALONG, RICHARD?
WHY... CERTAINLY.
FAR BE IT FROM ME TO PASS UP AN OPPORTUNITY TO GO CLOTHES SHOPPING.
ESPECIALLY WITH A HUNKY DADDY LIKE YOU, MISTER.
SEE YOU LATER, EDUARDO.
RIGHT.
C'MON, LITTLE HEATH. LET'S GO WATCH SOME SAMURAI CYBORG VIDEOS.
SOMETHIN' TELLS ME THOSE TWO ARE GONNA' BE GONE FOR A WHILE...
SHORTLY...
YOU'RE SURE THIS SHIRT LOOKS O.K., RICHARD?
TRUST ME, ANDREW. I MAY NOT KNOW ANYTHING ABOUT BABIES, BUT I DO KNOW CLOTHES. AND THAT SHIRT IS YOU.
THOSE BICEPS DESERVE TO BE DISPLAYED.
I'LL TAKE YOUR WORD ON THAT.
GOD, THIS IS FUN. IT'S BEEN AGES SINCE I'VE HAD A CHANCE TO SPEND AN AFTERNOON RAIDING THE MALL... SHOPPING FOR MYSELF INSTEAD OF FOR BABY PRODUCTS.
I HAVE TO ASK... WHAT MADE YOU DECIDE TO ADOPT A KID, ANYWAY?
HAVE YOU EVER BEEN AT A PLACE IN YOUR LIFE WHERE EVERYTHING WAS RIGHT, RICHARD?
THE RIGHT RELATIONSHIP... THE RIGHT JOB ... THE RIGHT HOUSE?
PLEASE. I'M STILL WORKING ON THE RIGHT HAIR COLOR.
THAT OTHER STUFF HAS NEVER BEEN IN THE CARDS FOR ME.
DON'T BE TOO SURE OF THAT. IT CAN HAPPEN. AND WHEN IT DOES, YOU MAY FEEL LIKE I DID.
HOW?
LIKE YOU WANT TO SHARE THAT LOVE, THAT SENSE OF ABUNDANCE... WITH A CHILD.
I SUDDENLY JUST FELT VERY... PARENTAL.
GREG FOX © 2001
I THINK I'D START WITH A CAT, ANDREW.
CATS CAN'T TALK BACK TO YOU, RICHARD.
AND THIS IS A BAD THING?

Panel 1:
GOOD MORNING.

ANDREW! UM... GOOD MORNING.

YOU'RE UP EARLY.

Panel 2:
YEAH, I LIKE TO GET UP AT THIS HOUR, GET SOME WORK DONE...BEFORE HEATH WAKES UP.

WHEN YOU'RE A SINGLE PARENT, YOU HAVE TO BE CREATIVE WITH YOUR TIME ALLOTMENT.

Panel 3:
DID I JUST SAY "TIME ALLOTMENT"? GOOD GOD...I REALLY AM TURNING INTO THE GUPPIE SCUM I ALWAYS HAD NIGHTMARES ABOUT.

WELL, IF IT'S ANY CONSOLATION, YOU HAVE A GREAT WARDROBE.

WHICH, I'M HAPPY TO SEE, YOU'RE BARELY WEARING AT THE MOMENT.

Panel 4:
I KNOW. THANKS TO YOU.

OH, I ENJOYED OUR LITTLE CLOTHES-SHOPPING SPREE, ANDREW.

SO DID I, RICHARD.

Panel 5:
ANDREW, UM... I HOPE YOU DON'T THINK THAT BECAUSE I'M COMING IN AT 6:00 A.M., AFTER A NIGHT OF CLUBBING...

...THAT I WAS OUT HAVING SLUTTY GAY BAR SEX WITH SOME STRANGER.

NO, I DIDN'T THINK THAT.

GOOD.

UNTIL NOW.

Panel 6:
ANDREW...I WASN'T.

I JUST HAPPENED TO BE AT A PARTY THAT RAN RATHER LATE.

YOU DON'T OWE ME ANY EXPLANATIONS, RICHARD.

I KNOW, BUT...

...I JUST DIDN'T WANT YOU TO GET THE WRONG IDEA.

GREG FOX © 2001

Panel 7:
WELL, ACTUALLY...I AM A LITTLE RELIEVED.

WHY'S THAT?

BECAUSE I'D PREFER TO DO WHAT I'M ABOUT TO DO WITH SOMEONE WHO HASN'T BEEN OUT HAVING "SLUTTY GAY BAR SEX" ALL NIGHT.

WHA-WHAT ARE YOU ABOUT TO DO?!

Panel 8:

Panel 9:
I'D SAY THAT'S A CREATIVE USE OF TIME ALLOTMENT, ANDREW.

I'D HAVE TO AGREE. IN FACT--

YOU WANNA' SHUT UP AND CONTINUE?

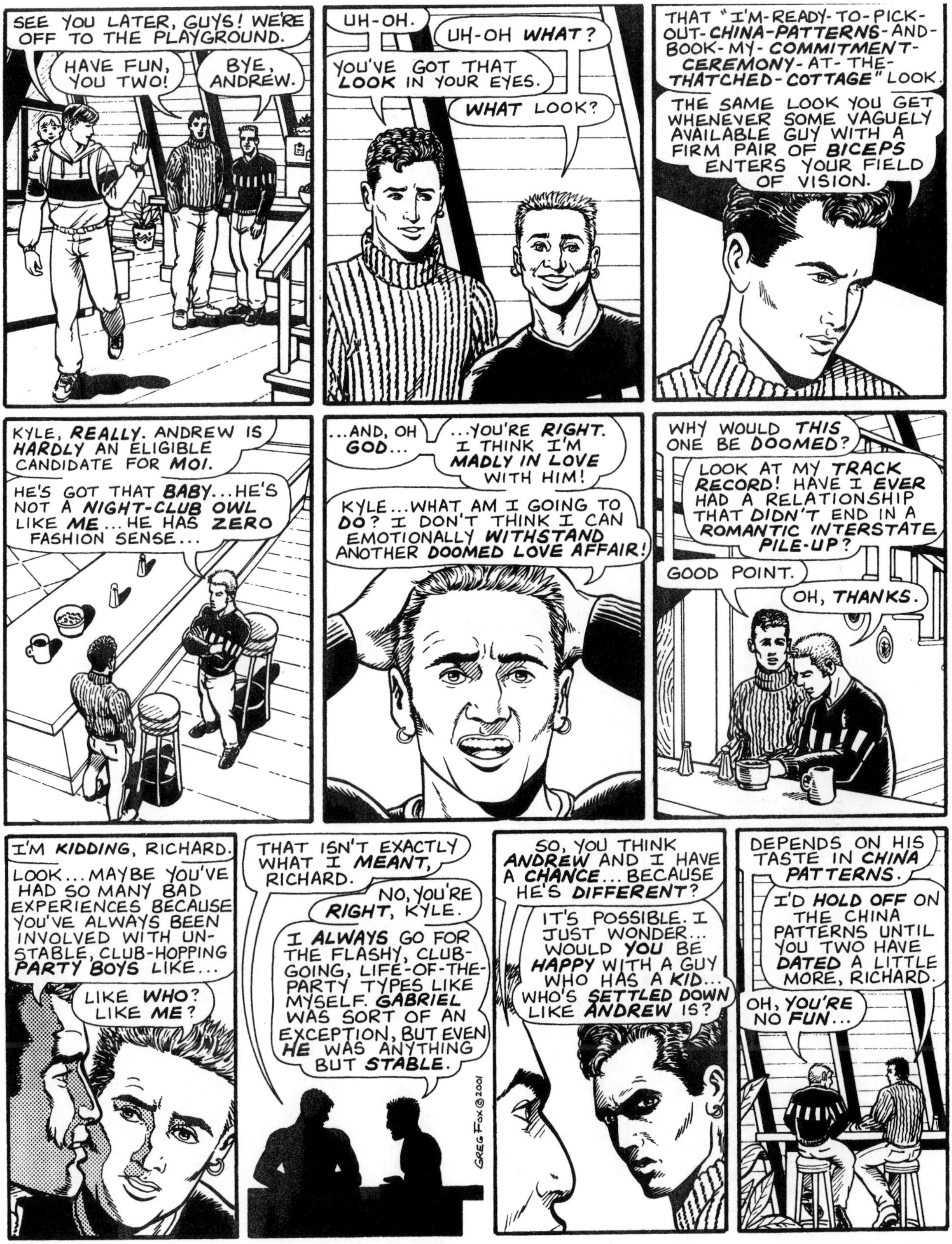
SEE YOU LATER, GUYS! WE'RE OFF TO THE PLAYGROUND.
HAVE FUN, YOU TWO!
BYE, ANDREW.
UH-OH.
UH-OH WHAT?
YOU'VE GOT THAT LOOK IN YOUR EYES.
WHAT LOOK?
THAT "I'M-READY-TO-PICK-OUT-CHINA-PATTERNS-AND-BOOK-MY-COMMITMENT-CEREMONY-AT-THE-THATCHED-COTTAGE" LOOK.
THE SAME LOOK YOU GET WHENEVER SOME VAGUELY AVAILABLE GUY WITH A FIRM PAIR OF BICEPS ENTERS YOUR FIELD OF VISION.
KYLE, REALLY. ANDREW IS HARDLY AN ELIGIBLE CANDIDATE FOR MOI.
HE'S GOT THAT BABY... HE'S NOT A NIGHT-CLUB OWL LIKE ME... HE HAS ZERO FASHION SENSE...
...AND, OH GOD...
...YOU'RE RIGHT. I THINK I'M MADLY IN LOVE WITH HIM!
KYLE... WHAT AM I GOING TO DO? I DON'T THINK I CAN EMOTIONALLY WITHSTAND ANOTHER DOOMED LOVE AFFAIR!
WHY WOULD THIS ONE BE DOOMED?
LOOK AT MY TRACK RECORD! HAVE I EVER HAD A RELATIONSHIP THAT DIDN'T END IN A ROMANTIC INTERSTATE PILE-UP?
GOOD POINT.
OH, THANKS.
I'M KIDDING, RICHARD.
LOOK... MAYBE YOU'VE HAD SO MANY BAD EXPERIENCES BECAUSE YOU'VE ALWAYS BEEN INVOLVED WITH UN-STABLE, CLUB-HOPPING PARTY BOYS LIKE...
LIKE WHO? LIKE ME?
THAT ISN'T EXACTLY WHAT I MEANT, RICHARD.
NO, YOU'RE RIGHT, KYLE.
I ALWAYS GO FOR THE FLASHY, CLUB-GOING, LIFE-OF-THE-PARTY TYPES LIKE MYSELF. GABRIEL WAS SORT OF AN EXCEPTION, BUT EVEN HE WAS ANYTHING BUT STABLE.
GREG FOX © 2001
SO, YOU THINK ANDREW AND I HAVE A CHANCE... BECAUSE HE'S DIFFERENT?
IT'S POSSIBLE. I JUST WONDER... WOULD YOU BE HAPPY WITH A GUY WHO HAS A KID... WHO'S SETTLED DOWN LIKE ANDREW IS?
DEPENDS ON HIS TASTE IN CHINA PATTERNS.
I'D HOLD OFF ON THE CHINA PATTERNS UNTIL YOU TWO HAVE DATED A LITTLE MORE, RICHARD.
OH, YOU'RE NO FUN...

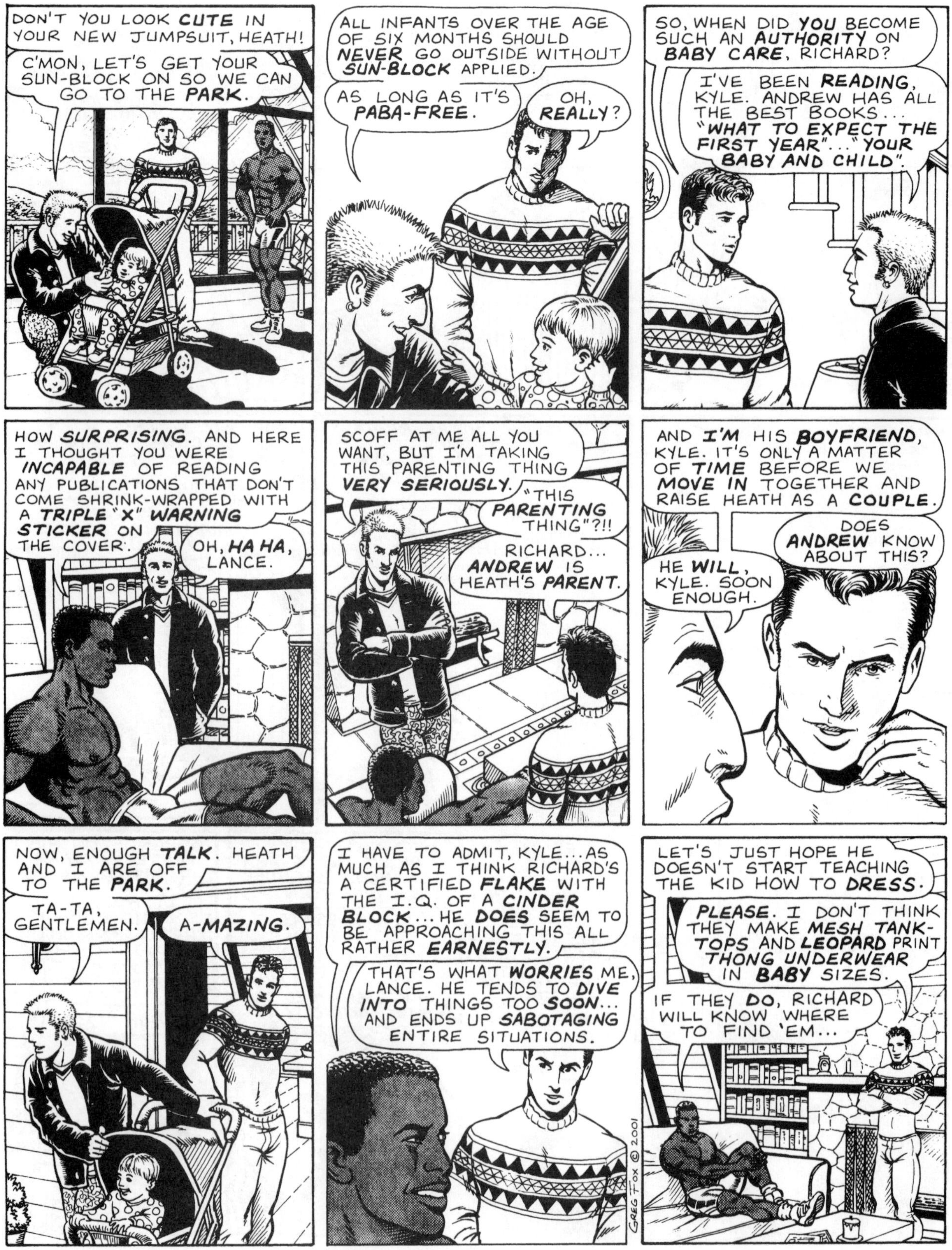
DON'T YOU LOOK CUTE IN YOUR NEW JUMPSUIT, HEATH!
C'MON, LET'S GET YOUR SUN-BLOCK ON SO WE CAN GO TO THE PARK.
ALL INFANTS OVER THE AGE OF SIX MONTHS SHOULD NEVER GO OUTSIDE WITHOUT SUN-BLOCK APPLIED.
AS LONG AS IT'S PABA-FREE.
OH, REALLY?
SO, WHEN DID YOU BECOME SUCH AN AUTHORITY ON BABY CARE, RICHARD?
I'VE BEEN READING, KYLE. ANDREW HAS ALL THE BEST BOOKS... "WHAT TO EXPECT THE FIRST YEAR"..."YOUR BABY AND CHILD".
HOW SURPRISING. AND HERE I THOUGHT YOU WERE INCAPABLE OF READING ANY PUBLICATIONS THAT DON'T COME SHRINK-WRAPPED WITH A TRIPLE "X" WARNING STICKER ON THE COVER.
OH, HA HA, LANCE.
SCOFF AT ME ALL YOU WANT, BUT I'M TAKING THIS PARENTING THING VERY SERIOUSLY.
"THIS PARENTING THING"?!!
RICHARD... ANDREW IS HEATH'S PARENT.
AND I'M HIS BOYFRIEND, KYLE. IT'S ONLY A MATTER OF TIME BEFORE WE MOVE IN TOGETHER AND RAISE HEATH AS A COUPLE.
DOES ANDREW KNOW ABOUT THIS?
HE WILL, KYLE. SOON ENOUGH.
NOW, ENOUGH TALK. HEATH AND I ARE OFF TO THE PARK.
TA-TA, GENTLEMEN.
A-MAZING.
I HAVE TO ADMIT, KYLE... AS MUCH AS I THINK RICHARD'S A CERTIFIED FLAKE WITH THE I.Q. OF A CINDER BLOCK... HE DOES SEEM TO BE APPROACHING THIS ALL RATHER EARNESTLY.
THAT'S WHAT WORRIES ME, LANCE. HE TENDS TO DIVE INTO THINGS TOO SOON... AND ENDS UP SABOTAGING ENTIRE SITUATIONS.
GREG FOX © 2001
LET'S JUST HOPE HE DOESN'T START TEACHING THE KID HOW TO DRESS.
PLEASE. I DON'T THINK THEY MAKE MESH TANK-TOPS AND LEOPARD PRINT THONG UNDERWEAR IN BABY SIZES.
IF THEY DO, RICHARD WILL KNOW WHERE TO FIND 'EM...

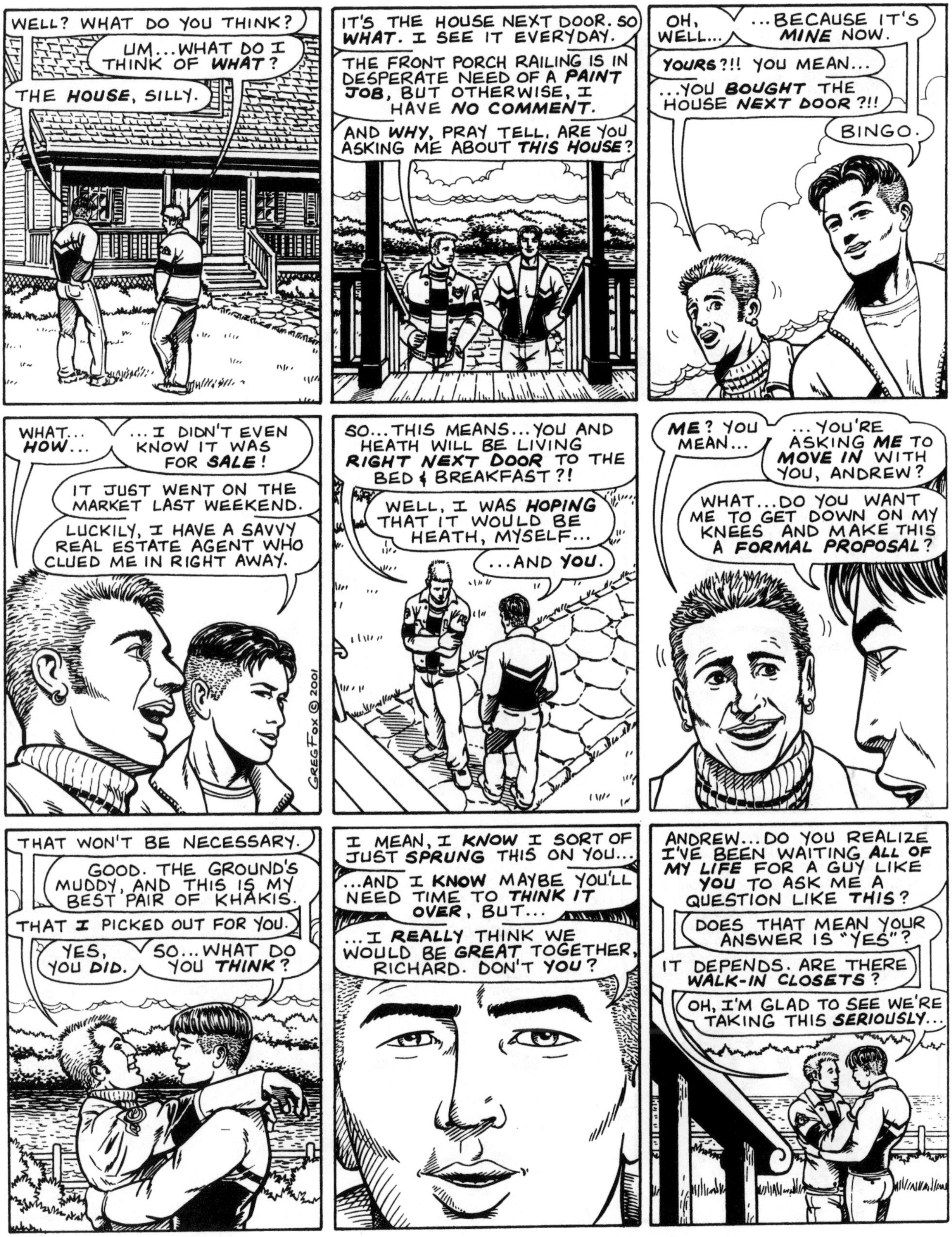
WELL? WHAT DO YOU THINK?
UM...WHAT DO I THINK OF WHAT?
THE HOUSE, SILLY.
IT'S THE HOUSE NEXT DOOR. SO WHAT. I SEE IT EVERYDAY.
THE FRONT PORCH RAILING IS IN DESPERATE NEED OF A PAINT JOB, BUT OTHERWISE, I HAVE NO COMMENT.
AND WHY, PRAY TELL, ARE YOU ASKING ME ABOUT THIS HOUSE?
OH, WELL...
...BECAUSE IT'S MINE NOW.
YOURS?!! YOU MEAN...
...YOU BOUGHT THE HOUSE NEXT DOOR?!!
BINGO.
WHAT... HOW...
...I DIDN'T EVEN KNOW IT WAS FOR SALE!
IT JUST WENT ON THE MARKET LAST WEEKEND.
LUCKILY, I HAVE A SAVVY REAL ESTATE AGENT WHO CLUED ME IN RIGHT AWAY.
GREG FOX © 2001
SO...THIS MEANS...YOU AND HEATH WILL BE LIVING RIGHT NEXT DOOR TO THE BED & BREAKFAST?!
WELL, I WAS HOPING THAT IT WOULD BE HEATH, MYSELF...
...AND YOU.
ME? YOU MEAN...
...YOU'RE ASKING ME TO MOVE IN WITH YOU, ANDREW?
WHAT...DO YOU WANT ME TO GET DOWN ON MY KNEES AND MAKE THIS A FORMAL PROPOSAL?
THAT WON'T BE NECESSARY.
GOOD. THE GROUND'S MUDDY, AND THIS IS MY BEST PAIR OF KHAKIS.
THAT I PICKED OUT FOR YOU.
YES, YOU DID.
SO...WHAT DO YOU THINK?
I MEAN, I KNOW I SORT OF JUST SPRUNG THIS ON YOU...
...AND I KNOW MAYBE YOU'LL NEED TIME TO THINK IT OVER, BUT...
...I REALLY THINK WE WOULD BE GREAT TOGETHER, RICHARD. DON'T YOU?
ANDREW...DO YOU REALIZE I'VE BEEN WAITING ALL OF MY LIFE FOR A GUY LIKE YOU TO ASK ME A QUESTION LIKE THIS?
DOES THAT MEAN YOUR ANSWER IS "YES"?
IT DEPENDS. ARE THERE WALK-IN CLOSETS?
OH, I'M GLAD TO SEE WE'RE TAKING THIS SERIOUSLY...

HEY, RICHARD.

BRAD...?! YOU'RE *BACK* FROM *BRAZIL?!!*

AND YOU'RE...

NAKED. I KNOW.

ALL MY *CLOTHES* ARE IN THE *WASHING MACHINE* AND *DRYER.*

MAYBE I SHOULD BORROW SOME *SWEATPANTS* FROM KYLE 'TIL THEY'RE DONE.

WHAT ON EARTH *FOR?*

I JUST WISH I HAD MY *CAMERA.*

WELL, ANYWAY... I CAME DOWN HERE TO GET SOME *BOXES.* I'M *MOVING OUT.*

YEAH, I HEARD. YOU'RE *MOVIN'* IN WITH THAT *ORIENTAL GUY* WITH THE *BABY?*

ASIAN IS THE PROPER TERM, BRAD.

AND *REALLY...* HE'S *FOURTH GENERATION.*

CALLING HIM "THAT *ASIAN* GUY" IS LIKE CALLING *YOU* "THAT *GERMAN* GUY" BECAUSE YOUR *GREAT-GRANDPARENTS* IMMIGRATED HERE FROM GERMANY.

WHATEVER. HE DOESN'T SEEM LIKE YOUR *TYPE.*

OH? SINCE WHEN DID THE *VIRGIN BRAD STEELE* BECOME AN *EXPERT* ON *GAY* RELATIONSHIPS?

ALL I'M SAYIN' IS... HE'S *SETTLED DOWN...* HE HAS A *BABY SON...*

AND?

...AND *YOU'RE,* LIKE... THIS CLUB-GOIN', CIRCUS-PARTY *FREAK.*

THEY'RE CALLED *CIRCUIT PARTIES,* NOT "*CIRCUS PARTIES*". ALTHOUGH THAT *MAY NOT* BE AN INACCURATE DESCRIPTION.

ANYWAY... I'VE *CHANGED* SINCE YOU'VE BEEN AWAY, BRAD. I *HAVE* SETTLED DOWN. ANDREW AND I ARE *PERFECT* FOR EACH OTHER.

UH-HUH.

AND *BESIDES...* WE STILL HAVE *FUN.* ANDREW AND I ARE ACTUALLY *GOING* TO A *CIRCUIT PARTY* TOGETHER IN A FEW WEEKS... "THE *MIRROR BALL*".

YEAH, WELL... *GOOD LUCK.*

GREG FOX © 2001

ALL RIGHT, I'M OFF TO *PACK.* OH, BY THE WAY... I *DID* LEARN *TWO THINGS* FROM THIS CONVERSATION.

WHAT?

YOU *ARE* A *REAL BLOND...*

...AND YOU *DON'T* STUFF YOUR BRIEFS, AFTER ALL.

JEEZ...

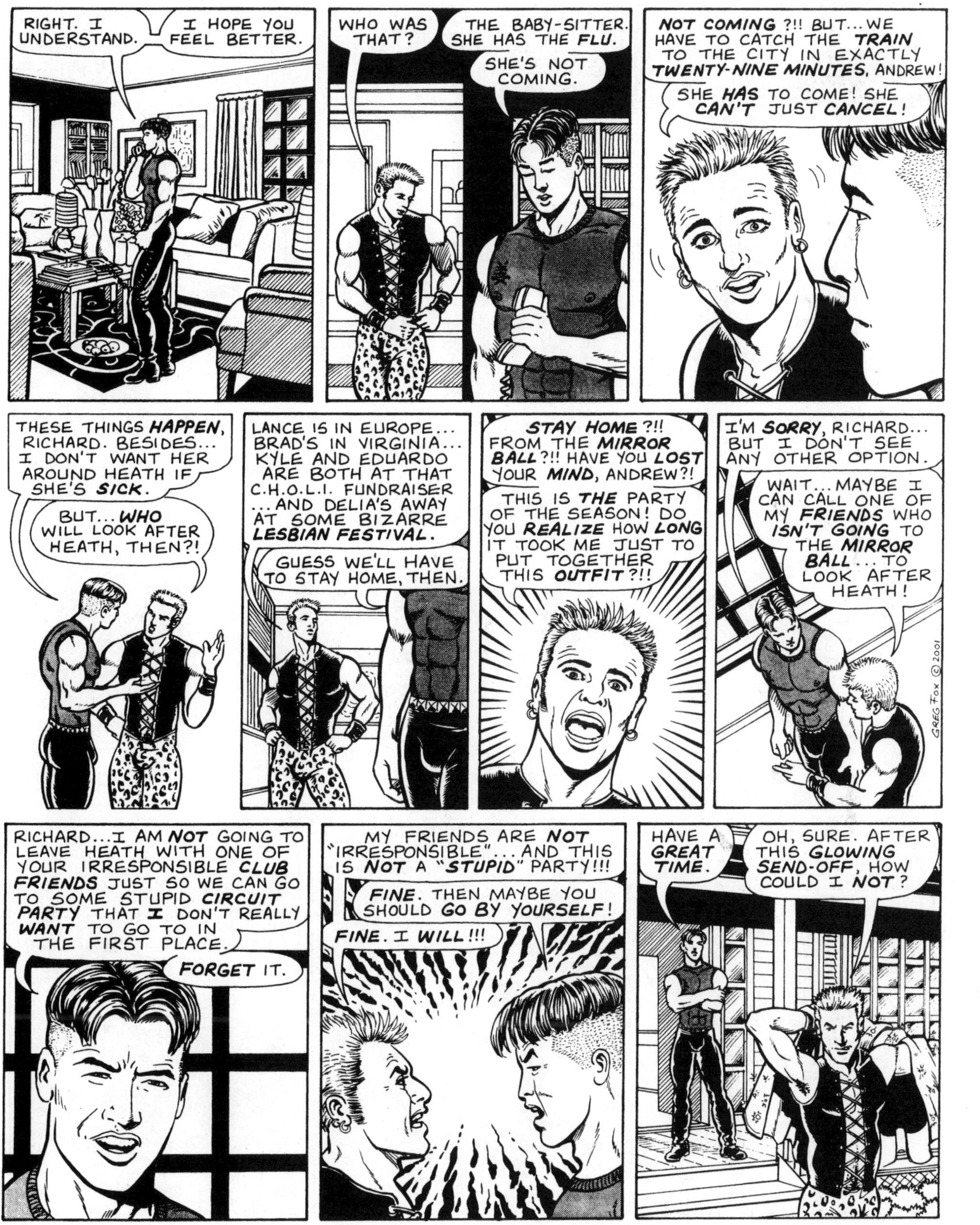
RIGHT. I UNDERSTAND.
I HOPE YOU FEEL BETTER.
WHO WAS THAT?
THE BABY-SITTER. SHE HAS THE FLU.
SHE'S NOT COMING.
NOT COMING?!! BUT...WE HAVE TO CATCH THE TRAIN TO THE CITY IN EXACTLY TWENTY-NINE MINUTES, ANDREW!
SHE HAS TO COME! SHE CAN'T JUST CANCEL!
THESE THINGS HAPPEN, RICHARD. BESIDES... I DON'T WANT HER AROUND HEATH IF SHE'S SICK.
BUT...WHO WILL LOOK AFTER HEATH, THEN?!
LANCE IS IN EUROPE... BRAD'S IN VIRGINIA... KYLE AND EDUARDO ARE BOTH AT THAT C.H.O.L.I. FUNDRAISER ...AND DELIA'S AWAY AT SOME BIZARRE LESBIAN FESTIVAL.
GUESS WE'LL HAVE TO STAY HOME, THEN.
STAY HOME?!! FROM THE MIRROR BALL?!! HAVE YOU LOST YOUR MIND, ANDREW?!
THIS IS THE PARTY OF THE SEASON! DO YOU REALIZE HOW LONG IT TOOK ME JUST TO PUT TOGETHER THIS OUTFIT?!!
I'M SORRY, RICHARD... BUT I DON'T SEE ANY OTHER OPTION.
WAIT...MAYBE I CAN CALL ONE OF MY FRIENDS WHO ISN'T GOING TO THE MIRROR BALL...TO LOOK AFTER HEATH!
GREG FOX © 2001
RICHARD...I AM NOT GOING TO LEAVE HEATH WITH ONE OF YOUR IRRESPONSIBLE CLUB FRIENDS JUST SO WE CAN GO TO SOME STUPID CIRCUIT PARTY THAT I DON'T REALLY WANT TO GO TO IN THE FIRST PLACE.
FORGET IT.
MY FRIENDS ARE NOT "IRRESPONSIBLE"... AND THIS IS NOT A "STUPID" PARTY!!!
FINE. THEN MAYBE YOU SHOULD GO BY YOURSELF!
FINE. I WILL!!!
HAVE A GREAT TIME.
OH, SURE. AFTER THIS GLOWING SEND-OFF, HOW COULD I NOT?

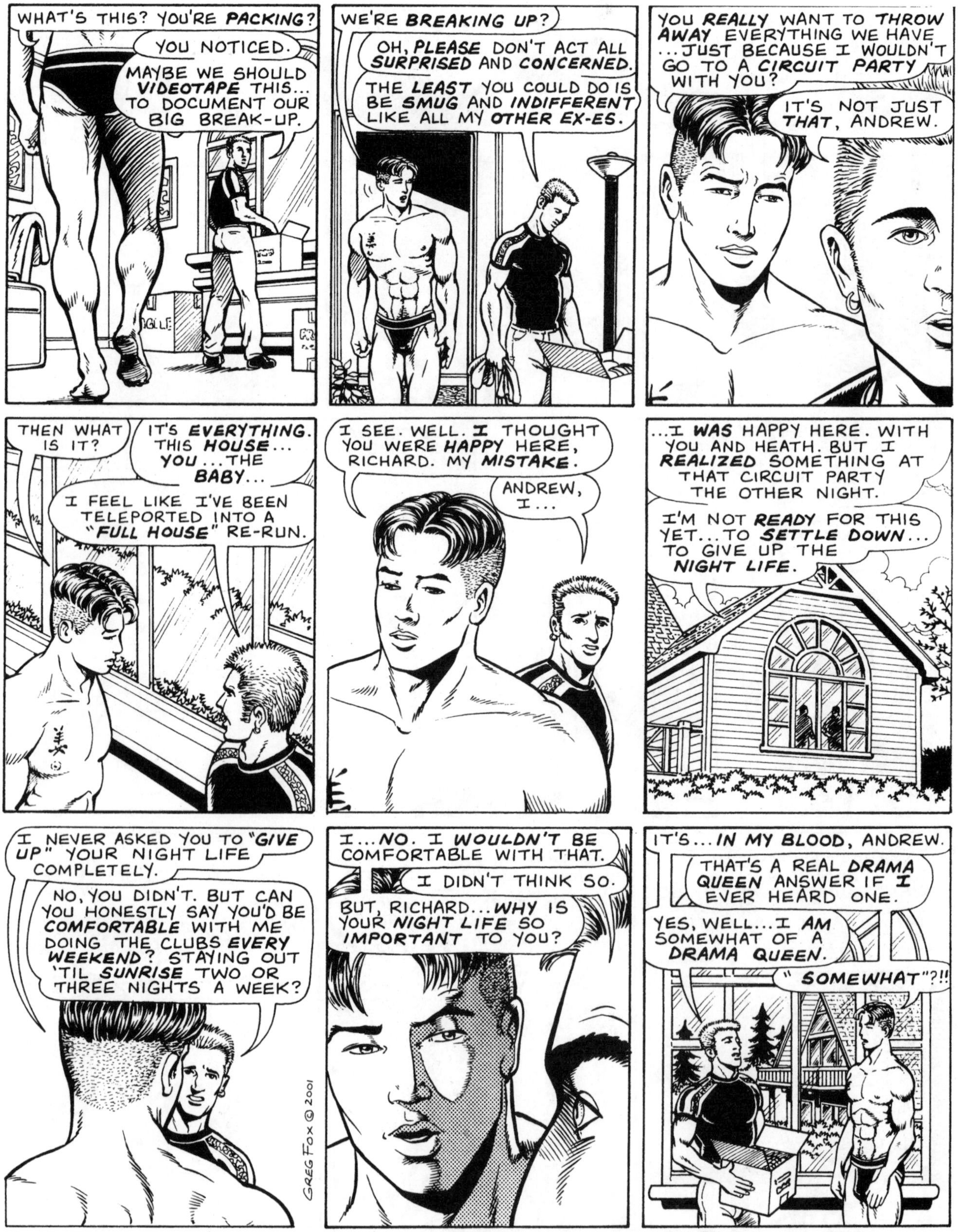
WHAT'S THIS? YOU'RE PACKING?
YOU NOTICED.
MAYBE WE SHOULD VIDEOTAPE THIS... TO DOCUMENT OUR BIG BREAK-UP.
WE'RE BREAKING UP?
OH, PLEASE DON'T ACT ALL SURPRISED AND CONCERNED.
THE LEAST YOU COULD DO IS BE SMUG AND INDIFFERENT LIKE ALL MY OTHER EX-ES.
YOU REALLY WANT TO THROW AWAY EVERYTHING WE HAVE ...JUST BECAUSE I WOULDN'T GO TO A CIRCUIT PARTY WITH YOU?
IT'S NOT JUST THAT, ANDREW.
THEN WHAT IS IT?
IT'S EVERYTHING. THIS HOUSE... YOU... THE BABY...
I FEEL LIKE I'VE BEEN TELEPORTED INTO A "FULL HOUSE" RE-RUN.
I SEE. WELL. I THOUGHT YOU WERE HAPPY HERE, RICHARD. MY MISTAKE.
ANDREW, I...
...I WAS HAPPY HERE. WITH YOU AND HEATH. BUT I REALIZED SOMETHING AT THAT CIRCUIT PARTY THE OTHER NIGHT.
I'M NOT READY FOR THIS YET... TO SETTLE DOWN... TO GIVE UP THE NIGHT LIFE.
I NEVER ASKED YOU TO "GIVE UP" YOUR NIGHT LIFE COMPLETELY.
NO, YOU DIDN'T. BUT CAN YOU HONESTLY SAY YOU'D BE COMFORTABLE WITH ME DOING THE CLUBS EVERY WEEKEND? STAYING OUT 'TIL SUNRISE TWO OR THREE NIGHTS A WEEK?
GREG FOX © 2001
I... NO. I WOULDN'T BE COMFORTABLE WITH THAT.
I DIDN'T THINK SO.
BUT, RICHARD... WHY IS YOUR NIGHT LIFE SO IMPORTANT TO YOU?
IT'S... IN MY BLOOD, ANDREW.
THAT'S A REAL DRAMA QUEEN ANSWER IF I EVER HEARD ONE.
YES, WELL... I AM SOMEWHAT OF A DRAMA QUEEN.
"SOMEWHAT"?!!

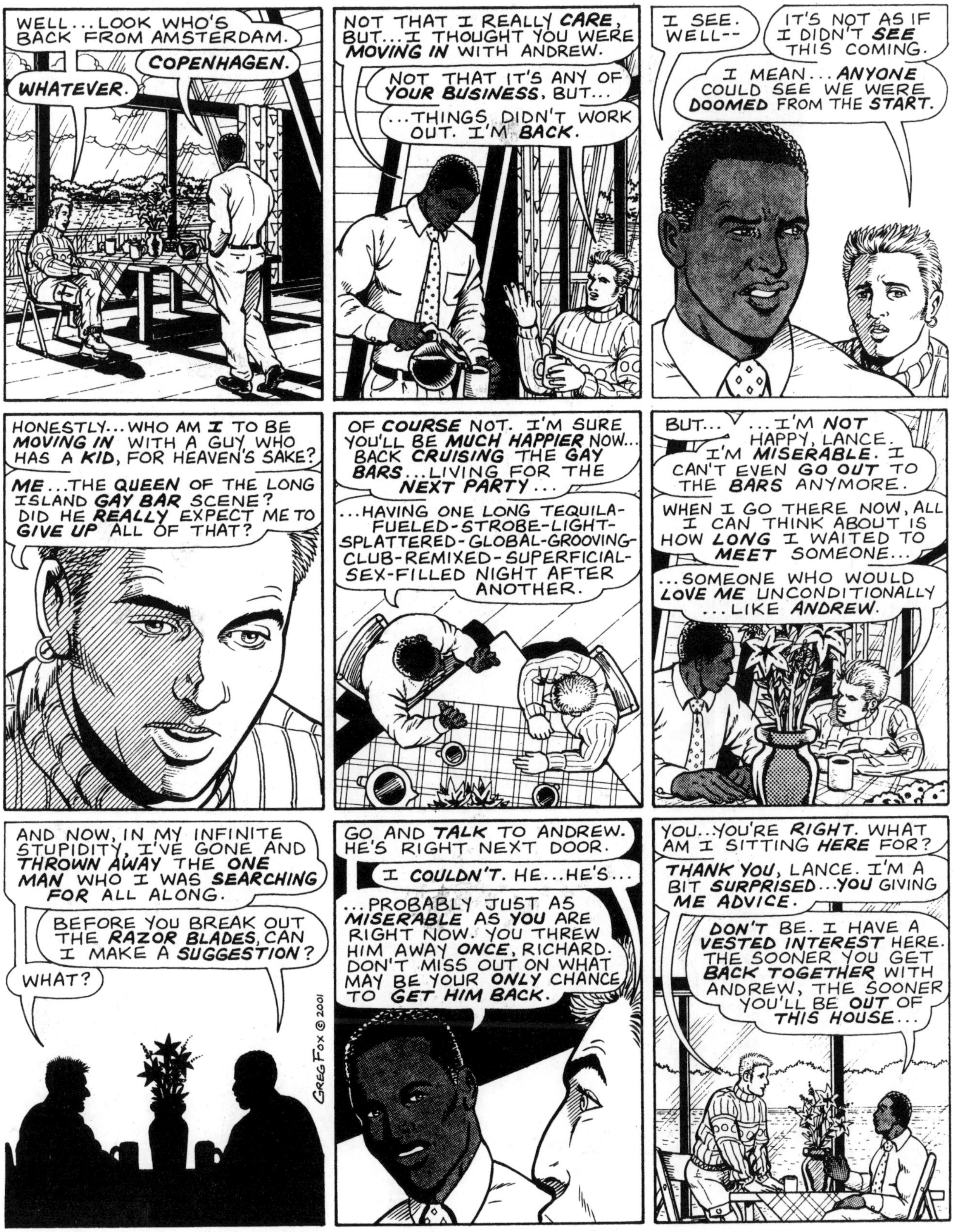
WELL... LOOK WHO'S BACK FROM AMSTERDAM.
COPENHAGEN.
WHATEVER.
NOT THAT I REALLY CARE, BUT... I THOUGHT YOU WERE MOVING IN WITH ANDREW.
NOT THAT IT'S ANY OF YOUR BUSINESS, BUT...
...THINGS DIDN'T WORK OUT. I'M BACK.
I SEE. WELL--
IT'S NOT AS IF I DIDN'T SEE THIS COMING.
I MEAN... ANYONE COULD SEE WE WERE DOOMED FROM THE START.
HONESTLY... WHO AM I TO BE MOVING IN WITH A GUY WHO HAS A KID, FOR HEAVEN'S SAKE?
ME... THE QUEEN OF THE LONG ISLAND GAY BAR SCENE? DID HE REALLY EXPECT ME TO GIVE UP ALL OF THAT?
OF COURSE NOT. I'M SURE YOU'LL BE MUCH HAPPIER NOW... BACK CRUISING THE GAY BARS... LIVING FOR THE NEXT PARTY...
...HAVING ONE LONG TEQUILA-FUELED-STROBE-LIGHT-SPLATTERED-GLOBAL-GROOVING-CLUB-REMIXED-SUPERFICIAL-SEX-FILLED NIGHT AFTER ANOTHER.
BUT...
...I'M NOT HAPPY, LANCE. I'M MISERABLE. I CAN'T EVEN GO OUT TO THE BARS ANYMORE.
WHEN I GO THERE NOW, ALL I CAN THINK ABOUT IS HOW LONG I WAITED TO MEET SOMEONE...
...SOMEONE WHO WOULD LOVE ME UNCONDITIONALLY ...LIKE ANDREW.
AND NOW, IN MY INFINITE STUPIDITY, I'VE GONE AND THROWN AWAY THE ONE MAN WHO I WAS SEARCHING FOR ALL ALONG.
BEFORE YOU BREAK OUT THE RAZOR BLADES, CAN I MAKE A SUGGESTION?
WHAT?
GREG FOX © 2001
GO AND TALK TO ANDREW. HE'S RIGHT NEXT DOOR.
I COULDN'T. HE... HE'S...
...PROBABLY JUST AS MISERABLE AS YOU ARE RIGHT NOW. YOU THREW HIM AWAY ONCE, RICHARD. DON'T MISS OUT ON WHAT MAY BE YOUR ONLY CHANCE TO GET HIM BACK.
YOU... YOU'RE RIGHT. WHAT AM I SITTING HERE FOR?
THANK YOU, LANCE. I'M A BIT SURPRISED... YOU GIVING ME ADVICE.
DON'T BE. I HAVE A VESTED INTEREST HERE. THE SOONER YOU GET BACK TOGETHER WITH ANDREW, THE SOONER YOU'LL BE OUT OF THIS HOUSE...

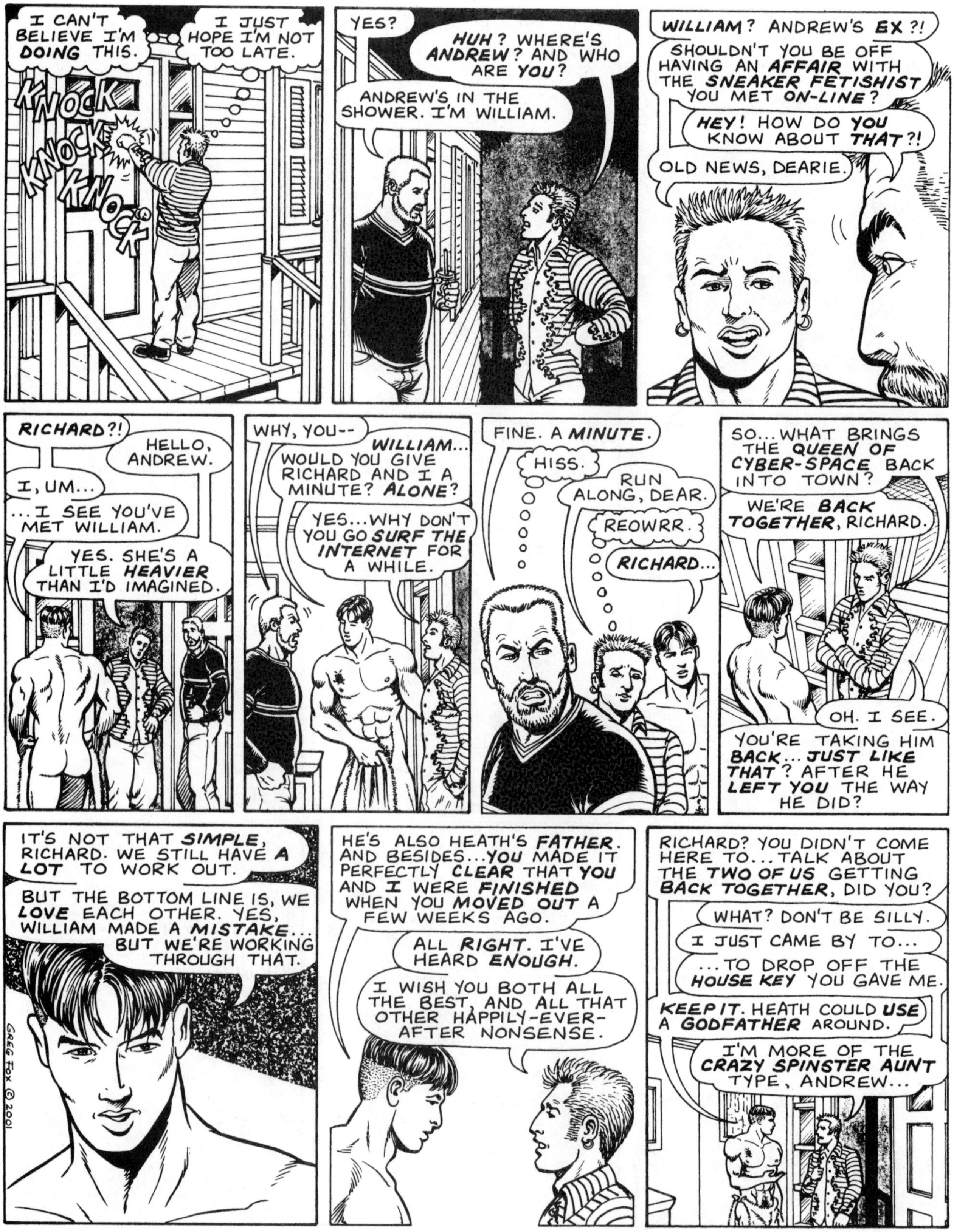
I CAN'T BELIEVE I'M DOING THIS.
I JUST HOPE I'M NOT TOO LATE.
KNOCK KNOCK KNOCK
YES?
HUH? WHERE'S ANDREW? AND WHO ARE YOU?
ANDREW'S IN THE SHOWER. I'M WILLIAM.
WILLIAM? ANDREW'S EX?!
SHOULDN'T YOU BE OFF HAVING AN AFFAIR WITH THE SNEAKER FETISHIST YOU MET ON-LINE?
HEY! HOW DO YOU KNOW ABOUT THAT?!
OLD NEWS, DEARIE.
RICHARD?!
HELLO, ANDREW.
I, UM...
...I SEE YOU'VE MET WILLIAM.
YES. SHE'S A LITTLE HEAVIER THAN I'D IMAGINED.
WHY, YOU--
WILLIAM... WOULD YOU GIVE RICHARD AND I A MINUTE? ALONE?
YES... WHY DON'T YOU GO SURF THE INTERNET FOR A WHILE.
FINE. A MINUTE.
HISS.
RUN ALONG, DEAR.
REOWRR.
RICHARD...
SO... WHAT BRINGS THE QUEEN OF CYBER-SPACE BACK INTO TOWN?
WE'RE BACK TOGETHER, RICHARD.
OH. I SEE.
YOU'RE TAKING HIM BACK... JUST LIKE THAT? AFTER HE LEFT YOU THE WAY HE DID?
IT'S NOT THAT SIMPLE, RICHARD. WE STILL HAVE A LOT TO WORK OUT.
BUT THE BOTTOM LINE IS, WE LOVE EACH OTHER. YES, WILLIAM MADE A MISTAKE... BUT WE'RE WORKING THROUGH THAT.
GREG FOX © 2001
HE'S ALSO HEATH'S FATHER. AND BESIDES... YOU MADE IT PERFECTLY CLEAR THAT YOU AND I WERE FINISHED WHEN YOU MOVED OUT A FEW WEEKS AGO.
ALL RIGHT. I'VE HEARD ENOUGH.
I WISH YOU BOTH ALL THE BEST, AND ALL THAT OTHER HAPPILY-EVER-AFTER NONSENSE.
RICHARD? YOU DIDN'T COME HERE TO... TALK ABOUT THE TWO OF US GETTING BACK TOGETHER, DID YOU?
WHAT? DON'T BE SILLY.
I JUST CAME BY TO...
...TO DROP OFF THE HOUSE KEY YOU GAVE ME.
KEEP IT. HEATH COULD USE A GODFATHER AROUND.
I'M MORE OF THE CRAZY SPINSTER AUNT TYPE, ANDREW...

YEAH? CAN I HELP YOU? YOU NEED A *ROOM*?

ER... *NO*. I'M HERE FOR *KYLE*.

OH. YOU'RE "*THE DATE*". C'MON IN.

SO...WHERE DO YOU PLAN ON GOIN' WITH KYLE TONIGHT?

I THOUGHT WE'D HAVE DINNER AND THEN SEE A MOVIE.

UH-HUH. YOU KNOW, KYLE'S REAL *PARTICULAR* ABOUT WHAT HE *EATS*. HE'S SORT OF A *HEALTH FOOD WHACKO*.

OH, SO AM *I*. IN FACT, THAT'S HOW I *MET* KYLE...AT THE CHECK-OUT COUNTER AT THE *HEALTH FOOD STORE*!

OH YEAH? IS THAT WHAT YOU DO? GO AROUND *PICKIN' UP* GUYS IN HEALTH FOOD STORES?

NO, I *DON'T*.

LOOK... JUST *WHO ARE YOU*, ANYWAY?

I'M *BRAD*. KYLE'S *FRIEND*.

KYLE'S *VERY CLOSE* FRIEND.

AND I'M *WARNIN'* YOU... IF YOU DO *ANYTHING* TO *MESS* WITH KYLE, YOU'LL HAVE TO ANSWER TO *ME*. GOT THAT?

G-GOT IT.

I'LL TAKE IT FROM HERE, "*DAD*".

HI, BARRY.

UH...CAN WE *GO*, KYLE?

DON'T STAY OUT *TOO LATE* WITH THIS GUY, KYLE.

SURE, BRAD. SEE YOU LATER.

RIGHT.

LATER.

SO...WHEN ARE YOU GONNA' *TELL* HIM?

HUH?! TELL HIM *WHAT*, EDUARDO?

THAT YOU'RE, LIKE, *MADLY IN LOVE* WITH HIM?

KID, I DON'T KNOW WHAT YOU--

SAVE IT, JOCK-FACE. I BEEN WATCHIN' YOU STUMBLE OVER YOUR INFATUATION FOR KYLE FOR OVER A *YEAR* NOW.

YOU WAIT ANY *LONGER* AND HE MIGHT FIND *SOMEBODY ELSE*. YOU COULD LOSE HIM *FOREVER*.

JEEZ. YOU THINK KYLE AND THIS GUY BARRY MIGHT GET *SERIOUS*?

I *DOUBT* IT. BARRY ACTUALLY SEEMS *COOL* AND *INTERESTING*. FROM WHAT I'VE SEEN, KYLE ONLY GETS SERIOUSLY *INVOLVED* WITH UPTIGHT, BORING, *DOPEY* GUYS.

YOU'RE IN LUCK.

WELL, *THAT'S* A RELIEF.

HEY... *WAIT* A MINUTE...

GregFox © 2001

WOW. ORGANIC BROCCOLI'S *TWO* FOR *THREE DOLLARS.*

KYLE...WE GOTTA' *TALK.*

ABOUT THE *BROCCOLI?*

SCREW THE BROCCOLI. I MEAN...THAT *IS* A GOOD PRICE. BUT THIS IS *IMPORTANT.*

ALL RIGHT.

LOOK, KYLE...THIS HAS BEEN BUILDIN' UP FOR A *LONG TIME.* AND WHEN I WAS IN *BRAZIL,* IT ALL BECAME *CRYSTAL CLEAR* TO ME. I'M JUST GONNA' COME RIGHT OUT N' *SAY* IT.

I THINK WE SHOULD BE *GOIN' OUT,* KYLE.

YOU...YOU DO? YEAH. I DO.

C'MON, KYLE...YOU GOTTA' ADMIT THERE'S BEEN *SPARKS FLYIN'* BETWEEN US SINCE THAT *FIRST DAY* I WALKED INTO THE B&B.

GREG FOX © 2001

BRAD... I -- AND BEFORE YOU SAY ANYTHING... I *DON'T CARE* ABOUT THE *HUGE AGE DIFFERENCE* BETWEEN US. THAT *DOESN'T MATTER* TO ME...NO MATTER WHAT *ANYBODY ELSE* SAYS.

WOW. *"HUGE* AGE DIFFERENCE". HOW... *FLATTERING.*

AW...YOU *KNOW* WHAT I MEANT, KYLE. C'MON ...WE'RE *PERFECT* FOR EACH OTHER.

I NEVER MET ANOTHER *GAY GUY* LIKE YOU. YOU'RE *REGULAR*...YOU'RE NOT A CLUB-GOIN' *FREAK* ...YOU EVEN LIKE *LED ZEPPELIN,* FOR CHRISSAKES.

SALE 99¢ LB

BRAD, I LIKE YOU *TOO.* A *LOT.* BUT...

BUT *WHAT?!*

YOU'VE *NEVER* BEEN IN A *RELATIONSHIP* BEFORE. THIS IS STILL ALL *NEW* TO YOU.

SO? WHAT DOES *THAT* MATTER?

IT MATTERS *TO ME,* BRAD... I'M *PAST* THE POINT OF *EXPERIMENTING*...OF HAVING *CASUAL RELATIONSHIPS.*

THE NEXT PERSON I GET *INVOLVED* WITH... I WANT TO HAVE A *SERIOUS COMMITMENT* WITH. TO BUILD A *LIFE* TOGETHER.

BUT...THAT'S *GOOD* KYLE. SO DO I!

BRAD...YOU CAN'T POSSIBLY EVEN *KNOW* THAT YET. YOU'RE A 20 YEAR OLD *VIRGIN.* I'M NOT GOING TO RISK *MY* FUTURE SO YOU CAN *DUMP ME* IN FIVE YEARS WHEN YOU REALIZE YOU MADE A COMMITMENT TOO *YOUNG.*

THAT AIN'T GONNA' *HAPPEN,* KYLE.

YOU'RE *RIGHT* IT'S NOT. BECAUSE WE'RE JUST GOING TO REMAIN *FRIENDS* AND *FORGET* ABOUT THIS CONVERSATION.

YOU CAN'T JUST MAKE AN *IMPORTANT DECISION* LIKE THIS AT THE *SUPERMARKET,* KYLE!

HEY...*YOU'RE* THE ONE WHO *BROUGHT IT UP* AT THE *SUPERMARKET...*

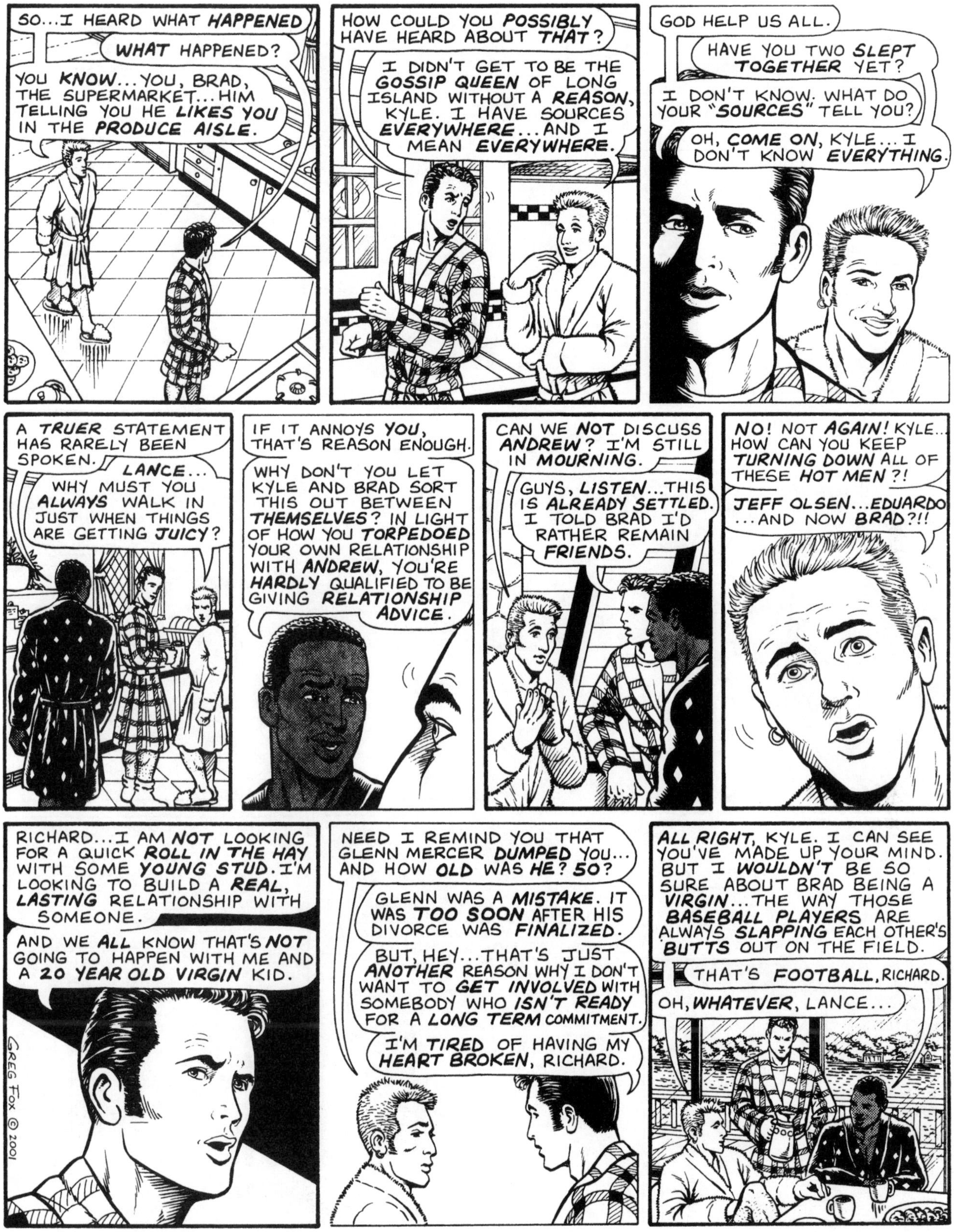
SO... I HEARD WHAT HAPPENED
WHAT HAPPENED?
YOU KNOW... YOU, BRAD, THE SUPERMARKET... HIM TELLING YOU HE LIKES YOU IN THE PRODUCE AISLE.
HOW COULD YOU POSSIBLY HAVE HEARD ABOUT THAT?
I DIDN'T GET TO BE THE GOSSIP QUEEN OF LONG ISLAND WITHOUT A REASON, KYLE. I HAVE SOURCES EVERYWHERE... AND I MEAN EVERYWHERE.
GOD HELP US ALL.
HAVE YOU TWO SLEPT TOGETHER YET?
I DON'T KNOW. WHAT DO YOUR "SOURCES" TELL YOU?
OH, COME ON, KYLE... I DON'T KNOW EVERYTHING.
A TRUER STATEMENT HAS RARELY BEEN SPOKEN.
LANCE... WHY MUST YOU ALWAYS WALK IN JUST WHEN THINGS ARE GETTING JUICY?
IF IT ANNOYS YOU, THAT'S REASON ENOUGH.
WHY DON'T YOU LET KYLE AND BRAD SORT THIS OUT BETWEEN THEMSELVES? IN LIGHT OF HOW YOU TORPEDOED YOUR OWN RELATIONSHIP WITH ANDREW, YOU'RE HARDLY QUALIFIED TO BE GIVING RELATIONSHIP ADVICE.
CAN WE NOT DISCUSS ANDREW? I'M STILL IN MOURNING.
GUYS, LISTEN... THIS IS ALREADY SETTLED. I TOLD BRAD I'D RATHER REMAIN FRIENDS.
NO! NOT AGAIN! KYLE... HOW CAN YOU KEEP TURNING DOWN ALL OF THESE HOT MEN?!
JEFF OLSEN... EDUARDO ...AND NOW BRAD?!!
RICHARD... I AM NOT LOOKING FOR A QUICK ROLL IN THE HAY WITH SOME YOUNG STUD. I'M LOOKING TO BUILD A REAL, LASTING RELATIONSHIP WITH SOMEONE.
AND WE ALL KNOW THAT'S NOT GOING TO HAPPEN WITH ME AND A 20 YEAR OLD VIRGIN KID.
GREG FOX © 2001
NEED I REMIND YOU THAT GLENN MERCER DUMPED YOU... AND HOW OLD WAS HE? 50?
GLENN WAS A MISTAKE. IT WAS TOO SOON AFTER HIS DIVORCE WAS FINALIZED.
BUT, HEY... THAT'S JUST ANOTHER REASON WHY I DON'T WANT TO GET INVOLVED WITH SOMEBODY WHO ISN'T READY FOR A LONG TERM COMMITMENT.
I'M TIRED OF HAVING MY HEART BROKEN, RICHARD.
ALL RIGHT, KYLE. I CAN SEE YOU'VE MADE UP YOUR MIND. BUT I WOULDN'T BE SO SURE ABOUT BRAD BEING A VIRGIN... THE WAY THOSE BASEBALL PLAYERS ARE ALWAYS SLAPPING EACH OTHER'S BUTTS OUT ON THE FIELD.
THAT'S FOOTBALL, RICHARD.
OH, WHATEVER, LANCE...

GOOD MORNING, BRAD!

OH, UH...HEY, KYLE.

YOU'RE UP *EARLY*.

YEAH, UH...I THOUGHT I'D JUST GRAB A QUICK COFFEE AND HEAD OUT TO PRACTICE EARLY TODAY.

UH-HUH. GEE...I WISH YOU'D STICK AROUND FOR *BREAKFAST*. I'M MAKING YOUR *FAVORITE*...BLUEBERRY WALNUT PANCAKES.

UM...I'D *LIKE* TO. BUT...I REALLY OUGHTA' GET GOIN'. BIG GAME AGAINST SAN ANTONIO ON SATURDAY. GOTTA' MAKE THE *MOST* OF THESE NEXT FEW PRACTICES.

I UNDERSTAND.

HEY, BRAD... ARE WE O.K.?

GREG FOX © 2001

"O.K."? ABOUT *WHAT*?

YOU KNOW...ABOUT WHAT YOU *SAID*...

ABOUT ME *LIKING* YOU AS *MORE* THAN A *FRIEND*, KYLE?

UH... YEAH.

ABOUT *THAT*.

I'M OVER IT.

OH?

IT'S NOT A *BIG DEAL*, KYLE. *JEEZ*. SO YOU AIN'T INTERESTED IN ME. I'LL LIVE.

WELL...O.K....

NOT THAT I *UNDERSTAND* IT. I MEAN, HOW OFTEN DO YOU GET THE CHANCE TO GO OUT WITH A *HOT STUD* LIKE *ME*?

BUT, HEY...THAT'S *YOUR* LOSS.

RIGHT. WELL...I'M *GLAD* YOU'RE *OVER* IT.

OH, YEAH. I DEFINITELY AM.

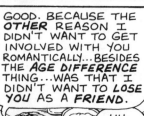

GOOD. BECAUSE THE *OTHER* REASON I DIDN'T WANT TO GET INVOLVED WITH YOU ROMANTICALLY...BESIDES THE *AGE DIFFERENCE* THING...WAS THAT I DIDN'T WANT TO *LOSE YOU* AS A *FRIEND*.

UH-HUH...

SO CAN YOU START ACTING LIKE MY *FRIEND* AGAIN? 'CAUSE LATELY IT FEELS LIKE I LOST YOU *ANYWAY*...

...AND WE DIDN'T EVEN SLEEP TOGETHER.

YEAH, WELL...

YOU *KNOW* I'M *CRAZY* ABOUT YOU, DON'T YOU?

JUST BECAUSE I DON'T WANT A *ROMANTIC INVOLVEMENT* WITH YOU DOESN'T MEAN I DON'T THINK YOU'RE *AMAZING*.

AND IF I SOMEHOW MESSED UP OUR *FRIENDSHIP* HERE...OR IF I'VE *HURT YOU* IN ANY WAY, I... WELL...I DON'T THINK I COULD *LIVE* WITH MYSELF.

SO, PLEASE... CAN WE BE *FRIENDS* AGAIN? I *MISS YOU*, YOU BIG *JERK*.

I MISS YOU *TOO*!

THANK *GOD*.

SO ARE YOU STAYING FOR THOSE PANCAKES OR *WHAT*?

JUST TRY N' *STOP* ME...

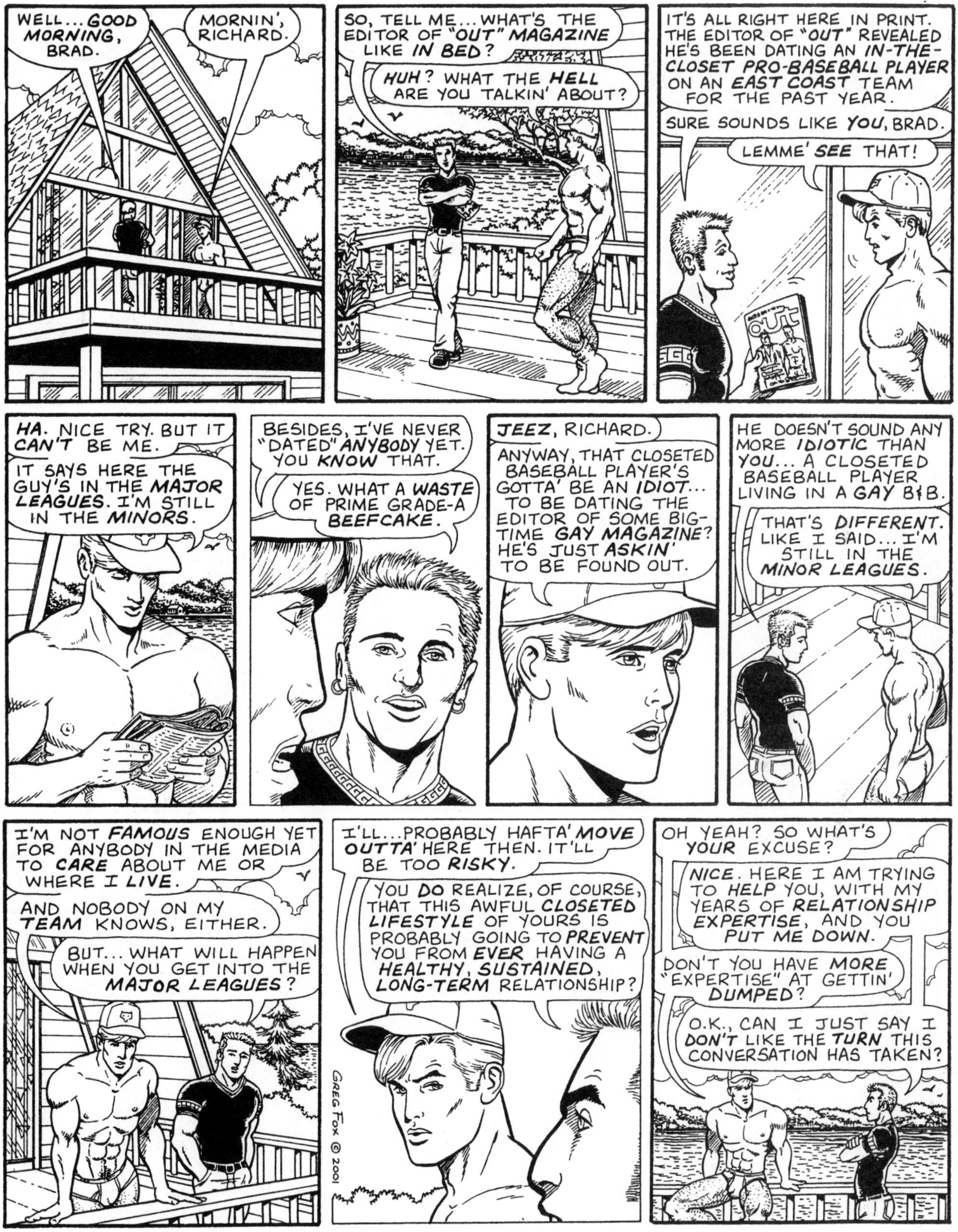
WELL... GOOD MORNING, BRAD.
MORNIN', RICHARD.
SO, TELL ME... WHAT'S THE EDITOR OF "OUT" MAGAZINE LIKE IN BED?
HUH? WHAT THE HELL ARE YOU TALKIN' ABOUT?
IT'S ALL RIGHT HERE IN PRINT. THE EDITOR OF "OUT" REVEALED HE'S BEEN DATING AN IN-THE-CLOSET PRO-BASEBALL PLAYER ON AN EAST COAST TEAM FOR THE PAST YEAR.
SURE SOUNDS LIKE YOU, BRAD.
LEMME' SEE THAT!
HA. NICE TRY. BUT IT CAN'T BE ME.
IT SAYS HERE THE GUY'S IN THE MAJOR LEAGUES. I'M STILL IN THE MINORS.
BESIDES, I'VE NEVER "DATED" ANYBODY YET. YOU KNOW THAT.
YES. WHAT A WASTE OF PRIME GRADE-A BEEFCAKE.
JEEZ, RICHARD.
ANYWAY, THAT CLOSETED BASEBALL PLAYER'S GOTTA' BE AN IDIOT... TO BE DATING THE EDITOR OF SOME BIG-TIME GAY MAGAZINE? HE'S JUST ASKIN' TO BE FOUND OUT.
HE DOESN'T SOUND ANY MORE IDIOTIC THAN YOU... A CLOSETED BASEBALL PLAYER LIVING IN A GAY B&B.
THAT'S DIFFERENT. LIKE I SAID... I'M STILL IN THE MINOR LEAGUES.
I'M NOT FAMOUS ENOUGH YET FOR ANYBODY IN THE MEDIA TO CARE ABOUT ME OR WHERE I LIVE.
AND NOBODY ON MY TEAM KNOWS, EITHER.
BUT... WHAT WILL HAPPEN WHEN YOU GET INTO THE MAJOR LEAGUES?
I'LL... PROBABLY HAFTA' MOVE OUTTA' HERE THEN. IT'LL BE TOO RISKY.
YOU DO REALIZE, OF COURSE, THAT THIS AWFUL CLOSETED LIFESTYLE OF YOURS IS PROBABLY GOING TO PREVENT YOU FROM EVER HAVING A HEALTHY, SUSTAINED, LONG-TERM RELATIONSHIP?
GREG FOX © 2001
OH YEAH? SO WHAT'S YOUR EXCUSE?
NICE. HERE I AM TRYING TO HELP YOU, WITH MY YEARS OF RELATIONSHIP EXPERTISE, AND YOU PUT ME DOWN.
DON'T YOU HAVE MORE "EXPERTISE" AT GETTIN' DUMPED?
O.K., CAN I JUST SAY I DON'T LIKE THE TURN THIS CONVERSATION HAS TAKEN?

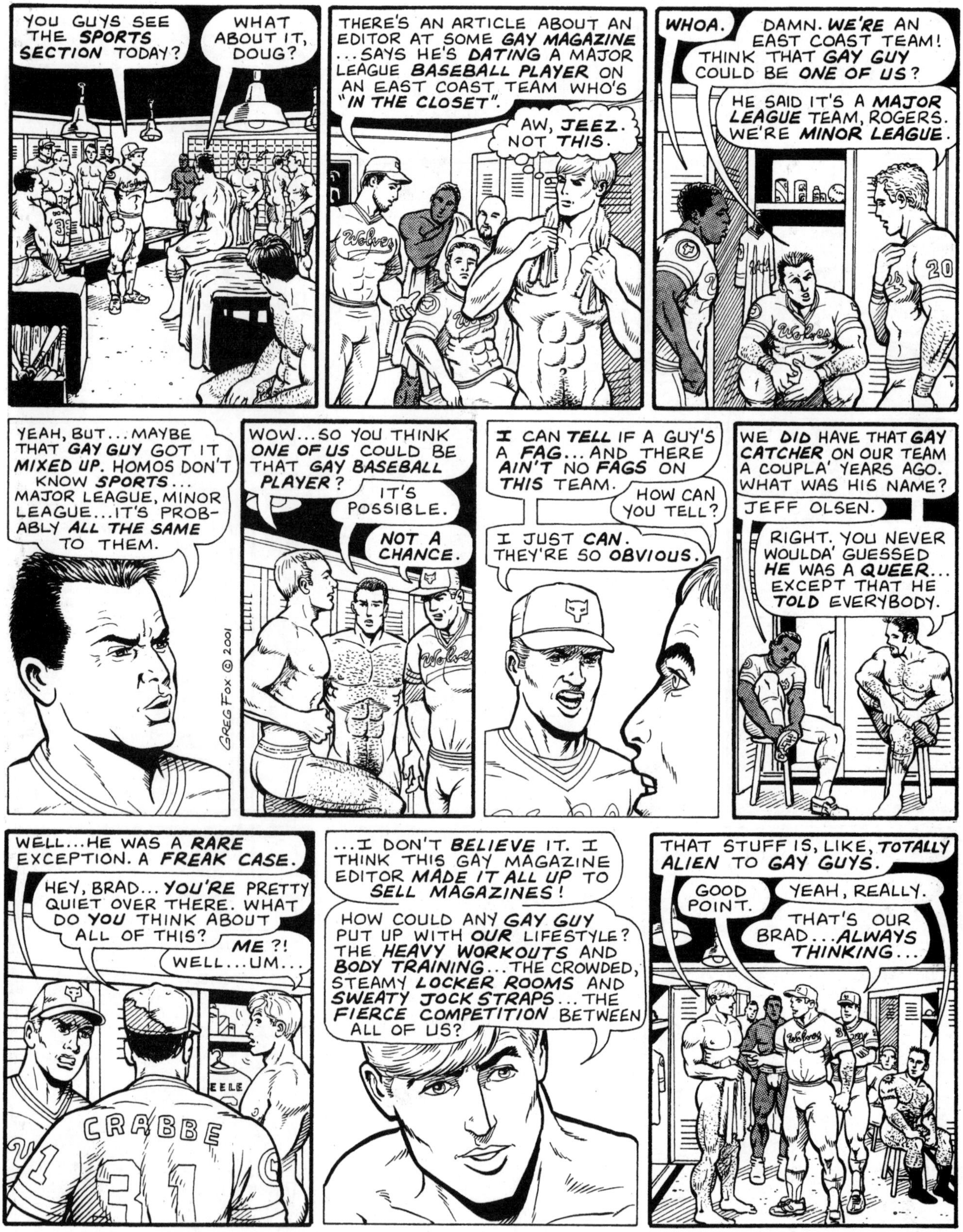
YOU GUYS SEE THE SPORTS SECTION TODAY?
WHAT ABOUT IT, DOUG?
THERE'S AN ARTICLE ABOUT AN EDITOR AT SOME GAY MAGAZINE ...SAYS HE'S DATING A MAJOR LEAGUE BASEBALL PLAYER ON AN EAST COAST TEAM WHO'S "IN THE CLOSET".
AW, JEEZ. NOT THIS.
WHOA.
DAMN. WE'RE AN EAST COAST TEAM! THINK THAT GAY GUY COULD BE ONE OF US?
HE SAID IT'S A MAJOR LEAGUE TEAM, ROGERS. WE'RE MINOR LEAGUE.
YEAH, BUT... MAYBE THAT GAY GUY GOT IT MIXED UP. HOMOS DON'T KNOW SPORTS... MAJOR LEAGUE, MINOR LEAGUE...IT'S PROBABLY ALL THE SAME TO THEM.
GREG FOX © 2001
WOW...SO YOU THINK ONE OF US COULD BE THAT GAY BASEBALL PLAYER?
IT'S POSSIBLE.
NOT A CHANCE.
I CAN TELL IF A GUY'S A FAG... AND THERE AIN'T NO FAGS ON THIS TEAM.
HOW CAN YOU TELL?
I JUST CAN. THEY'RE SO OBVIOUS.
WE DID HAVE THAT GAY CATCHER ON OUR TEAM A COUPLA' YEARS AGO. WHAT WAS HIS NAME?
JEFF OLSEN.
RIGHT. YOU NEVER WOULDA' GUESSED HE WAS A QUEER... EXCEPT THAT HE TOLD EVERYBODY.
WELL...HE WAS A RARE EXCEPTION. A FREAK CASE.
HEY, BRAD... YOU'RE PRETTY QUIET OVER THERE. WHAT DO YOU THINK ABOUT ALL OF THIS?
ME?!
WELL...UM...
CRABBE 31
...I DON'T BELIEVE IT. I THINK THIS GAY MAGAZINE EDITOR MADE IT ALL UP TO SELL MAGAZINES!
HOW COULD ANY GAY GUY PUT UP WITH OUR LIFESTYLE? THE HEAVY WORKOUTS AND BODY TRAINING... THE CROWDED, STEAMY LOCKER ROOMS AND SWEATY JOCK STRAPS... THE FIERCE COMPETITION BETWEEN ALL OF US?
THAT STUFF IS, LIKE, TOTALLY ALIEN TO GAY GUYS.
GOOD POINT.
YEAH, REALLY.
THAT'S OUR BRAD... ALWAYS THINKING...

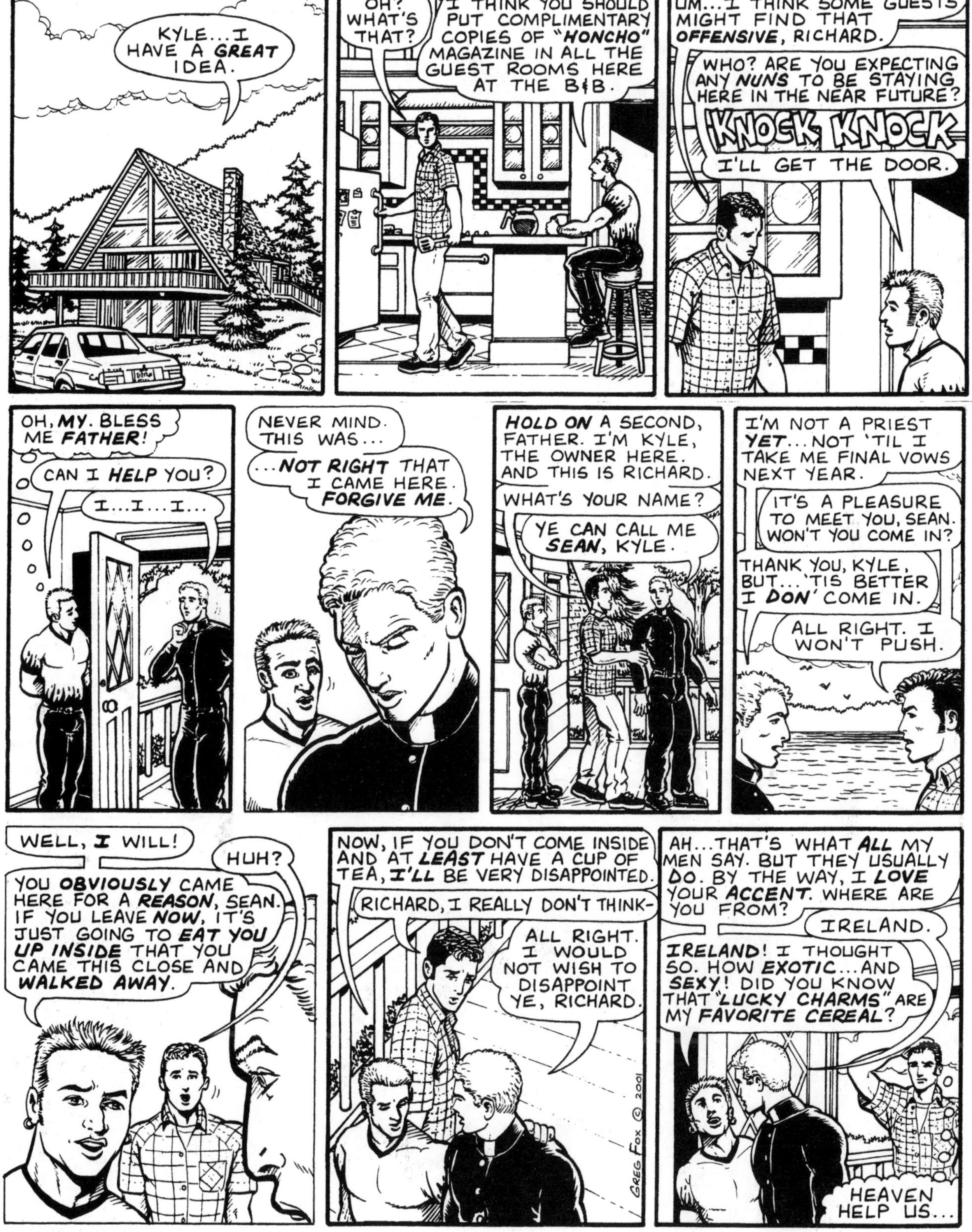

KYLE... I HAVE A GREAT IDEA.
OH? WHAT'S THAT?
I THINK YOU SHOULD PUT COMPLIMENTARY COPIES OF "HONCHO" MAGAZINE IN ALL THE GUEST ROOMS HERE AT THE B&B.
UM... I THINK SOME GUESTS MIGHT FIND THAT OFFENSIVE, RICHARD.
WHO? ARE YOU EXPECTING ANY NUNS TO BE STAYING HERE IN THE NEAR FUTURE?
KNOCK KNOCK
I'LL GET THE DOOR.
OH, MY. BLESS ME FATHER!
CAN I HELP YOU?
I... I... I...
NEVER MIND. THIS WAS...
...NOT RIGHT THAT I CAME HERE. FORGIVE ME.
HOLD ON A SECOND, FATHER. I'M KYLE, THE OWNER HERE. AND THIS IS RICHARD.
WHAT'S YOUR NAME?
YE CAN CALL ME SEAN, KYLE.
I'M NOT A PRIEST YET... NOT 'TIL I TAKE ME FINAL VOWS NEXT YEAR.
IT'S A PLEASURE TO MEET YOU, SEAN. WON'T YOU COME IN?
THANK YOU, KYLE, BUT... 'TIS BETTER I DON' COME IN.
ALL RIGHT. I WON'T PUSH.
WELL, I WILL!
HUH?
YOU OBVIOUSLY CAME HERE FOR A REASON, SEAN. IF YOU LEAVE NOW, IT'S JUST GOING TO EAT YOU UP INSIDE THAT YOU CAME THIS CLOSE AND WALKED AWAY.
NOW, IF YOU DON'T COME INSIDE AND AT LEAST HAVE A CUP OF TEA, I'LL BE VERY DISAPPOINTED.
RICHARD, I REALLY DON'T THINK-
ALL RIGHT. I WOULD NOT WISH TO DISAPPOINT YE, RICHARD.
GREG FOX © 2001
AH... THAT'S WHAT ALL MY MEN SAY. BUT THEY USUALLY DO. BY THE WAY, I LOVE YOUR ACCENT. WHERE ARE YOU FROM?
IRELAND.
IRELAND! I THOUGHT SO. HOW EXOTIC... AND SEXY! DID YOU KNOW THAT "LUCKY CHARMS" ARE MY FAVORITE CEREAL?
HEAVEN HELP US...

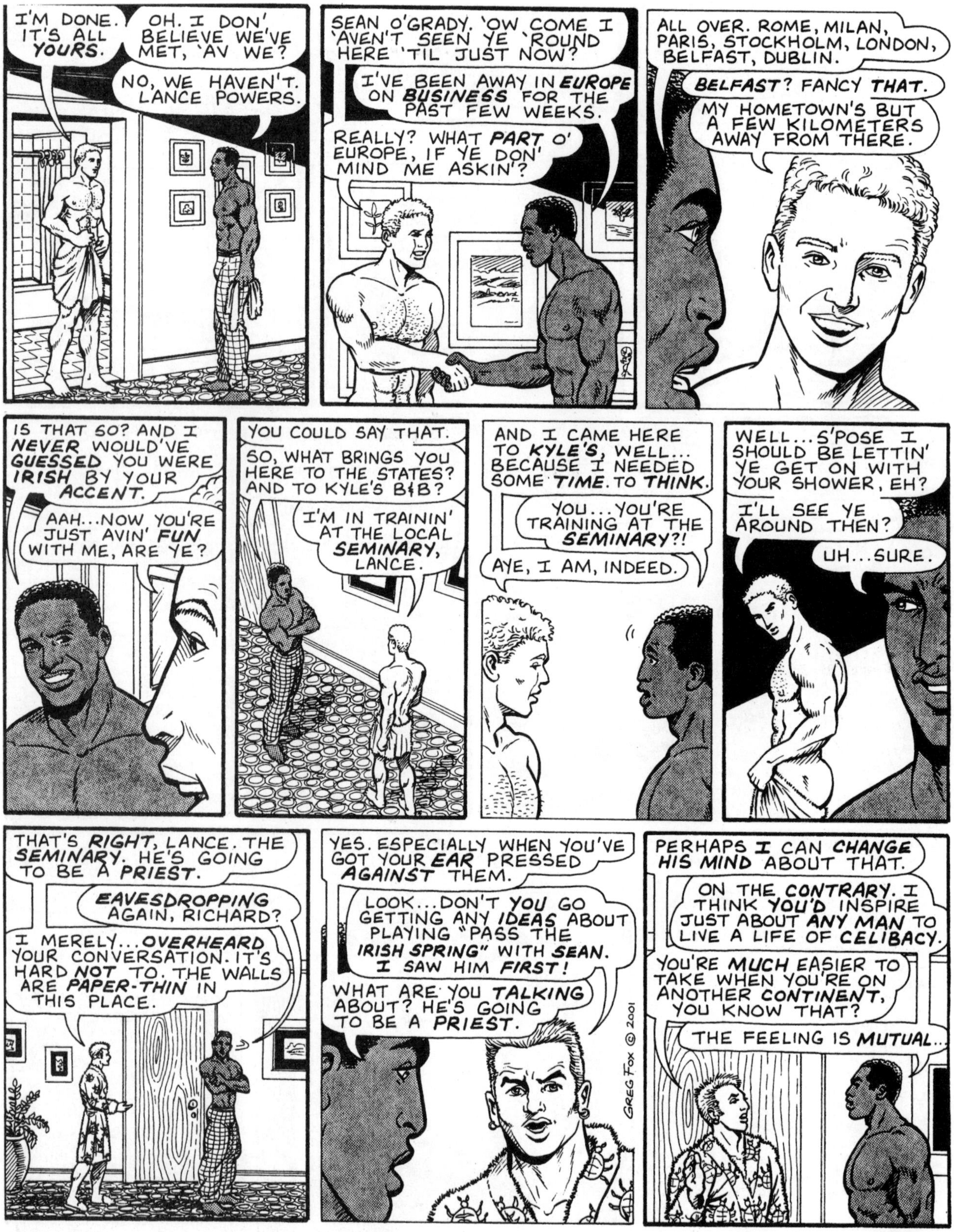
I'M DONE. IT'S ALL YOURS.
OH. I DON' BELIEVE WE'VE MET, 'AV WE?
NO, WE HAVEN'T. LANCE POWERS.
SEAN O'GRADY. 'OW COME I 'AVEN'T SEEN YE 'ROUND HERE 'TIL JUST NOW?
I'VE BEEN AWAY IN EUROPE ON BUSINESS FOR THE PAST FEW WEEKS.
REALLY? WHAT PART O' EUROPE, IF YE DON' MIND ME ASKIN'?
ALL OVER. ROME, MILAN, PARIS, STOCKHOLM, LONDON, BELFAST, DUBLIN.
BELFAST? FANCY THAT.
MY HOMETOWN'S BUT A FEW KILOMETERS AWAY FROM THERE.
IS THAT SO? AND I NEVER WOULD'VE GUESSED YOU WERE IRISH BY YOUR ACCENT.
AAH...NOW YOU'RE JUST AVIN' FUN WITH ME, ARE YE?
YOU COULD SAY THAT.
SO, WHAT BRINGS YOU HERE TO THE STATES? AND TO KYLE'S B&B?
I'M IN TRAININ' AT THE LOCAL SEMINARY, LANCE.
AND I CAME HERE TO KYLE'S, WELL... BECAUSE I NEEDED SOME TIME. TO THINK.
YOU...YOU'RE TRAINING AT THE SEMINARY?!
AYE, I AM, INDEED.
WELL...S'POSE I SHOULD BE LETTIN' YE GET ON WITH YOUR SHOWER, EH?
I'LL SEE YE AROUND THEN?
UH...SURE.
THAT'S RIGHT, LANCE. THE SEMINARY. HE'S GOING TO BE A PRIEST.
EAVESDROPPING AGAIN, RICHARD?
I MERELY...OVERHEARD YOUR CONVERSATION. IT'S HARD NOT TO. THE WALLS ARE PAPER-THIN IN THIS PLACE.
YES. ESPECIALLY WHEN YOU'VE GOT YOUR EAR PRESSED AGAINST THEM.
LOOK...DON'T YOU GO GETTING ANY IDEAS ABOUT PLAYING "PASS THE IRISH SPRING" WITH SEAN. I SAW HIM FIRST!
WHAT ARE YOU TALKING ABOUT? HE'S GOING TO BE A PRIEST.
GREG FOX © 2001
PERHAPS I CAN CHANGE HIS MIND ABOUT THAT.
ON THE CONTRARY. I THINK YOU'D INSPIRE JUST ABOUT ANY MAN TO LIVE A LIFE OF CELIBACY.
YOU'RE MUCH EASIER TO TAKE WHEN YOU'RE ON ANOTHER CONTINENT, YOU KNOW THAT?
THE FEELING IS MUTUAL...

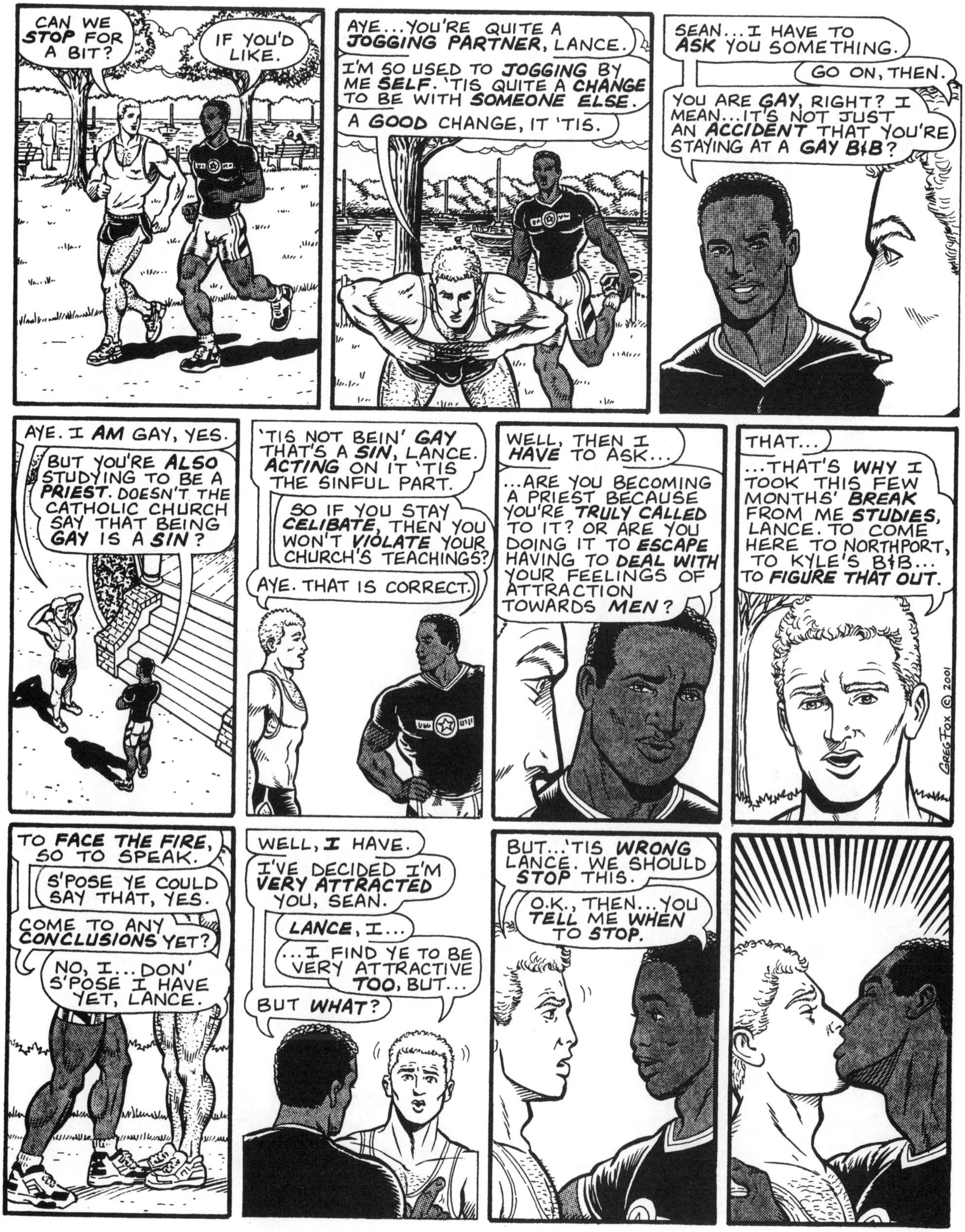
CAN WE STOP FOR A BIT?
IF YOU'D LIKE.
AYE... YOU'RE QUITE A JOGGING PARTNER, LANCE.
I'M SO USED TO JOGGING BY ME SELF. 'TIS QUITE A CHANGE TO BE WITH SOMEONE ELSE.
A GOOD CHANGE, IT 'TIS.
SEAN... I HAVE TO ASK YOU SOMETHING.
GO ON, THEN.
YOU ARE GAY, RIGHT? I MEAN... IT'S NOT JUST AN ACCIDENT THAT YOU'RE STAYING AT A GAY B&B?
AYE. I AM GAY, YES.
BUT YOU'RE ALSO STUDYING TO BE A PRIEST. DOESN'T THE CATHOLIC CHURCH SAY THAT BEING GAY IS A SIN?
'TIS NOT BEIN' GAY THAT'S A SIN, LANCE. ACTING ON IT 'TIS THE SINFUL PART.
SO IF YOU STAY CELIBATE, THEN YOU WON'T VIOLATE YOUR CHURCH'S TEACHINGS?
AYE. THAT IS CORRECT.
WELL, THEN I HAVE TO ASK...
...ARE YOU BECOMING A PRIEST BECAUSE YOU'RE TRULY CALLED TO IT? OR ARE YOU DOING IT TO ESCAPE HAVING TO DEAL WITH YOUR FEELINGS OF ATTRACTION TOWARDS MEN?
THAT...
...THAT'S WHY I TOOK THIS FEW MONTHS' BREAK FROM ME STUDIES, LANCE. TO COME HERE TO NORTHPORT, TO KYLE'S B&B... TO FIGURE THAT OUT.
GREG FOX © 2001
TO FACE THE FIRE, SO TO SPEAK.
S'POSE YE COULD SAY THAT, YES.
COME TO ANY CONCLUSIONS YET?
NO, I... DON' S'POSE I HAVE YET, LANCE.
WELL, I HAVE.
I'VE DECIDED I'M VERY ATTRACTED YOU, SEAN.
LANCE, I...
...I FIND YE TO BE VERY ATTRACTIVE TOO, BUT...
BUT WHAT?
BUT...'TIS WRONG LANCE. WE SHOULD STOP THIS.
O.K., THEN... YOU TELL ME WHEN TO STOP.

Panel 1:
SEAN? YOU O.K.?

AYE. I WAS JUST *THINKIN'*, LANCE.

Panel 2:
UH-OH. NEVER A GOOD THING TO DO BEFORE YOUR MORNING *INFUSION* OF CAFFEINE.

I'M SURE HEALTH-FOOD NUT *KYLE* WOULD BE *APPALLED* TO HEAR ME SAY THAT, BY THE WAY.

SO, WHAT'S UP?

Panel 3:
I S'POSE I'M 'AVIN'... *MIXED EMOTIONS* 'BOUT OUR ...*RELATIONSHIP*, LANCE.

WELL, *I'M* NOT. IT FEELS *RIGHT* TO ME.

Panel 4:
YOU'RE NOT THE ONE WHO'S TO BE *ORDAINED* AS A *PRIEST* NEXT YEAR.

OH, YOU MEAN... YOU'RE *STILL* GOING TO *GO THROUGH* WITH THAT, HUH?

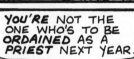

Panel 5:
I... ...I DON' *KNOW*, LANCE. IT'S ALL SO *CON-FUSIN'*, ISN'T IT?

IT DOESN'T *HAVE* TO BE.

Panel 6:
YE DON' *UNDERSTAND*, LANCE. I'VE BEEN PLANNIN' THIS SINCE I WAS A WEE LAD.

RIGHT. SO YOU COULD *ESCAPE* YOUR ATTRACTION TOWARDS *MEN*.

I NEVER SAID FOR SURE THAT'S *WHY* I'M DOIN' IT.

Panel 7:
YOU NEVER SAID THAT *ISN'T* WHY YOU'RE DOING IT EITHER, SEAN.

MAYBE I'M JUST NOT SURE YET ME SELF.

GOOD GOD...THIS IS *BREAKING* ONE OF MY CARDINAL *RULES*.

Panel 8:
WHAT WOULD *THAT* BE, THEN?

TO NEVER GET *INVOLVED* WITH ANYONE WHO'S STILL *QUESTIONING* THEIR *SEXUAL ORIENTATION*.

THERE'S NO *QUESTION*, LANCE. I *KNOW* I'M *GAY*.

I JUST DON' KNOW IF I WANT TO *ACT* ON IT.

Panel 9:
I THINK IT'S *TOO LATE* FOR *THAT*. WE'VE "ACTED" ON IT TOGETHER...*MULTIPLE TIMES*.

WELL, THEN...IF I WANT TO *CONTINUE* ACTIN' ON IT.

ALL RIGHT...SO MAYBE UNTIL YOU *FIGURE THAT OUT*...WE SHOULD *STOP SEEING EACH OTHER*.

Panel 10:
THAT'S THE *LAST THING* I WANT TO HAPPEN.

YOU *ARE* CONFUSING, YOU KNOW THAT?

GregFox © 2001

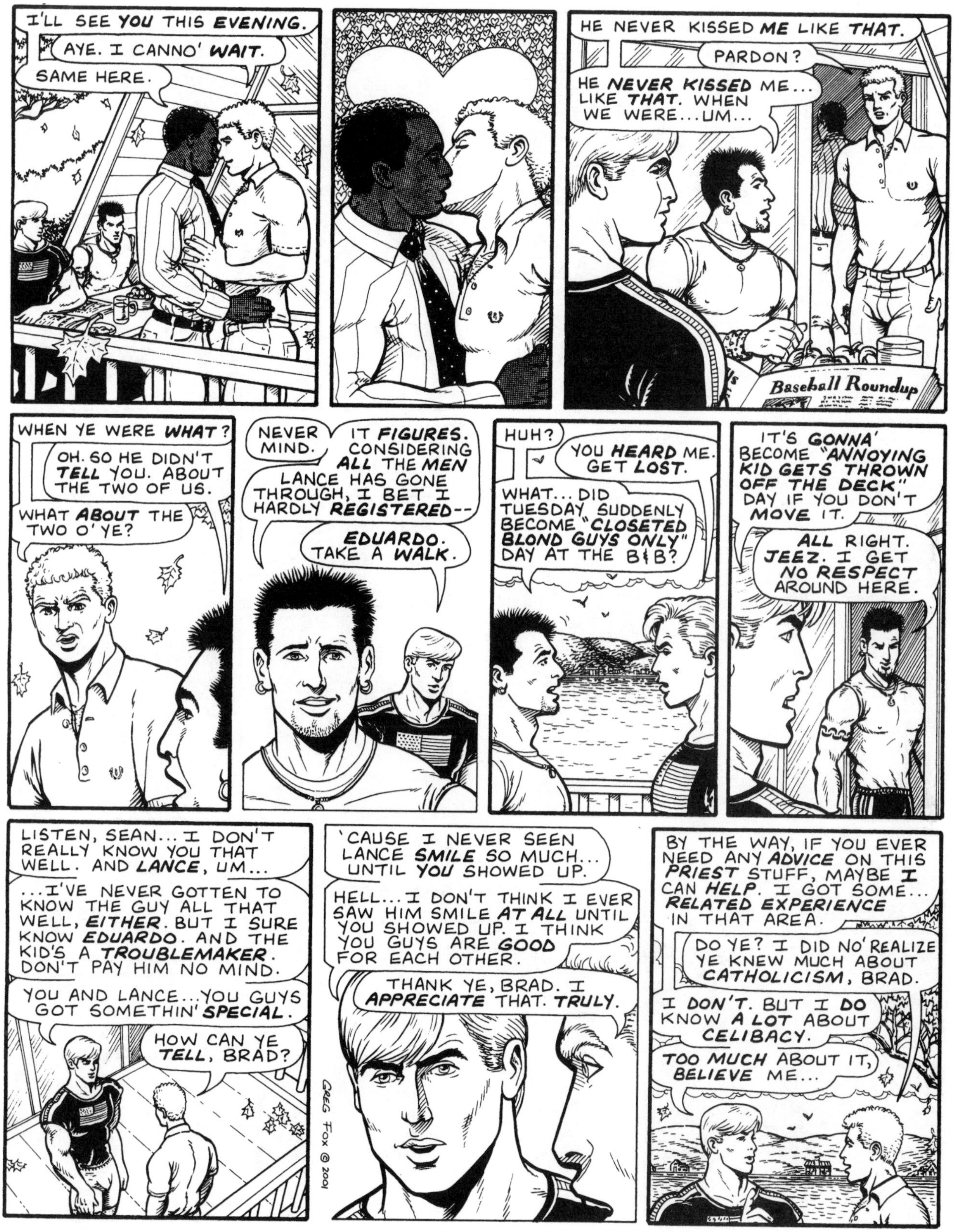
I'LL SEE YOU THIS EVENING.
AYE. I CANNO' WAIT.
SAME HERE.
HE NEVER KISSED ME LIKE THAT.
PARDON?
HE NEVER KISSED ME... LIKE THAT. WHEN WE WERE...UM...
Baseball Roundup
WHEN YE WERE WHAT?
OH. SO HE DIDN'T TELL YOU. ABOUT THE TWO OF US.
WHAT ABOUT THE TWO O' YE?
NEVER MIND.
IT FIGURES. CONSIDERING ALL THE MEN LANCE HAS GONE THROUGH, I BET I HARDLY REGISTERED--
EDUARDO. TAKE A WALK.
HUH?
YOU HEARD ME. GET LOST.
WHAT... DID TUESDAY SUDDENLY BECOME "CLOSETED BLOND GUYS ONLY" DAY AT THE B&B?
IT'S GONNA' BECOME "ANNOYING KID GETS THROWN OFF THE DECK" DAY IF YOU DON'T MOVE IT.
ALL RIGHT. JEEZ. I GET NO RESPECT AROUND HERE.
LISTEN, SEAN... I DON'T REALLY KNOW YOU THAT WELL. AND LANCE, UM...
...I'VE NEVER GOTTEN TO KNOW THE GUY ALL THAT WELL, EITHER. BUT I SURE KNOW EDUARDO. AND THE KID'S A TROUBLEMAKER. DON'T PAY HIM NO MIND.
YOU AND LANCE...YOU GUYS GOT SOMETHIN' SPECIAL.
HOW CAN YE TELL, BRAD?
'CAUSE I NEVER SEEN LANCE SMILE SO MUCH... UNTIL YOU SHOWED UP.
HELL... I DON'T THINK I EVER SAW HIM SMILE AT ALL UNTIL YOU SHOWED UP. I THINK YOU GUYS ARE GOOD FOR EACH OTHER.
THANK YE, BRAD. I APPRECIATE THAT. TRULY.
GREG FOX © 2001
BY THE WAY, IF YOU EVER NEED ANY ADVICE ON THIS PRIEST STUFF, MAYBE I CAN HELP. I GOT SOME... RELATED EXPERIENCE IN THAT AREA.
DO YE? I DID NO' REALIZE YE KNEW MUCH ABOUT CATHOLICISM, BRAD.
I DON'T. BUT I DO KNOW A LOT ABOUT CELIBACY.
TOO MUCH ABOUT IT, BELIEVE ME...

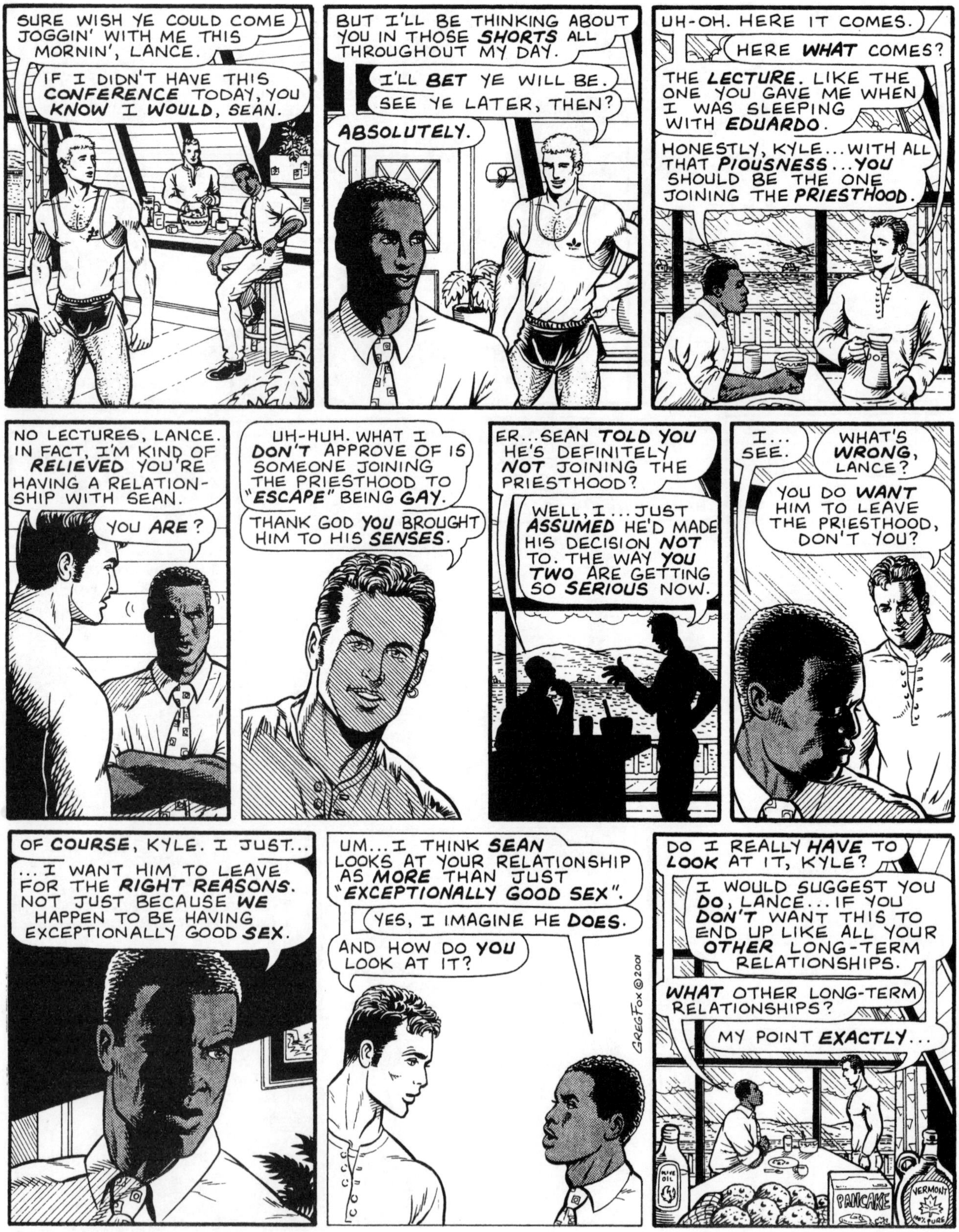
SURE WISH YE COULD COME JOGGIN' WITH ME THIS MORNIN', LANCE.
IF I DIDN'T HAVE THIS CONFERENCE TODAY, YOU KNOW I WOULD, SEAN.
BUT I'LL BE THINKING ABOUT YOU IN THOSE SHORTS ALL THROUGHOUT MY DAY.
I'LL BET YE WILL BE.
SEE YE LATER, THEN?
ABSOLUTELY.
UH-OH. HERE IT COMES.
HERE WHAT COMES?
THE LECTURE. LIKE THE ONE YOU GAVE ME WHEN I WAS SLEEPING WITH EDUARDO.
HONESTLY, KYLE... WITH ALL THAT PIOUSNESS... YOU SHOULD BE THE ONE JOINING THE PRIESTHOOD.
NO LECTURES, LANCE. IN FACT, I'M KIND OF RELIEVED YOU'RE HAVING A RELATIONSHIP WITH SEAN.
YOU ARE?
UH-HUH. WHAT I DON'T APPROVE OF IS SOMEONE JOINING THE PRIESTHOOD TO "ESCAPE" BEING GAY.
THANK GOD YOU BROUGHT HIM TO HIS SENSES.
ER... SEAN TOLD YOU HE'S DEFINITELY NOT JOINING THE PRIESTHOOD?
WELL, I... JUST ASSUMED HE'D MADE HIS DECISION NOT TO. THE WAY YOU TWO ARE GETTING SO SERIOUS NOW.
I... SEE.
WHAT'S WRONG, LANCE?
YOU DO WANT HIM TO LEAVE THE PRIESTHOOD, DON'T YOU?
OF COURSE, KYLE. I JUST...
... I WANT HIM TO LEAVE FOR THE RIGHT REASONS. NOT JUST BECAUSE WE HAPPEN TO BE HAVING EXCEPTIONALLY GOOD SEX.
UM... I THINK SEAN LOOKS AT YOUR RELATIONSHIP AS MORE THAN JUST "EXCEPTIONALLY GOOD SEX".
YES, I IMAGINE HE DOES.
AND HOW DO YOU LOOK AT IT?
GREGFOX © 2001
DO I REALLY HAVE TO LOOK AT IT, KYLE?
I WOULD SUGGEST YOU DO, LANCE... IF YOU DON'T WANT THIS TO END UP LIKE ALL YOUR OTHER LONG-TERM RELATIONSHIPS.
WHAT OTHER LONG-TERM RELATIONSHIPS?
MY POINT EXACTLY...
PANCAKE
VERMONT

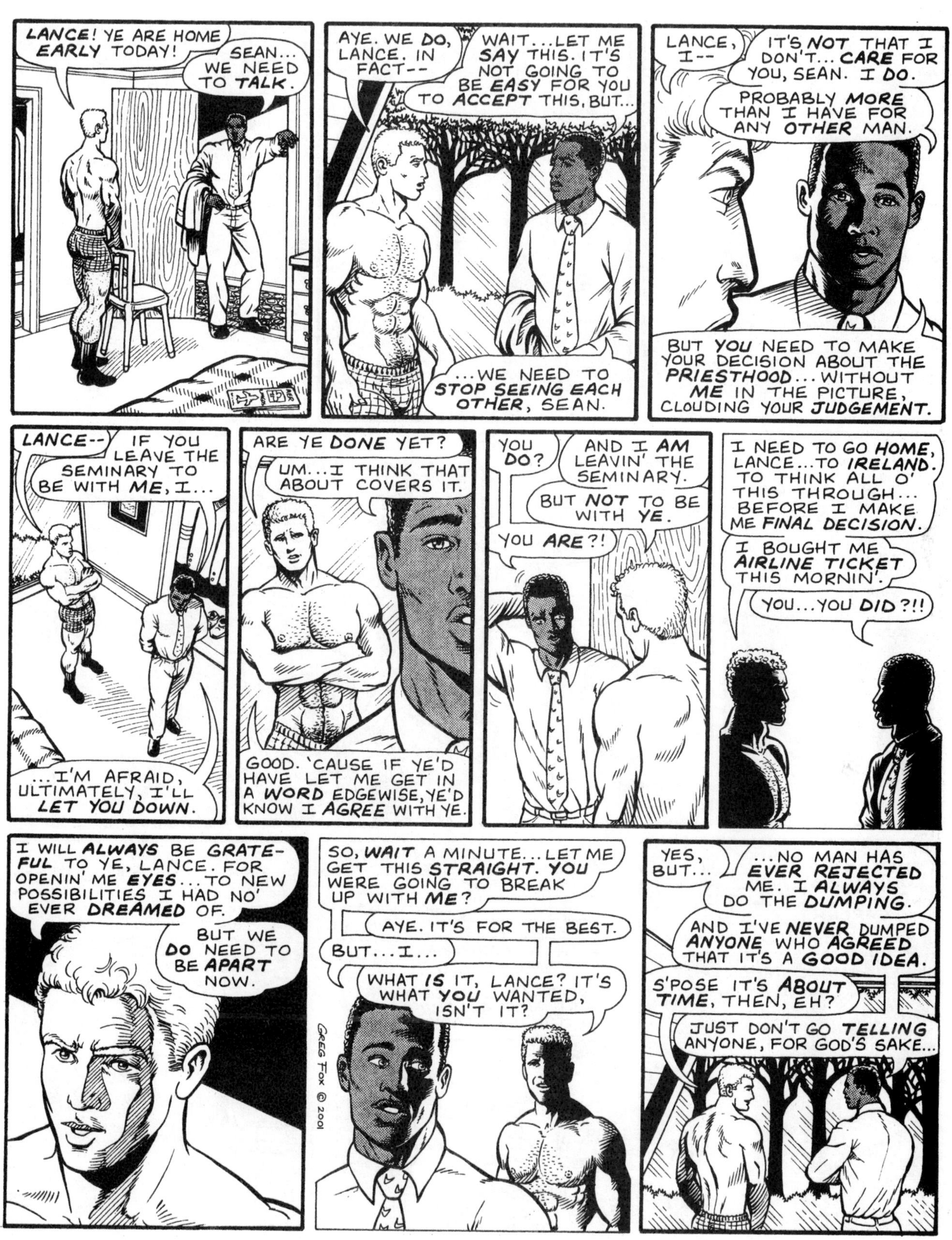
LANCE! YE ARE HOME EARLY TODAY!
SEAN... WE NEED TO TALK.
AYE. WE DO, LANCE. IN FACT--
WAIT...LET ME SAY THIS. IT'S NOT GOING TO BE EASY FOR YOU TO ACCEPT THIS, BUT...
...WE NEED TO STOP SEEING EACH OTHER, SEAN.
LANCE, I--
IT'S NOT THAT I DON'T... CARE FOR YOU, SEAN. I DO.
PROBABLY MORE THAN I HAVE FOR ANY OTHER MAN.
BUT YOU NEED TO MAKE YOUR DECISION ABOUT THE PRIESTHOOD... WITHOUT ME IN THE PICTURE, CLOUDING YOUR JUDGEMENT.
LANCE--
IF YOU LEAVE THE SEMINARY TO BE WITH ME, I...
...I'M AFRAID, ULTIMATELY, I'LL LET YOU DOWN.
ARE YE DONE YET?
UM...I THINK THAT ABOUT COVERS IT.
GOOD. 'CAUSE IF YE'D HAVE LET ME GET IN A WORD EDGEWISE, YE'D KNOW I AGREE WITH YE.
YOU DO?
AND I AM LEAVIN' THE SEMINARY.
BUT NOT TO BE WITH YE.
YOU ARE?!
I NEED TO GO HOME, LANCE...TO IRELAND. TO THINK ALL O' THIS THROUGH... BEFORE I MAKE ME FINAL DECISION.
I BOUGHT ME AIRLINE TICKET THIS MORNIN'.
YOU...YOU DID?!!
I WILL ALWAYS BE GRATEFUL TO YE, LANCE. FOR OPENIN' ME EYES...TO NEW POSSIBILITIES I HAD NO' EVER DREAMED OF.
BUT WE DO NEED TO BE APART NOW.
SO, WAIT A MINUTE...LET ME GET THIS STRAIGHT. YOU WERE GOING TO BREAK UP WITH ME?
AYE. IT'S FOR THE BEST.
BUT...I...
WHAT IS IT, LANCE? IT'S WHAT YOU WANTED, ISN'T IT?
GREG FOX © 2001
YES, BUT...
...NO MAN HAS EVER REJECTED ME. I ALWAYS DO THE DUMPING.
AND I'VE NEVER DUMPED ANYONE WHO AGREED THAT IT'S A GOOD IDEA.
S'POSE IT'S ABOUT TIME, THEN, EH?
JUST DON'T GO TELLING ANYONE, FOR GOD'S SAKE...

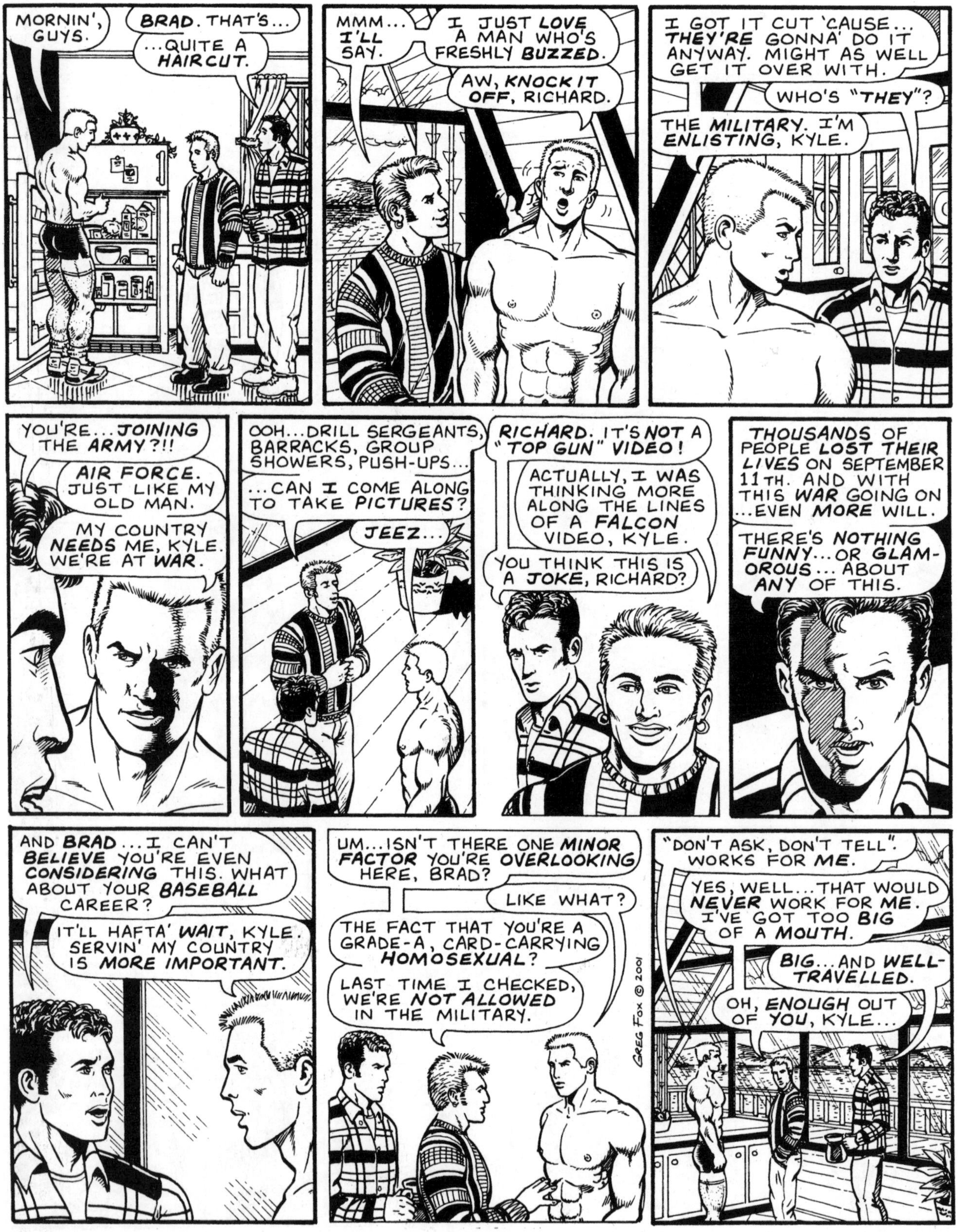
MORNIN', GUYS.
BRAD. THAT'S...
...QUITE A HAIRCUT.
MMM... I'LL SAY.
I JUST LOVE A MAN WHO'S FRESHLY BUZZED.
AW, KNOCK IT OFF, RICHARD.
I GOT IT CUT 'CAUSE... THEY'RE GONNA' DO IT ANYWAY. MIGHT AS WELL GET IT OVER WITH.
WHO'S "THEY"?
THE MILITARY. I'M ENLISTING, KYLE.
YOU'RE... JOINING THE ARMY?!!
AIR FORCE. JUST LIKE MY OLD MAN.
MY COUNTRY NEEDS ME, KYLE. WE'RE AT WAR.
OOH... DRILL SERGEANTS, BARRACKS, GROUP SHOWERS, PUSH-UPS...
...CAN I COME ALONG TO TAKE PICTURES?
JEEZ...
RICHARD. IT'S NOT A "TOP GUN" VIDEO!
ACTUALLY, I WAS THINKING MORE ALONG THE LINES OF A FALCON VIDEO, KYLE.
YOU THINK THIS IS A JOKE, RICHARD?
THOUSANDS OF PEOPLE LOST THEIR LIVES ON SEPTEMBER 11TH. AND WITH THIS WAR GOING ON ...EVEN MORE WILL.
THERE'S NOTHING FUNNY... OR GLAMOROUS... ABOUT ANY OF THIS.
AND BRAD... I CAN'T BELIEVE YOU'RE EVEN CONSIDERING THIS. WHAT ABOUT YOUR BASEBALL CAREER?
IT'LL HAFTA' WAIT, KYLE. SERVIN' MY COUNTRY IS MORE IMPORTANT.
UM... ISN'T THERE ONE MINOR FACTOR YOU'RE OVERLOOKING HERE, BRAD?
LIKE WHAT?
THE FACT THAT YOU'RE A GRADE-A, CARD-CARRYING HOMOSEXUAL?
LAST TIME I CHECKED, WE'RE NOT ALLOWED IN THE MILITARY.
GREG FOX © 2001
"DON'T ASK, DON'T TELL". WORKS FOR ME.
YES, WELL... THAT WOULD NEVER WORK FOR ME. I'VE GOT TOO BIG OF A MOUTH.
BIG... AND WELL-TRAVELLED.
OH, ENOUGH OUT OF YOU, KYLE...

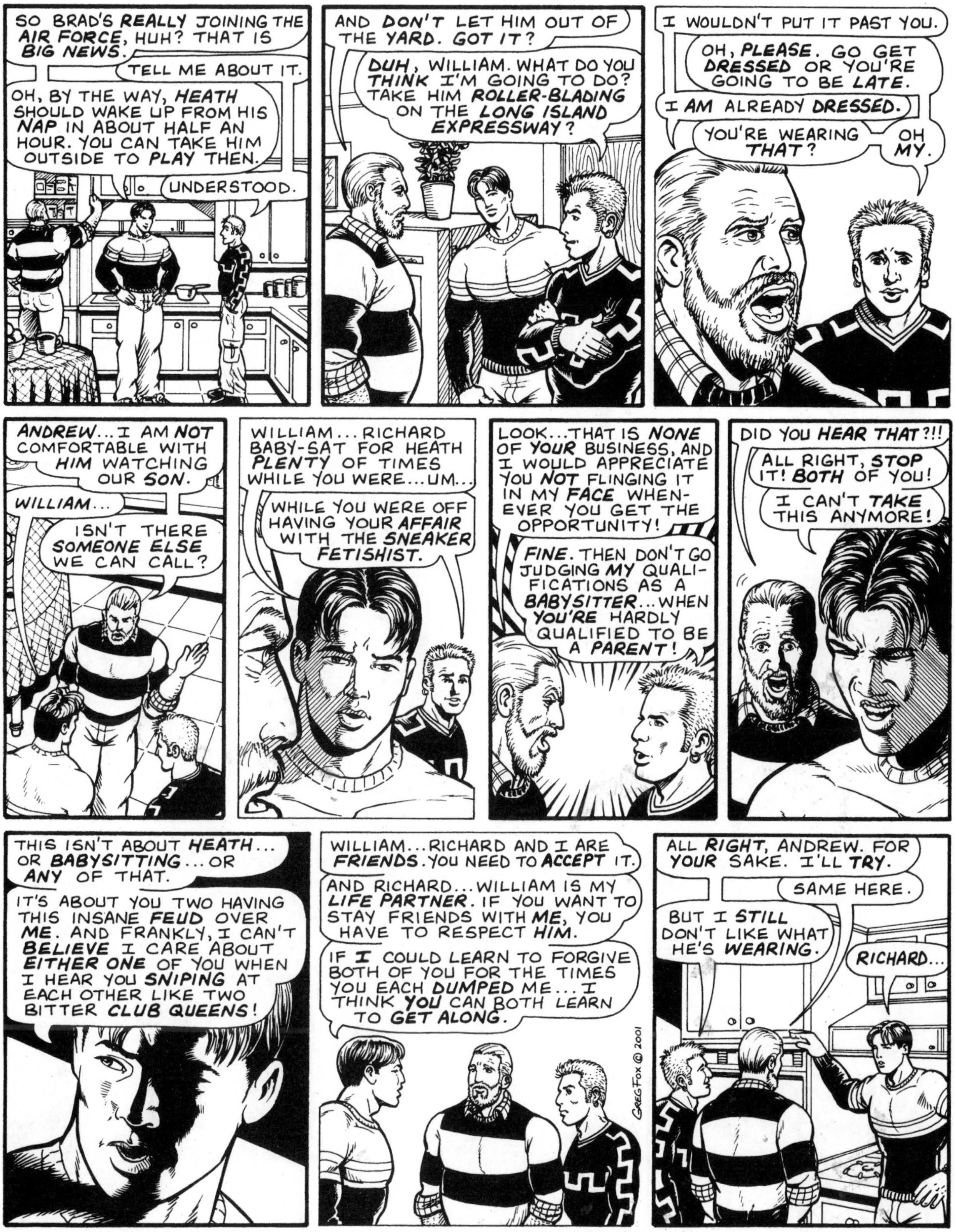
SO BRAD'S REALLY JOINING THE AIR FORCE, HUH? THAT IS BIG NEWS.
TELL ME ABOUT IT.
OH, BY THE WAY, HEATH SHOULD WAKE UP FROM HIS NAP IN ABOUT HALF AN HOUR. YOU CAN TAKE HIM OUTSIDE TO PLAY THEN.
UNDERSTOOD.
AND DON'T LET HIM OUT OF THE YARD. GOT IT?
DUH, WILLIAM. WHAT DO YOU THINK I'M GOING TO DO? TAKE HIM ROLLER-BLADING ON THE LONG ISLAND EXPRESSWAY?
I WOULDN'T PUT IT PAST YOU.
OH, PLEASE. GO GET DRESSED OR YOU'RE GOING TO BE LATE.
I AM ALREADY DRESSED.
YOU'RE WEARING THAT?
OH MY.
ANDREW... I AM NOT COMFORTABLE WITH HIM WATCHING OUR SON.
WILLIAM...
ISN'T THERE SOMEONE ELSE WE CAN CALL?
WILLIAM... RICHARD BABY-SAT FOR HEATH PLENTY OF TIMES WHILE YOU WERE... UM...
WHILE YOU WERE OFF HAVING YOUR AFFAIR WITH THE SNEAKER FETISHIST.
LOOK... THAT IS NONE OF YOUR BUSINESS, AND I WOULD APPRECIATE YOU NOT FLINGING IT IN MY FACE WHEN-EVER YOU GET THE OPPORTUNITY!
FINE. THEN DON'T GO JUDGING MY QUALI-FICATIONS AS A BABYSITTER... WHEN YOU'RE HARDLY QUALIFIED TO BE A PARENT!
DID YOU HEAR THAT?!!
ALL RIGHT, STOP IT! BOTH OF YOU!
I CAN'T TAKE THIS ANYMORE!
THIS ISN'T ABOUT HEATH... OR BABYSITTING... OR ANY OF THAT.
IT'S ABOUT YOU TWO HAVING THIS INSANE FEUD OVER ME. AND FRANKLY, I CAN'T BELIEVE I CARE ABOUT EITHER ONE OF YOU WHEN I HEAR YOU SNIPING AT EACH OTHER LIKE TWO BITTER CLUB QUEENS!
WILLIAM... RICHARD AND I ARE FRIENDS. YOU NEED TO ACCEPT IT.
AND RICHARD... WILLIAM IS MY LIFE PARTNER. IF YOU WANT TO STAY FRIENDS WITH ME, YOU HAVE TO RESPECT HIM.
IF I COULD LEARN TO FORGIVE BOTH OF YOU FOR THE TIMES YOU EACH DUMPED ME... I THINK YOU CAN BOTH LEARN TO GET ALONG.
GREG FOX © 2001
ALL RIGHT, ANDREW. FOR YOUR SAKE. I'LL TRY.
SAME HERE.
BUT I STILL DON'T LIKE WHAT HE'S WEARING.
RICHARD...

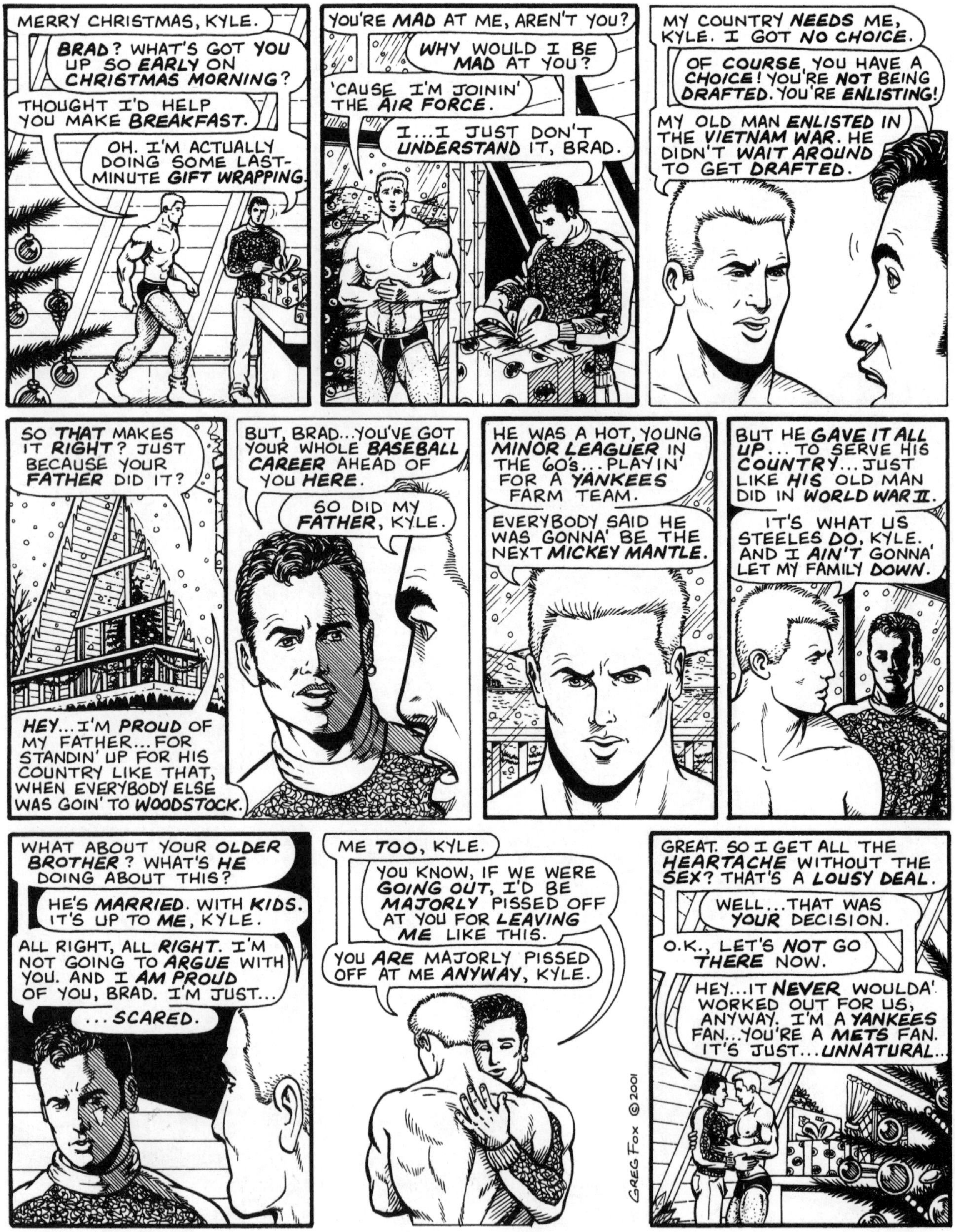

MERRY CHRISTMAS, KYLE.
BRAD? WHAT'S GOT YOU UP SO EARLY ON CHRISTMAS MORNING?
THOUGHT I'D HELP YOU MAKE BREAKFAST.
OH. I'M ACTUALLY DOING SOME LAST-MINUTE GIFT WRAPPING.
YOU'RE MAD AT ME, AREN'T YOU?
WHY WOULD I BE MAD AT YOU?
'CAUSE I'M JOININ' THE AIR FORCE.
I...I JUST DON'T UNDERSTAND IT, BRAD.
MY COUNTRY NEEDS ME, KYLE. I GOT NO CHOICE.
OF COURSE YOU HAVE A CHOICE! YOU'RE NOT BEING DRAFTED. YOU'RE ENLISTING!
MY OLD MAN ENLISTED IN THE VIETNAM WAR. HE DIDN'T WAIT AROUND TO GET DRAFTED.
SO THAT MAKES IT RIGHT? JUST BECAUSE YOUR FATHER DID IT?
HEY...I'M PROUD OF MY FATHER...FOR STANDIN' UP FOR HIS COUNTRY LIKE THAT, WHEN EVERYBODY ELSE WAS GOIN' TO WOODSTOCK.
BUT, BRAD...YOU'VE GOT YOUR WHOLE BASEBALL CAREER AHEAD OF YOU HERE.
SO DID MY FATHER, KYLE.
HE WAS A HOT, YOUNG MINOR LEAGUER IN THE 60'S...PLAYIN' FOR A YANKEES FARM TEAM.
EVERYBODY SAID HE WAS GONNA' BE THE NEXT MICKEY MANTLE.
BUT HE GAVE IT ALL UP...TO SERVE HIS COUNTRY...JUST LIKE HIS OLD MAN DID IN WORLD WAR II.
IT'S WHAT US STEELES DO, KYLE. AND I AIN'T GONNA' LET MY FAMILY DOWN.
WHAT ABOUT YOUR OLDER BROTHER? WHAT'S HE DOING ABOUT THIS?
HE'S MARRIED. WITH KIDS. IT'S UP TO ME, KYLE.
ALL RIGHT, ALL RIGHT. I'M NOT GOING TO ARGUE WITH YOU. AND I AM PROUD OF YOU, BRAD. I'M JUST...
...SCARED.
ME TOO, KYLE.
YOU KNOW, IF WE WERE GOING OUT, I'D BE MAJORLY PISSED OFF AT YOU FOR LEAVING ME LIKE THIS.
YOU ARE MAJORLY PISSED OFF AT ME ANYWAY, KYLE.
GREG FOX ©2001
GREAT. SO I GET ALL THE HEARTACHE WITHOUT THE SEX? THAT'S A LOUSY DEAL.
WELL...THAT WAS YOUR DECISION.
O.K., LET'S NOT GO THERE NOW.
HEY...IT NEVER WOULDA' WORKED OUT FOR US, ANYWAY. I'M A YANKEES FAN...YOU'RE A METS FAN. IT'S JUST...UNNATURAL...

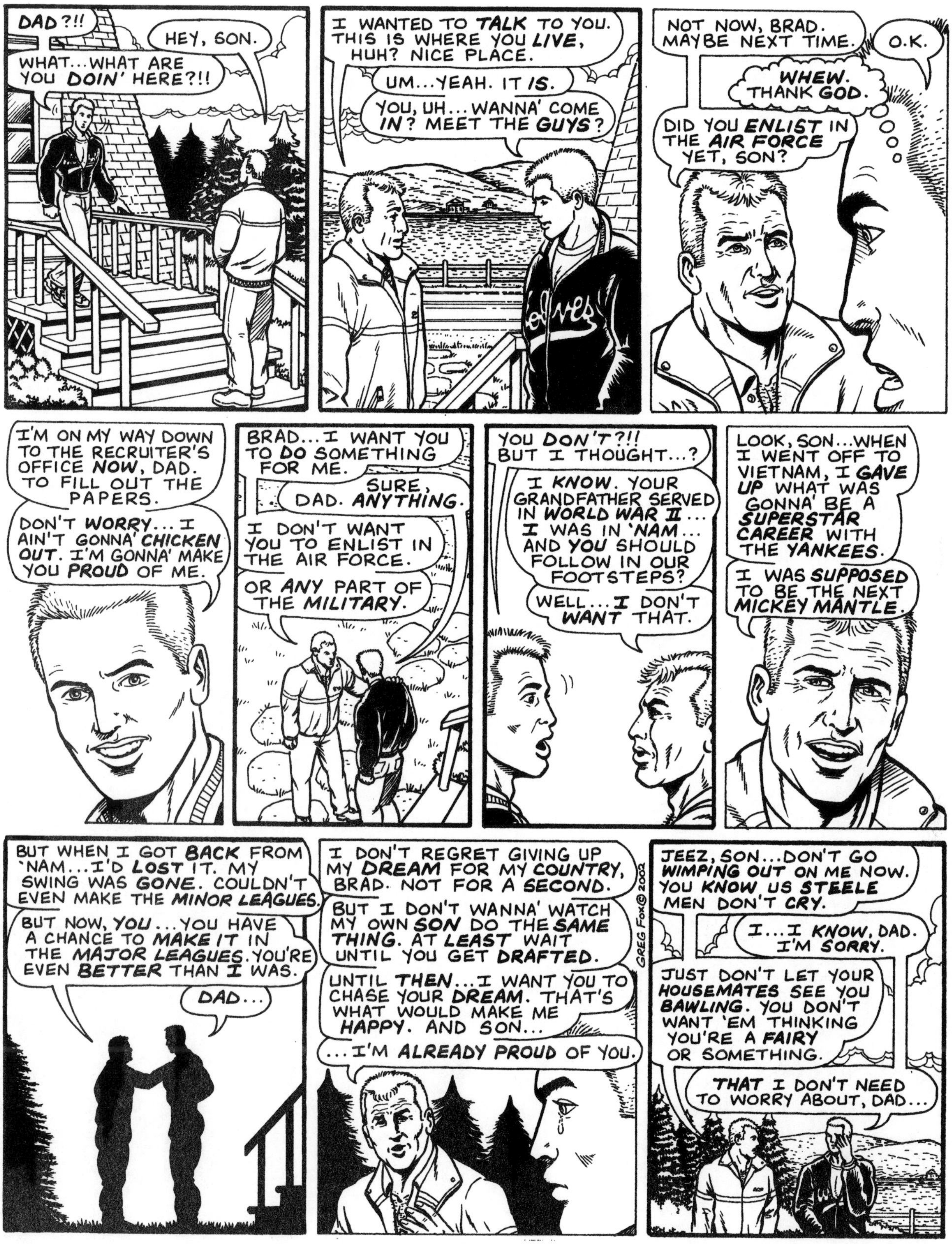
DAD?!!
WHAT...WHAT ARE YOU DOIN' HERE?!!
HEY, SON.
I WANTED TO TALK TO YOU. THIS IS WHERE YOU LIVE, HUH? NICE PLACE.
UM...YEAH. IT IS.
YOU, UH...WANNA' COME IN? MEET THE GUYS?
NOT NOW, BRAD. MAYBE NEXT TIME.
O.K.
WHEW. THANK GOD.
DID YOU ENLIST IN THE AIR FORCE YET, SON?
I'M ON MY WAY DOWN TO THE RECRUITER'S OFFICE NOW, DAD. TO FILL OUT THE PAPERS.
DON'T WORRY... I AIN'T GONNA' CHICKEN OUT. I'M GONNA' MAKE YOU PROUD OF ME.
BRAD... I WANT YOU TO DO SOMETHING FOR ME.
SURE, DAD. ANYTHING.
I DON'T WANT YOU TO ENLIST IN THE AIR FORCE.
OR ANY PART OF THE MILITARY.
YOU DON'T?!! BUT I THOUGHT...?
I KNOW. YOUR GRANDFATHER SERVED IN WORLD WAR II... I WAS IN 'NAM... AND YOU SHOULD FOLLOW IN OUR FOOTSTEPS?
WELL... I DON'T WANT THAT.
LOOK, SON...WHEN I WENT OFF TO VIETNAM, I GAVE UP WHAT WAS GONNA' BE A SUPERSTAR CAREER WITH THE YANKEES.
I WAS SUPPOSED TO BE THE NEXT MICKEY MANTLE.
BUT WHEN I GOT BACK FROM 'NAM...I'D LOST IT. MY SWING WAS GONE. COULDN'T EVEN MAKE THE MINOR LEAGUES.
BUT NOW, YOU...YOU HAVE A CHANCE TO MAKE IT IN THE MAJOR LEAGUES. YOU'RE EVEN BETTER THAN I WAS.
DAD...
I DON'T REGRET GIVING UP MY DREAM FOR MY COUNTRY, BRAD. NOT FOR A SECOND.
BUT I DON'T WANNA' WATCH MY OWN SON DO THE SAME THING. AT LEAST WAIT UNTIL YOU GET DRAFTED.
UNTIL THEN...I WANT YOU TO CHASE YOUR DREAM. THAT'S WHAT WOULD MAKE ME HAPPY. AND SON...
...I'M ALREADY PROUD OF YOU.
GREG FOX © 2002
JEEZ, SON...DON'T GO WIMPING OUT ON ME NOW. YOU KNOW US STEELE MEN DON'T CRY.
I...I KNOW, DAD. I'M SORRY.
JUST DON'T LET YOUR HOUSEMATES SEE YOU BAWLING. YOU DON'T WANT 'EM THINKING YOU'RE A FAIRY OR SOMETHING.
THAT I DON'T NEED TO WORRY ABOUT, DAD...

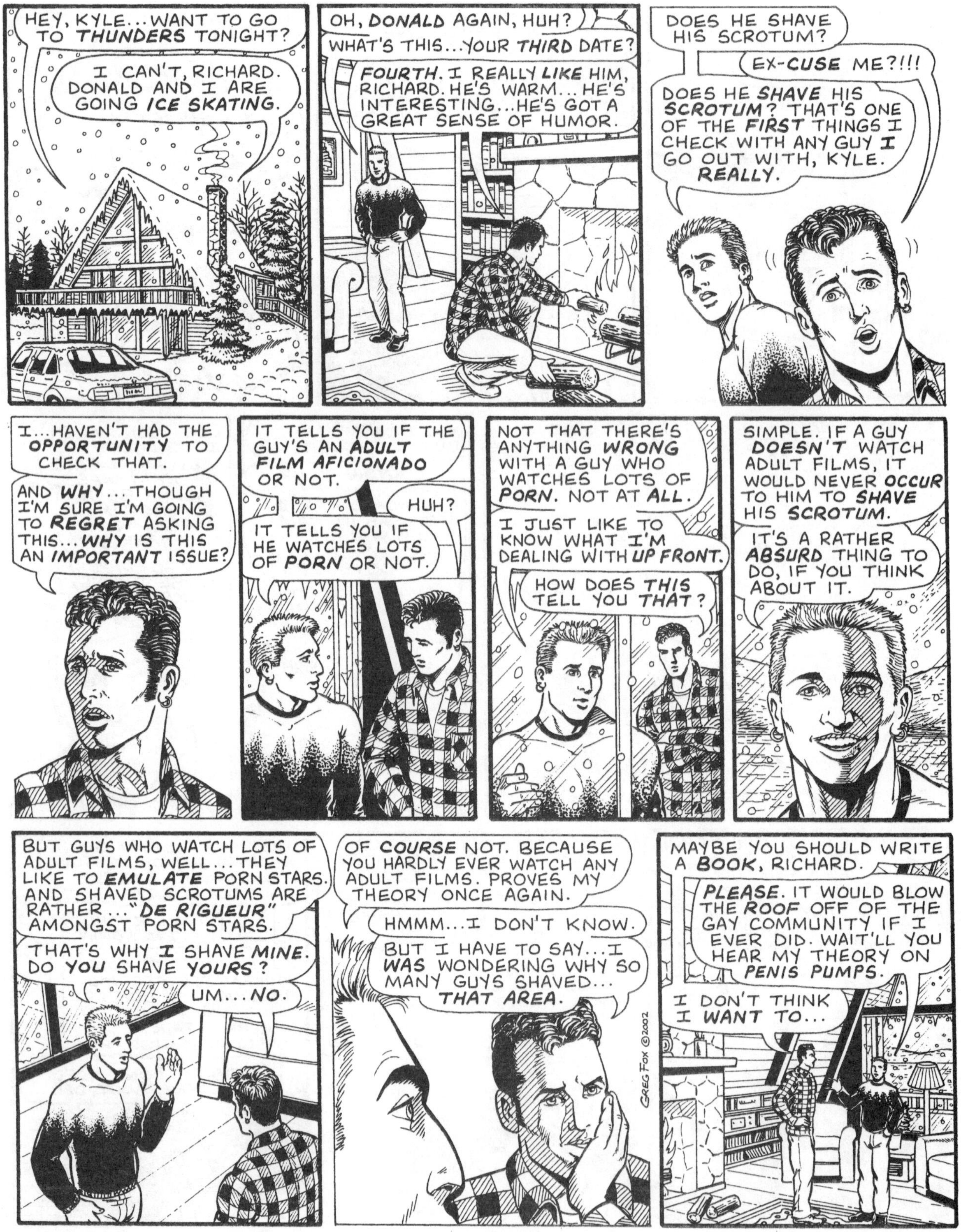
HEY, KYLE... WANT TO GO TO THUNDERS TONIGHT?
I CAN'T, RICHARD. DONALD AND I ARE GOING ICE SKATING.
OH, DONALD AGAIN, HUH?
WHAT'S THIS... YOUR THIRD DATE?
FOURTH. I REALLY LIKE HIM, RICHARD. HE'S WARM... HE'S INTERESTING... HE'S GOT A GREAT SENSE OF HUMOR.
DOES HE SHAVE HIS SCROTUM?
EX-CUSE ME?!!!
DOES HE SHAVE HIS SCROTUM? THAT'S ONE OF THE FIRST THINGS I CHECK WITH ANY GUY I GO OUT WITH, KYLE. REALLY.
I... HAVEN'T HAD THE OPPORTUNITY TO CHECK THAT.
AND WHY... THOUGH I'M SURE I'M GOING TO REGRET ASKING THIS... WHY IS THIS AN IMPORTANT ISSUE?
IT TELLS YOU IF THE GUY'S AN ADULT FILM AFICIONADO OR NOT.
HUH?
IT TELLS YOU IF HE WATCHES LOTS OF PORN OR NOT.
NOT THAT THERE'S ANYTHING WRONG WITH A GUY WHO WATCHES LOTS OF PORN. NOT AT ALL.
I JUST LIKE TO KNOW WHAT I'M DEALING WITH UP FRONT.
HOW DOES THIS TELL YOU THAT?
SIMPLE. IF A GUY DOESN'T WATCH ADULT FILMS, IT WOULD NEVER OCCUR TO HIM TO SHAVE HIS SCROTUM.
IT'S A RATHER ABSURD THING TO DO, IF YOU THINK ABOUT IT.
BUT GUYS WHO WATCH LOTS OF ADULT FILMS, WELL... THEY LIKE TO EMULATE PORN STARS. AND SHAVED SCROTUMS ARE RATHER... "DE RIGUEUR" AMONGST PORN STARS.
THAT'S WHY I SHAVE MINE. DO YOU SHAVE YOURS?
UM... NO.
OF COURSE NOT. BECAUSE YOU HARDLY EVER WATCH ANY ADULT FILMS. PROVES MY THEORY ONCE AGAIN.
HMMM... I DON'T KNOW.
BUT I HAVE TO SAY... I WAS WONDERING WHY SO MANY GUYS SHAVED... THAT AREA.
GREG FOX ©2002
MAYBE YOU SHOULD WRITE A BOOK, RICHARD.
PLEASE. IT WOULD BLOW THE ROOF OFF OF THE GAY COMMUNITY IF I EVER DID. WAIT'LL YOU HEAR MY THEORY ON PENIS PUMPS.
I DON'T THINK I WANT TO...

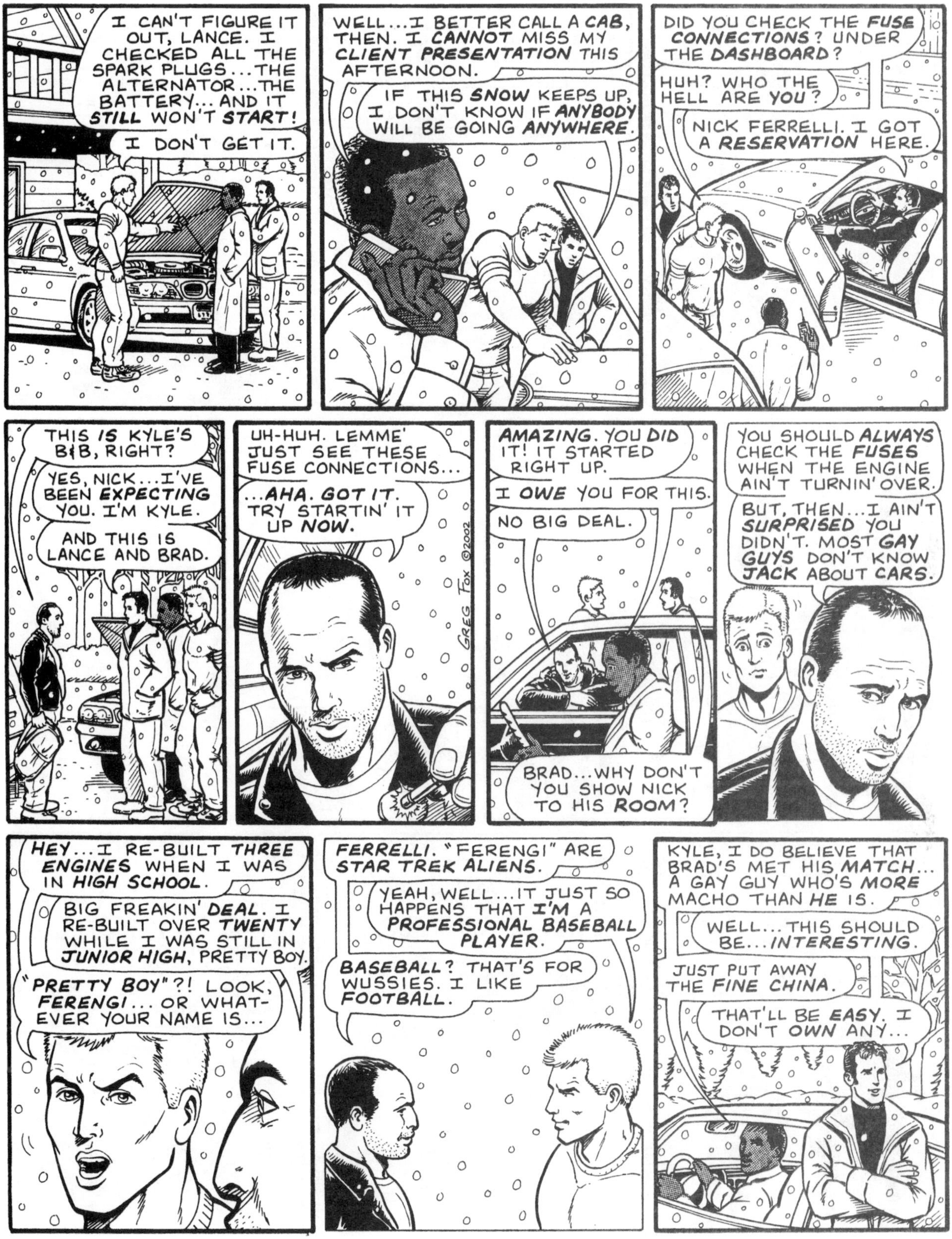

I CAN'T FIGURE IT OUT, LANCE. I CHECKED ALL THE SPARK PLUGS... THE ALTERNATOR... THE BATTERY... AND IT **STILL** WON'T **START**!
I DON'T GET IT.
WELL... I BETTER CALL A **CAB**, THEN. I **CANNOT** MISS MY **CLIENT PRESENTATION** THIS AFTERNOON.
IF THIS **SNOW** KEEPS UP, I DON'T KNOW IF **ANYBODY** WILL BE GOING **ANYWHERE**.
DID YOU CHECK THE **FUSE CONNECTIONS**? UNDER THE **DASHBOARD**?
HUH? WHO THE HELL ARE **YOU**?
NICK FERRELLI. I GOT A **RESERVATION** HERE.
THIS **IS** KYLE'S B&B, RIGHT?
YES, NICK... I'VE BEEN **EXPECTING** YOU. I'M KYLE.
AND THIS IS LANCE AND BRAD.
UH-HUH. LEMME' JUST SEE THESE FUSE CONNECTIONS...
...**AHA. GOT IT.** TRY STARTIN' IT UP **NOW**.
GREG FOX ©2002
AMAZING. YOU **DID** IT! IT STARTED RIGHT UP.
I **OWE** YOU FOR THIS.
NO BIG DEAL.
BRAD... WHY DON'T YOU SHOW NICK TO HIS **ROOM**?
YOU SHOULD **ALWAYS** CHECK THE **FUSES** WHEN THE ENGINE AIN'T TURNIN' OVER.
BUT, THEN... I AIN'T **SURPRISED** YOU DIDN'T. MOST **GAY GUYS** DON'T KNOW **JACK** ABOUT **CARS**.
HEY... I RE-BUILT **THREE ENGINES** WHEN I WAS IN **HIGH SCHOOL**.
BIG FREAKIN' **DEAL**. I RE-BUILT OVER **TWENTY** WHILE I WAS STILL IN **JUNIOR HIGH**, PRETTY BOY.
"**PRETTY BOY**"?! LOOK, **FERENGI**... OR WHAT-EVER YOUR NAME IS...
FERRELLI. "FERENGI" ARE **STAR TREK ALIENS**.
YEAH, WELL... IT JUST SO HAPPENS THAT **I'M** A **PROFESSIONAL BASEBALL PLAYER**.
BASEBALL? THAT'S FOR WUSSIES. I LIKE **FOOTBALL**.
KYLE, I DO BELIEVE THAT BRAD'S MET HIS **MATCH**... A GAY GUY WHO'S **MORE** MACHO THAN **HE** IS.
WELL... THIS SHOULD BE... **INTERESTING**.
JUST PUT AWAY THE **FINE CHINA**.
THAT'LL BE **EASY**. I DON'T **OWN** ANY...

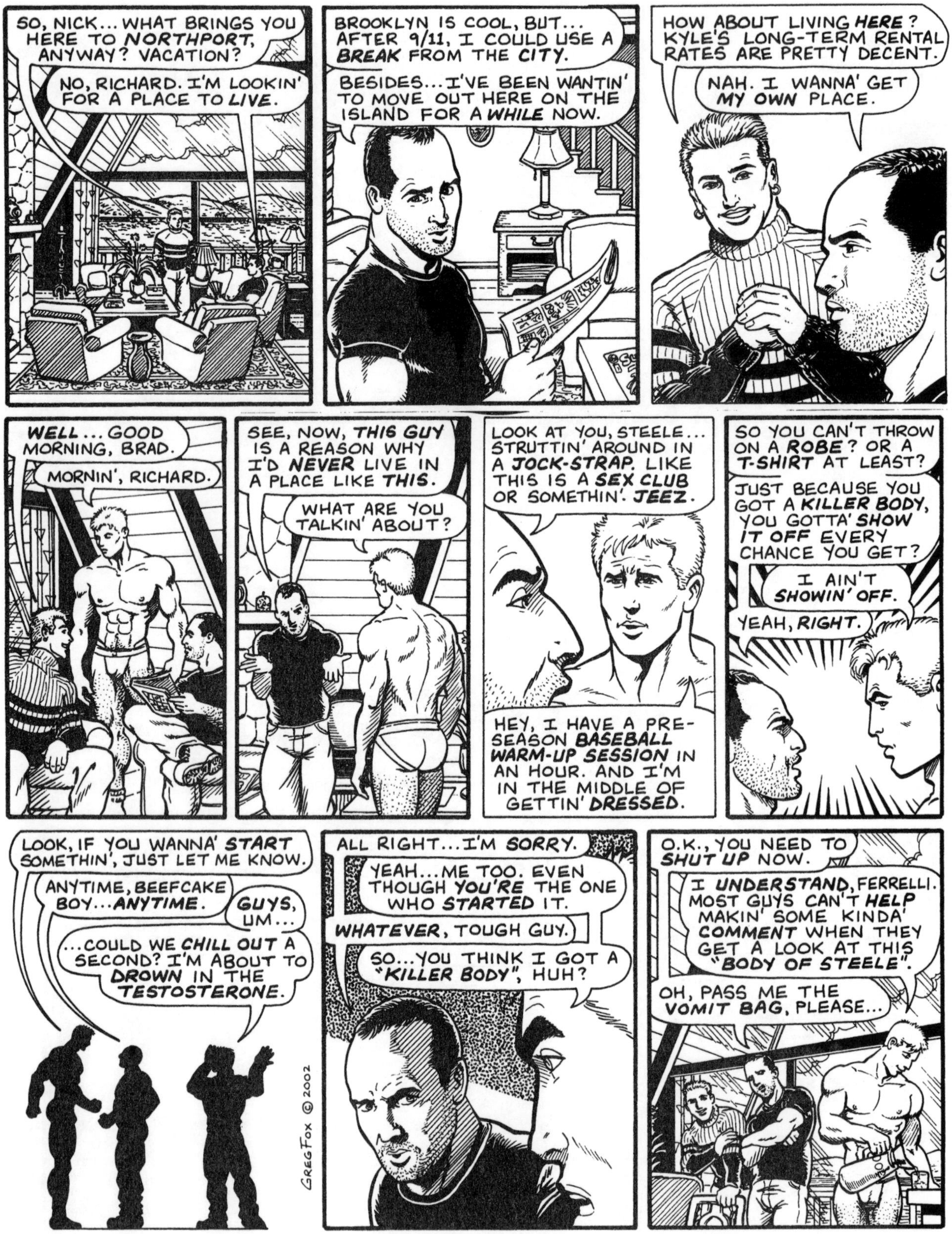
SO, NICK... WHAT BRINGS YOU HERE TO NORTHPORT, ANYWAY? VACATION?
NO, RICHARD. I'M LOOKIN' FOR A PLACE TO LIVE.
BROOKLYN IS COOL, BUT... AFTER 9/11, I COULD USE A BREAK FROM THE CITY.
BESIDES... I'VE BEEN WANTIN' TO MOVE OUT HERE ON THE ISLAND FOR A WHILE NOW.
HOW ABOUT LIVING HERE? KYLE'S LONG-TERM RENTAL RATES ARE PRETTY DECENT.
NAH. I WANNA' GET MY OWN PLACE.
WELL... GOOD MORNING, BRAD.
MORNIN', RICHARD.
SEE, NOW, THIS GUY IS A REASON WHY I'D NEVER LIVE IN A PLACE LIKE THIS.
WHAT ARE YOU TALKIN' ABOUT?
LOOK AT YOU, STEELE... STRUTTIN' AROUND IN A JOCK-STRAP, LIKE THIS IS A SEX CLUB OR SOMETHIN'. JEEZ.
HEY, I HAVE A PRE-SEASON BASEBALL WARM-UP SESSION IN AN HOUR. AND I'M IN THE MIDDLE OF GETTIN' DRESSED.
SO YOU CAN'T THROW ON A ROBE? OR A T-SHIRT AT LEAST?
JUST BECAUSE YOU GOT A KILLER BODY, YOU GOTTA' SHOW IT OFF EVERY CHANCE YOU GET?
I AIN'T SHOWIN' OFF.
YEAH, RIGHT.
LOOK, IF YOU WANNA' START SOMETHIN', JUST LET ME KNOW.
ANYTIME, BEEFCAKE BOY... ANYTIME.
GUYS, UM...
...COULD WE CHILL OUT A SECOND? I'M ABOUT TO DROWN IN THE TESTOSTERONE.
GREG FOX © 2002
ALL RIGHT... I'M SORRY.
YEAH... ME TOO. EVEN THOUGH YOU'RE THE ONE WHO STARTED IT.
WHATEVER, TOUGH GUY.
SO... YOU THINK I GOT A "KILLER BODY", HUH?
O.K., YOU NEED TO SHUT UP NOW.
I UNDERSTAND, FERRELLI. MOST GUYS CAN'T HELP MAKIN' SOME KINDA' COMMENT WHEN THEY GET A LOOK AT THIS "BODY OF STEELE".
OH, PASS ME THE VOMIT BAG, PLEASE...

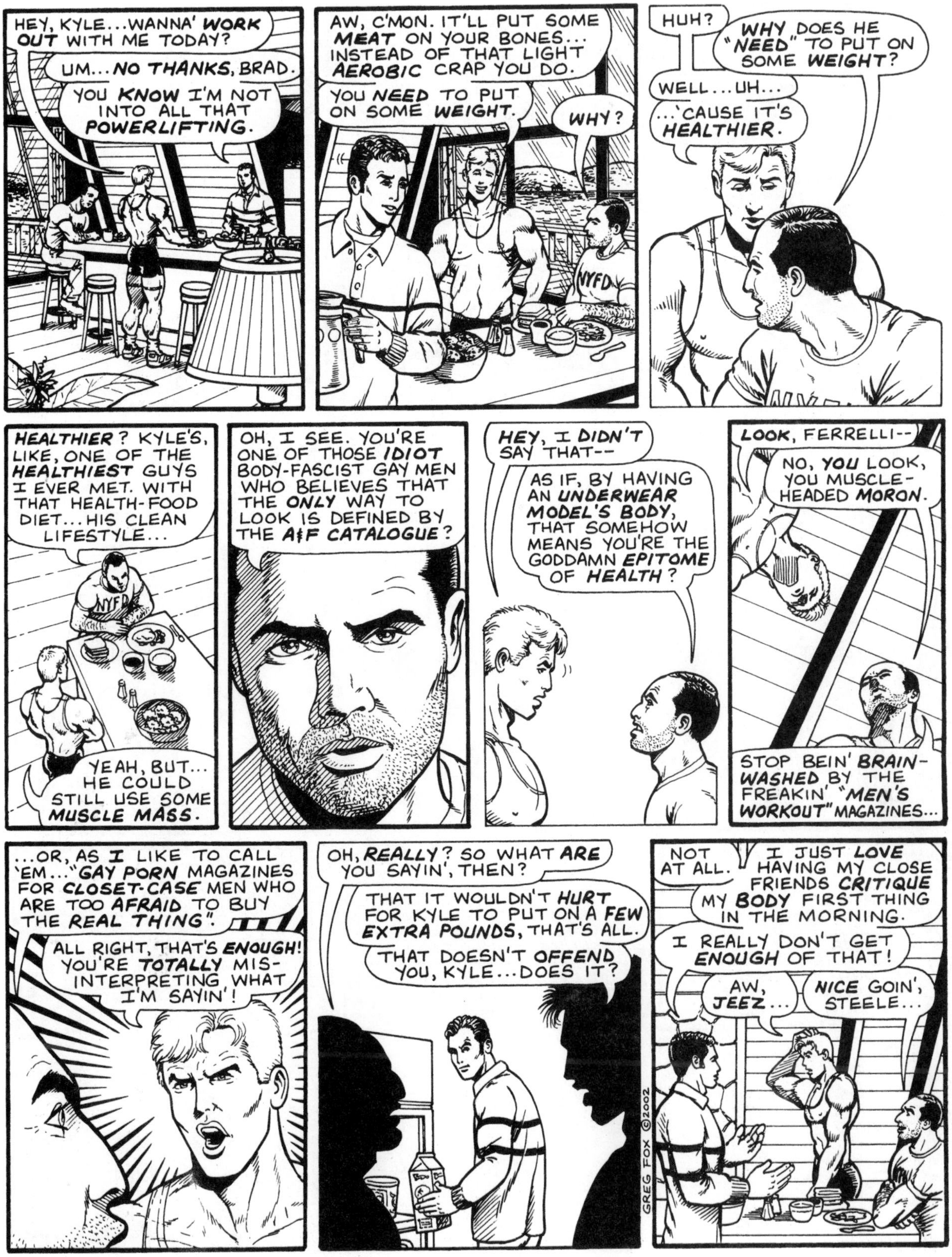
HEY, KYLE...WANNA' WORK OUT WITH ME TODAY?
UM... NO THANKS, BRAD.
YOU KNOW I'M NOT INTO ALL THAT POWERLIFTING.
AW, C'MON. IT'LL PUT SOME MEAT ON YOUR BONES... INSTEAD OF THAT LIGHT AEROBIC CRAP YOU DO.
YOU NEED TO PUT ON SOME WEIGHT.
WHY?
HUH?
WHY DOES HE "NEED" TO PUT ON SOME WEIGHT?
WELL...UH...
...'CAUSE IT'S HEALTHIER.
NYFD
HEALTHIER? KYLE'S, LIKE, ONE OF THE HEALTHIEST GUYS I EVER MET. WITH THAT HEALTH-FOOD DIET...HIS CLEAN LIFESTYLE...
NYFD
YEAH, BUT... HE COULD STILL USE SOME MUSCLE MASS.
OH, I SEE. YOU'RE ONE OF THOSE IDIOT BODY-FASCIST GAY MEN WHO BELIEVES THAT THE ONLY WAY TO LOOK IS DEFINED BY THE A&F CATALOGUE?
HEY, I DIDN'T SAY THAT--
AS IF, BY HAVING AN UNDERWEAR MODEL'S BODY, THAT SOMEHOW MEANS YOU'RE THE GODDAMN EPITOME OF HEALTH?
LOOK, FERRELLI--
NO, YOU LOOK, YOU MUSCLE-HEADED MORON.
STOP BEIN' BRAIN-WASHED BY THE FREAKIN' "MEN'S WORKOUT" MAGAZINES...
...OR, AS I LIKE TO CALL 'EM..."GAY PORN MAGAZINES FOR CLOSET-CASE MEN WHO ARE TOO AFRAID TO BUY THE REAL THING".
ALL RIGHT, THAT'S ENOUGH! YOU'RE TOTALLY MIS-INTERPRETING WHAT I'M SAYIN'!
OH, REALLY? SO WHAT ARE YOU SAYIN', THEN?
THAT IT WOULDN'T HURT FOR KYLE TO PUT ON A FEW EXTRA POUNDS, THAT'S ALL.
THAT DOESN'T OFFEND YOU, KYLE...DOES IT?
GREG FOX ©2002
NOT AT ALL.
I JUST LOVE HAVING MY CLOSE FRIENDS CRITIQUE MY BODY FIRST THING IN THE MORNING.
I REALLY DON'T GET ENOUGH OF THAT!
AW, JEEZ...
NICE GOIN', STEELE...

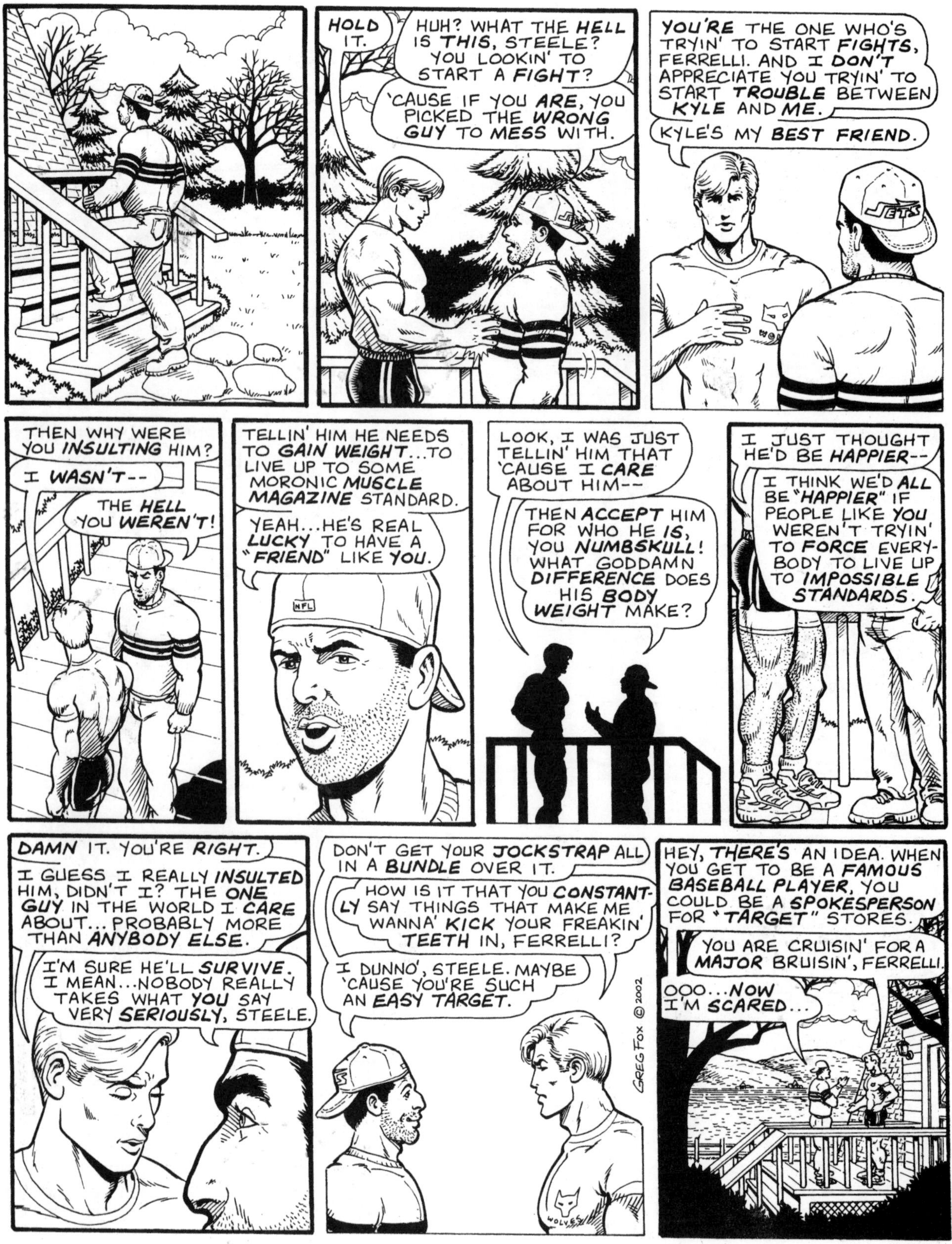
HOLD IT.
HUH? WHAT THE HELL IS THIS, STEELE? YOU LOOKIN' TO START A FIGHT?
'CAUSE IF YOU ARE, YOU PICKED THE WRONG GUY TO MESS WITH.
YOU'RE THE ONE WHO'S TRYIN' TO START FIGHTS, FERRELLI. AND I DON'T APPRECIATE YOU TRYIN' TO START TROUBLE BETWEEN KYLE AND ME.
KYLE'S MY BEST FRIEND.
JETS
THEN WHY WERE YOU INSULTING HIM?
I WASN'T--
THE HELL YOU WEREN'T!
TELLIN' HIM HE NEEDS TO GAIN WEIGHT...TO LIVE UP TO SOME MORONIC MUSCLE MAGAZINE STANDARD.
YEAH...HE'S REAL LUCKY TO HAVE A "FRIEND" LIKE YOU.
NFL
LOOK, I WAS JUST TELLIN' HIM THAT 'CAUSE I CARE ABOUT HIM--
THEN ACCEPT HIM FOR WHO HE IS, YOU NUMBSKULL! WHAT GODDAMN DIFFERENCE DOES HIS BODY WEIGHT MAKE?
I JUST THOUGHT HE'D BE HAPPIER--
I THINK WE'D ALL BE "HAPPIER" IF PEOPLE LIKE YOU WEREN'T TRYIN' TO FORCE EVERYBODY TO LIVE UP TO IMPOSSIBLE STANDARDS.
DAMN IT. YOU'RE RIGHT.
I GUESS I REALLY INSULTED HIM, DIDN'T I? THE ONE GUY IN THE WORLD I CARE ABOUT... PROBABLY MORE THAN ANYBODY ELSE.
I'M SURE HE'LL SURVIVE. I MEAN...NOBODY REALLY TAKES WHAT YOU SAY VERY SERIOUSLY, STEELE.
DON'T GET YOUR JOCKSTRAP ALL IN A BUNDLE OVER IT.
HOW IS IT THAT YOU CONSTANTLY SAY THINGS THAT MAKE ME WANNA' KICK YOUR FREAKIN' TEETH IN, FERRELLI?
I DUNNO', STEELE. MAYBE 'CAUSE YOU'RE SUCH AN EASY TARGET.
GREG FOX © 2002
WOLVES
HEY, THERE'S AN IDEA. WHEN YOU GET TO BE A FAMOUS BASEBALL PLAYER, YOU COULD BE A SPOKESPERSON FOR "TARGET" STORES.
YOU ARE CRUISIN' FOR A MAJOR BRUISIN', FERRELLI.
OOO...NOW I'M SCARED...

"SLAM"

I HATE ALL MEN.

KYLE? WHAT'S GOIN' ON?

I JUST BROKE UP WITH DONALD.

DONALD? THE GUY YOU'VE BEEN DATING FOR THE PAST FEW MONTHS?

HOW COME I NEVER MET THIS GUY, ANYWAY?

MAYBE BECAUSE HE WAS TOO BUSY SLEEPING WITH HIS COMPUTER REPAIRMAN. SOMETHING HE "NEGLECTED" TO TELL ME ABOUT UNTIL TODAY.

AND, PLEASE...SPARE ME THE "HARD DRIVE" JOKES.

AW, JEEZ, KYLE. THAT SUCKS.

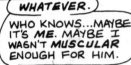

WHATEVER.

WHO KNOWS...MAYBE IT'S ME. MAYBE I WASN'T MUSCULAR ENOUGH FOR HIM.

KYLE...ONLY A COMPLETE IDIOT WOULD THINK SOMETHIN' LIKE THAT. YOU'RE PERFECT JUST THE WAY YOU ARE.

YEAH, RIGHT.

YOU ARE, KYLE!

BRAD...EVEN YOU SAID I NEEDED TO PUT ON WEIGHT.

WELL...I WAS WRONG. I'M A BIG, MUSCLE-HEADED IDIOT! AND I'M SORRY I EVER SAID THAT.

CHRIST. NOT EVERYBODY'S GOTTA' BE A MUSCLE-MAGAZINE MODEL, KYLE. THERE'S ALL KINDS OF GOOD LOOKIN' GUYS.

THE IMPORTANT THING IS TO BE HEALTHY. AND YOU ARE.

I...I BELIEVE THAT. I JUST WISH THE REST OF THE WORLD DID.

LOOK...I FELL IN LOVE WITH YOU JUST THE WAY YOU ARE. JUST BE YOURSELF, KYLE. THAT'S ENOUGH FOR ANY GUY.

YOU..."FELL IN LOVE" WITH ME?!

YOU KNOW I DID. AND I'M OVER IT. C'MON...WE TALKED THIS ALL OUT MONTHS AGO. WE'RE BETTER OFF AS FRIENDS. I CAN SEE THAT NOW.

BUT PART OF ME IS ALWAYS GONNA' LOVE YOU.

GregFox ©2002

YOU KNOW, FOR A "BIG, MUSCLE-HEADED IDIOT"...

...YOU'RE PRETTY AWESOME.

THANKS. SO...YOU WANT ME TO BEAT UP THIS GUY DONALD FOR YOU OR WHAT?

NO, THAT'S O.K. I THINK MY PEELING OUT ON HIS FRONT LAWN GOT THE MESSAGE ACROSS.

UM, YEAH, THAT PROBABLY DID...

DONALD?! WHAT ARE YOU *DOING* HERE?!

WE HAVE TO *TALK*, KYLE.

OH? DO WE?

YES... WE *DO.*

WELL, LET'S SEE... WE WERE HAVING A *MONOGAMOUS* RELATIONSHIP...

...I WALKED IN ON YOU HAVING *SEX* WITH YOUR *COMPUTER REPAIRMAN*...

...AND NOW IT'S *OVER.* WHAT *ELSE* IS THERE TO *TALK* ABOUT?

KYLE, IT DIDN'T *MEAN* ANYTHING. HE WAS JUST A *CUTE BOY* I SLEPT WITH A COUPLE OF TIMES.

IT WAS *JUST SEX.*

THAT *MIGHT* FLY IF WE WERE HAVING AN *OPEN* RELATIONSHIP, DONALD. BUT WE *WEREN'T.* UNLESS THERE'S SOME NEW DEFINITION OF "MONOGAMY" I'M UNAWARE OF.

KYLE, PLEASE...YOU HAVE TO UNDERSTAND ...I'VE *ALWAYS* HAD A THING FOR *YOUNGER MEN.*

OBVIOUSLY. I'M OVER *TEN YEARS* YOUNGER THAN YOU.

BUT THIS *BOY*, KYLE ...HE WAS *REALLY* YOUNG. *NINETEEN.*

I JUST *COULDN'T* PASS UP AN OPPORTUNITY WITH *HIM.*

WELL, O.K...*THAT* JUSTIFIES *EVERYTHING.* HOW *SILLY* OF ME TO EVEN BE *UPSET!*

CAN I *GET YOU* ANYTHING, DONALD? COFFEE...TEA...

...A SUBSCRIPTION TO XY MAGAZINE?

KYLE...I THINK YOU'RE *OVERREACTING* A BIT.

LOOK, DONALD... YOU JUST *DON'T GET IT.* WE HAD AN *AGREEMENT*... TO BE *MONOGAMOUS* WITH EACH OTHER. I TOOK THAT *SERIOUSLY.* I THOUGHT *YOU* DID, TOO.

I *DID*, KYLE. BUT THIS *BOY*...HE MADE ME FEEL SO...*YOUNG.*

YOU *SCARE* ME, DONALD. I THINK YOU'D PROBABLY SAY JUST ABOUT *ANYTHING* TO GET *LAID.* INCLUDING MAKING PROMISES OF MONOGAMY TO ME...THAT YOU HAD *NO INTENTION* OF KEEPING.

AND ONE MORE THING...ALL THIS TALK ABOUT "*BOYS*" IS *DISTURBING.* YOU'RE A LITTLE TOO OBSESSED WITH *YOUTH* AND USING *OTHER PEOPLE* TO MAKE YOU FEEL *YOUNG.*

I WANT TO BE WITH A *MAN*, DONALD...NOT A *BOY.* AND *YOU*, WELL...

...I THINK YOU NEED TO DO SOME *GROWING UP.*

GREG FOX ©2002

DOES THIS MEAN IT'S REALLY *OVER* BETWEEN US?

BINGO!

CAN WE AT LEAST HAVE *ORAL SEX?*

OH, WE ARE SO OVER *NOW*...

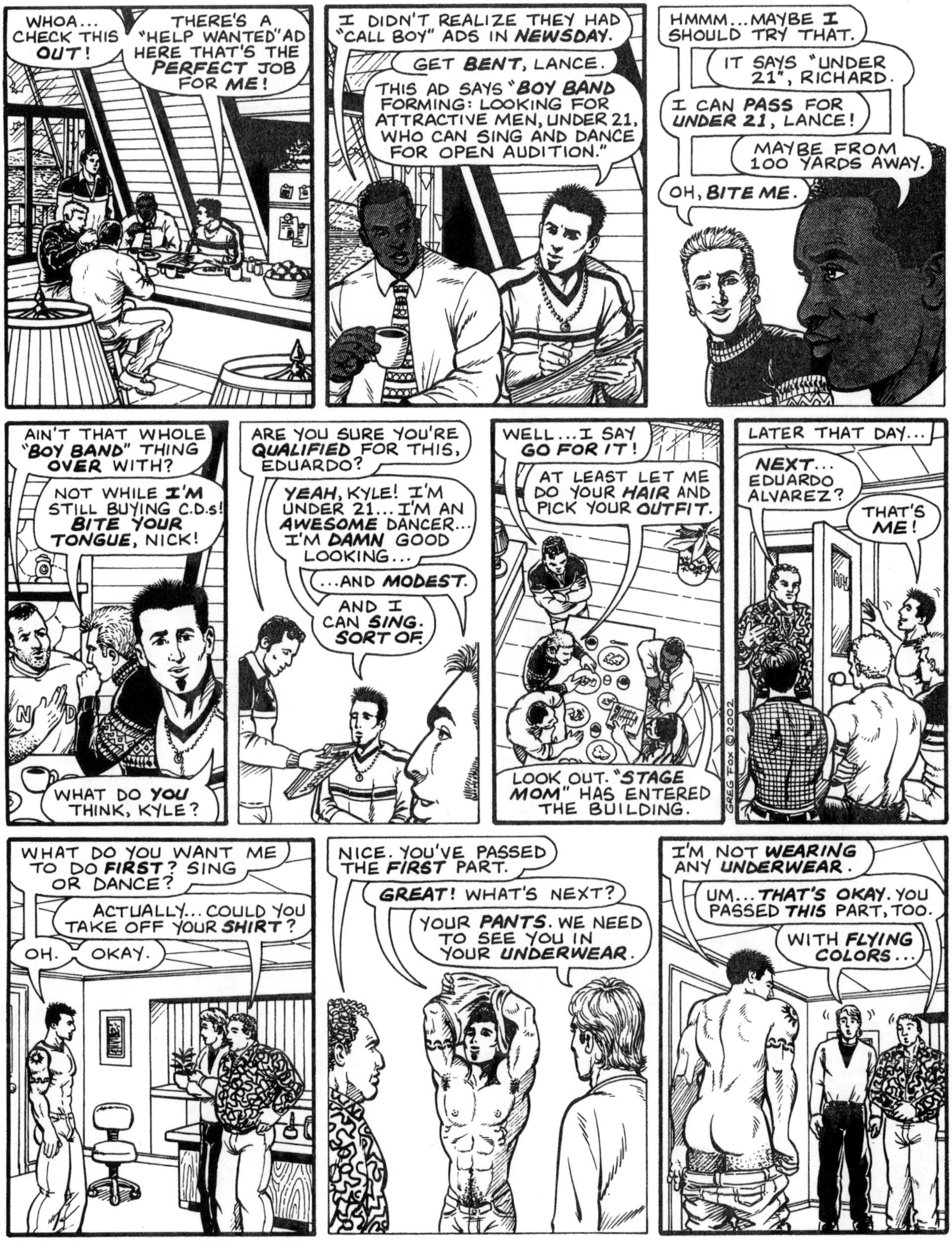
WHOA... CHECK THIS OUT!
THERE'S A "HELP WANTED" AD HERE THAT'S THE PERFECT JOB FOR ME!
I DIDN'T REALIZE THEY HAD "CALL BOY" ADS IN NEWSDAY.
GET BENT, LANCE.
THIS AD SAYS "BOY BAND FORMING: LOOKING FOR ATTRACTIVE MEN, UNDER 21, WHO CAN SING AND DANCE FOR OPEN AUDITION."
HMMM... MAYBE I SHOULD TRY THAT.
IT SAYS "UNDER 21", RICHARD.
I CAN PASS FOR UNDER 21, LANCE!
MAYBE FROM 100 YARDS AWAY.
OH, BITE ME.
AIN'T THAT WHOLE "BOY BAND" THING OVER WITH?
NOT WHILE I'M STILL BUYING C.D.s! BITE YOUR TONGUE, NICK!
WHAT DO YOU THINK, KYLE?
ARE YOU SURE YOU'RE QUALIFIED FOR THIS, EDUARDO?
YEAH, KYLE! I'M UNDER 21... I'M AN AWESOME DANCER... I'M DAMN GOOD LOOKING...
...AND MODEST.
AND I CAN SING. SORT OF.
WELL... I SAY GO FOR IT!
AT LEAST LET ME DO YOUR HAIR AND PICK YOUR OUTFIT.
LOOK OUT. "STAGE MOM" HAS ENTERED THE BUILDING.
GREG FOX © 2002
LATER THAT DAY...
NEXT... EDUARDO ALVAREZ?
THAT'S ME!
WHAT DO YOU WANT ME TO DO FIRST? SING OR DANCE?
ACTUALLY... COULD YOU TAKE OFF YOUR SHIRT?
OH.
OKAY.
NICE. YOU'VE PASSED THE FIRST PART.
GREAT! WHAT'S NEXT?
YOUR PANTS. WE NEED TO SEE YOU IN YOUR UNDERWEAR.
I'M NOT WEARING ANY UNDERWEAR.
UM... THAT'S OKAY. YOU PASSED THIS PART, TOO.
WITH FLYING COLORS...

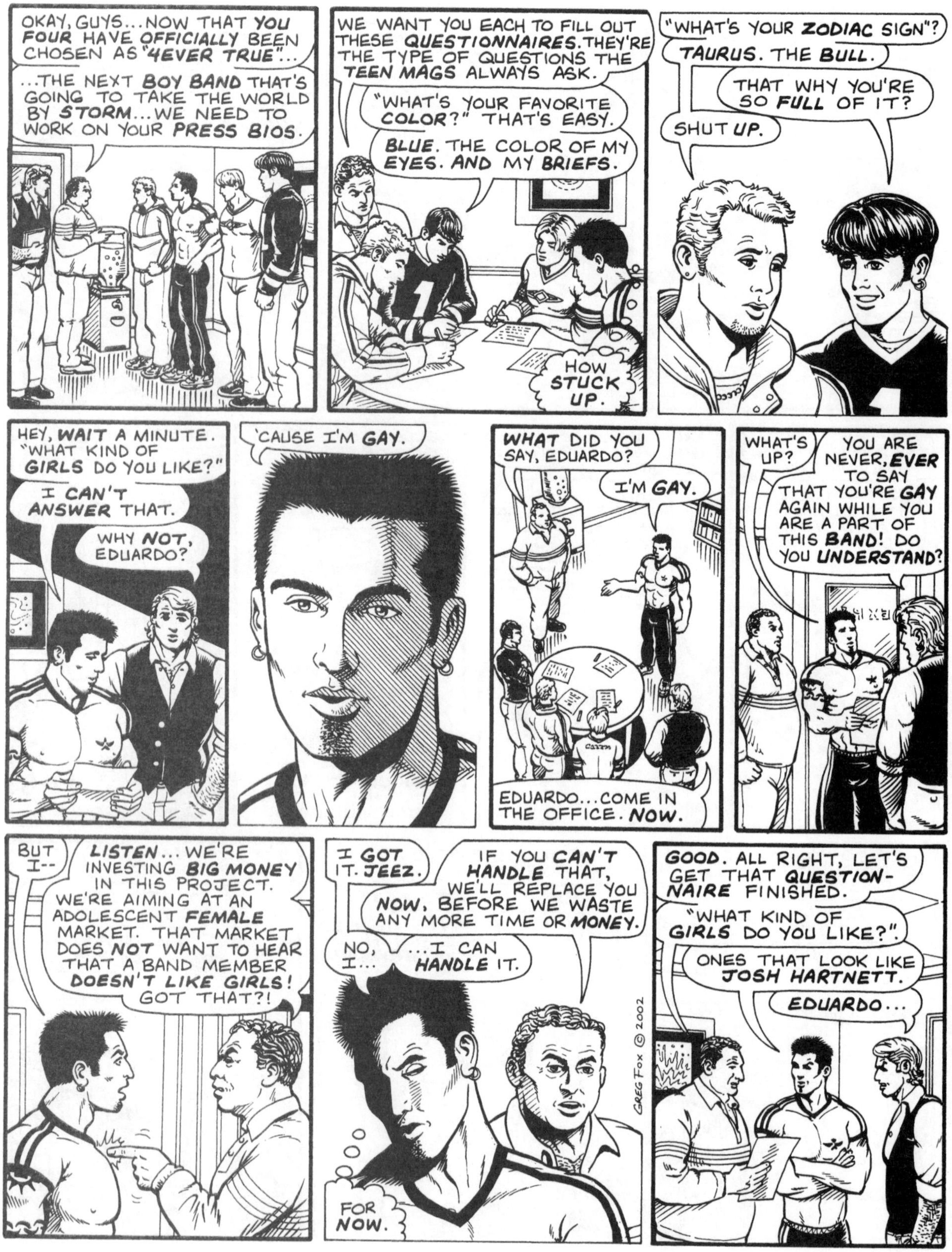
OKAY, GUYS...NOW THAT YOU FOUR HAVE OFFICIALLY BEEN CHOSEN AS "4EVER TRUE"...
...THE NEXT BOY BAND THAT'S GOING TO TAKE THE WORLD BY STORM...WE NEED TO WORK ON YOUR PRESS BIOS.
WE WANT YOU EACH TO FILL OUT THESE QUESTIONNAIRES. THEY'RE THE TYPE OF QUESTIONS THE TEEN MAGS ALWAYS ASK.
"WHAT'S YOUR FAVORITE COLOR?" THAT'S EASY.
BLUE. THE COLOR OF MY EYES. AND MY BRIEFS.
HOW STUCK UP.
"WHAT'S YOUR ZODIAC SIGN"?
TAURUS. THE BULL.
THAT WHY YOU'RE SO FULL OF IT?
SHUT UP.
HEY, WAIT A MINUTE. "WHAT KIND OF GIRLS DO YOU LIKE?"
I CAN'T ANSWER THAT.
WHY NOT, EDUARDO?
'CAUSE I'M GAY.
WHAT DID YOU SAY, EDUARDO?
I'M GAY.
EDUARDO...COME IN THE OFFICE. NOW.
WHAT'S UP?
YOU ARE NEVER, EVER TO SAY THAT YOU'RE GAY AGAIN WHILE YOU ARE A PART OF THIS BAND! DO YOU UNDERSTAND?
BUT I--
LISTEN... WE'RE INVESTING BIG MONEY IN THIS PROJECT. WE'RE AIMING AT AN ADOLESCENT FEMALE MARKET. THAT MARKET DOES NOT WANT TO HEAR THAT A BAND MEMBER DOESN'T LIKE GIRLS! GOT THAT?!
I GOT IT. JEEZ.
IF YOU CAN'T HANDLE THAT, WE'LL REPLACE YOU NOW, BEFORE WE WASTE ANY MORE TIME OR MONEY.
NO, I...
...I CAN HANDLE IT.
FOR NOW.
GREG FOX © 2002
GOOD. ALL RIGHT, LET'S GET THAT QUESTIONNAIRE FINISHED.
"WHAT KIND OF GIRLS DO YOU LIKE?"
ONES THAT LOOK LIKE JOSH HARTNETT.
EDUARDO...

...BABY...YOU'VE GOT EVERYTHING I NE-E-E-E-E-ED...
ALL RIGHT, GUYS...THAT'S IT FOR TODAY.
SEE YOU ALL BRIGHT AND EARLY TOMORROW MORNING!
HOW ARE WE DOING, MR. WATTS?
YOU'RE DOING GREAT, TIM. YOU GUYS'LL HAVE NSYNC RUNNING SCARED IN NO TIME.
NOW, GO HOME AND GET SOME SLEEP! NO GOING OUT AND GETTING INTO TROUBLE, OKAY?
HEY, EDUARDO... COULD I TALK TO YOU A SECOND?
I GOTTA' RUN, CAMERON...OR I'LL MISS THE LAST BUS BACK TO NORTHPORT.
HOW ABOUT IF I GIVE YOU A RIDE?
OH. OKAY. COOL.
SO...WHAT'S UP? WHAT'D YOU WANNA' TALK ABOUT?
WHAT YOU SAID THE OTHER DAY AT REHEARSAL. ABOUT YOU BEING...
GAY?
UH...YEAH.
LOOK, I AIN'T SUPPOSED TO TALK ABOUT THAT.
MR. WATTS SAID HE'D FIRE ME FROM THE BAND IF I EVER MEN-TIONED IT AGAIN.
OH.
WHAT?
NOTHING. NEVER MIND.
YOU ARE TOO, AREN'T YOU?
YEAH, I AM.
IS IT OBVIOUS?
NOT REALLY. BUT I'VE GOT A PRETTY NOTORIOUS SENSE OF GAYDAR. AND BESIDES... I KINDA' ASSUME THAT ANY GUY WHO JOINS A BOY BAND HAS A HIGH CHANCE OF BEIN' AT LEAST PARTIALLY QUEER.
GREG FOX ©2002
HAVE YOU TOLD YOUR PARENTS YOU'RE GAY YET, EDUARDO?
UM, YEAH, CAMERON. THEY KNOW.
WOW. THAT'S SO COOL. LUCKY YOU.
"LUCKY"?!
DRIVE, CAMERON. WE GOT A LOT TO TALK ABOUT...

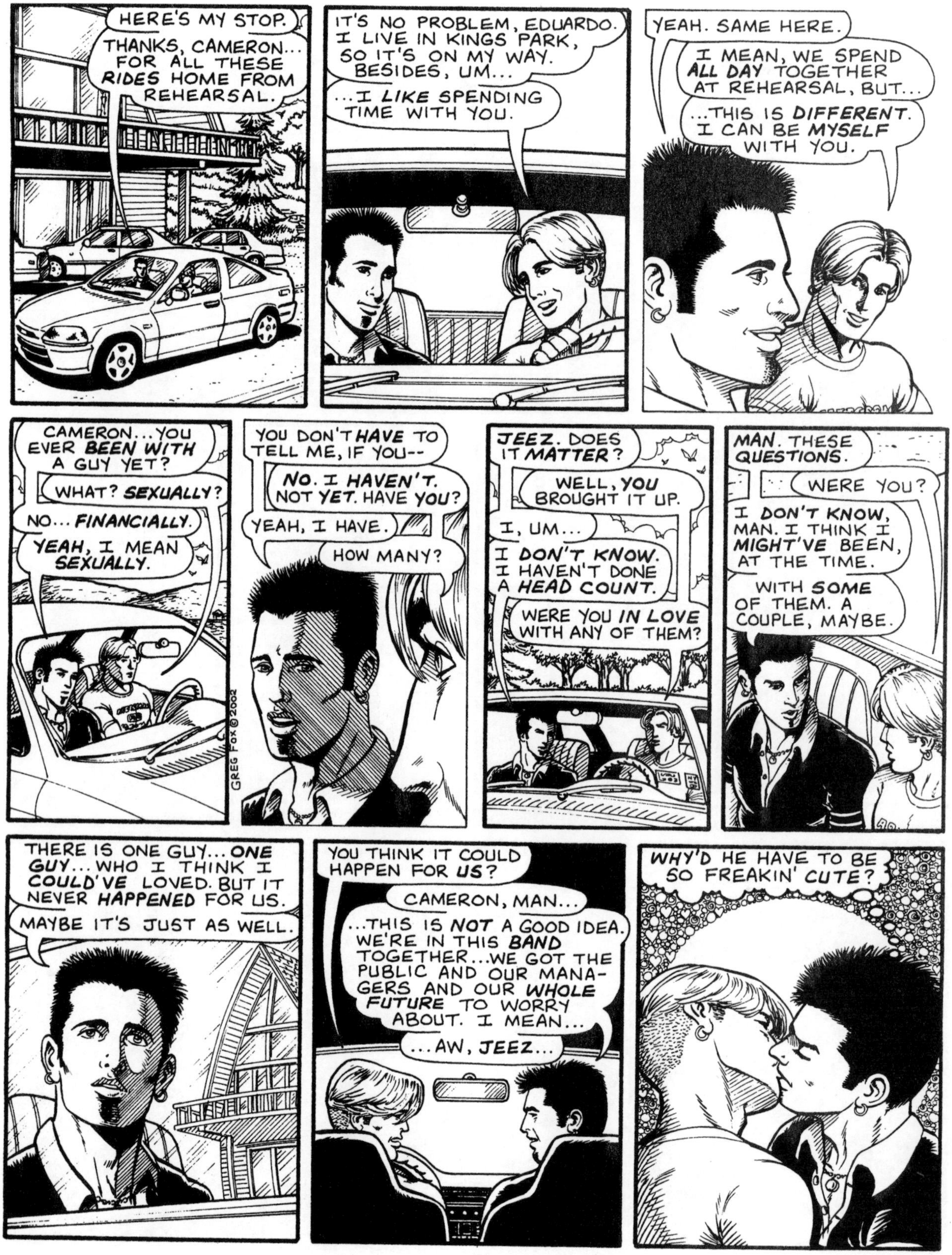
HERE'S MY STOP.
THANKS, CAMERON... FOR ALL THESE RIDES HOME FROM REHEARSAL.
IT'S NO PROBLEM, EDUARDO. I LIVE IN KINGS PARK, SO IT'S ON MY WAY. BESIDES, UM...
...I LIKE SPENDING TIME WITH YOU.
YEAH. SAME HERE.
I MEAN, WE SPEND ALL DAY TOGETHER AT REHEARSAL, BUT...
...THIS IS DIFFERENT. I CAN BE MYSELF WITH YOU.
CAMERON...YOU EVER BEEN WITH A GUY YET?
WHAT? SEXUALLY?
NO... FINANCIALLY.
YEAH, I MEAN SEXUALLY.
GREG FOX © 2002
YOU DON'T HAVE TO TELL ME, IF YOU--
NO. I HAVEN'T. NOT YET. HAVE YOU?
YEAH, I HAVE.
HOW MANY?
JEEZ. DOES IT MATTER?
WELL, YOU BROUGHT IT UP.
I, UM...
I DON'T KNOW. I HAVEN'T DONE A HEAD COUNT.
WERE YOU IN LOVE WITH ANY OF THEM?
MAN. THESE QUESTIONS.
WERE YOU?
I DON'T KNOW, MAN. I THINK I MIGHT'VE BEEN, AT THE TIME.
WITH SOME OF THEM. A COUPLE, MAYBE.
THERE IS ONE GUY... ONE GUY... WHO I THINK I COULD'VE LOVED. BUT IT NEVER HAPPENED FOR US.
MAYBE IT'S JUST AS WELL.
YOU THINK IT COULD HAPPEN FOR US?
CAMERON, MAN...
...THIS IS NOT A GOOD IDEA. WE'RE IN THIS BAND TOGETHER...WE GOT THE PUBLIC AND OUR MANAGERS AND OUR WHOLE FUTURE TO WORRY ABOUT. I MEAN...
...AW, JEEZ...
WHY'D HE HAVE TO BE SO FREAKIN' CUTE?

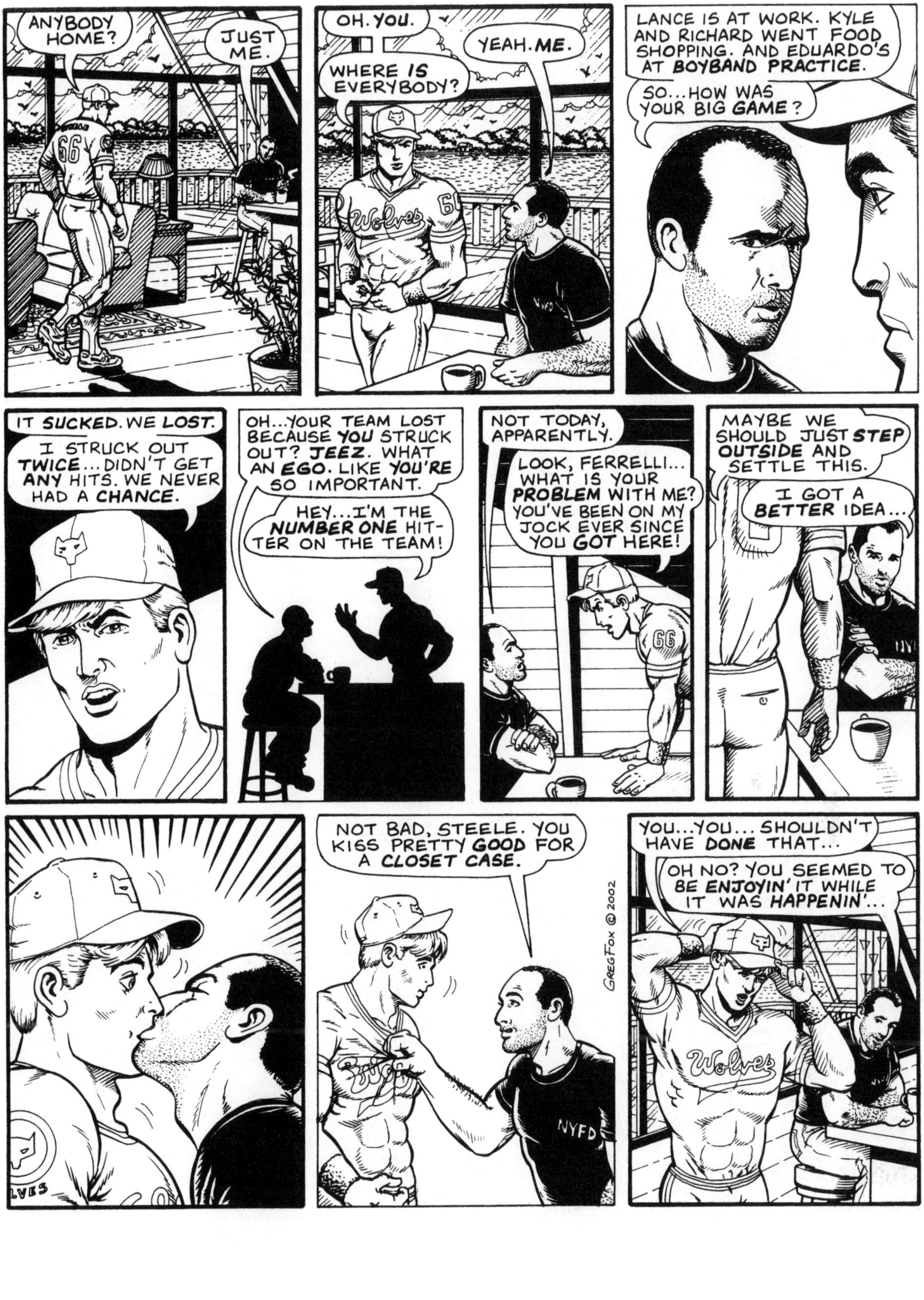
ANYBODY HOME?
JUST ME.
OH. YOU.
WHERE IS EVERYBODY?
YEAH. ME.
LANCE IS AT WORK. KYLE AND RICHARD WENT FOOD SHOPPING. AND EDUARDO'S AT BOYBAND PRACTICE.
SO...HOW WAS YOUR BIG GAME?
IT SUCKED. WE LOST.
I STRUCK OUT TWICE...DIDN'T GET ANY HITS. WE NEVER HAD A CHANCE.
OH...YOUR TEAM LOST BECAUSE YOU STRUCK OUT? JEEZ. WHAT AN EGO. LIKE YOU'RE SO IMPORTANT.
HEY...I'M THE NUMBER ONE HITTER ON THE TEAM!
NOT TODAY, APPARENTLY.
LOOK, FERRELLI... WHAT IS YOUR PROBLEM WITH ME? YOU'VE BEEN ON MY JOCK EVER SINCE YOU GOT HERE!
MAYBE WE SHOULD JUST STEP OUTSIDE AND SETTLE THIS.
I GOT A BETTER IDEA...
NOT BAD, STEELE. YOU KISS PRETTY GOOD FOR A CLOSET CASE.
GREGFOX © 2002
YOU...YOU... SHOULDN'T HAVE DONE THAT...
OH NO? YOU SEEMED TO BE ENJOYIN' IT WHILE IT WAS HAPPENIN'...

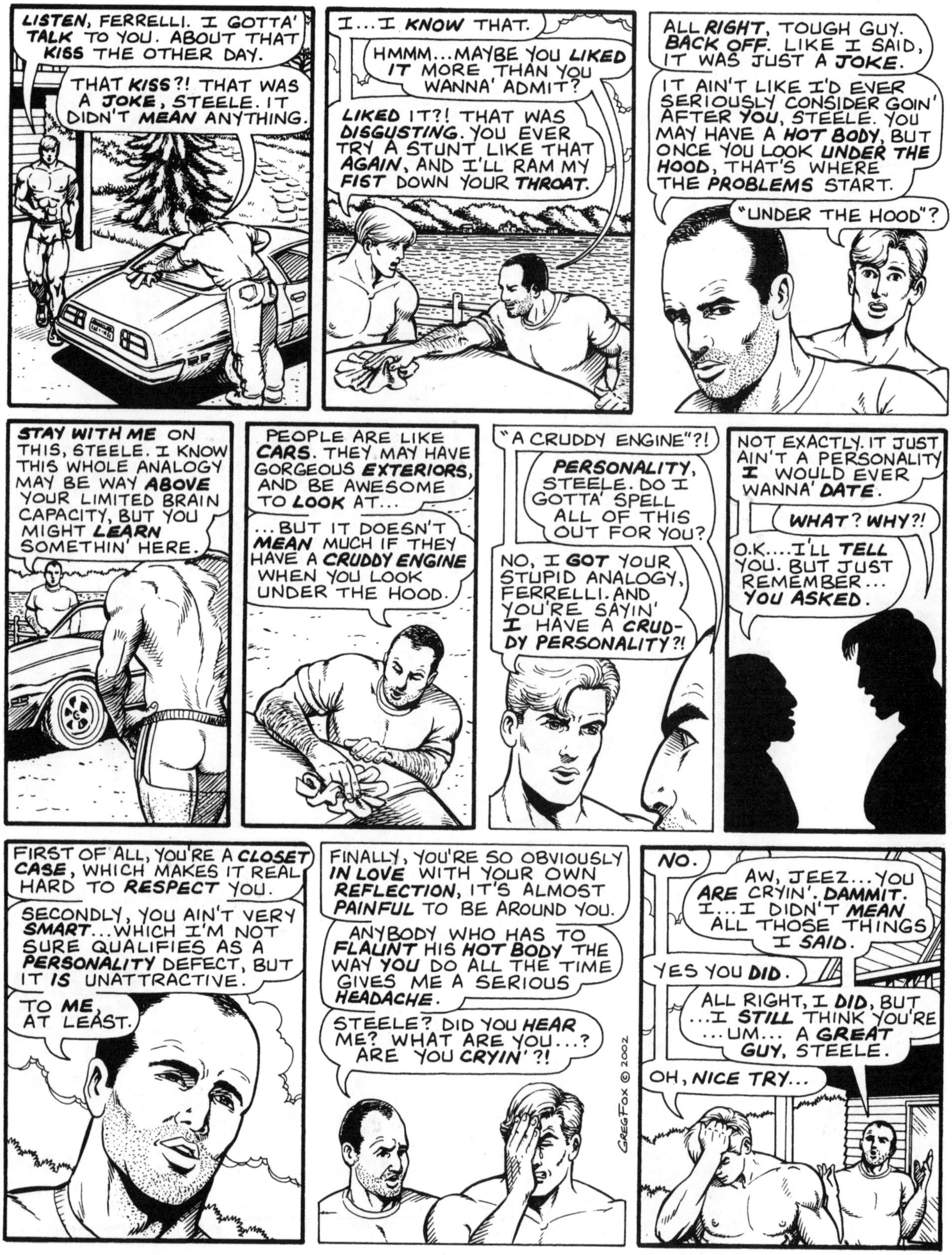

LISTEN, FERRELLI. I GOTTA' TALK TO YOU. ABOUT THAT KISS THE OTHER DAY.
THAT KISS?! THAT WAS A JOKE, STEELE. IT DIDN'T MEAN ANYTHING.
I... I KNOW THAT.
HMMM...MAYBE YOU LIKED IT MORE THAN YOU WANNA' ADMIT?
LIKED IT?! THAT WAS DISGUSTING. YOU EVER TRY A STUNT LIKE THAT AGAIN, AND I'LL RAM MY FIST DOWN YOUR THROAT.
ALL RIGHT, TOUGH GUY. BACK OFF. LIKE I SAID, IT WAS JUST A JOKE.
IT AIN'T LIKE I'D EVER SERIOUSLY CONSIDER GOIN' AFTER YOU, STEELE. YOU MAY HAVE A HOT BODY, BUT ONCE YOU LOOK UNDER THE HOOD, THAT'S WHERE THE PROBLEMS START.
"UNDER THE HOOD"?
STAY WITH ME ON THIS, STEELE. I KNOW THIS WHOLE ANALOGY MAY BE WAY ABOVE YOUR LIMITED BRAIN CAPACITY, BUT YOU MIGHT LEARN SOMETHIN' HERE.
PEOPLE ARE LIKE CARS. THEY MAY HAVE GORGEOUS EXTERIORS, AND BE AWESOME TO LOOK AT...
...BUT IT DOESN'T MEAN MUCH IF THEY HAVE A CRUDDY ENGINE WHEN YOU LOOK UNDER THE HOOD.
"A CRUDDY ENGINE"?!
PERSONALITY, STEELE. DO I GOTTA' SPELL ALL OF THIS OUT FOR YOU?
NO, I GOT YOUR STUPID ANALOGY, FERRELLI. AND YOU'RE SAYIN' I HAVE A CRUDDY PERSONALITY?!
NOT EXACTLY. IT JUST AIN'T A PERSONALITY I WOULD EVER WANNA' DATE.
WHAT? WHY?!
O.K.... I'LL TELL YOU. BUT JUST REMEMBER... YOU ASKED.
FIRST OF ALL, YOU'RE A CLOSET CASE, WHICH MAKES IT REAL HARD TO RESPECT YOU.
SECONDLY, YOU AIN'T VERY SMART...WHICH I'M NOT SURE QUALIFIES AS A PERSONALITY DEFECT, BUT IT IS UNATTRACTIVE.
TO ME, AT LEAST.
FINALLY, YOU'RE SO OBVIOUSLY IN LOVE WITH YOUR OWN REFLECTION, IT'S ALMOST PAINFUL TO BE AROUND YOU.
ANYBODY WHO HAS TO FLAUNT HIS HOT BODY THE WAY YOU DO ALL THE TIME GIVES ME A SERIOUS HEADACHE.
STEELE? DID YOU HEAR ME? WHAT ARE YOU...? ARE YOU CRYIN'?!
GREG FOX © 2002
NO.
AW, JEEZ... YOU ARE CRYIN'. DAMMIT. I... I DIDN'T MEAN ALL THOSE THINGS I SAID.
YES YOU DID.
ALL RIGHT, I DID, BUT ...I STILL THINK YOU'RE ...UM... A GREAT GUY, STEELE.
OH, NICE TRY...

A **METS** CAP?

WHAT ABOUT IT?

I THOUGHT YOU **DIDN'T LIKE** BASEBALL.

I DIDN'T SAY THAT. I SAID I **PREFER FOOTBALL.** BUT I LIKE BASEBALL, TOO.

O.K... BUT WHY THE **METS**?

WHAT. ARE YOU A **YANKEE** FAN?

DAMN RIGHT I AM.

FIGURES. YOU KNOW, PEOPLE ALL OVER THE **COUNTRY** LIKE THE **YANKEES.** BUT ONLY **TRUE NEW YORKERS** ARE METS FANS.

OH, THAT'S A LOAD OF **CRAP,** FERRELLI. AND BESIDES... **I'M** ABOUT AS **NEW YORK** AS THEY COME.

NOW **THAT'S** A HUMOROUS STATEMENT.

JEEZ, FERRELLI! WHY DO WE **ALWAYS** GOTTA' GET INTO THESE **STUPID ARGUMENTS**?!

I... ...I DON'T KNOW.

LOOK, STEELE... I GUESS I SHOULD **APOLOGIZE.** FOR SAYIN' THOSE THINGS LAST WEEK... THAT MADE YOU **CRY.**

I **WASN'T CRYIN'**!!!

O.K., WHATEVER, TOUGH GUY. BUT I'M **SORRY,** ANYWAY.

IT'S NOT JUST **YOU.** I RANK ON **EVERY-BODY.** SOMETIMES MAYBE I GO TOO **FAR.** I'M SORRY IF I... YOU KNOW...

...HURT YOU.

ALL RIGHT. BUT...

BUT **WHAT**?

FERRELLI... I **KNOW** WE'D **NEVER** WORK OUT AS A **COUPLE** OR ANYTHING, BUT...

...CAN'T WE AT LEAST BE **FRIENDS?** I MEAN, WE GOT SO MUCH IN COMMON. **SPORTS... FIXIN' CARS... METALLICA... COMIC BOOKS.**

MAYBE THAT'S WHY WHAT YOU SAID LAST WEEK **HURT** ME SO MUCH.

'CAUSE, WELL... YOU'RE SOMEBODY I **RESPECT.** SOMEBODY I'D **WANT** TO HAVE... AS A **BUDDY.**

YOU THINK THERE'S **ANY** POSSIBILITY THAT COULD EVER HAPPEN?

THE **METS GAME** IS ABOUT TO START. FEEL LIKE WATCHIN' IT WITH ME?

ME? WATCH A **METS** GAME?

FRIENDS **DO** THAT, STEELE. THEY **COMPROMISE.**

C'MON, IT'S **BASEBALL.** I'LL WATCH THE **YANKEE** GAME WITH YOU LATER... IF YOU'D LIKE.

YEAH. I'D LIKE.

O.K.

I GOTTA' ADMIT, PIAZZA **IS** A GREAT CATCHER.

HE'S ALSO GOT A **GREAT ASS.**

WELL... YEAH. THAT **TOO.**

NOW WE'RE TALKIN'...

GREG FOX ©2002

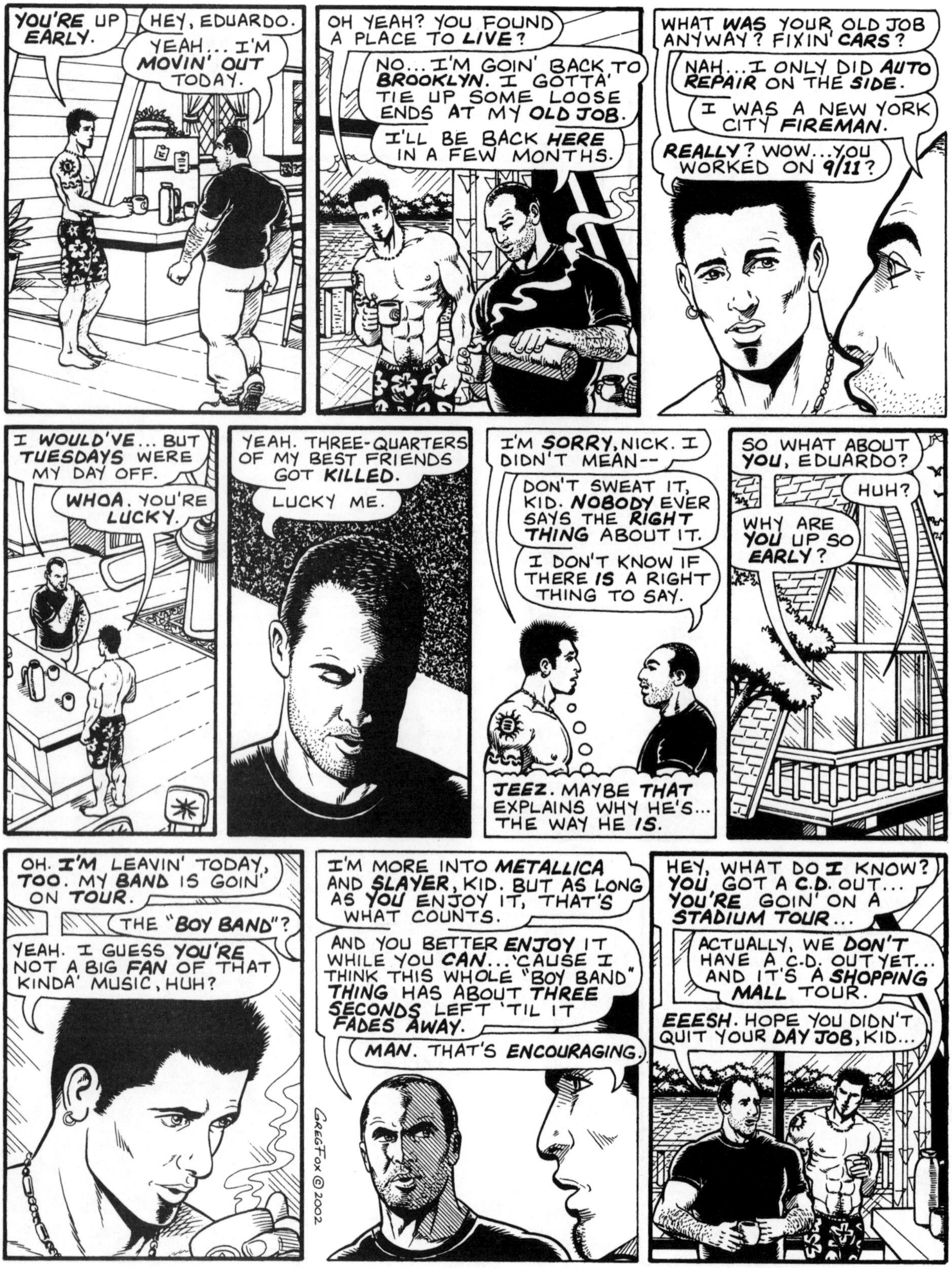
YOU'RE UP EARLY.
HEY, EDUARDO.
YEAH... I'M MOVIN' OUT TODAY.
OH YEAH? YOU FOUND A PLACE TO LIVE?
NO... I'M GOIN' BACK TO BROOKLYN. I GOTTA' TIE UP SOME LOOSE ENDS AT MY OLD JOB.
I'LL BE BACK HERE IN A FEW MONTHS.
WHAT WAS YOUR OLD JOB ANYWAY? FIXIN' CARS?
NAH... I ONLY DID AUTO REPAIR ON THE SIDE.
I WAS A NEW YORK CITY FIREMAN.
REALLY? WOW... YOU WORKED ON 9/11?
I WOULD'VE... BUT TUESDAYS WERE MY DAY OFF.
WHOA. YOU'RE LUCKY.
YEAH. THREE-QUARTERS OF MY BEST FRIENDS GOT KILLED.
LUCKY ME.
I'M SORRY, NICK. I DIDN'T MEAN--
DON'T SWEAT IT, KID. NOBODY EVER SAYS THE RIGHT THING ABOUT IT.
I DON'T KNOW IF THERE IS A RIGHT THING TO SAY.
JEEZ. MAYBE THAT EXPLAINS WHY HE'S... THE WAY HE IS.
SO WHAT ABOUT YOU, EDUARDO?
HUH?
WHY ARE YOU UP SO EARLY?
OH. I'M LEAVIN' TODAY, TOO. MY BAND IS GOIN' ON TOUR.
THE "BOY BAND"?
YEAH. I GUESS YOU'RE NOT A BIG FAN OF THAT KINDA' MUSIC, HUH?
I'M MORE INTO METALLICA AND SLAYER, KID. BUT AS LONG AS YOU ENJOY IT, THAT'S WHAT COUNTS.
AND YOU BETTER ENJOY IT WHILE YOU CAN... 'CAUSE I THINK THIS WHOLE "BOY BAND" THING HAS ABOUT THREE SECONDS LEFT 'TIL IT FADES AWAY.
MAN. THAT'S ENCOURAGING.
GREGFOX © 2002
HEY, WHAT DO I KNOW? YOU GOT A C.D. OUT... YOU'RE GOIN' ON A STADIUM TOUR...
ACTUALLY, WE DON'T HAVE A C.D. OUT YET... AND IT'S A SHOPPING MALL TOUR.
EEESH. HOPE YOU DIDN'T QUIT YOUR DAY JOB, KID...

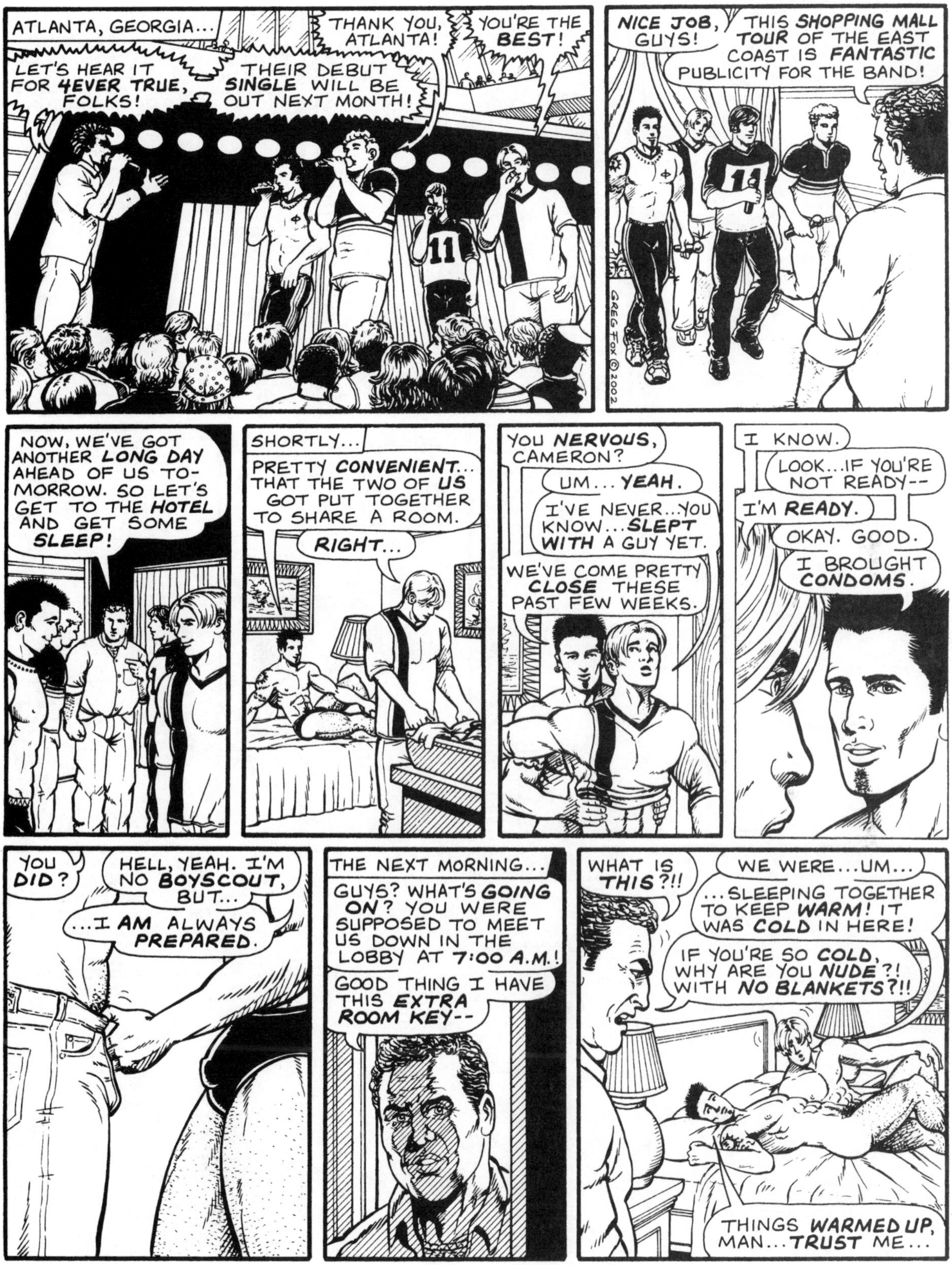
ATLANTA, GEORGIA...
THANK YOU, ATLANTA!
YOU'RE THE BEST!
LET'S HEAR IT FOR 4EVER TRUE, FOLKS!
THEIR DEBUT SINGLE WILL BE OUT NEXT MONTH!
11
GREG FOX © 2002
NICE JOB, GUYS!
THIS SHOPPING MALL TOUR OF THE EAST COAST IS FANTASTIC PUBLICITY FOR THE BAND!
11
NOW, WE'VE GOT ANOTHER LONG DAY AHEAD OF US TO-MORROW. SO LET'S GET TO THE HOTEL AND GET SOME SLEEP!
SHORTLY...
PRETTY CONVENIENT... THAT THE TWO OF US GOT PUT TOGETHER TO SHARE A ROOM.
RIGHT...
YOU NERVOUS, CAMERON?
UM... YEAH.
I'VE NEVER... YOU KNOW... SLEPT WITH A GUY YET.
WE'VE COME PRETTY CLOSE THESE PAST FEW WEEKS.
I KNOW.
LOOK... IF YOU'RE NOT READY--
I'M READY.
OKAY. GOOD.
I BROUGHT CONDOMS.
YOU DID?
HELL, YEAH. I'M NO BOYSCOUT, BUT...
...I AM ALWAYS PREPARED.
THE NEXT MORNING...
GUYS? WHAT'S GOING ON? YOU WERE SUPPOSED TO MEET US DOWN IN THE LOBBY AT 7:00 A.M.!
GOOD THING I HAVE THIS EXTRA ROOM KEY--
WHAT IS THIS?!!
WE WERE... UM...
...SLEEPING TOGETHER TO KEEP WARM! IT WAS COLD IN HERE!
IF YOU'RE SO COLD, WHY ARE YOU NUDE?! WITH NO BLANKETS?!!
THINGS WARMED UP, MAN... TRUST ME...

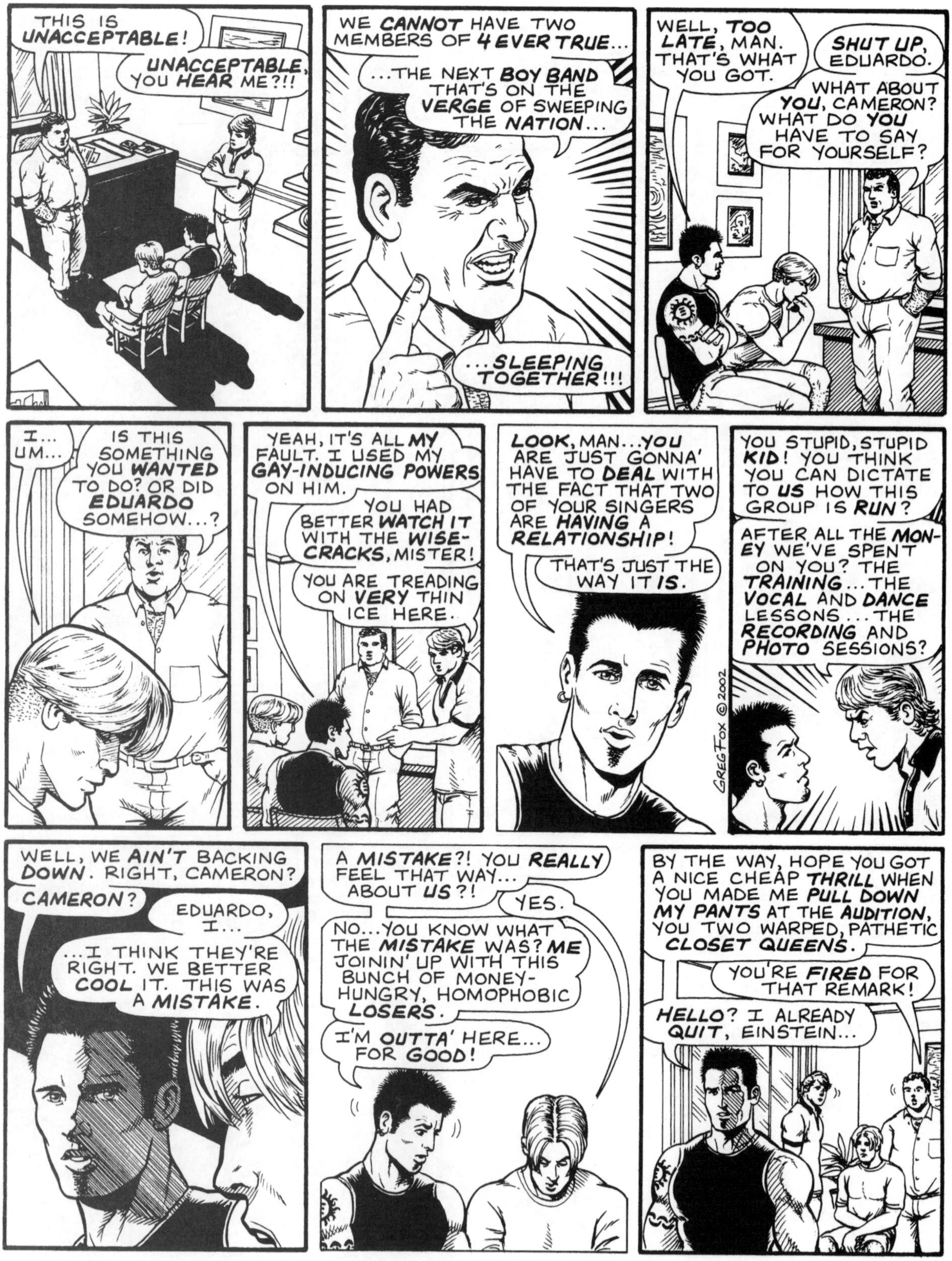

THIS IS UNACCEPTABLE!
UNACCEPTABLE, YOU HEAR ME?!!
WE CANNOT HAVE TWO MEMBERS OF 4 EVER TRUE...
...THE NEXT BOY BAND THAT'S ON THE VERGE OF SWEEPING THE NATION...
...SLEEPING TOGETHER!!!
WELL, TOO LATE, MAN. THAT'S WHAT YOU GOT.
SHUT UP, EDUARDO.
WHAT ABOUT YOU, CAMERON? WHAT DO YOU HAVE TO SAY FOR YOURSELF?
I... UM...
IS THIS SOMETHING YOU WANTED TO DO? OR DID EDUARDO SOMEHOW...?
YEAH, IT'S ALL MY FAULT. I USED MY GAY-INDUCING POWERS ON HIM.
YOU HAD BETTER WATCH IT WITH THE WISE-CRACKS, MISTER!
YOU ARE TREADING ON VERY THIN ICE HERE.
LOOK, MAN...YOU ARE JUST GONNA' HAVE TO DEAL WITH THE FACT THAT TWO OF YOUR SINGERS ARE HAVING A RELATIONSHIP!
THAT'S JUST THE WAY IT IS.
GREG FOX © 2002
YOU STUPID, STUPID KID! YOU THINK YOU CAN DICTATE TO US HOW THIS GROUP IS RUN?
AFTER ALL THE MONEY WE'VE SPENT ON YOU? THE TRAINING... THE VOCAL AND DANCE LESSONS... THE RECORDING AND PHOTO SESSIONS?
WELL, WE AIN'T BACKING DOWN. RIGHT, CAMERON?
CAMERON?
EDUARDO, I...
...I THINK THEY'RE RIGHT. WE BETTER COOL IT. THIS WAS A MISTAKE.
A MISTAKE?! YOU REALLY FEEL THAT WAY... ABOUT US?!
YES.
NO...YOU KNOW WHAT THE MISTAKE WAS? ME JOININ' UP WITH THIS BUNCH OF MONEY-HUNGRY, HOMOPHOBIC LOSERS.
I'M OUTTA' HERE... FOR GOOD!
BY THE WAY, HOPE YOU GOT A NICE CHEAP THRILL WHEN YOU MADE ME PULL DOWN MY PANTS AT THE AUDITION, YOU TWO WARPED, PATHETIC CLOSET QUEENS.
YOU'RE FIRED FOR THAT REMARK!
HELLO? I ALREADY QUIT, EINSTEIN...

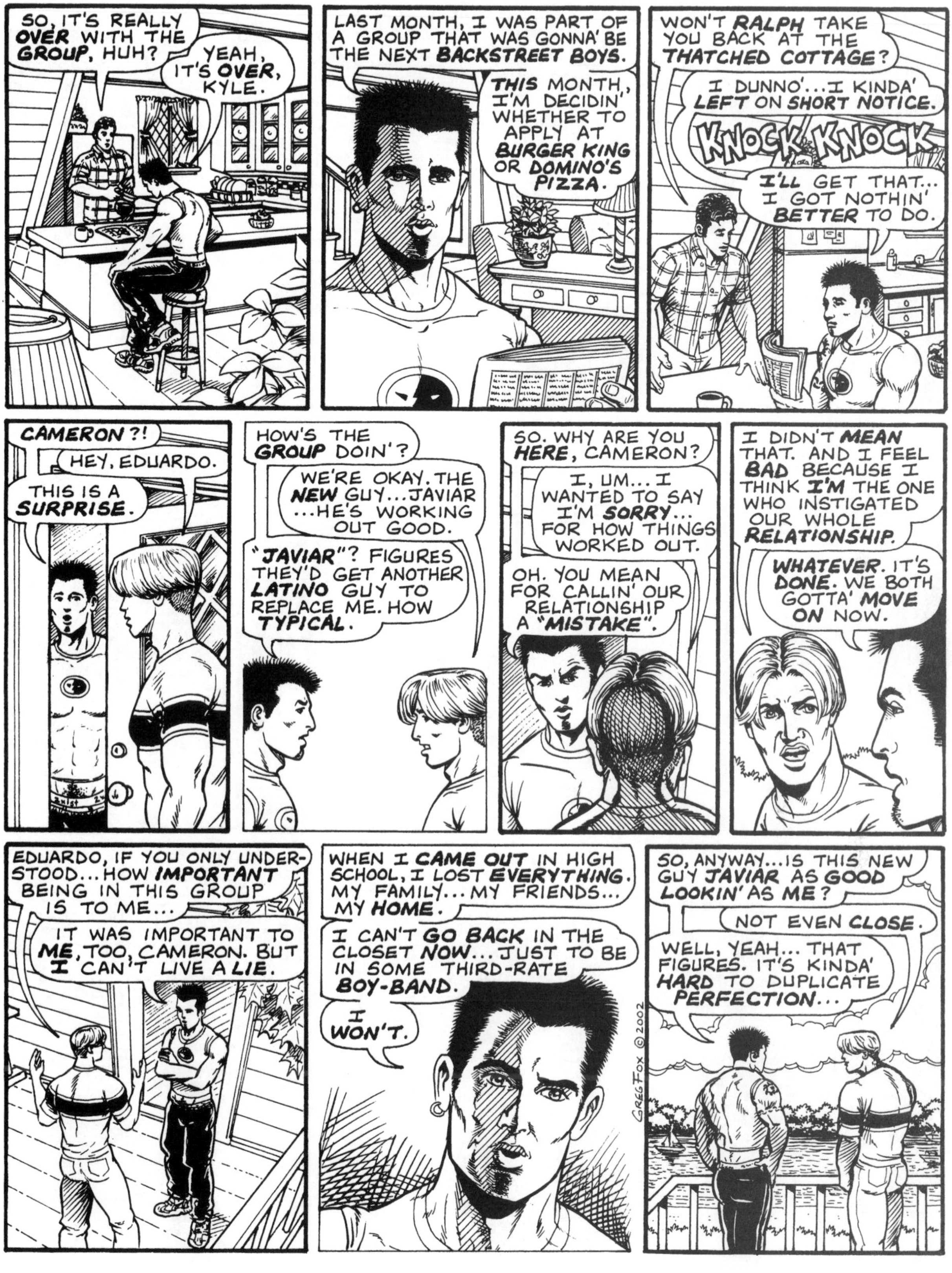

SO, IT'S REALLY OVER WITH THE GROUP, HUH?
YEAH, IT'S OVER, KYLE.
LAST MONTH, I WAS PART OF A GROUP THAT WAS GONNA' BE THE NEXT BACKSTREET BOYS.
THIS MONTH, I'M DECIDIN' WHETHER TO APPLY AT BURGER KING OR DOMINO'S PIZZA.
WON'T RALPH TAKE YOU BACK AT THE THATCHED COTTAGE?
I DUNNO'... I KINDA' LEFT ON SHORT NOTICE.
KNOCK KNOCK
I'LL GET THAT... I GOT NOTHIN' BETTER TO DO.
CAMERON?!
HEY, EDUARDO.
THIS IS A SURPRISE.
HOW'S THE GROUP DOIN'?
WE'RE OKAY. THE NEW GUY... JAVIAR ...HE'S WORKING OUT GOOD.
"JAVIAR"? FIGURES THEY'D GET ANOTHER LATINO GUY TO REPLACE ME. HOW TYPICAL.
SO. WHY ARE YOU HERE, CAMERON?
I, UM... I WANTED TO SAY I'M SORRY... FOR HOW THINGS WORKED OUT.
OH. YOU MEAN FOR CALLIN' OUR RELATIONSHIP A "MISTAKE".
I DIDN'T MEAN THAT. AND I FEEL BAD BECAUSE I THINK I'M THE ONE WHO INSTIGATED OUR WHOLE RELATIONSHIP.
WHATEVER. IT'S DONE. WE BOTH GOTTA' MOVE ON NOW.
EDUARDO, IF YOU ONLY UNDERSTOOD... HOW IMPORTANT BEING IN THIS GROUP IS TO ME...
IT WAS IMPORTANT TO ME, TOO, CAMERON. BUT I CAN'T LIVE A LIE.
WHEN I CAME OUT IN HIGH SCHOOL, I LOST EVERYTHING. MY FAMILY... MY FRIENDS... MY HOME.
I CAN'T GO BACK IN THE CLOSET NOW... JUST TO BE IN SOME THIRD-RATE BOY-BAND.
I WON'T.
GREG FOX © 2002
SO, ANYWAY... IS THIS NEW GUY JAVIAR AS GOOD LOOKIN' AS ME?
NOT EVEN CLOSE.
WELL, YEAH... THAT FIGURES. IT'S KINDA' HARD TO DUPLICATE PERFECTION...

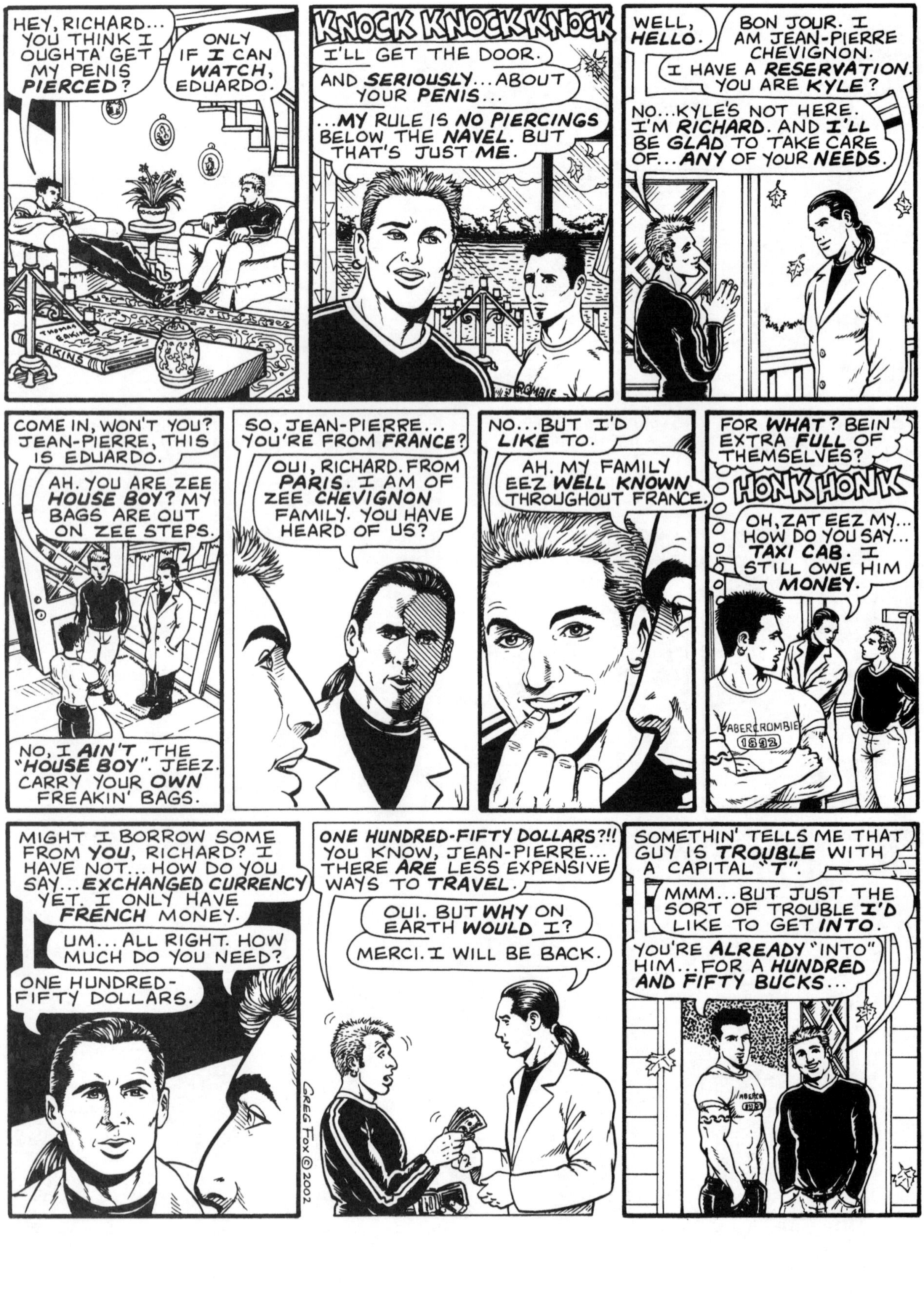
HEY, RICHARD... YOU THINK I OUGHTA' GET MY PENIS PIERCED?
ONLY IF I CAN WATCH, EDUARDO.
THOMAS EAKINS
EAKINS
KNOCK KNOCK KNOCK
I'LL GET THE DOOR.
AND SERIOUSLY... ABOUT YOUR PENIS...
...MY RULE IS NO PIERCINGS BELOW THE NAVEL. BUT THAT'S JUST ME.
ROMBIE
WELL, HELLO.
BON JOUR. I AM JEAN-PIERRE CHEVIGNON.
I HAVE A RESERVATION. YOU ARE KYLE?
NO...KYLE'S NOT HERE. I'M RICHARD. AND I'LL BE GLAD TO TAKE CARE OF... ANY OF YOUR NEEDS.
COME IN, WON'T YOU? JEAN-PIERRE, THIS IS EDUARDO.
AH. YOU ARE ZEE HOUSE BOY? MY BAGS ARE OUT ON ZEE STEPS.
NO, I AIN'T THE "HOUSE BOY". JEEZ. CARRY YOUR OWN FREAKIN' BAGS.
SO, JEAN-PIERRE... YOU'RE FROM FRANCE?
OUI, RICHARD. FROM PARIS. I AM OF ZEE CHEVIGNON FAMILY. YOU HAVE HEARD OF US?
NO...BUT I'D LIKE TO.
AH. MY FAMILY EEZ WELL KNOWN THROUGHOUT FRANCE.
FOR WHAT? BEIN' EXTRA FULL OF THEMSELVES?
HONK HONK
OH, ZAT EEZ MY... HOW DO YOU SAY... TAXI CAB. I STILL OWE HIM MONEY.
ABERCROMBIE 1892
MIGHT I BORROW SOME FROM YOU, RICHARD? I HAVE NOT... HOW DO YOU SAY... EXCHANGED CURRENCY YET. I ONLY HAVE FRENCH MONEY.
UM... ALL RIGHT. HOW MUCH DO YOU NEED?
ONE HUNDRED-FIFTY DOLLARS.
GREG FOX © 2002
ONE HUNDRED-FIFTY DOLLARS?!! YOU KNOW, JEAN-PIERRE... THERE ARE LESS EXPENSIVE WAYS TO TRAVEL.
OUI. BUT WHY ON EARTH WOULD I?
MERCI. I WILL BE BACK.
SOMETHIN' TELLS ME THAT GUY IS TROUBLE WITH A CAPITAL "T".
MMM... BUT JUST THE SORT OF TROUBLE I'D LIKE TO GET INTO.
YOU'RE ALREADY "INTO" HIM... FOR A HUNDRED AND FIFTY BUCKS...

YOU LIKE TO RIDE ZEE BULL, EH? HOLD ON!
HAHAHA! MAN FUNNY!
WOW. CAN JEAN-PIERRE COME LIVE NEXT DOOR WITH US FOR A FEW WEEKS? I'VE NEVER SEEN HEATH SO ENTERTAINED!
YOU CAN ASK! ALTHOUGH, I DON'T THINK JEAN-PIERRE CAME TO THE U.S.A. TO BE A NANNY, ANDREW.
WHY IS HE HERE, KYLE?
HE'S A GUEST PROFESSOR AT STONYBROOK UNIVERSITY. HE'S ACTUALLY AN EXPERT IN THE HISTORY OF FRENCH ART.
HMM... I BET THAT'S NOT THE ONLY "ART" HE'S AN "EXPERT" AT. HE SEEMS LIKE QUITE A CATCH.
CAREFUL, ANDREW. YOU ALREADY HAVE A HUSBAND.
I MEANT FOR YOU, KYLE.
I DON'T THINK SO.
OH, C'MON, KYLE.
US MARRIED MEN NEED TO LIVE VICARIOUSLY THROUGH SINGLE GUYS LIKE YOU.
YOU KNOW, AFTER MY LAST FEW DATING DISASTERS, I THINK I'M TAKING A BREAK ON MEN FOR A WHILE.
OH? THINKING OF TRYING WOMEN?
SORRY... MY ELEVATOR DOESN'T STOP ON THAT FLOOR.
THEN WHAT? ARE YOU TAKING UP CELIBACY?
I'M TAKING UP SENSIBILITY. LIKE... TAKING SOME TIME BEFORE I LEAP INTO ANOTHER RELATIONSHIP AND END UP GETTING MY HEART BROKEN AGAIN.
NEXT TIME... I WANT IT TO BE RIGHT.
HOW DO YOU KNOW JEAN-PIERRE WOULDN'T BE "RIGHT"?
PLEASE, ANDREW... HE'S GOING BACK TO FRANCE IN A FEW MONTHS. I'M NOT INTERESTED IN HAVING A TRANSATLANTIC RELATIONSHIP.
I COULD BARELY KEEP IT TOGETHER WHEN I WAS DATING A GUY FROM NEW JERSEY.
THIS JEAN-PIERRE MIGHT BE WORTH TRAVELLING FOR, KYLE.
YEAH, WELL... IF HE MOVES TO JERSEY, I'LL CONSIDER IT...

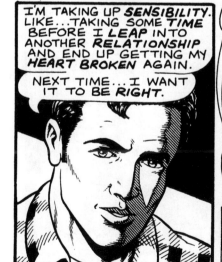

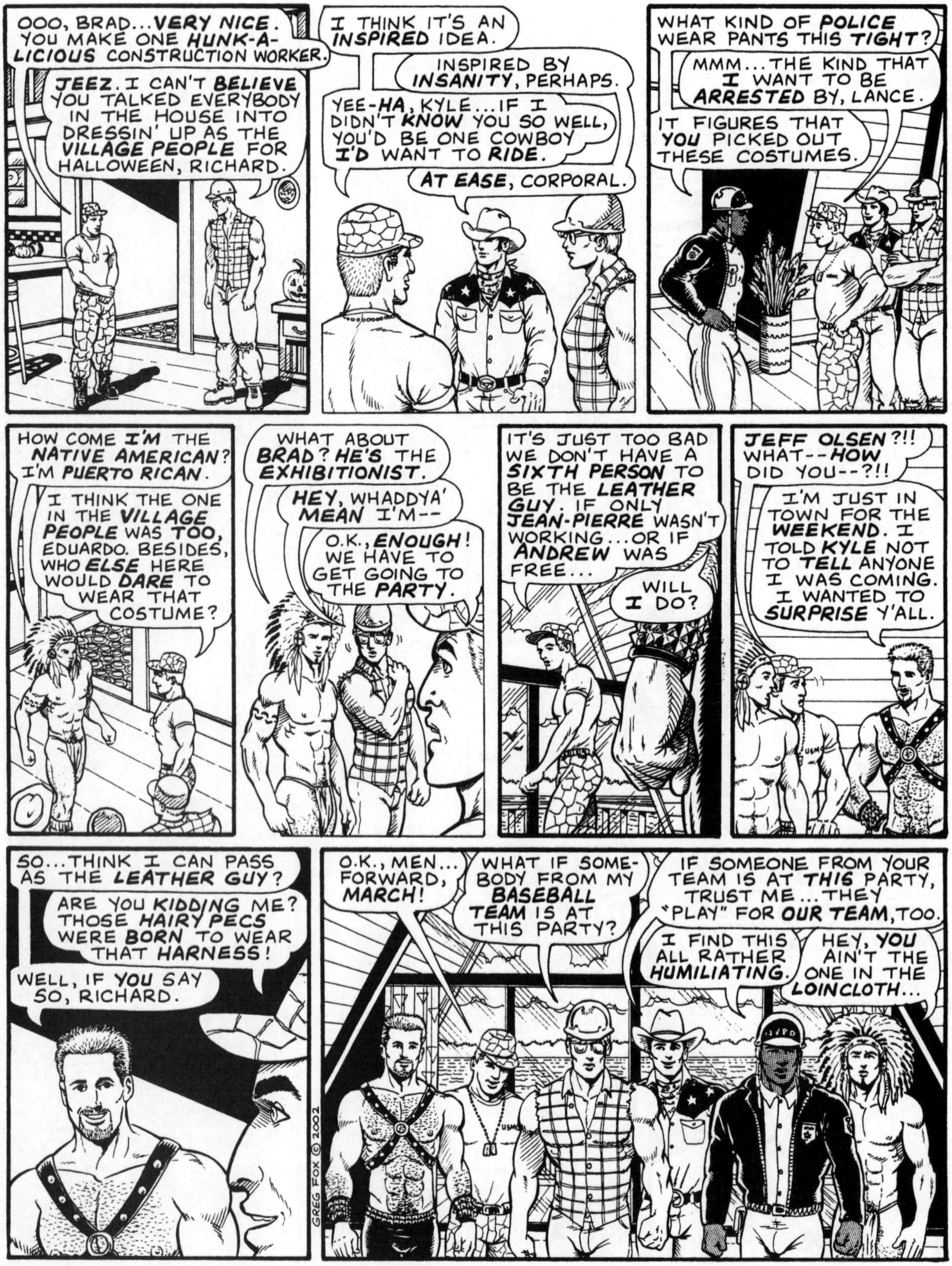
OOO, BRAD...VERY NICE. YOU MAKE ONE HUNK-A-LICIOUS CONSTRUCTION WORKER.
JEEZ. I CAN'T BELIEVE YOU TALKED EVERYBODY IN THE HOUSE INTO DRESSIN' UP AS THE VILLAGE PEOPLE FOR HALLOWEEN, RICHARD.
I THINK IT'S AN INSPIRED IDEA.
INSPIRED BY INSANITY, PERHAPS.
YEE-HA, KYLE...IF I DIDN'T KNOW YOU SO WELL, YOU'D BE ONE COWBOY I'D WANT TO RIDE.
AT EASE, CORPORAL.
WHAT KIND OF POLICE WEAR PANTS THIS TIGHT?
MMM...THE KIND THAT I WANT TO BE ARRESTED BY, LANCE.
IT FIGURES THAT YOU PICKED OUT THESE COSTUMES.
HOW COME I'M THE NATIVE AMERICAN? I'M PUERTO RICAN.
I THINK THE ONE IN THE VILLAGE PEOPLE WAS TOO, EDUARDO. BESIDES, WHO ELSE HERE WOULD DARE TO WEAR THAT COSTUME?
WHAT ABOUT BRAD? HE'S THE EXHIBITIONIST.
HEY, WHADDYA' MEAN I'M--
O.K., ENOUGH! WE HAVE TO GET GOING TO THE PARTY.
IT'S JUST TOO BAD WE DON'T HAVE A SIXTH PERSON TO BE THE LEATHER GUY. IF ONLY JEAN-PIERRE WASN'T WORKING...OR IF ANDREW WAS FREE...
WILL I DO?
JEFF OLSEN?!! WHAT--HOW DID YOU--?!!
I'M JUST IN TOWN FOR THE WEEKEND. I TOLD KYLE NOT TO TELL ANYONE I WAS COMING. I WANTED TO SURPRISE Y'ALL.
SO...THINK I CAN PASS AS THE LEATHER GUY?
ARE YOU KIDDING ME? THOSE HAIRY PECS WERE BORN TO WEAR THAT HARNESS!
WELL, IF YOU SAY SO, RICHARD.
GREG FOX © 2002
O.K., MEN... FORWARD, MARCH!
WHAT IF SOMEBODY FROM MY BASEBALL TEAM IS AT THIS PARTY?
IF SOMEONE FROM YOUR TEAM IS AT THIS PARTY, TRUST ME...THEY "PLAY" FOR OUR TEAM, TOO.
I FIND THIS ALL RATHER HUMILIATING.
HEY, YOU AIN'T THE ONE IN THE LOINCLOTH...

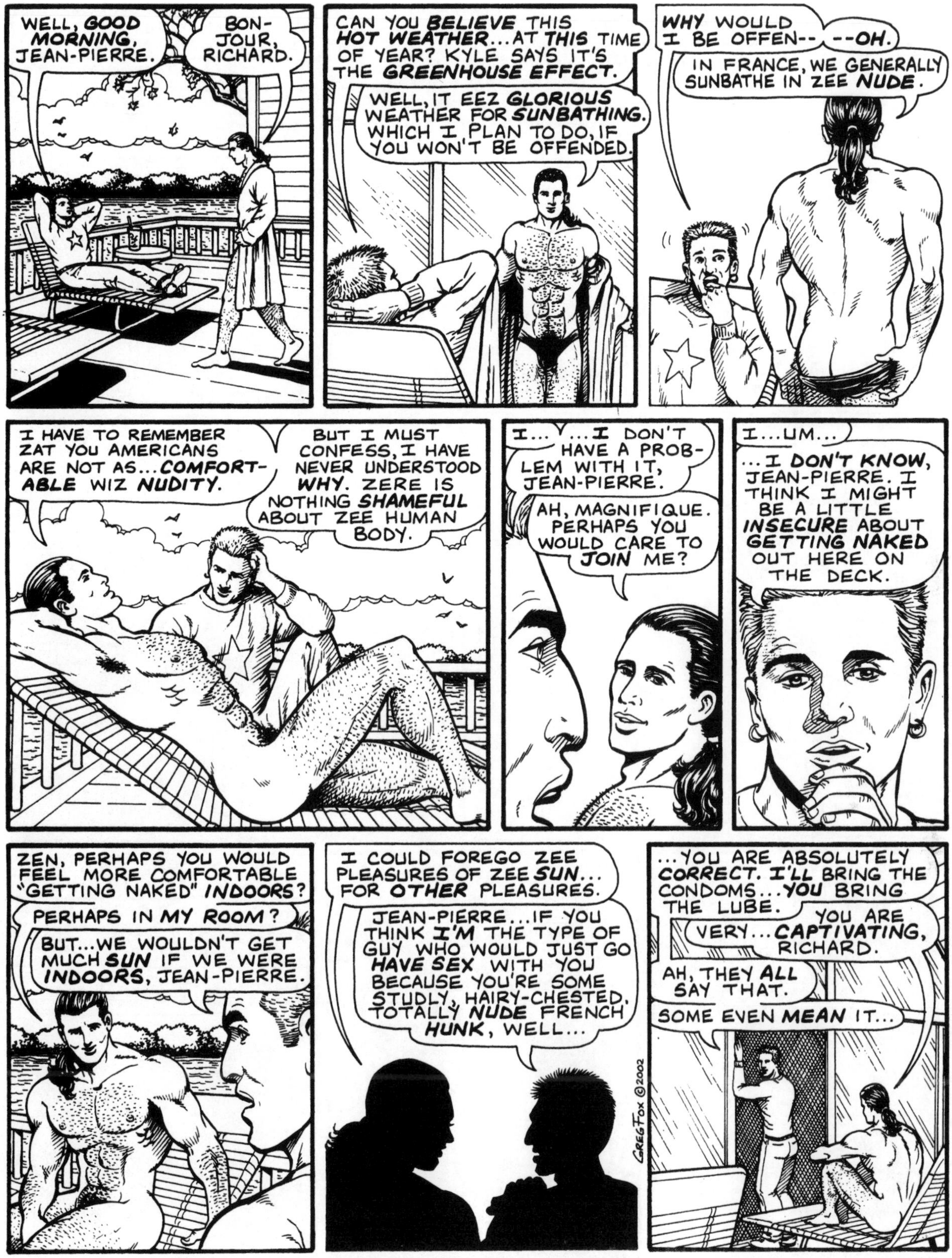
WELL, GOOD MORNING, JEAN-PIERRE.
BON-JOUR, RICHARD.
CAN YOU BELIEVE THIS HOT WEATHER...AT THIS TIME OF YEAR? KYLE SAYS IT'S THE GREENHOUSE EFFECT.
WELL, IT EEZ GLORIOUS WEATHER FOR SUNBATHING. WHICH I PLAN TO DO, IF YOU WON'T BE OFFENDED.
WHY WOULD I BE OFFEN--
--OH.
IN FRANCE, WE GENERALLY SUNBATHE IN ZEE NUDE.
I HAVE TO REMEMBER ZAT YOU AMERICANS ARE NOT AS...COMFORTABLE WIZ NUDITY.
BUT I MUST CONFESS, I HAVE NEVER UNDERSTOOD WHY. ZERE IS NOTHING SHAMEFUL ABOUT ZEE HUMAN BODY.
I...
...I DON'T HAVE A PROBLEM WITH IT, JEAN-PIERRE.
AH, MAGNIFIQUE. PERHAPS YOU WOULD CARE TO JOIN ME?
I...UM...
...I DON'T KNOW, JEAN-PIERRE. I THINK I MIGHT BE A LITTLE INSECURE ABOUT GETTING NAKED OUT HERE ON THE DECK.
ZEN, PERHAPS YOU WOULD FEEL MORE COMFORTABLE "GETTING NAKED" INDOORS?
PERHAPS IN MY ROOM?
BUT...WE WOULDN'T GET MUCH SUN IF WE WERE INDOORS, JEAN-PIERRE.
I COULD FOREGO ZEE PLEASURES OF ZEE SUN... FOR OTHER PLEASURES.
JEAN-PIERRE...IF YOU THINK I'M THE TYPE OF GUY WHO WOULD JUST GO HAVE SEX WITH YOU BECAUSE YOU'RE SOME STUDLY, HAIRY-CHESTED, TOTALLY NUDE FRENCH HUNK, WELL...
GREG FOX ©2002
...YOU ARE ABSOLUTELY CORRECT. I'LL BRING THE CONDOMS...YOU BRING THE LUBE.
YOU ARE VERY...CAPTIVATING, RICHARD.
AH, THEY ALL SAY THAT.
SOME EVEN MEAN IT...

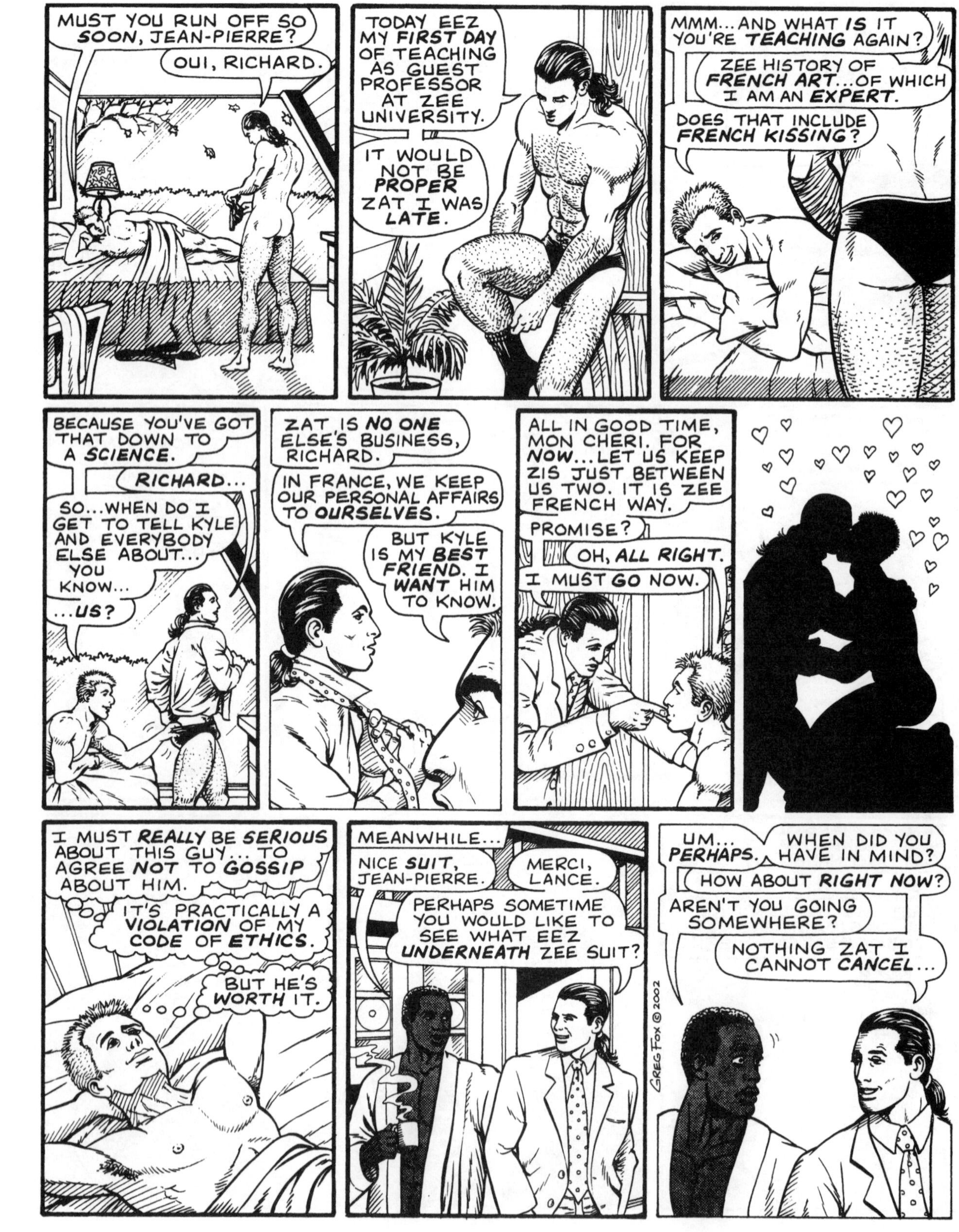
MUST YOU RUN OFF SO SOON, JEAN-PIERRE?
OUI, RICHARD.
TODAY EEZ MY FIRST DAY OF TEACHING AS GUEST PROFESSOR AT ZEE UNIVERSITY.
IT WOULD NOT BE PROPER ZAT I WAS LATE.
MMM... AND WHAT IS IT YOU'RE TEACHING AGAIN?
ZEE HISTORY OF FRENCH ART...OF WHICH I AM AN EXPERT.
DOES THAT INCLUDE FRENCH KISSING?
BECAUSE YOU'VE GOT THAT DOWN TO A SCIENCE.
RICHARD...
SO...WHEN DO I GET TO TELL KYLE AND EVERYBODY ELSE ABOUT... YOU KNOW...
...US?
ZAT IS NO ONE ELSE'S BUSINESS, RICHARD.
IN FRANCE, WE KEEP OUR PERSONAL AFFAIRS TO OURSELVES.
BUT KYLE IS MY BEST FRIEND. I WANT HIM TO KNOW.
ALL IN GOOD TIME, MON CHERI. FOR NOW... LET US KEEP ZIS JUST BETWEEN US TWO. IT IS ZEE FRENCH WAY.
PROMISE?
OH, ALL RIGHT.
I MUST GO NOW.
I MUST REALLY BE SERIOUS ABOUT THIS GUY... TO AGREE NOT TO GOSSIP ABOUT HIM.
IT'S PRACTICALLY A VIOLATION OF MY CODE OF ETHICS.
BUT HE'S WORTH IT.
MEANWHILE...
NICE SUIT, JEAN-PIERRE.
MERCI, LANCE.
PERHAPS SOMETIME YOU WOULD LIKE TO SEE WHAT EEZ UNDERNEATH ZEE SUIT?
GREG FOX © 2002
UM... PERHAPS.
WHEN DID YOU HAVE IN MIND?
HOW ABOUT RIGHT NOW?
AREN'T YOU GOING SOMEWHERE?
NOTHING ZAT I CANNOT CANCEL...

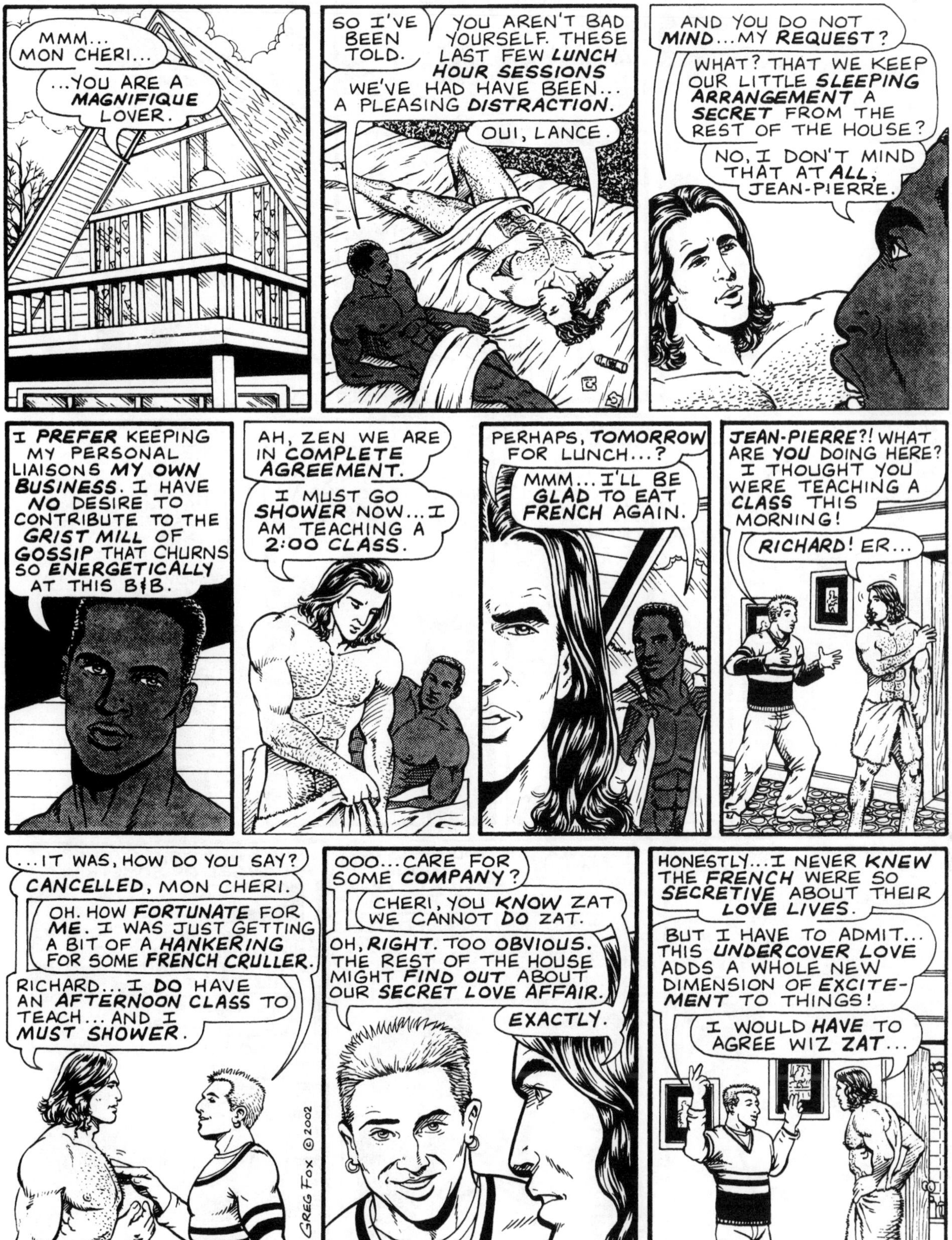
MMM... MON CHERI...
...YOU ARE A MAGNIFIQUE LOVER.
SO I'VE BEEN TOLD.
YOU AREN'T BAD YOURSELF. THESE LAST FEW LUNCH HOUR SESSIONS WE'VE HAD HAVE BEEN... A PLEASING DISTRACTION.
OUI, LANCE.
AND YOU DO NOT MIND...MY REQUEST?
WHAT? THAT WE KEEP OUR LITTLE SLEEPING ARRANGEMENT A SECRET FROM THE REST OF THE HOUSE?
NO, I DON'T MIND THAT AT ALL, JEAN-PIERRE.
I PREFER KEEPING MY PERSONAL LIAISONS MY OWN BUSINESS. I HAVE NO DESIRE TO CONTRIBUTE TO THE GRIST MILL OF GOSSIP THAT CHURNS SO ENERGETICALLY AT THIS B&B.
AH, ZEN WE ARE IN COMPLETE AGREEMENT.
I MUST GO SHOWER NOW...I AM TEACHING A 2:00 CLASS.
PERHAPS, TOMORROW FOR LUNCH...?
MMM... I'LL BE GLAD TO EAT FRENCH AGAIN.
JEAN-PIERRE?! WHAT ARE YOU DOING HERE? I THOUGHT YOU WERE TEACHING A CLASS THIS MORNING!
RICHARD! ER...
...IT WAS, HOW DO YOU SAY? CANCELLED, MON CHERI.
OH. HOW FORTUNATE FOR ME. I WAS JUST GETTING A BIT OF A HANKERING FOR SOME FRENCH CRULLER.
RICHARD... I DO HAVE AN AFTERNOON CLASS TO TEACH... AND I MUST SHOWER.
GREG FOX ©2002
OOO... CARE FOR SOME COMPANY?
CHERI, YOU KNOW ZAT WE CANNOT DO ZAT.
OH, RIGHT. TOO OBVIOUS. THE REST OF THE HOUSE MIGHT FIND OUT ABOUT OUR SECRET LOVE AFFAIR.
EXACTLY.
HONESTLY...I NEVER KNEW THE FRENCH WERE SO SECRETIVE ABOUT THEIR LOVE LIVES.
BUT I HAVE TO ADMIT... THIS UNDERCOVER LOVE ADDS A WHOLE NEW DIMENSION OF EXCITEMENT TO THINGS!
I WOULD HAVE TO AGREE WIZ ZAT...

OH, MAN. I CAN'T BELIEVE I FORGOT MY WALLET.

OF ALL TIMES... ON CHRISTMAS MORNING!

I WANTED FRESH STRAWBERRIES SO I COULD MAKE THE GUYS MY SPECIAL HOLIDAY STRAWBERRY WAFFLE SUPREME.

BUT NOW... BY THE TIME I DRIVE ALL THE WAY BACK TO THE B&B...

...GET MY WALLET... DRIVE BACK HERE... AND BACK HOME AGAIN... IT'LL BE TOO LATE FOR BREAKFAST.

MAN...I RUINED EVERYTHING.

WILL TWENTY DOLLARS COVER IT?

HUH?! YOU LOOK LIKE YOU NEED TO BORROW SOME MONEY.

WILL TWENTY DOLLARS DO?

I... ...WOW. I COULDN'T JUST BORROW MONEY FROM A STRANGER.

I'M STEVE. NOW I'M NOT A STRANGER.

UM...I'M KYLE.

I KNOW.

YOU KNOW?!

YEAH...I THINK WE WENT TO THE SAME COLLEGE. GENESEO, RIGHT?

RIGHT. BUT--

HERE... WOULD YOU TAKE THIS MONEY? YOU CAN PAY ME BACK NEXT TIME WE RUN INTO EACH OTHER.

NOW...HAVE A MERRY CHRISTMAS, KYLE.

HEY, WAIT A MINUTE, STEVE.

HOW ABOUT COMING BY MY B&B FOR BREAKFAST TODAY? THAT WAY I CAN PAY YOU BACK RIGHT AWAY.

KYLE, YOU DON'T HAVE TO--

I WANT TO. I INSIST.

GREG FOX © 2002

WELL, O.K., IF YOU INSIST. I AM KIND OF CURIOUS ABOUT YOUR HOLIDAY STRAWBERRY WAFFLE SUPREME.

HUH?! HOW ON EARTH COULD YOU KNOW I'M MAKING THAT FOR BREAKFAST?

UH...LUCKY GUESS?

WHAT ARE YOU, STEVE? AN ANGEL OR SOMETHING?

DO I LOOK LIKE AN ANGEL?

YOU LOOK LIKE A CHIPPENDALES STRIPPER. BUT THAT'S BESIDE THE POINT.

IS THAT SUPPOSED TO BE A COMPLIMENT?

IT'S NOT AN INSULT...

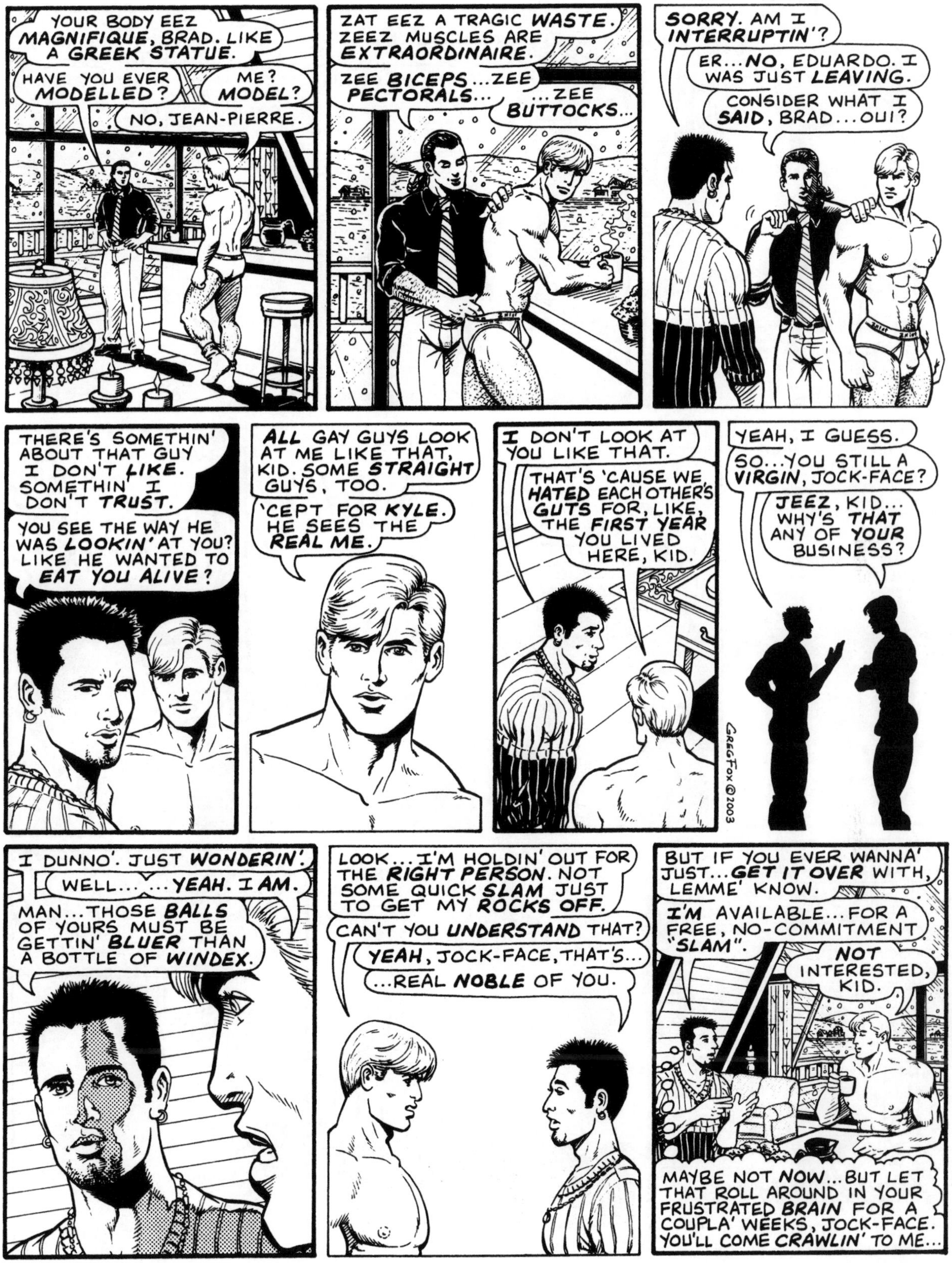
YOUR BODY EEZ MAGNIFIQUE, BRAD. LIKE A GREEK STATUE.
HAVE YOU EVER MODELLED?
ME? MODEL?
NO, JEAN-PIERRE.
ZAT EEZ A TRAGIC WASTE. ZEEZ MUSCLES ARE EXTRAORDINAIRE.
ZEE BICEPS...ZEE PECTORALS...
...ZEE BUTTOCKS...
SORRY. AM I INTERRUPTIN'?
ER...NO, EDUARDO. I WAS JUST LEAVING.
CONSIDER WHAT I SAID, BRAD...OUI?
THERE'S SOMETHIN' ABOUT THAT GUY I DON'T LIKE. SOMETHIN' I DON'T TRUST.
YOU SEE THE WAY HE WAS LOOKIN' AT YOU? LIKE HE WANTED TO EAT YOU ALIVE?
ALL GAY GUYS LOOK AT ME LIKE THAT, KID. SOME STRAIGHT GUYS, TOO.
'CEPT FOR KYLE. HE SEES THE REAL ME.
I DON'T LOOK AT YOU LIKE THAT.
THAT'S 'CAUSE WE HATED EACH OTHER'S GUTS FOR, LIKE, THE FIRST YEAR YOU LIVED HERE, KID.
GREGFOX ©2003
YEAH, I GUESS.
SO...YOU STILL A VIRGIN, JOCK-FACE?
JEEZ, KID... WHY'S THAT ANY OF YOUR BUSINESS?
I DUNNO'. JUST WONDERIN'.
WELL...
...YEAH. I AM.
MAN...THOSE BALLS OF YOURS MUST BE GETTIN' BLUER THAN A BOTTLE OF WINDEX.
LOOK...I'M HOLDIN' OUT FOR THE RIGHT PERSON. NOT SOME QUICK SLAM JUST TO GET MY ROCKS OFF.
CAN'T YOU UNDERSTAND THAT?
YEAH, JOCK-FACE, THAT'S...
...REAL NOBLE OF YOU.
BUT IF YOU EVER WANNA' JUST...GET IT OVER WITH, LEMME' KNOW.
I'M AVAILABLE...FOR A FREE, NO-COMMITMENT "SLAM".
NOT INTERESTED, KID.
MAYBE NOT NOW...BUT LET THAT ROLL AROUND IN YOUR FRUSTRATED BRAIN FOR A COUPLA' WEEKS, JOCK-FACE. YOU'LL COME CRAWLIN' TO ME...

WHAT'S GOT YOU SO DOWN?

OH...AS IF YOU CARE, LANCE.

I DON'T, TRUTHFULLY. I WAS JUST MAKING CONVERSATION.

HOW MAGNANIMOUS OF YOU.

DON'T MENTION IT.

ALL RIGHT...I DON'T KNOW WHY I'M TELLING YOU THIS, BUT...

...I THINK JEAN-PIERRE IS SLEEPING WITH SOMEONE ELSE.

OH, PLEASE.

I THINK I WOULD NOTICE SOMETHING LIKE THAT.

HUH? WHY WOULD YOU--?

AND I DON'T SEE HOW IT'S ANY OF YOUR CONCERN, ANYWAY.

WELL...WHOSE CONCERN SHOULD IT BE?

MINE. THAT'S BETWEEN HIM AND ME.

WHAT?! BUT I'M THE ONE WHO'S...

HOLD ON A MINUTE...ARE YOU SAYING...?

...YOU'RE SLEEPING WITH JEAN-PIERRE?!!!

WHERE IS HE?!!!

MEANWHILE, AT STONYBROOK UNIVERSITY...

ARE YOU SURE IT'S OKAY I SIT IN ON THIS FIGURE DRAWING CLASS, MARK? I DON'T EVEN GO TO SCHOOL HERE.

YEAH, IT'S COOL, EDUARDO. YOU GOTTA' SEE THIS HOT NUDE GUY WE'VE BEEN DRAWING.

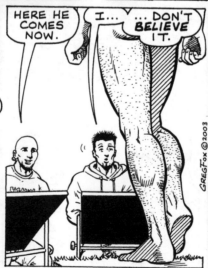

HERE HE COMES NOW.

I... ...DON'T BELIEVE IT.

GREGFOX ©2003

JEAN-PIERRE?!!

EDUARDO?!!

MON DIEU!!!

YEAH, YOU CAN SAY THAT AGAIN.

WHATEVER "THAT" MEANS...

EDUARDO! I AM GLAD YOU ARE HERE. I NEED TO...EXPLAIN.

OH YEAH? WHADDYA' NEED TO EXPLAIN, JEAN-PIERRE?

THE REASON WHY YOU'VE BEEN NUDE MODELLING FOR MY FRIEND'S DRAWING CLASS... AFTER YOU'D TOLD EVERYBODY HERE AT THE B&B THAT YOU'RE SOME BIG-TIME "GUEST PROFESSOR" AT THE COLLEGE?

OUI. PLEASE...IT EEZ NOT AS YOU THINK...

OH, I'M SURE IT IS "AS I THINK", FRENCHIE. I HAD YOU PEGGED AS A SCAM ARTIST FROM THE MOMENT YOU WALTZED YOUR PRETENTIOUS PARISIAN BUTT INTO THIS PLACE WEEKS AGO.

AND I AIN'T SURPRISED AT ALL THAT I CAUGHT YOU WITH YOUR... HEHE... PANTS DOWN.

PLEASE...YOU MUST NOT TELL RICHARD OR LANCE ABOUT ZIS!

TOO LATE FOR THAT. BUT THEN...I THINK THEY ALREADY GOT YOUR NUMBER WITHOUT MY HELP.

WHAT DO YOU MEAN?

WHAT HE MEANS IS THAT LANCE AND I ALREADY DISCOVERED THAT YOU'VE BEEN TWO-TIMING US, JEAN-PIERRE.

YES. AND THIS LATEST DISCOVERY ABOUT YOUR FALSE CREDENTIALS IS JUST THE ICING ON A VERY BAD-TASTING FRENCH PASTRY.

LANCE...RICHARD ...YOU DO NOT UNDERSTAND! I WAS SO IN LOVE WIZ YOU BOTH...

OH, SAVE THE "TORN BETWEEN TWO LOVERS" SPIEL, PEPÉ LÉ PEW.

WE HAVE MORE IMPORTANT THINGS TO DISCUSS.

WHAT "THINGS"?

THE MONEY YOU OWE US. RICHARD AND I HAVE DETERMINED THAT BETWEEN US BOTH, YOU'VE BORROWED OVER THREE THOUSAND DOLLARS. WE WANT IT BACK.

GREG FOX © 2003

AND IN CASH, TOO. I'M SURE ANY CHECK YOU'D WRITE WOULD BOUNCE HIGHER THAN THE EIFFEL TOWER.

BUT...HOW AM I TO RAISE SUCH A SUM?

I'M SURE, LIKE ANY GOOD WHORE, YOU'LL FIND A WAY. I MUST SAY, YOU'RE VERSATILE.

ISN'T HE? SO COMMAND-ING AS A "TOP".

YET SO CONVINCING AS A "BOTTOM".

MUST WE DISCUSS ZIS?

OH, I THINK WE MUST...

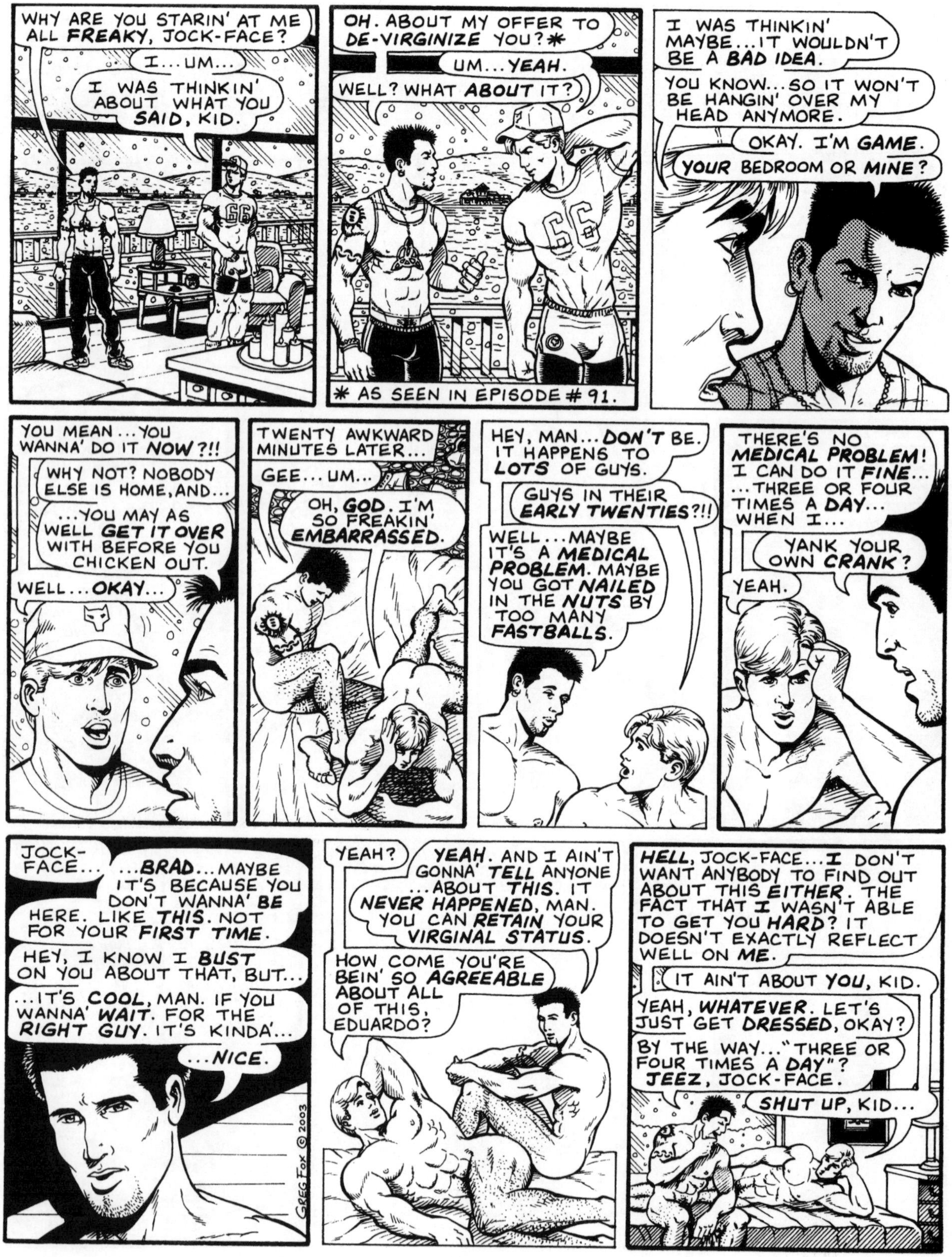
WHY ARE YOU STARIN' AT ME ALL FREAKY, JOCK-FACE?
I... UM...
I WAS THINKIN' ABOUT WHAT YOU SAID, KID.
OH. ABOUT MY OFFER TO DE-VIRGINIZE YOU?*
UM... YEAH.
WELL? WHAT ABOUT IT?
* AS SEEN IN EPISODE #91.
I WAS THINKIN' MAYBE... IT WOULDN'T BE A BAD IDEA.
YOU KNOW... SO IT WON'T BE HANGIN' OVER MY HEAD ANYMORE.
OKAY. I'M GAME.
YOUR BEDROOM OR MINE?
YOU MEAN... YOU WANNA' DO IT NOW?!!
WHY NOT? NOBODY ELSE IS HOME, AND...
...YOU MAY AS WELL GET IT OVER WITH BEFORE YOU CHICKEN OUT.
WELL... OKAY...
TWENTY AWKWARD MINUTES LATER...
GEE... UM...
OH, GOD. I'M SO FREAKIN' EMBARRASSED.
HEY, MAN... DON'T BE. IT HAPPENS TO LOTS OF GUYS.
GUYS IN THEIR EARLY TWENTIES?!!
WELL... MAYBE IT'S A MEDICAL PROBLEM. MAYBE YOU GOT NAILED IN THE NUTS BY TOO MANY FASTBALLS.
THERE'S NO MEDICAL PROBLEM! I CAN DO IT FINE... ...THREE OR FOUR TIMES A DAY... WHEN I...
YANK YOUR OWN CRANK?
YEAH.
JOCK-FACE...
...BRAD... MAYBE IT'S BECAUSE YOU DON'T WANNA' BE HERE. LIKE THIS. NOT FOR YOUR FIRST TIME.
HEY, I KNOW I BUST ON YOU ABOUT THAT, BUT...
...IT'S COOL, MAN. IF YOU WANNA' WAIT. FOR THE RIGHT GUY. IT'S KINDA'...
...NICE.
GREG FOX © 2003
YEAH?
YEAH. AND I AIN'T GONNA' TELL ANYONE ...ABOUT THIS. IT NEVER HAPPENED, MAN. YOU CAN RETAIN YOUR VIRGINAL STATUS.
HOW COME YOU'RE BEIN' SO AGREEABLE ABOUT ALL OF THIS, EDUARDO?
HELL, JOCK-FACE... I DON'T WANT ANYBODY TO FIND OUT ABOUT THIS EITHER. THE FACT THAT I WASN'T ABLE TO GET YOU HARD? IT DOESN'T EXACTLY REFLECT WELL ON ME.
IT AIN'T ABOUT YOU, KID.
YEAH, WHATEVER. LET'S JUST GET DRESSED, OKAY?
BY THE WAY... "THREE OR FOUR TIMES A DAY"? JEEZ, JOCK-FACE.
SHUT UP, KID...

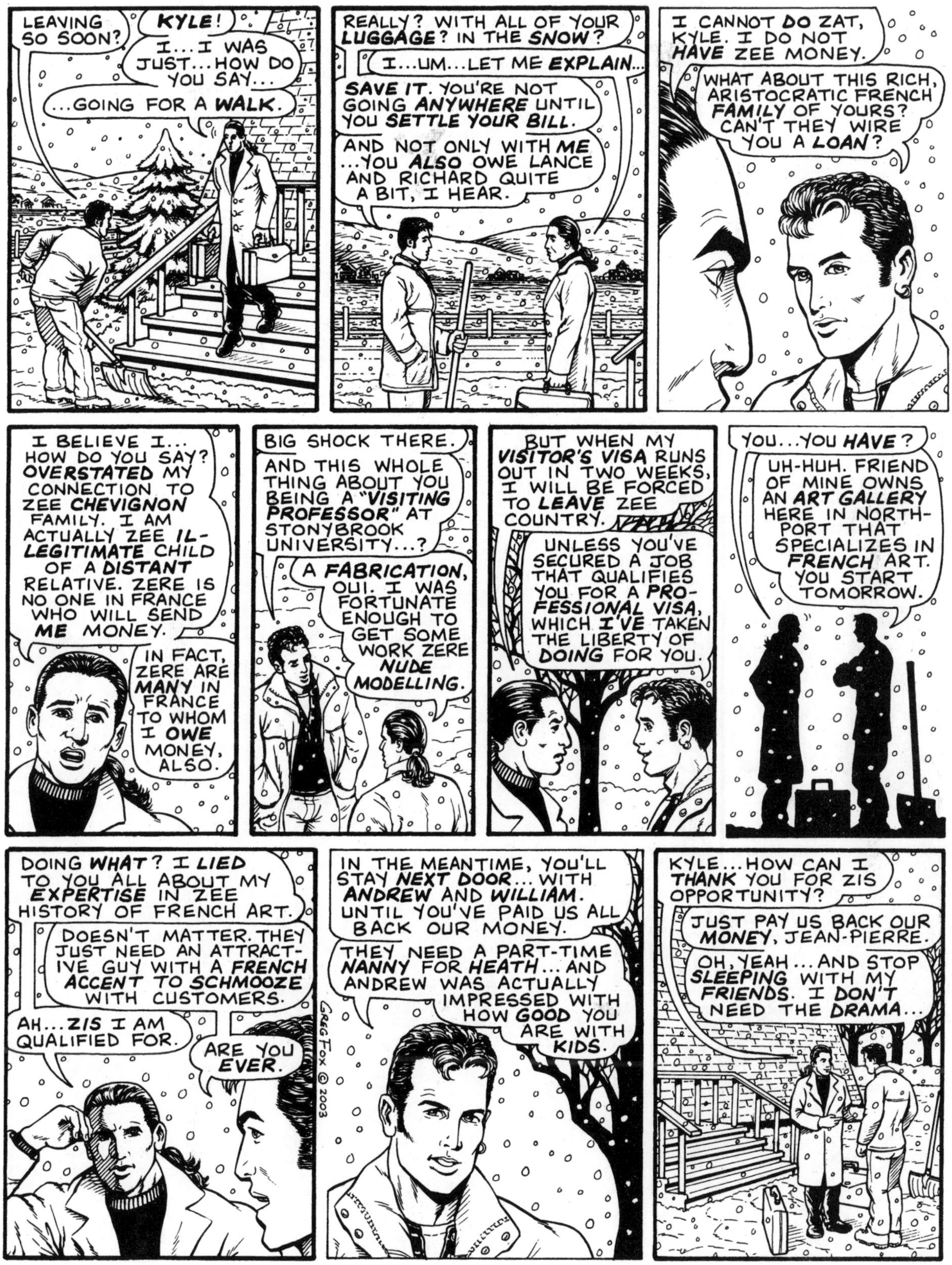
LEAVING SO SOON?
KYLE!
I... I WAS JUST... HOW DO YOU SAY...
...GOING FOR A WALK.
REALLY? WITH ALL OF YOUR LUGGAGE? IN THE SNOW?
I...UM...LET ME EXPLAIN...
SAVE IT. YOU'RE NOT GOING ANYWHERE UNTIL YOU SETTLE YOUR BILL.
AND NOT ONLY WITH ME ...YOU ALSO OWE LANCE AND RICHARD QUITE A BIT, I HEAR.
I CANNOT DO ZAT, KYLE. I DO NOT HAVE ZEE MONEY.
WHAT ABOUT THIS RICH, ARISTOCRATIC FRENCH FAMILY OF YOURS? CAN'T THEY WIRE YOU A LOAN?
I BELIEVE I... HOW DO YOU SAY? OVERSTATED MY CONNECTION TO ZEE CHEVIGNON FAMILY. I AM ACTUALLY ZEE IL-LEGITIMATE CHILD OF A DISTANT RELATIVE. ZERE IS NO ONE IN FRANCE WHO WILL SEND ME MONEY.
IN FACT, ZERE ARE MANY IN FRANCE TO WHOM I OWE MONEY, ALSO.
BIG SHOCK THERE.
AND THIS WHOLE THING ABOUT YOU BEING A "VISITING PROFESSOR" AT STONYBROOK UNIVERSITY...?
A FABRICATION, OUI. I WAS FORTUNATE ENOUGH TO GET SOME WORK ZERE NUDE MODELLING.
BUT WHEN MY VISITOR'S VISA RUNS OUT IN TWO WEEKS, I WILL BE FORCED TO LEAVE ZEE COUNTRY.
UNLESS YOU'VE SECURED A JOB THAT QUALIFIES YOU FOR A PRO-FESSIONAL VISA, WHICH I'VE TAKEN THE LIBERTY OF DOING FOR YOU.
YOU...YOU HAVE?
UH-HUH. FRIEND OF MINE OWNS AN ART GALLERY HERE IN NORTH-PORT THAT SPECIALIZES IN FRENCH ART. YOU START TOMORROW.
DOING WHAT? I LIED TO YOU ALL ABOUT MY EXPERTISE IN ZEE HISTORY OF FRENCH ART.
DOESN'T MATTER. THEY JUST NEED AN ATTRACT-IVE GUY WITH A FRENCH ACCENT TO SCHMOOZE WITH CUSTOMERS.
AH... ZIS I AM QUALIFIED FOR.
ARE YOU EVER.
GREG FOX © 2003
IN THE MEANTIME, YOU'LL STAY NEXT DOOR... WITH ANDREW AND WILLIAM. UNTIL YOU'VE PAID US ALL BACK OUR MONEY.
THEY NEED A PART-TIME NANNY FOR HEATH... AND ANDREW WAS ACTUALLY IMPRESSED WITH HOW GOOD YOU ARE WITH KIDS.
KYLE... HOW CAN I THANK YOU FOR ZIS OPPORTUNITY?
JUST PAY US BACK OUR MONEY, JEAN-PIERRE.
OH, YEAH... AND STOP SLEEPING WITH MY FRIENDS. I DON'T NEED THE DRAMA...

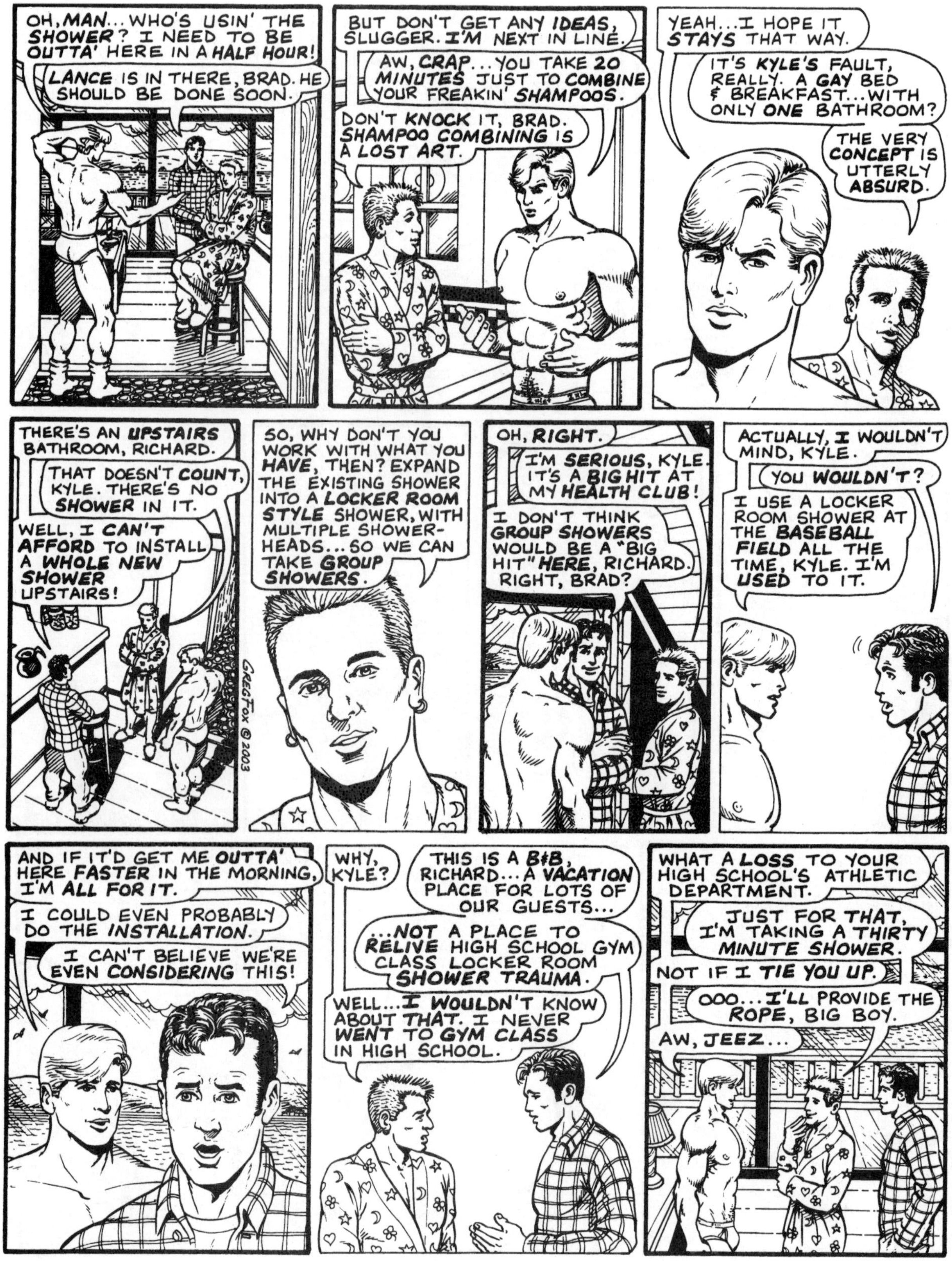

OH, MAN... WHO'S USIN' THE SHOWER? I NEED TO BE OUTTA' HERE IN A HALF HOUR!
LANCE IS IN THERE, BRAD. HE SHOULD BE DONE SOON.
BUT DON'T GET ANY IDEAS, SLUGGER. I'M NEXT IN LINE.
AW, CRAP... YOU TAKE 20 MINUTES JUST TO COMBINE YOUR FREAKIN' SHAMPOOS.
DON'T KNOCK IT, BRAD. SHAMPOO COMBINING IS A LOST ART.
YEAH... I HOPE IT STAYS THAT WAY.
IT'S KYLE'S FAULT, REALLY. A GAY BED & BREAKFAST... WITH ONLY ONE BATHROOM?
THE VERY CONCEPT IS UTTERLY ABSURD.
THERE'S AN UPSTAIRS BATHROOM, RICHARD.
THAT DOESN'T COUNT, KYLE. THERE'S NO SHOWER IN IT.
WELL, I CAN'T AFFORD TO INSTALL A WHOLE NEW SHOWER UPSTAIRS!
GREG FOX © 2003
SO, WHY DON'T YOU WORK WITH WHAT YOU HAVE, THEN? EXPAND THE EXISTING SHOWER INTO A LOCKER ROOM STYLE SHOWER, WITH MULTIPLE SHOWER-HEADS... SO WE CAN TAKE GROUP SHOWERS.
OH, RIGHT.
I'M SERIOUS, KYLE. IT'S A BIG HIT AT MY HEALTH CLUB!
I DON'T THINK GROUP SHOWERS WOULD BE A "BIG HIT" HERE, RICHARD. RIGHT, BRAD?
ACTUALLY, I WOULDN'T MIND, KYLE.
YOU WOULDN'T?
I USE A LOCKER ROOM SHOWER AT THE BASEBALL FIELD ALL THE TIME, KYLE. I'M USED TO IT.
AND IF IT'D GET ME OUTTA' HERE FASTER IN THE MORNING, I'M ALL FOR IT.
I COULD EVEN PROBABLY DO THE INSTALLATION.
I CAN'T BELIEVE WE'RE EVEN CONSIDERING THIS!
WHY, KYLE?
THIS IS A B&B, RICHARD... A VACATION PLACE FOR LOTS OF OUR GUESTS...
...NOT A PLACE TO RELIVE HIGH SCHOOL GYM CLASS LOCKER ROOM SHOWER TRAUMA.
WELL... I WOULDN'T KNOW ABOUT THAT. I NEVER WENT TO GYM CLASS IN HIGH SCHOOL.
WHAT A LOSS TO YOUR HIGH SCHOOL'S ATHLETIC DEPARTMENT.
JUST FOR THAT, I'M TAKING A THIRTY MINUTE SHOWER.
NOT IF I TIE YOU UP.
OOO... I'LL PROVIDE THE ROPE, BIG BOY.
AW, JEEZ...

DAMN, DELIA...YOU THROW PRETTY **HARD** FOR...UH...

FOR **WHAT**?!

DON'T YOU **DARE** SAY FOR A **GIRL**, STEELE...

...OR I'M GONNA' HAVE TO COME OVER THERE AND **SLAP** THOSE SCULPTED **BUNS** OF YOURS!

...FOR A **NON-PROFESSIONAL**.

NICE **SAVE**.

YEAH, I'M **KNOWN** FOR THAT.

TOO BAD YOU COULDN'T **SAVE** THAT OPENING GAME OF THE SEASON AGAINST **LEXINGTON** LAST WEEK.

DON'T **REMIND** ME. I GAVE IT **ALL** I COULD.

YEAH, BUT WITH **BLAKESLEY** PITCHING, IT WAS A LOST CAUSE.

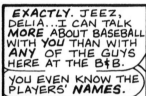

EXACTLY. JEEZ, DELIA...I CAN TALK **MORE** ABOUT BASEBALL WITH **YOU** THAN WITH **ANY** OF THE GUYS HERE AT THE B&B.

YOU EVEN KNOW THE PLAYERS' **NAMES**.

WELL, **HELL**, STEELE ...I'M AT ALMOST EVERY **HOME GAME**.

I **KNOW**. AND I **APPRECIATE** THAT.

DON'T TAKE IT AS A **PERSONAL COMPLIMENT**, STEELE. I'M NOT THERE JUST TO WATCH **YOU** PLAY. I'M THERE FOR THE **TEAM**.

AS MUCH AS THEY **SUCK** SOMETIMES.

TOO BAD YOU'RE NOT A **GUY**.

HUH?! WHAT IS **THAT** SUPPOSED TO MEAN?

I MEAN...UM...

...IF YOU WERE A **GUY**, I'D PROBABLY WANNA' **DATE** YOU. WE GOT SO MUCH IN **COMMON**.

WELL, SORRY TO DISAPPOINT YOU, BUT IF I WAS A **GUY**, I **WOULDN'T** WANT TO DATE YOU.

WHAT? WHY **NOT**?!

'CAUSE I LIKE **WOMEN**, REMEMBER?

OH. YEAH. WELL, THAT'D BE A **PROBLEM**.

GregFox © 2003

HOW ABOUT IF **YOU** WERE A **WOMAN**? YOU COULD PLAY ON MY **LESBIAN SOFTBALL** TEAM.

YEAH, RIGHT.

YOU'D BE REAL **PRETTY**, YOU KNOW THAT?

O.K., **SHUT UP** NOW...

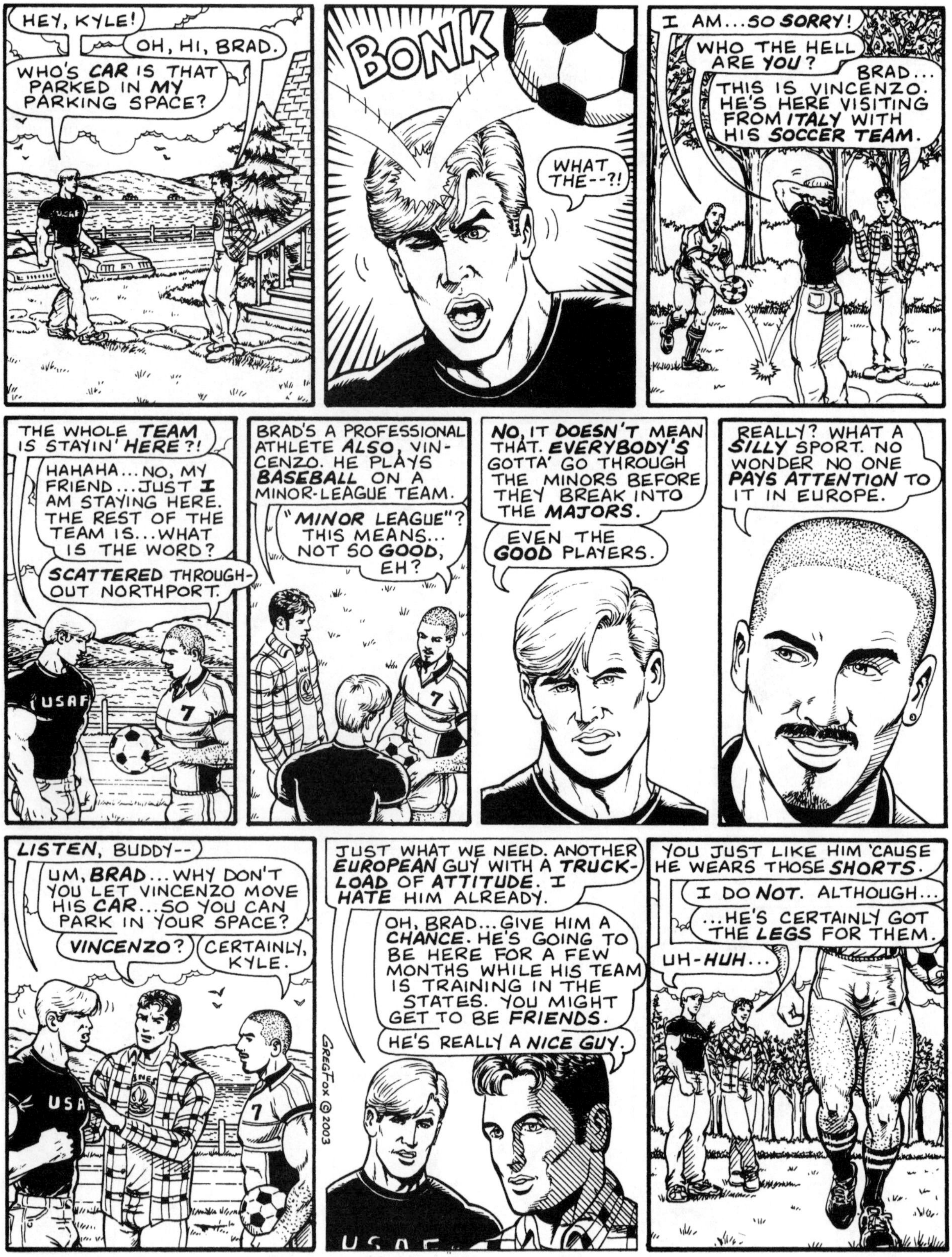
HEY, KYLE!
OH, HI, BRAD.
WHO'S CAR IS THAT PARKED IN MY PARKING SPACE?
BONK
WHAT THE--?!
I AM...SO SORRY!
WHO THE HELL ARE YOU?
BRAD... THIS IS VINCENZO. HE'S HERE VISITING FROM ITALY WITH HIS SOCCER TEAM.
USAF
7
THE WHOLE TEAM IS STAYIN' HERE?!
HAHAHA... NO, MY FRIEND... JUST I AM STAYING HERE. THE REST OF THE TEAM IS... WHAT IS THE WORD?
SCATTERED THROUGHOUT NORTHPORT.
BRAD'S A PROFESSIONAL ATHLETE ALSO, VINCENZO. HE PLAYS BASEBALL ON A MINOR-LEAGUE TEAM.
"MINOR LEAGUE"? THIS MEANS... NOT SO GOOD, EH?
NO, IT DOESN'T MEAN THAT. EVERYBODY'S GOTTA' GO THROUGH THE MINORS BEFORE THEY BREAK INTO THE MAJORS.
EVEN THE GOOD PLAYERS.
REALLY? WHAT A SILLY SPORT. NO WONDER NO ONE PAYS ATTENTION TO IT IN EUROPE.
LISTEN, BUDDY--
UM, BRAD... WHY DON'T YOU LET VINCENZO MOVE HIS CAR... SO YOU CAN PARK IN YOUR SPACE?
VINCENZO?
CERTAINLY, KYLE.
GREGFOX © 2003
JUST WHAT WE NEED. ANOTHER EUROPEAN GUY WITH A TRUCK-LOAD OF ATTITUDE. I HATE HIM ALREADY.
OH, BRAD... GIVE HIM A CHANCE. HE'S GOING TO BE HERE FOR A FEW MONTHS WHILE HIS TEAM IS TRAINING IN THE STATES. YOU MIGHT GET TO BE FRIENDS.
HE'S REALLY A NICE GUY.
YOU JUST LIKE HIM 'CAUSE HE WEARS THOSE SHORTS.
I DO NOT. ALTHOUGH...
...HE'S CERTAINLY GOT THE LEGS FOR THEM.
UH-HUH...

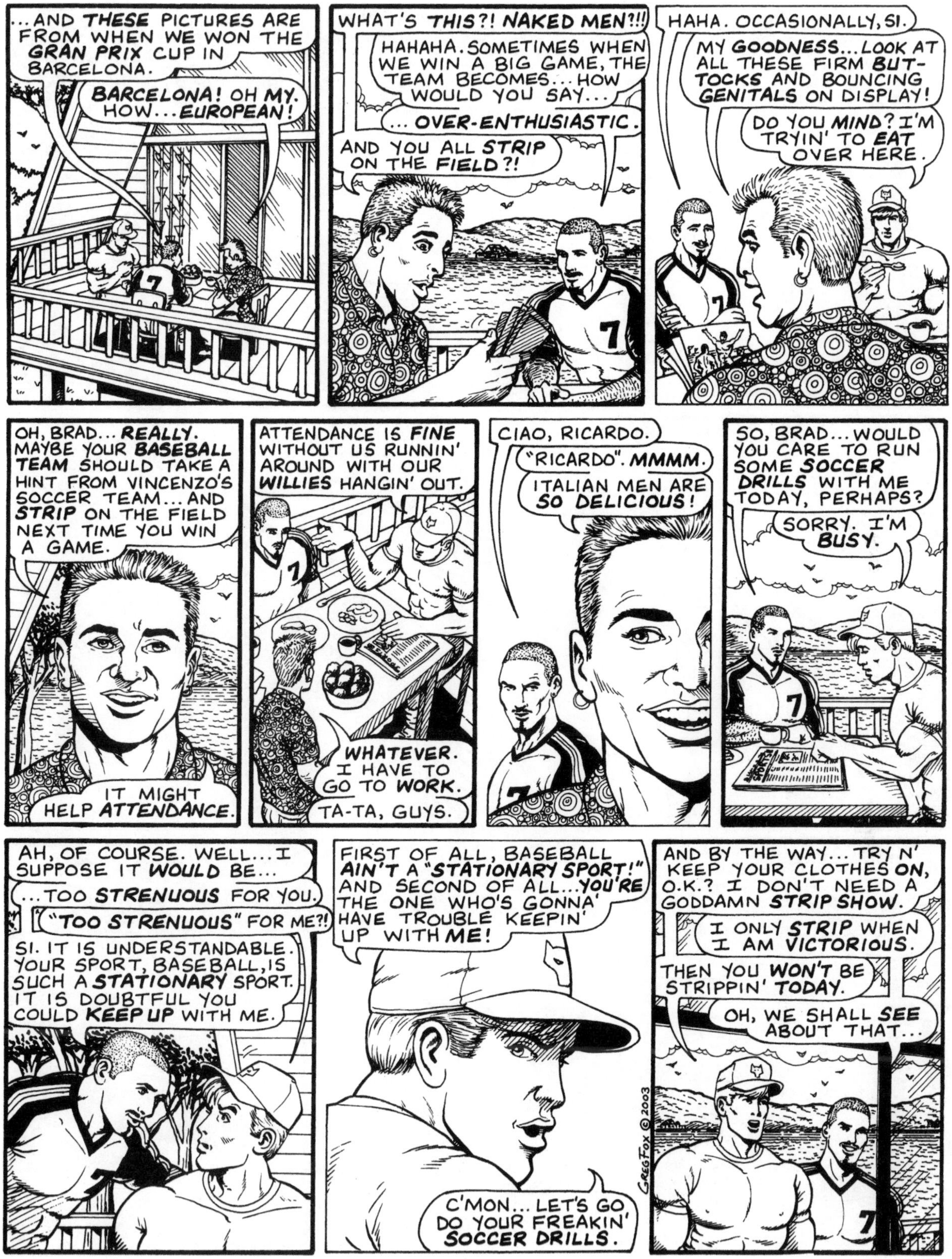
...AND THESE PICTURES ARE FROM WHEN WE WON THE GRAN PRIX CUP IN BARCELONA.
BARCELONA! OH MY. HOW... EUROPEAN!
WHAT'S THIS?! NAKED MEN?!!
HAHAHA. SOMETIMES WHEN WE WIN A BIG GAME, THE TEAM BECOMES... HOW WOULD YOU SAY...
...OVER-ENTHUSIASTIC.
AND YOU ALL STRIP ON THE FIELD?!
HAHA. OCCASIONALLY, SI.
MY GOODNESS... LOOK AT ALL THESE FIRM BUTTOCKS AND BOUNCING GENITALS ON DISPLAY!
DO YOU MIND? I'M TRYIN' TO EAT OVER HERE.
OH, BRAD... REALLY. MAYBE YOUR BASEBALL TEAM SHOULD TAKE A HINT FROM VINCENZO'S SOCCER TEAM... AND STRIP ON THE FIELD NEXT TIME YOU WIN A GAME.
IT MIGHT HELP ATTENDANCE.
ATTENDANCE IS FINE WITHOUT US RUNNIN' AROUND WITH OUR WILLIES HANGIN' OUT.
WHATEVER. I HAVE TO GO TO WORK.
TA-TA, GUYS.
CIAO, RICARDO.
"RICARDO". MMMM.
ITALIAN MEN ARE SO DELICIOUS!
SO, BRAD... WOULD YOU CARE TO RUN SOME SOCCER DRILLS WITH ME TODAY, PERHAPS?
SORRY. I'M BUSY.
AH, OF COURSE. WELL... I SUPPOSE IT WOULD BE...
...TOO STRENUOUS FOR YOU.
"TOO STRENUOUS" FOR ME?!
SI. IT IS UNDERSTANDABLE. YOUR SPORT, BASEBALL, IS SUCH A STATIONARY SPORT. IT IS DOUBTFUL YOU COULD KEEP UP WITH ME.
FIRST OF ALL, BASEBALL AIN'T A "STATIONARY SPORT!" AND SECOND OF ALL... YOU'RE THE ONE WHO'S GONNA' HAVE TROUBLE KEEPIN' UP WITH ME!
C'MON... LET'S GO DO YOUR FREAKIN' SOCCER DRILLS.
GREG FOX © 2003
AND BY THE WAY... TRY N' KEEP YOUR CLOTHES ON, O.K.? I DON'T NEED A GODDAMN STRIP SHOW.
I ONLY STRIP WHEN I AM VICTORIOUS.
THEN YOU WON'T BE STRIPPIN' TODAY.
OH, WE SHALL SEE ABOUT THAT...

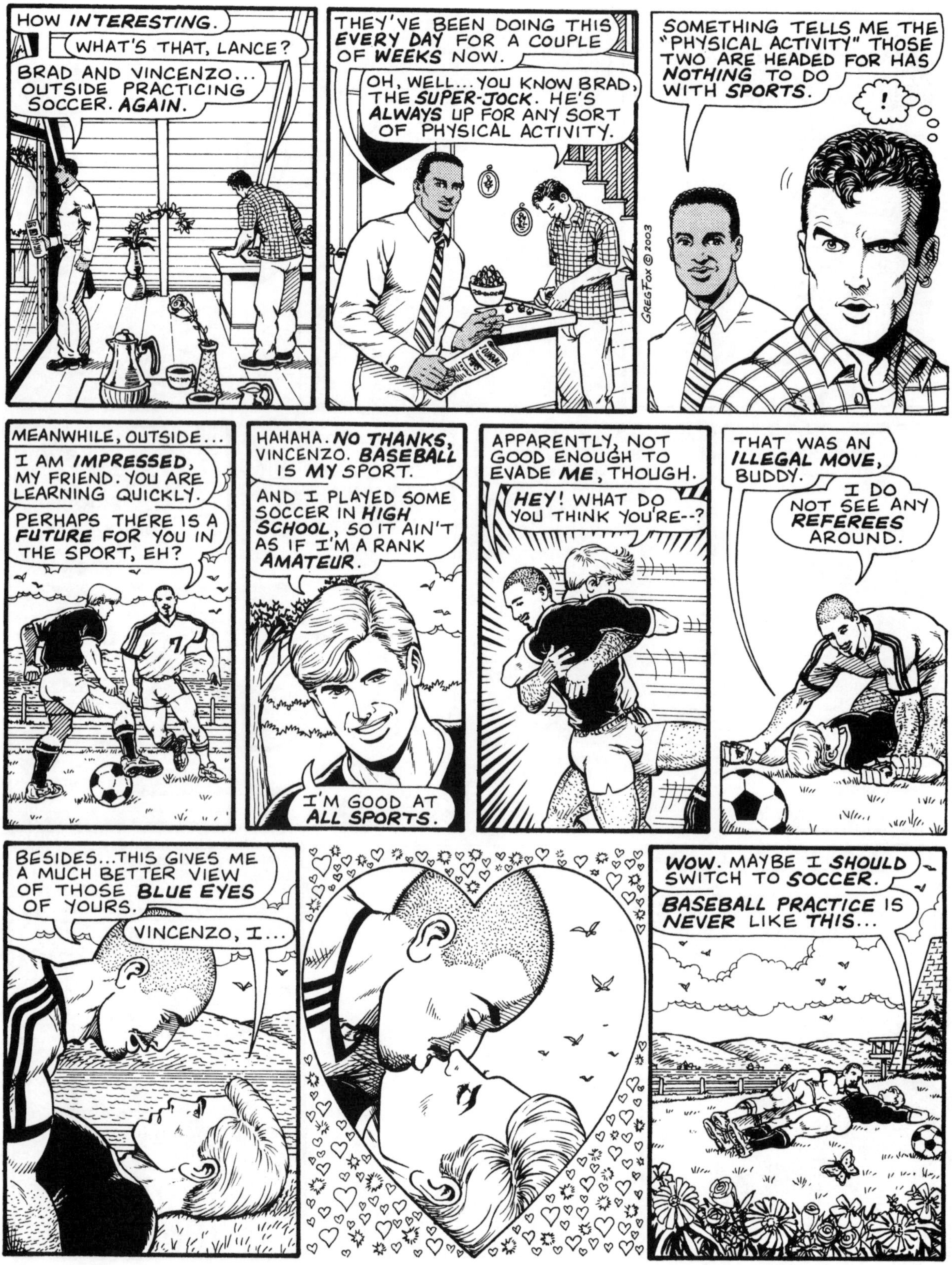
HOW INTERESTING.
WHAT'S THAT, LANCE?
BRAD AND VINCENZO... OUTSIDE PRACTICING SOCCER. AGAIN.
THEY'VE BEEN DOING THIS EVERY DAY FOR A COUPLE OF WEEKS NOW.
OH, WELL... YOU KNOW BRAD, THE SUPER-JOCK. HE'S ALWAYS UP FOR ANY SORT OF PHYSICAL ACTIVITY.
SOMETHING TELLS ME THE "PHYSICAL ACTIVITY" THOSE TWO ARE HEADED FOR HAS NOTHING TO DO WITH SPORTS.
!
GREGFOX © 2003
MEANWHILE, OUTSIDE...
I AM IMPRESSED, MY FRIEND. YOU ARE LEARNING QUICKLY.
PERHAPS THERE IS A FUTURE FOR YOU IN THE SPORT, EH?
HAHAHA. NO THANKS, VINCENZO. BASEBALL IS MY SPORT.
AND I PLAYED SOME SOCCER IN HIGH SCHOOL, SO IT AIN'T AS IF I'M A RANK AMATEUR.
I'M GOOD AT ALL SPORTS.
APPARENTLY, NOT GOOD ENOUGH TO EVADE ME, THOUGH.
HEY! WHAT DO YOU THINK YOU'RE--?
THAT WAS AN ILLEGAL MOVE, BUDDY.
I DO NOT SEE ANY REFEREES AROUND.
BESIDES... THIS GIVES ME A MUCH BETTER VIEW OF THOSE BLUE EYES OF YOURS.
VINCENZO, I...
WOW. MAYBE I SHOULD SWITCH TO SOCCER.
BASEBALL PRACTICE IS NEVER LIKE THIS...

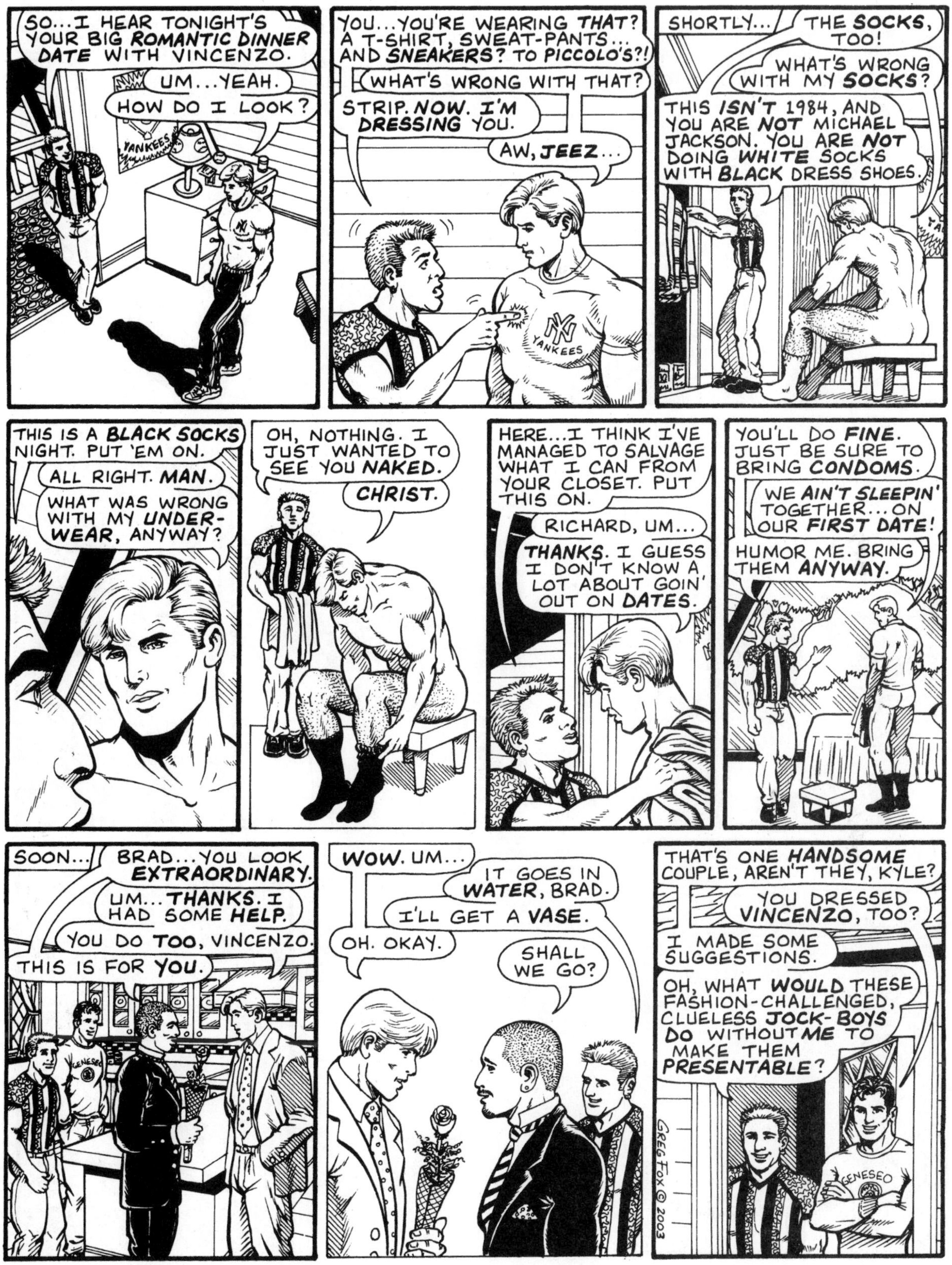
SO...I HEAR TONIGHT'S YOUR BIG ROMANTIC DINNER DATE WITH VINCENZO.
UM...YEAH.
HOW DO I LOOK?
YANKEES
YOU...YOU'RE WEARING THAT? A T-SHIRT, SWEAT-PANTS... AND SNEAKERS? TO PICCOLO'S?!
WHAT'S WRONG WITH THAT?
STRIP. NOW. I'M DRESSING YOU.
AW, JEEZ...
NY YANKEES
SHORTLY...
THE SOCKS, TOO!
WHAT'S WRONG WITH MY SOCKS?
THIS ISN'T 1984, AND YOU ARE NOT MICHAEL JACKSON. YOU ARE NOT DOING WHITE SOCKS WITH BLACK DRESS SHOES.
THIS IS A BLACK SOCKS NIGHT. PUT 'EM ON.
ALL RIGHT. MAN.
WHAT WAS WRONG WITH MY UNDER-WEAR, ANYWAY?
OH, NOTHING. I JUST WANTED TO SEE YOU NAKED.
CHRIST.
HERE...I THINK I'VE MANAGED TO SALVAGE WHAT I CAN FROM YOUR CLOSET. PUT THIS ON.
RICHARD, UM...
THANKS. I GUESS I DON'T KNOW A LOT ABOUT GOIN' OUT ON DATES.
YOU'LL DO FINE. JUST BE SURE TO BRING CONDOMS.
WE AIN'T SLEEPIN' TOGETHER...ON OUR FIRST DATE!
HUMOR ME. BRING THEM ANYWAY.
SOON...
BRAD...YOU LOOK EXTRAORDINARY.
UM...THANKS. I HAD SOME HELP.
YOU DO TOO, VINCENZO.
THIS IS FOR YOU.
GENESEO
WOW. UM...
IT GOES IN WATER, BRAD.
I'LL GET A VASE.
OH. OKAY.
SHALL WE GO?
GREG FOX © 2003
THAT'S ONE HANDSOME COUPLE, AREN'T THEY, KYLE?
YOU DRESSED VINCENZO, TOO?
I MADE SOME SUGGESTIONS.
OH, WHAT WOULD THESE FASHION-CHALLENGED, CLUELESS JOCK-BOYS DO WITHOUT ME TO MAKE THEM PRESENTABLE?
GENESEO

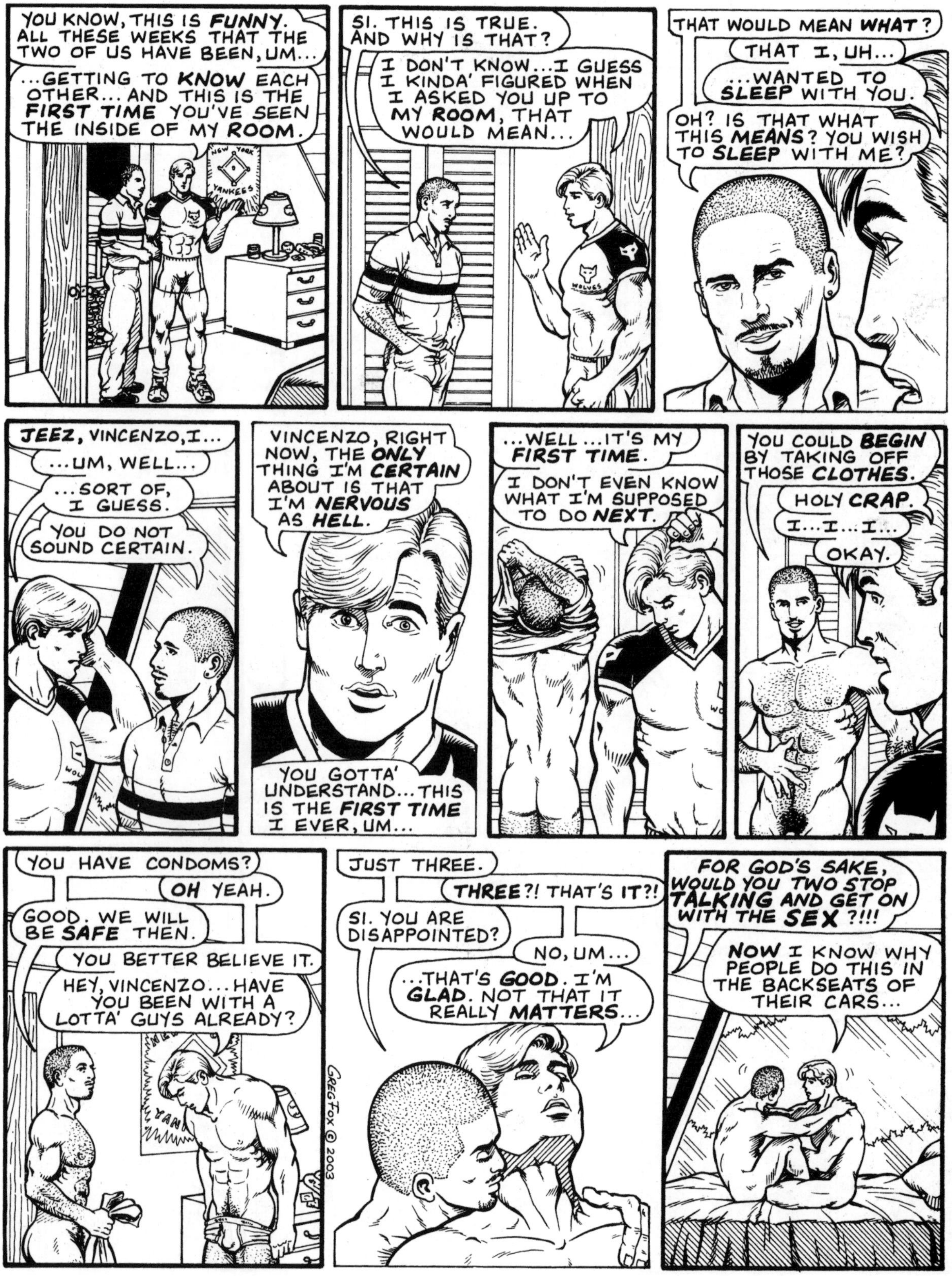
YOU KNOW, THIS IS FUNNY. ALL THESE WEEKS THAT THE TWO OF US HAVE BEEN, UM...
...GETTING TO KNOW EACH OTHER... AND THIS IS THE FIRST TIME YOU'VE SEEN THE INSIDE OF MY ROOM.
NEW YORK YANKEES
SI. THIS IS TRUE. AND WHY IS THAT?
I DON'T KNOW...I GUESS I KINDA' FIGURED WHEN I ASKED YOU UP TO MY ROOM, THAT WOULD MEAN...
WOLVES
THAT WOULD MEAN WHAT?
THAT I, UH...
...WANTED TO SLEEP WITH YOU.
OH? IS THAT WHAT THIS MEANS? YOU WISH TO SLEEP WITH ME?
JEEZ, VINCENZO, I...
...UM, WELL...
...SORT OF, I GUESS.
YOU DO NOT SOUND CERTAIN.
VINCENZO, RIGHT NOW, THE ONLY THING I'M CERTAIN ABOUT IS THAT I'M NERVOUS AS HELL.
YOU GOTTA' UNDERSTAND... THIS IS THE FIRST TIME I EVER, UM...
...WELL ...IT'S MY FIRST TIME.
I DON'T EVEN KNOW WHAT I'M SUPPOSED TO DO NEXT.
YOU COULD BEGIN BY TAKING OFF THOSE CLOTHES.
HOLY CRAP.
I...I...I...
OKAY.
YOU HAVE CONDOMS?
OH YEAH.
GOOD. WE WILL BE SAFE THEN.
YOU BETTER BELIEVE IT.
HEY, VINCENZO... HAVE YOU BEEN WITH A LOTTA' GUYS ALREADY?
GREG FOX © 2003
JUST THREE.
THREE?! THAT'S IT?!
SI. YOU ARE DISAPPOINTED?
NO, UM...
...THAT'S GOOD. I'M GLAD. NOT THAT IT REALLY MATTERS...
FOR GOD'S SAKE, WOULD YOU TWO STOP TALKING AND GET ON WITH THE SEX?!!!
NOW I KNOW WHY PEOPLE DO THIS IN THE BACKSEATS OF THEIR CARS...

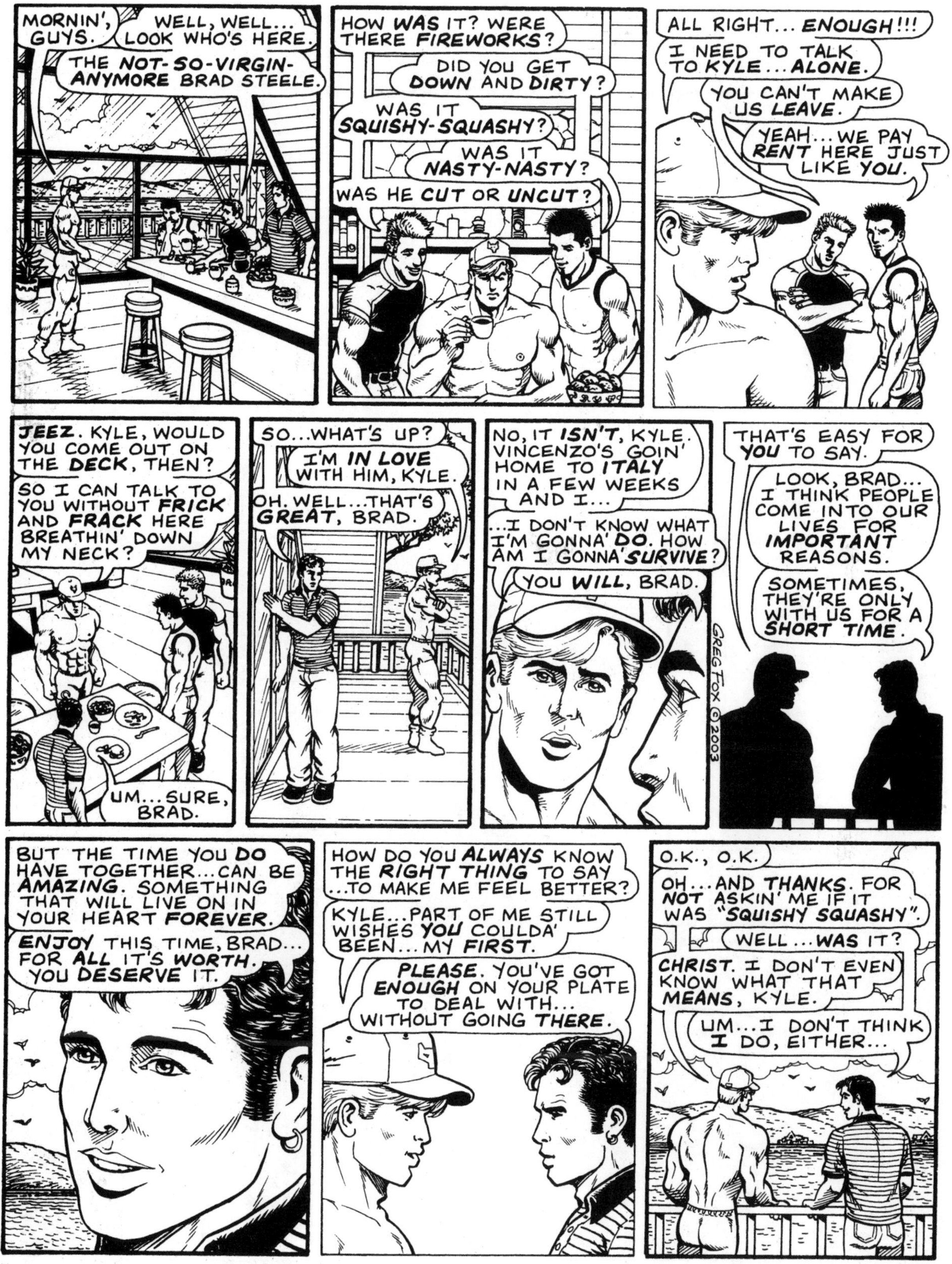
MORNIN', GUYS.
WELL, WELL... LOOK WHO'S HERE.
THE NOT-SO-VIRGIN-ANYMORE BRAD STEELE.
HOW WAS IT? WERE THERE FIREWORKS?
DID YOU GET DOWN AND DIRTY?
WAS IT SQUISHY-SQUASHY?
WAS IT NASTY-NASTY?
WAS HE CUT OR UNCUT?
ALL RIGHT... ENOUGH!!!
I NEED TO TALK TO KYLE... ALONE.
YOU CAN'T MAKE US LEAVE.
YEAH... WE PAY RENT HERE JUST LIKE YOU.
JEEZ. KYLE, WOULD YOU COME OUT ON THE DECK, THEN?
SO I CAN TALK TO YOU WITHOUT FRICK AND FRACK HERE BREATHIN' DOWN MY NECK?
UM... SURE, BRAD.
SO...WHAT'S UP?
I'M IN LOVE WITH HIM, KYLE.
OH. WELL...THAT'S GREAT, BRAD.
NO, IT ISN'T, KYLE. VINCENZO'S GOIN' HOME TO ITALY IN A FEW WEEKS AND I...
...I DON'T KNOW WHAT I'M GONNA' DO. HOW AM I GONNA' SURVIVE?
YOU WILL, BRAD.
GREG FOX © 2003
THAT'S EASY FOR YOU TO SAY.
LOOK, BRAD... I THINK PEOPLE COME INTO OUR LIVES FOR IMPORTANT REASONS.
SOMETIMES, THEY'RE ONLY WITH US FOR A SHORT TIME.
BUT THE TIME YOU DO HAVE TOGETHER...CAN BE AMAZING. SOMETHING THAT WILL LIVE ON IN YOUR HEART FOREVER.
ENJOY THIS TIME, BRAD... FOR ALL IT'S WORTH. YOU DESERVE IT.
HOW DO YOU ALWAYS KNOW THE RIGHT THING TO SAY ...TO MAKE ME FEEL BETTER?
KYLE...PART OF ME STILL WISHES YOU COULDA' BEEN... MY FIRST.
PLEASE. YOU'VE GOT ENOUGH ON YOUR PLATE TO DEAL WITH... WITHOUT GOING THERE.
O.K., O.K.
OH... AND THANKS. FOR NOT ASKIN' ME IF IT WAS "SQUISHY SQUASHY".
WELL... WAS IT?
CHRIST. I DON'T EVEN KNOW WHAT THAT MEANS, KYLE.
UM... I DON'T THINK I DO, EITHER...

YOU DID NOT NEED TO DRIVE ME TO THE AIRPORT, BRAD. I COULD HAVE TAKEN THE SHUTTLE WITH THE REST OF MY SOCCER TEAM.

I WANTED TO TO DRIVE YOU, VINCENZO. IS THAT O.K.?

SI, MY FRIEND. IT IS VERY..."O.K."

WE BETTER MOVE IT, OR YOU'RE GONNA' MISS YOUR--

AW, JEEZ.

WHAT IS WRONG?

I JUST REALIZED, I'M NOT GONNA' BE ABLE TO KISS YOU GOODBYE.

WHY NOT?

'CAUSE WE'RE IN A PUBLIC PLACE, VINCENZO. THE T.W.A. TERMINAL AT KENNEDY AIRPORT IS ABOUT AS PUBLIC AS YOU CAN GET.

AND... THIS IS A PROBLEM?

OF COURSE IT'S A PROBLEM. YOU KNOW I'M A PRO-BASEBALL PLAYER... AND I'M STILL IN THE CLOSET.

PUBLICLY, AT LEAST.

I SEE. HOW... UNFORTUNATE YOU FEEL THIS WAY.

FLIGHT 342 TO ROME NOW BOARDING AT GATE 6.

THAT IS MY FLIGHT, BRAD...

VINCENZO... I...

...THERE'S SO MUCH I WANNA' SAY. I JUST...

...DAMN.

ARRIVEDERCI, BRAD.

GOODBYE, VINCENZO. IT WAS...

...AWESOME, MAN. I... I...

AW, JEEZ... WHAT THE HELL...

WHAT ABOUT THE "CLOSET"?

SCREW IT. I'M STILL IN THE MINOR LEAGUES, ANYWAY. NOBODY HERE KNOWS ME.

BESIDES... I WOULDA' REGRETTED IT FOR THE REST OF MY LIFE IF I LET YOU GO WITHOUT KISSING YOU GOODBYE.

I WILL ALWAYS TREASURE OUR TIME TOGETHER, MY GOLDEN AMERICAN BOY.

S-SAME HERE, VINCENZO.

ARRIVEDERCI, MY LOVE.

ARRIVEDERCI, VINCENZO...

...ARRIVEDERCI.

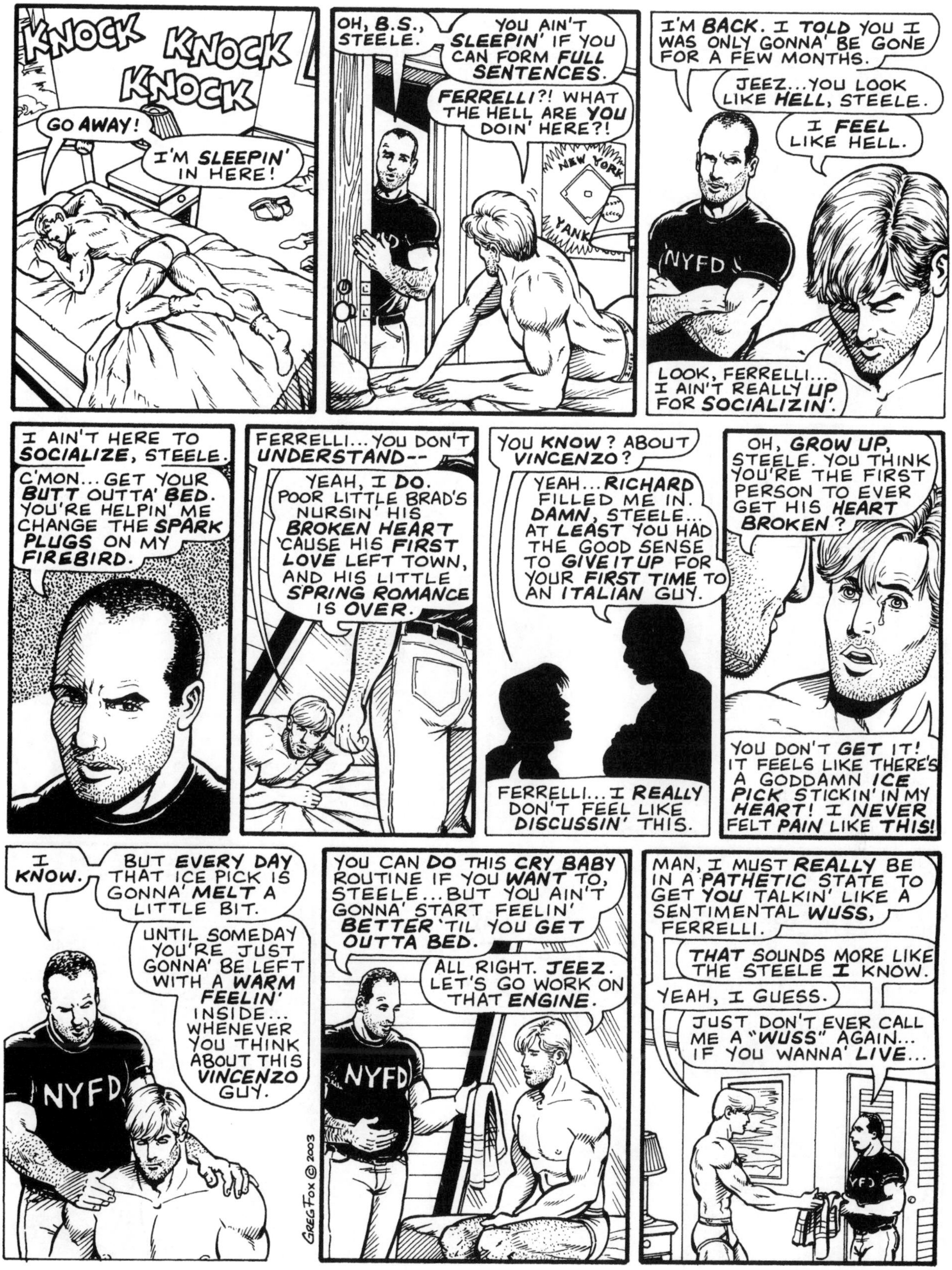
KNOCK KNOCK KNOCK
GO AWAY!
I'M SLEEPIN' IN HERE!
OH, B.S., STEELE.
YOU AIN'T SLEEPIN' IF YOU CAN FORM FULL SENTENCES.
FERRELLI?! WHAT THE HELL ARE YOU DOIN' HERE?!
NEW YORK
YANK
I'M BACK. I TOLD YOU I WAS ONLY GONNA' BE GONE FOR A FEW MONTHS.
JEEZ...YOU LOOK LIKE HELL, STEELE.
I FEEL LIKE HELL.
LOOK, FERRELLI... I AIN'T REALLY UP FOR SOCIALIZIN'.
I AIN'T HERE TO SOCIALIZE, STEELE.
C'MON... GET YOUR BUTT OUTTA' BED. YOU'RE HELPIN' ME CHANGE THE SPARK PLUGS ON MY FIREBIRD.
FERRELLI... YOU DON'T UNDERSTAND--
YEAH, I DO. POOR LITTLE BRAD'S NURSIN' HIS BROKEN HEART 'CAUSE HIS FIRST LOVE LEFT TOWN, AND HIS LITTLE SPRING ROMANCE IS OVER.
YOU KNOW? ABOUT VINCENZO?
YEAH... RICHARD FILLED ME IN. DAMN, STEELE... AT LEAST YOU HAD THE GOOD SENSE TO GIVE IT UP FOR YOUR FIRST TIME TO AN ITALIAN GUY.
FERRELLI... I REALLY DON'T FEEL LIKE DISCUSSIN' THIS.
OH, GROW UP, STEELE. YOU THINK YOU'RE THE FIRST PERSON TO EVER GET HIS HEART BROKEN?
YOU DON'T GET IT! IT FEELS LIKE THERE'S A GODDAMN ICE PICK STICKIN' IN MY HEART! I NEVER FELT PAIN LIKE THIS!
I KNOW.
BUT EVERY DAY THAT ICE PICK IS GONNA' MELT A LITTLE BIT.
UNTIL SOMEDAY YOU'RE JUST GONNA' BE LEFT WITH A WARM FEELIN' INSIDE... WHENEVER YOU THINK ABOUT THIS VINCENZO GUY.
GREG FOX © 2003
YOU CAN DO THIS CRY BABY ROUTINE IF YOU WANT TO, STEELE... BUT YOU AIN'T GONNA' START FEELIN' BETTER 'TIL YOU GET OUTTA BED.
ALL RIGHT. JEEZ. LET'S GO WORK ON THAT ENGINE.
MAN, I MUST REALLY BE IN A PATHETIC STATE TO GET YOU TALKIN' LIKE A SENTIMENTAL WUSS, FERRELLI.
THAT SOUNDS MORE LIKE THE STEELE I KNOW.
YEAH, I GUESS.
JUST DON'T EVER CALL ME A "WUSS" AGAIN... IF YOU WANNA' LIVE...

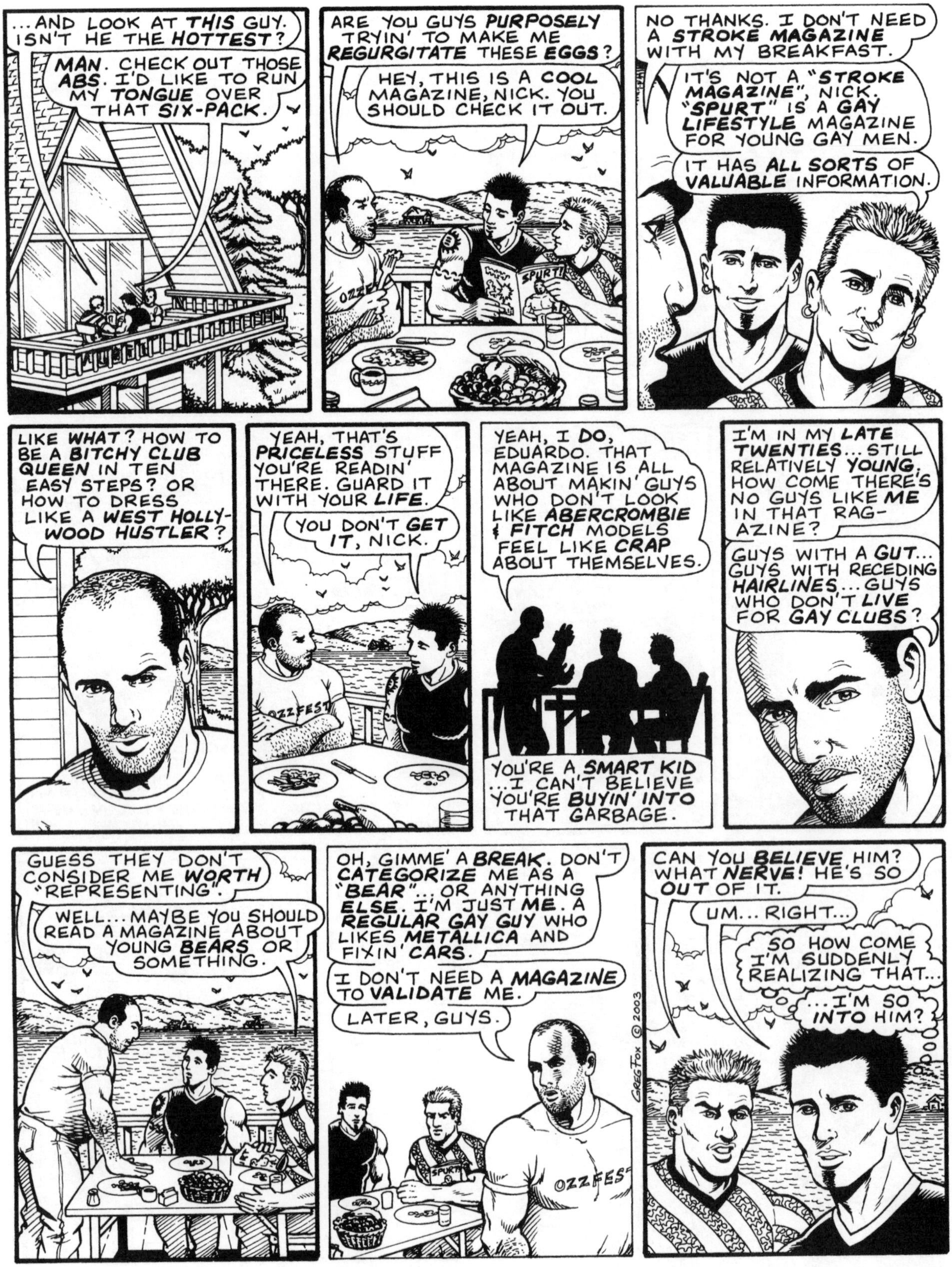
...AND LOOK AT THIS GUY. ISN'T HE THE HOTTEST?
MAN. CHECK OUT THOSE ABS. I'D LIKE TO RUN MY TONGUE OVER THAT SIX-PACK.
ARE YOU GUYS PURPOSELY TRYIN' TO MAKE ME REGURGITATE THESE EGGS?
HEY, THIS IS A COOL MAGAZINE, NICK. YOU SHOULD CHECK IT OUT.
SPURT
OZZF
NO THANKS. I DON'T NEED A STROKE MAGAZINE WITH MY BREAKFAST.
IT'S NOT A "STROKE MAGAZINE", NICK. "SPURT" IS A GAY LIFESTYLE MAGAZINE FOR YOUNG GAY MEN.
IT HAS ALL SORTS OF VALUABLE INFORMATION.
LIKE WHAT? HOW TO BE A BITCHY CLUB QUEEN IN TEN EASY STEPS? OR HOW TO DRESS LIKE A WEST HOLLY-WOOD HUSTLER?
YEAH, THAT'S PRICELESS STUFF YOU'RE READIN' THERE. GUARD IT WITH YOUR LIFE.
YOU DON'T GET IT, NICK.
OZZFEST
YEAH, I DO, EDUARDO. THAT MAGAZINE IS ALL ABOUT MAKIN' GUYS WHO DON'T LOOK LIKE ABERCROMBIE & FITCH MODELS FEEL LIKE CRAP ABOUT THEMSELVES.
YOU'RE A SMART KID ...I CAN'T BELIEVE YOU'RE BUYIN' INTO THAT GARBAGE.
I'M IN MY LATE TWENTIES... STILL RELATIVELY YOUNG. HOW COME THERE'S NO GUYS LIKE ME IN THAT RAG-AZINE?
GUYS WITH A GUT... GUYS WITH RECEDING HAIRLINES... GUYS WHO DON'T LIVE FOR GAY CLUBS?
GUESS THEY DON'T CONSIDER ME WORTH "REPRESENTING".
WELL... MAYBE YOU SHOULD READ A MAGAZINE ABOUT YOUNG BEARS OR SOMETHING.
OH, GIMME' A BREAK. DON'T CATEGORIZE ME AS A "BEAR"... OR ANYTHING ELSE. I'M JUST ME. A REGULAR GAY GUY WHO LIKES METALLICA AND FIXIN' CARS.
I DON'T NEED A MAGAZINE TO VALIDATE ME.
LATER, GUYS.
GREG FOX © 2003
SPURT
OZZFES
CAN YOU BELIEVE HIM? WHAT NERVE! HE'S SO OUT OF IT.
UM... RIGHT...
SO HOW COME I'M SUDDENLY REALIZING THAT...
...I'M SO INTO HIM?

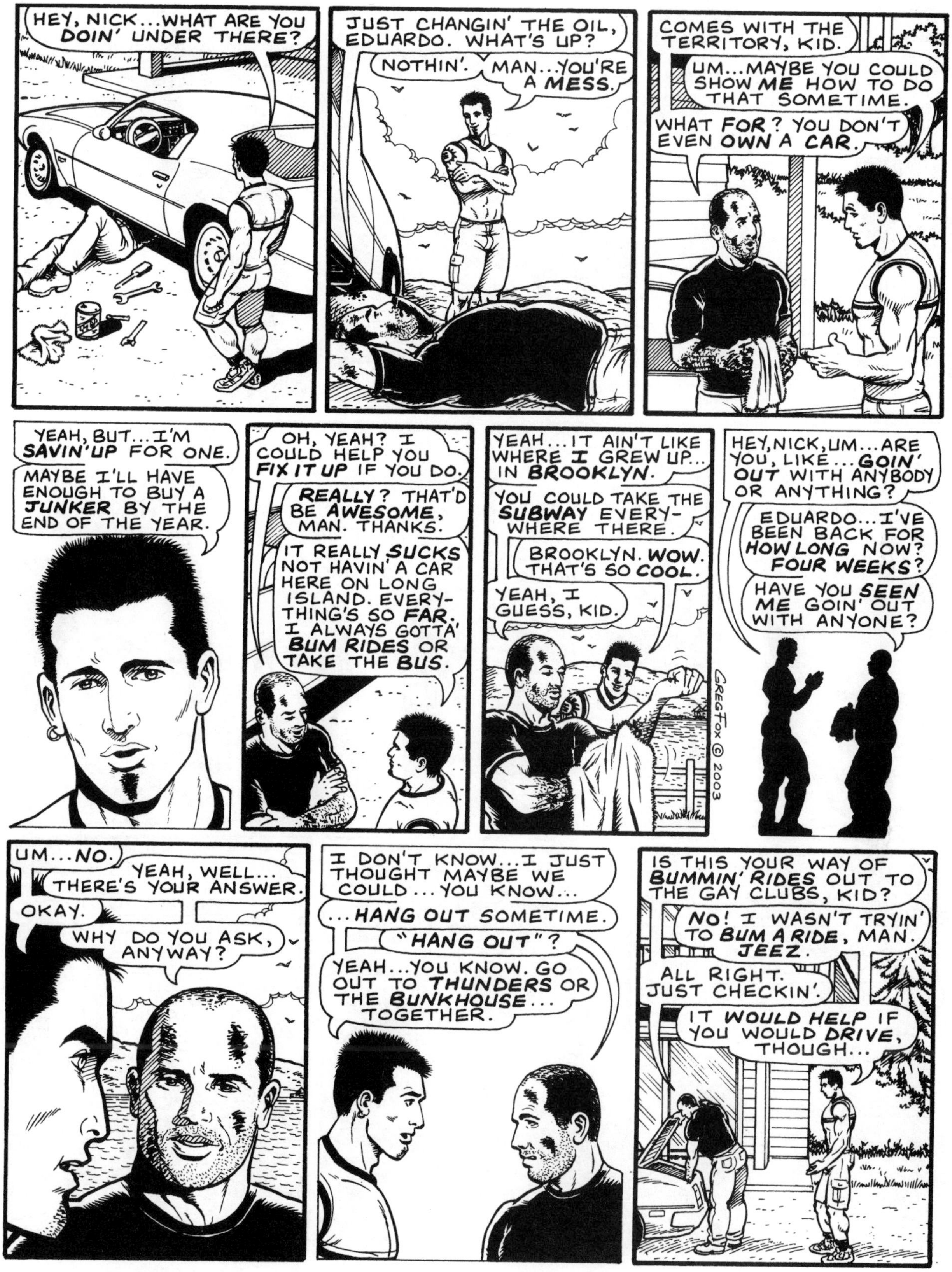
HEY, NICK...WHAT ARE YOU DOIN' UNDER THERE?
JUST CHANGIN' THE OIL, EDUARDO. WHAT'S UP?
NOTHIN'.
MAN...YOU'RE A MESS.
COMES WITH THE TERRITORY, KID.
UM...MAYBE YOU COULD SHOW ME HOW TO DO THAT SOMETIME.
WHAT FOR? YOU DON'T EVEN OWN A CAR.
YEAH, BUT...I'M SAVIN' UP FOR ONE.
MAYBE I'LL HAVE ENOUGH TO BUY A JUNKER BY THE END OF THE YEAR.
OH, YEAH? I COULD HELP YOU FIX IT UP IF YOU DO.
REALLY? THAT'D BE AWESOME, MAN. THANKS.
IT REALLY SUCKS NOT HAVIN' A CAR HERE ON LONG ISLAND. EVERY-THING'S SO FAR. I ALWAYS GOTTA' BUM RIDES OR TAKE THE BUS.
YEAH...IT AIN'T LIKE WHERE I GREW UP... IN BROOKLYN.
YOU COULD TAKE THE SUBWAY EVERY-WHERE THERE.
BROOKLYN. WOW. THAT'S SO COOL.
YEAH, I GUESS, KID.
GREG FOX © 2003
HEY, NICK, UM...ARE YOU, LIKE...GOIN' OUT WITH ANYBODY OR ANYTHING?
EDUARDO...I'VE BEEN BACK FOR HOW LONG NOW? FOUR WEEKS?
HAVE YOU SEEN ME GOIN' OUT WITH ANYONE?
UM...NO.
YEAH, WELL... THERE'S YOUR ANSWER.
OKAY.
WHY DO YOU ASK, ANYWAY?
I DON'T KNOW...I JUST THOUGHT MAYBE WE COULD...YOU KNOW...
...HANG OUT SOMETIME.
"HANG OUT"?
YEAH...YOU KNOW. GO OUT TO THUNDERS OR THE BUNKHOUSE... TOGETHER.
IS THIS YOUR WAY OF BUMMIN' RIDES OUT TO THE GAY CLUBS, KID?
NO! I WASN'T TRYIN' TO BUM A RIDE, MAN. JEEZ.
ALL RIGHT. JUST CHECKIN'.
IT WOULD HELP IF YOU WOULD DRIVE, THOUGH...

NICK?! WHERE ARE YOU GOIN'?!

HOME, KID. THIS SCENE AIN'T FOR ME.

YOU...YOU WERE JUST GONNA' LEAVE...WITHOUT TELLIN' ME?

YOU SEEMED TO BE DOIN' A PRETTY GOOD JOB OF IGNORIN' ME FOR THE PAST FORTY-FIVE MINUTES, EDUARDO...HANGIN' OUT WITH YOUR CATTY CLUB FRIENDS.

I...I'M SORRY. SOMETIMES I JUST GET SWEPT AWAY WHEN I HANG OUT WITH THOSE GUYS.

YEAH...I NOTICED.

DON'T YOU LIKE MY FRIENDS, NICK?

I DON'T THINK THEY LIKED ME TOO MUCH, EDUARDO. I'VE GOTTEN FRIENDLIER TREATMENT AT TRAFFIC COURT.

AAH...IT JUST TAKES A WHILE TO GET TO KNOW THEM, MAN.

SOMETHIN' TELLS ME THEY AIN'T WORTH THE EFFORT.

LOOK...THIS WAS PROBABLY A BAD IDEA...US COMIN' HERE TOGETHER.

ALL RIGHT. LET'S GO SOMEWHERE ELSE. HOW ABOUT THE BUNKHOUSE?

NO, KID...WHAT I MEANT WAS...

...THE TWO OF US... TOGETHER.

BAD IDEA.

BUT...WHY? I REALLY LIKE YOU, MAN.

IT'LL NEVER WORK OUT, KID. I'M NOT INTO THE SAME STUFF AS YOU. WHY WOULD YOU EVEN WANNA' BE WITH A GUY LIKE ME, ANYWAY?

'CAUSE YOU'RE REAL...'CAUSE YOU SAY WHAT'S ON YOUR MIND, AND YOU DON'T GIVE A CRAP ABOUT WHAT OTHER PEOPLE THINK. I LIKE THAT.

O.K., THEN. YOU WANNA' HONESTLY HEAR WHAT'S ON MY MIND RIGHT NOW?

GO AHEAD.

ALL RIGHT. YOU'RE SMART, EDUARDO...YOU'RE CUTE...

...AND YOU'RE ALSO MISSIN' YOUR FAMILY A WHOLE LOT MORE THAN YOU WANNA' ADMIT. I THINK YOU SEE ME AS SOME KINDA' FATHER FIGURE...

...AND THAT'S A ROLE I JUST DON'T WANNA' PLAY. ESPECIALLY WITH A GUY I'M DATING.

GREG FOX ©2003

I CAN BE YOUR FRIEND, EDUARDO...

...BUT NOTHIN' MORE THAN FRIENDS. GOT IT?

JEEZ. DO I HAVE ANY OTHER CHOICES?

WELL...WE COULD BE ENEMIES. BUT THAT'S NEVER FUN WHEN YOU'RE SHARIN' A BATHROOM WITH SOMEBODY...

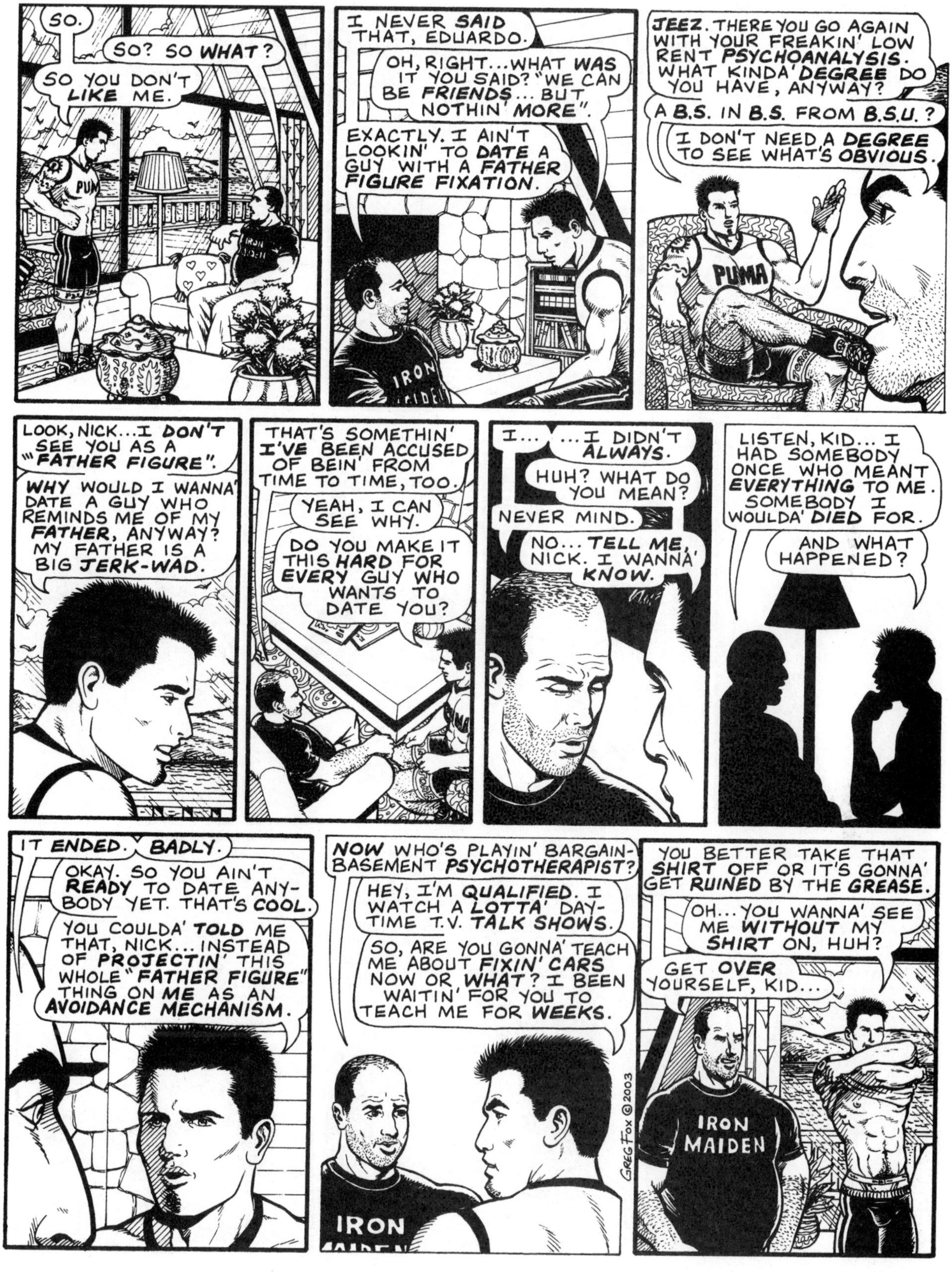
SO.
SO? SO WHAT?
SO YOU DON'T LIKE ME.
I NEVER SAID THAT, EDUARDO.
OH, RIGHT... WHAT WAS IT YOU SAID? "WE CAN BE FRIENDS... BUT NOTHIN' MORE".
EXACTLY. I AIN'T LOOKIN' TO DATE A GUY WITH A FATHER FIGURE FIXATION.
JEEZ. THERE YOU GO AGAIN WITH YOUR FREAKIN' LOW RENT PSYCHOANALYSIS. WHAT KINDA' DEGREE DO YOU HAVE, ANYWAY?
A B.S. IN B.S. FROM B.S.U.?
I DON'T NEED A DEGREE TO SEE WHAT'S OBVIOUS.
LOOK, NICK... I DON'T SEE YOU AS A "FATHER FIGURE".
WHY WOULD I WANNA' DATE A GUY WHO REMINDS ME OF MY FATHER, ANYWAY? MY FATHER IS A BIG JERK-WAD.
THAT'S SOMETHIN' I'VE BEEN ACCUSED OF BEIN' FROM TIME TO TIME, TOO.
YEAH, I CAN SEE WHY.
DO YOU MAKE IT THIS HARD FOR EVERY GUY WHO WANTS TO DATE YOU?
I...
...I DIDN'T ALWAYS.
HUH? WHAT DO YOU MEAN?
NEVER MIND.
NO... TELL ME, NICK. I WANNA' KNOW.
LISTEN, KID... I HAD SOMEBODY ONCE WHO MEANT EVERYTHING TO ME. SOMEBODY I WOULDA' DIED FOR.
AND WHAT HAPPENED?
IT ENDED.
BADLY.
OKAY. SO YOU AIN'T READY TO DATE ANYBODY YET. THAT'S COOL.
YOU COULDA' TOLD ME THAT, NICK... INSTEAD OF PROJECTIN' THIS WHOLE "FATHER FIGURE" THING ON ME AS AN AVOIDANCE MECHANISM.
NOW WHO'S PLAYIN' BARGAIN-BASEMENT PSYCHOTHERAPIST?
HEY, I'M QUALIFIED. I WATCH A LOTTA' DAYTIME T.V. TALK SHOWS.
SO, ARE YOU GONNA' TEACH ME ABOUT FIXIN' CARS NOW OR WHAT? I BEEN WAITIN' FOR YOU TO TEACH ME FOR WEEKS.
GREG FOX ©2003
YOU BETTER TAKE THAT SHIRT OFF OR IT'S GONNA' GET RUINED BY THE GREASE.
OH... YOU WANNA' SEE ME WITHOUT MY SHIRT ON, HUH?
GET OVER YOURSELF, KID...

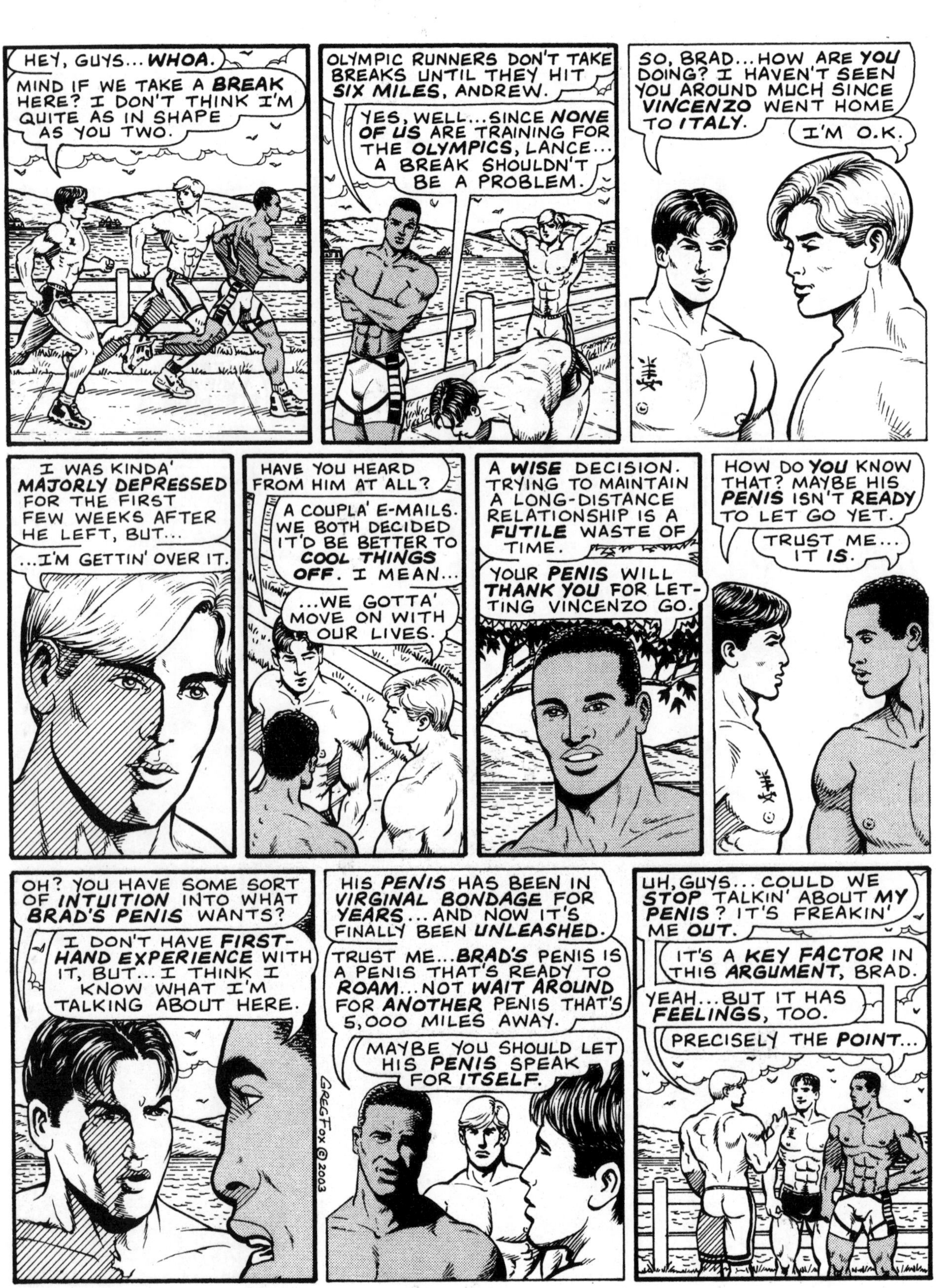
HEY, GUYS... WHOA.
MIND IF WE TAKE A BREAK HERE? I DON'T THINK I'M QUITE AS IN SHAPE AS YOU TWO.
OLYMPIC RUNNERS DON'T TAKE BREAKS UNTIL THEY HIT SIX MILES, ANDREW.
YES, WELL... SINCE NONE OF US ARE TRAINING FOR THE OLYMPICS, LANCE... A BREAK SHOULDN'T BE A PROBLEM.
SO, BRAD... HOW ARE YOU DOING? I HAVEN'T SEEN YOU AROUND MUCH SINCE VINCENZO WENT HOME TO ITALY.
I'M O.K.
I WAS KINDA' MAJORLY DEPRESSED FOR THE FIRST FEW WEEKS AFTER HE LEFT, BUT...
...I'M GETTIN' OVER IT.
HAVE YOU HEARD FROM HIM AT ALL?
A COUPLA' E-MAILS. WE BOTH DECIDED IT'D BE BETTER TO COOL THINGS OFF. I MEAN...
...WE GOTTA' MOVE ON WITH OUR LIVES.
A WISE DECISION. TRYING TO MAINTAIN A LONG-DISTANCE RELATIONSHIP IS A FUTILE WASTE OF TIME.
YOUR PENIS WILL THANK YOU FOR LETTING VINCENZO GO.
HOW DO YOU KNOW THAT? MAYBE HIS PENIS ISN'T READY TO LET GO YET.
TRUST ME... IT IS.
OH? YOU HAVE SOME SORT OF INTUITION INTO WHAT BRAD'S PENIS WANTS?
I DON'T HAVE FIRST-HAND EXPERIENCE WITH IT, BUT... I THINK I KNOW WHAT I'M TALKING ABOUT HERE.
HIS PENIS HAS BEEN IN VIRGINAL BONDAGE FOR YEARS... AND NOW IT'S FINALLY BEEN UNLEASHED.
TRUST ME... BRAD'S PENIS IS A PENIS THAT'S READY TO ROAM... NOT WAIT AROUND FOR ANOTHER PENIS THAT'S 5,000 MILES AWAY.
MAYBE YOU SHOULD LET HIS PENIS SPEAK FOR ITSELF.
GREG FOX © 2003
UH, GUYS... COULD WE STOP TALKIN' ABOUT MY PENIS? IT'S FREAKIN' ME OUT.
IT'S A KEY FACTOR IN THIS ARGUMENT, BRAD.
YEAH... BUT IT HAS FEELINGS, TOO.
PRECISELY THE POINT...

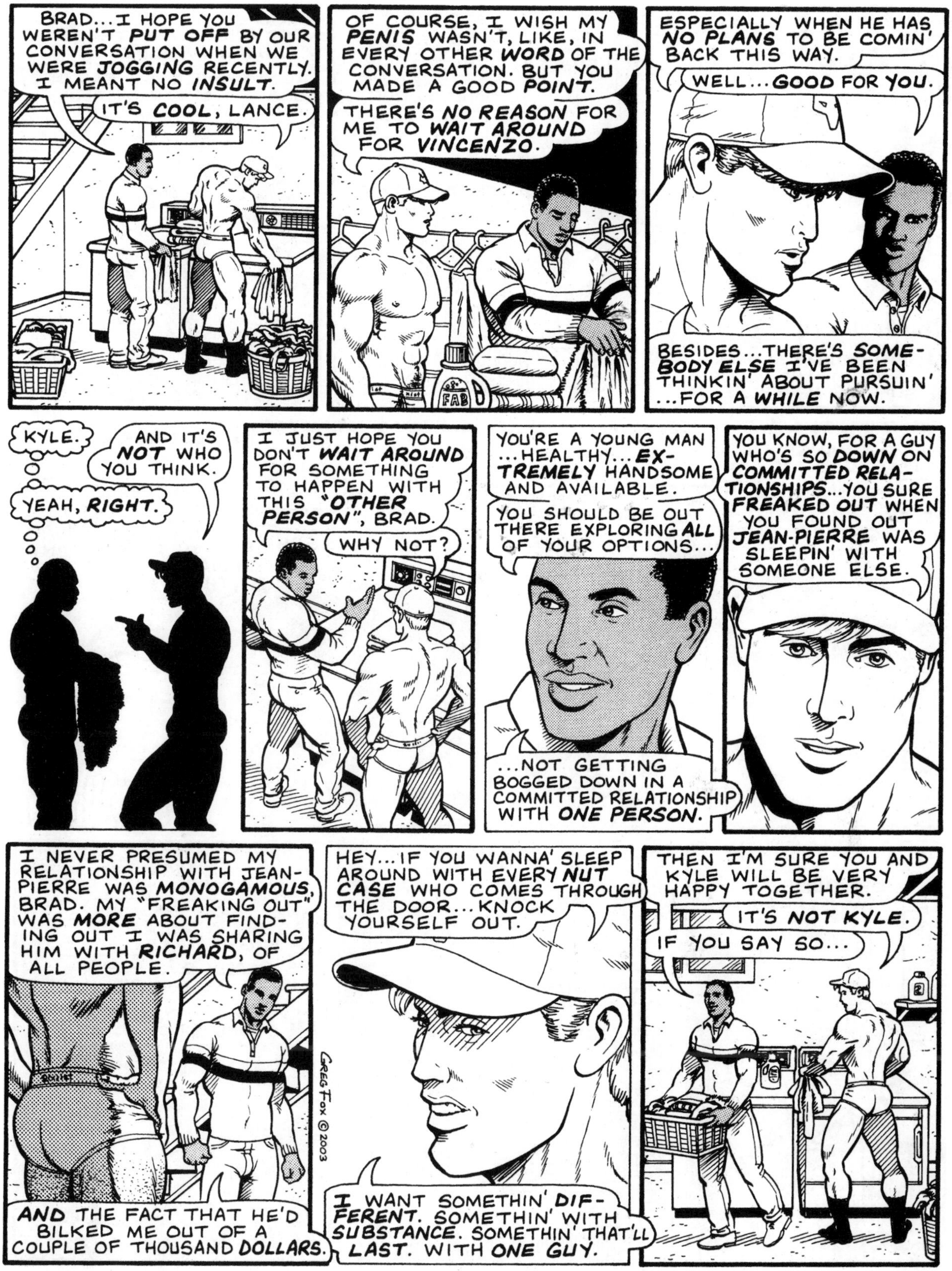
BRAD... I HOPE YOU WEREN'T PUT OFF BY OUR CONVERSATION WHEN WE WERE JOGGING RECENTLY. I MEANT NO INSULT.
IT'S COOL, LANCE.
OF COURSE, I WISH MY PENIS WASN'T, LIKE, IN EVERY OTHER WORD OF THE CONVERSATION. BUT YOU MADE A GOOD POINT.
THERE'S NO REASON FOR ME TO WAIT AROUND FOR VINCENZO.
FAB
ESPECIALLY WHEN HE HAS NO PLANS TO BE COMIN' BACK THIS WAY.
WELL... GOOD FOR YOU.
BESIDES... THERE'S SOMEBODY ELSE I'VE BEEN THINKIN' ABOUT PURSUIN' ...FOR A WHILE NOW.
KYLE.
AND IT'S NOT WHO YOU THINK.
YEAH, RIGHT.
I JUST HOPE YOU DON'T WAIT AROUND FOR SOMETHING TO HAPPEN WITH THIS "OTHER PERSON", BRAD.
WHY NOT?
YOU'RE A YOUNG MAN ...HEALTHY... EXTREMELY HANDSOME AND AVAILABLE.
YOU SHOULD BE OUT THERE EXPLORING ALL OF YOUR OPTIONS...
...NOT GETTING BOGGED DOWN IN A COMMITTED RELATIONSHIP WITH ONE PERSON.
YOU KNOW, FOR A GUY WHO'S SO DOWN ON COMMITTED RELATIONSHIPS...YOU SURE FREAKED OUT WHEN YOU FOUND OUT JEAN-PIERRE WAS SLEEPIN' WITH SOMEONE ELSE.
I NEVER PRESUMED MY RELATIONSHIP WITH JEAN-PIERRE WAS MONOGAMOUS, BRAD. MY "FREAKING OUT" WAS MORE ABOUT FINDING OUT I WAS SHARING HIM WITH RICHARD, OF ALL PEOPLE.
AND THE FACT THAT HE'D BILKED ME OUT OF A COUPLE OF THOUSAND DOLLARS.
GREG FOX © 2003
HEY... IF YOU WANNA' SLEEP AROUND WITH EVERY NUT CASE WHO COMES THROUGH THE DOOR... KNOCK YOURSELF OUT.
I WANT SOMETHIN' DIFFERENT. SOMETHIN' WITH SUBSTANCE. SOMETHIN' THAT'LL LAST. WITH ONE GUY.
THEN I'M SURE YOU AND KYLE WILL BE VERY HAPPY TOGETHER.
IT'S NOT KYLE.
IF YOU SAY SO...

WHA--? WHO ARE YOU *STRANGE MEN* IN MY BEDROOM?!

I'M JERRY!

I'M CLYDE!

I'M BIFF!

AND WE'RE ALL *HETEROSEXUAL!*

YOUR FRIENDS THINK YOU'RE *TOO GAY!*

WHAT?!

THAT'S WHY THEY HIRED *US* TO GIVE YOU OUR...

...STRAIGHT EYE for the QUEER GUY !!!

FIRST OF ALL, YOU NEED TO *GET RID* OF ALL THESE "STYLING PRODUCTS".

ALL YOU NEED IS A BAR OF SOAP, A SPEED STICK, AND A TOOTHBRUSH!

NO! NOT MY *MOISTURIZER!*

DUDE... *ESPECIALLY* THE *MOISTURIZER.*

NOW... ABOUT THIS WEIRD *ORANGE* HAIR COLOR? *WAY TOO GAY.*

HOW ABOUT A NICE *LIGHT BROWN* ?

"LIGHT BROWN"?!!

TESTIMONIAL: From Closeted, "Straight-acting" Housemate

HE'S ALWAYS TELLIN' *ME* WHAT TO WEAR.

BUT *HE* DRESSES LIKE A *FREAK!*

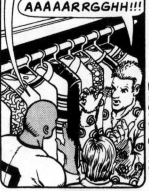

THESE CLOTHES? *WAY TOO GAY.* FROM NOW ON, YOU *ONLY* WEAR CLOTHES FROM THE *SPORTS AUTHORITY.*

AAAAARRGGHH!!!

TESTIMONIAL: From Housemate, Approaching 40

"*APPROACHING 40*"?! THANKS A *LOT.*

AND WHAT'S *WRONG* WITH RICHARD, ANYWAY? I LIKE HIM THE WAY HE *IS.*

WHAT?

YOU DO?

OH, *BLESS* YOU, KYLE!

AND HOW "*STRAIGHT*" ARE THESE GUYS, ANYWAY? HAVEN'T I SEEN YOU AT THE *EAGLE*, BIFF?

UM... I MIGHT'VE STOPPED IN THERE TO USE THE *RESTROOM* ONCE...

YEAH, *SURE*...

HUH ?!!

RICHARD? ARE YOU ALL RIGHT? YOU WERE TALKING IN YOUR SLEEP!

OH MY GOODNESS... IT WAS ALL A *DREAM*... A NIGHTMARE!

IT'S REALLY O.K. FOR ME TO BE GAY ?!!

LIKE ANYBODY COULD *STOP* YOU...

GREG FOX ©2003

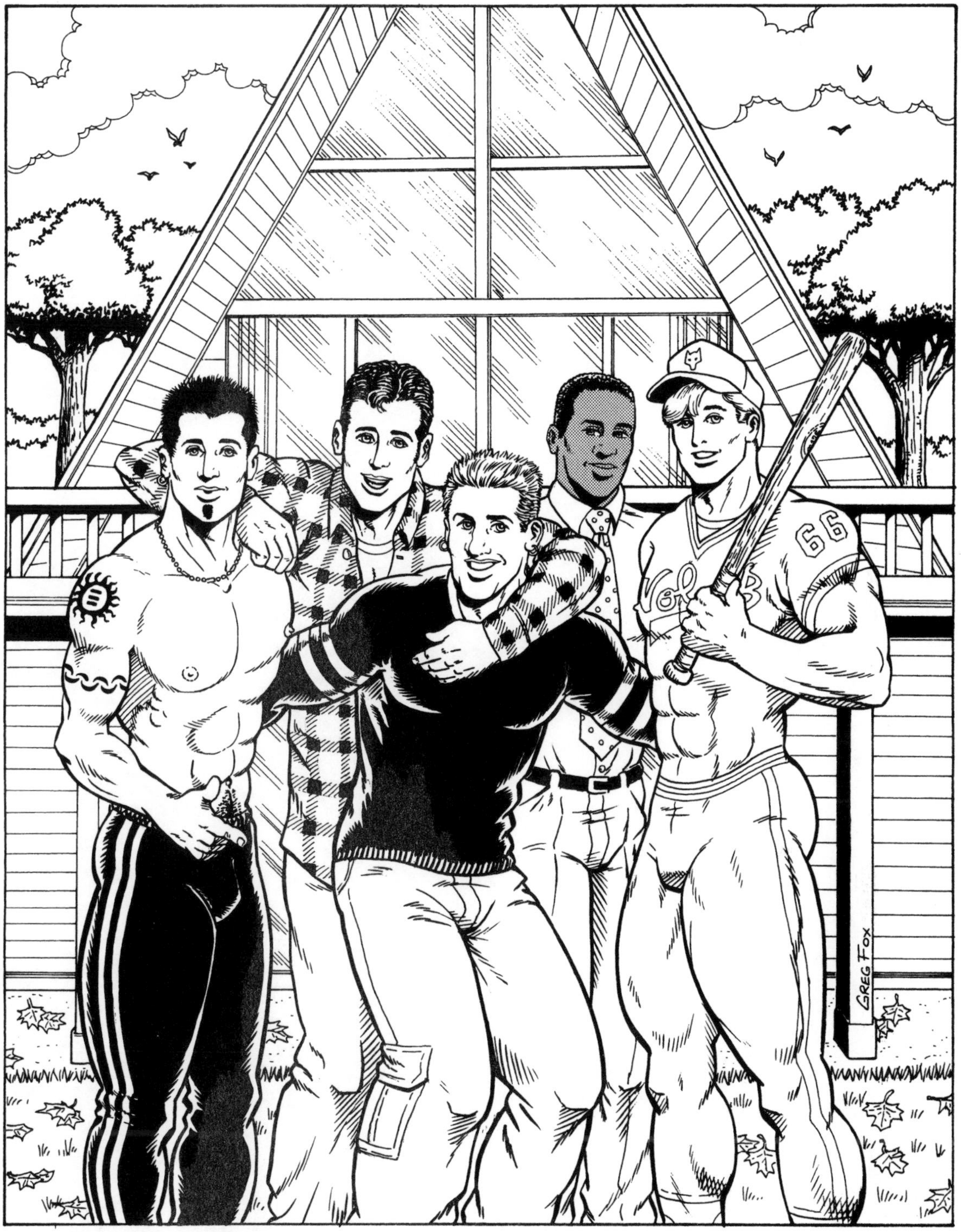
66
GREG FOX

Hold on!!! You thought we were done here? Uh-uh . . . here's a nice little surprise: an exclusive-to-this-book, all-new, never-before-published two-page episode of **Kyle's B&B!** And as if that isn't enough, following that are the never before seen **blueprints** to **Kyle's Bed & Breakfast!** But enough talking . . . let's get right to it, shall we?

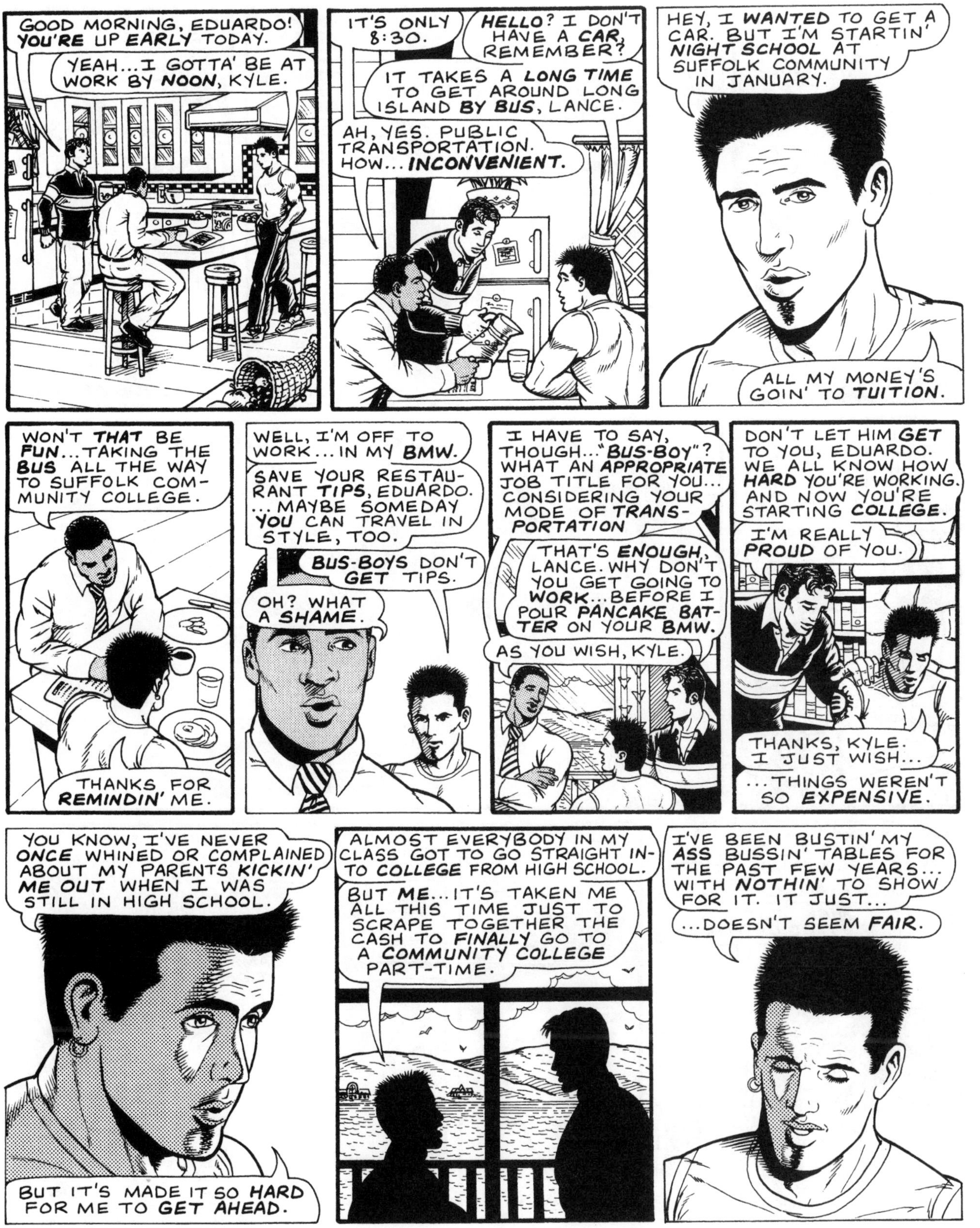
GOOD MORNING, EDUARDO! YOU'RE UP EARLY TODAY.
YEAH... I GOTTA' BE AT WORK BY NOON, KYLE.
IT'S ONLY 8:30.
HELLO? I DON'T HAVE A CAR, REMEMBER?
IT TAKES A LONG TIME TO GET AROUND LONG ISLAND BY BUS, LANCE.
AH, YES. PUBLIC TRANSPORTATION. HOW... INCONVENIENT.
HEY, I WANTED TO GET A CAR. BUT I'M STARTIN' NIGHT SCHOOL AT SUFFOLK COMMUNITY IN JANUARY.
ALL MY MONEY'S GOIN' TO TUITION.
WON'T THAT BE FUN... TAKING THE BUS ALL THE WAY TO SUFFOLK COMMUNITY COLLEGE.
THANKS FOR REMINDIN' ME.
WELL, I'M OFF TO WORK... IN MY BMW.
SAVE YOUR RESTAURANT TIPS, EDUARDO. ... MAYBE SOMEDAY YOU CAN TRAVEL IN STYLE, TOO.
BUS-BOYS DON'T GET TIPS.
OH? WHAT A SHAME.
I HAVE TO SAY, THOUGH... "BUS-BOY"? WHAT AN APPROPRIATE JOB TITLE FOR YOU... CONSIDERING YOUR MODE OF TRANSPORTATION
THAT'S ENOUGH, LANCE. WHY DON'T YOU GET GOING TO WORK... BEFORE I POUR PANCAKE BATTER ON YOUR BMW.
AS YOU WISH, KYLE.
DON'T LET HIM GET TO YOU, EDUARDO. WE ALL KNOW HOW HARD YOU'RE WORKING. AND NOW YOU'RE STARTING COLLEGE.
I'M REALLY PROUD OF YOU.
THANKS, KYLE. I JUST WISH...
...THINGS WEREN'T SO EXPENSIVE.
YOU KNOW, I'VE NEVER ONCE WHINED OR COMPLAINED ABOUT MY PARENTS KICKIN' ME OUT WHEN I WAS STILL IN HIGH SCHOOL.
BUT IT'S MADE IT SO HARD FOR ME TO GET AHEAD.
ALMOST EVERYBODY IN MY CLASS GOT TO GO STRAIGHT INTO COLLEGE FROM HIGH SCHOOL.
BUT ME... IT'S TAKEN ME ALL THIS TIME JUST TO SCRAPE TOGETHER THE CASH TO FINALLY GO TO A COMMUNITY COLLEGE PART-TIME.
I'VE BEEN BUSTIN' MY ASS BUSSIN' TABLES FOR THE PAST FEW YEARS... WITH NOTHIN' TO SHOW FOR IT. IT JUST...
...DOESN'T SEEM FAIR.

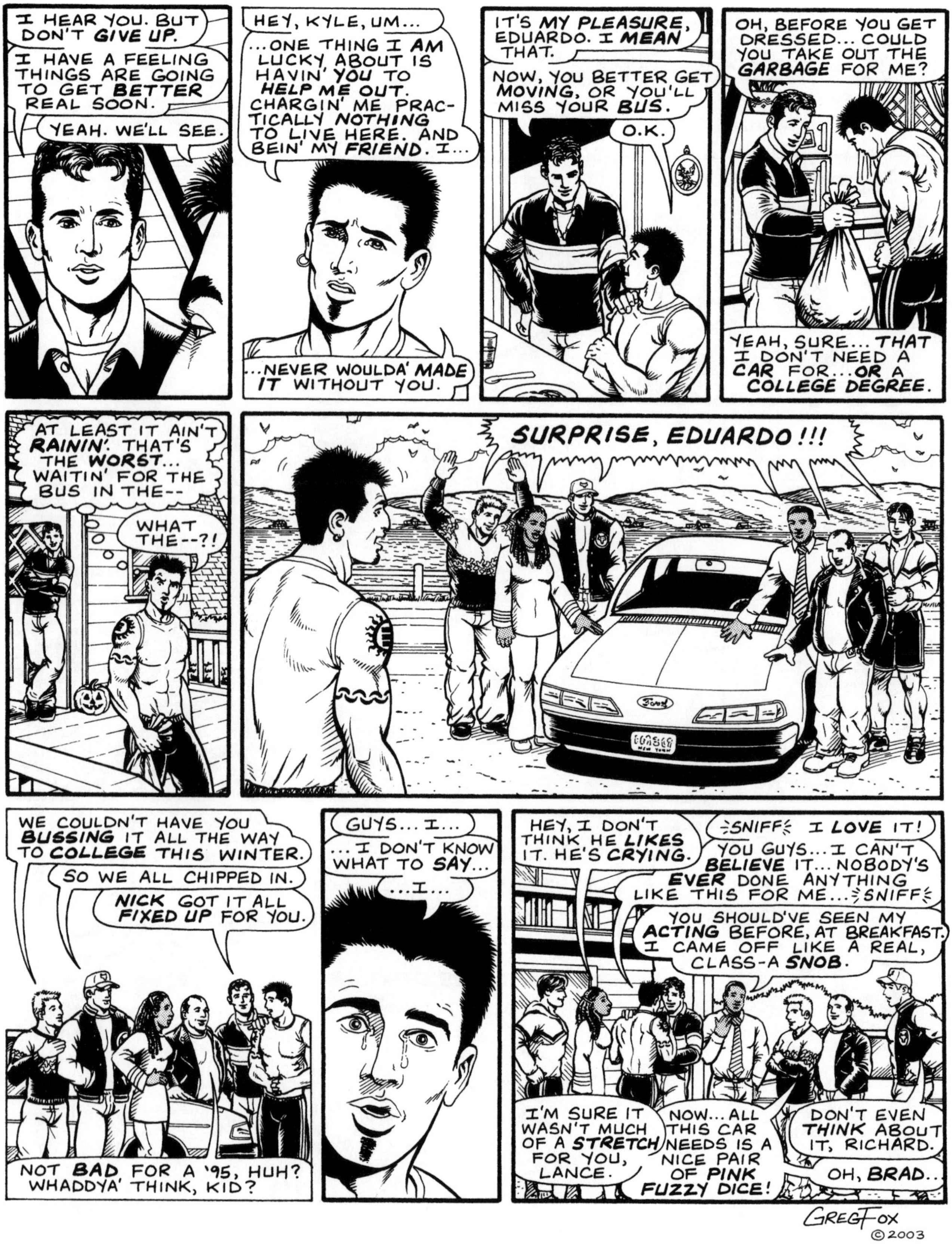
I HEAR YOU. BUT DON'T GIVE UP.
I HAVE A FEELING THINGS ARE GOING TO GET BETTER REAL SOON.
YEAH. WE'LL SEE.
HEY, KYLE, UM...
...ONE THING I AM LUCKY ABOUT IS HAVIN' YOU TO HELP ME OUT. CHARGIN' ME PRACTICALLY NOTHING TO LIVE HERE. AND BEIN' MY FRIEND. I...
...NEVER WOULDA' MADE IT WITHOUT YOU.
IT'S MY PLEASURE, EDUARDO. I MEAN THAT.
NOW, YOU BETTER GET MOVING, OR YOU'LL MISS YOUR BUS.
O.K.
OH, BEFORE YOU GET DRESSED... COULD YOU TAKE OUT THE GARBAGE FOR ME?
YEAH, SURE... THAT I DON'T NEED A CAR FOR... OR A COLLEGE DEGREE.
AT LEAST IT AIN'T RAININ'. THAT'S THE WORST... WAITIN' FOR THE BUS IN THE--
WHAT THE--?!
SURPRISE, EDUARDO!!!
WE COULDN'T HAVE YOU BUSSING IT ALL THE WAY TO COLLEGE THIS WINTER.
SO WE ALL CHIPPED IN.
NICK GOT IT ALL FIXED UP FOR YOU.
NOT BAD FOR A '95, HUH? WHADDYA' THINK, KID?
GUYS... I...
...I DON'T KNOW WHAT TO SAY...
...I...
HEY, I DON'T THINK HE LIKES IT. HE'S CRYING.
SNIFF I LOVE IT!
YOU GUYS... I CAN'T BELIEVE IT... NOBODY'S EVER DONE ANYTHING LIKE THIS FOR ME... SNIFF
YOU SHOULD'VE SEEN MY ACTING BEFORE, AT BREAKFAST. I CAME OFF LIKE A REAL, CLASS-A SNOB.
I'M SURE IT WASN'T MUCH OF A STRETCH FOR YOU, LANCE.
NOW... ALL THIS CAR NEEDS IS A NICE PAIR OF PINK FUZZY DICE!
DON'T EVEN THINK ABOUT IT, RICHARD.
OH, BRAD...
GREG FOX
©2003

Kyle's Bed & Breakfast:
The Blueprints

Yes, here at last are the frequently requested, but never-before-seen, **blueprints** of **Kyle's B&B!** Now, finally, you can see the floor plan of the entire B&B, from basement to roof, and everything in between. Wonder no longer about whose bedroom is next to whose, where that overworked bathroom shower is, and who has the largest closet space.

Join us now as we take a tour through **Kyle's B&B,** floor by floor, and answer all those questions floating around in your head! We'll start where most of the action is, on the main floor . . .

MAIN FLOOR

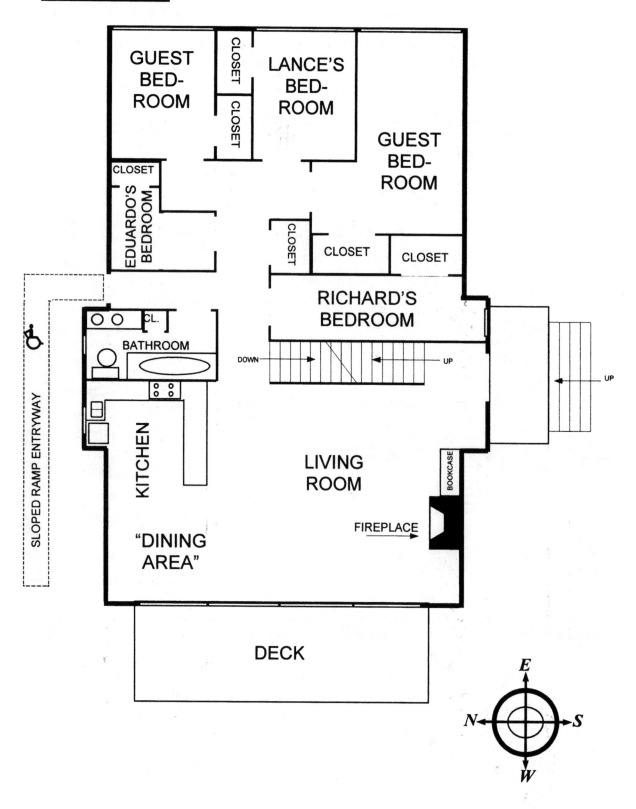

GUEST BED-ROOM

CLOSET

CLOSET

LANCE'S BED-ROOM

GUEST BED-ROOM

CLOSET

EDUARDO'S BEDROOM

CLOSET

CLOSET

CLOSET

RICHARD'S BEDROOM

DOWN

UP

UP

CL.

BATHROOM

SLOPED RAMP ENTRYWAY

KITCHEN

LIVING ROOM

BOOKCASE

"DINING AREA"

FIREPLACE

DECK

E

N — S

W

MAIN FLOOR

This is the floor where most of the activities, (and episodes), occur at **Kyle's B&B.** You can see the main entrance on the south side, leading into the large living room area, featuring an exposed cathedral-like A-frame ceiling to give the room an expansive feeling. The living room area features a loose circle of couches and chairs, and is where the TV is located, (you can often find Brad here monitoring his beloved Yankees games), as well as the fireplace, (often ablaze with a roaring fire during those snowy winter months). The largely glass-covered west wall, (featuring sliding glass doors which lead out onto the deck), face Northport harbor, and the hills of Centerport in the distance, often seen in the backgrounds of many **Kyle's B&B** episodes.

Immediately next to the living room area is the kitchen. Most often, guests at the B&B eat their meals at the "bar" which runs along the perimeter of the kitchen, though sometimes Kyle sets up a table in the dining area, for more formal meals. During warmer months, a table is set up out on the deck, so guests can enjoy their meals in the open air with the gorgeous harbor view.

The hallway running east from the living room leads to various bedrooms. Richard's bedroom, which is the closest of any of the bedrooms to the kitchen and living room, is situated ideally for someone with such a notorious gossip-gathering reputation. Eduardo has the distinction of having the smallest bedroom in the B&B, something he insisted on taking because of his inability, (at first), to afford to pay rent at the B&B. The guest bedroom in the northeast corner of the B&B is a popular room; both Glenn Mercer and Sean O'Grady stayed there during their respective stays. The large guest room in the southeast corner is considered the "deluxe" guestroom, reserved for special occasions. Also known as the "Michelangelo Room," Kyle is in the process of decorating it in Italian Renaissance style, with sculpture and framed prints by the great master. Look for this room to show up in future episodes of the strip! All three of the bedrooms on the east wall, (including Lance's), feature full-length, floor-to-ceiling windows looking out on the densely wooded hills behind the B&B, especially beautiful in the Fall when the maples are glowing all red and yellow and orange.

Down the hallway past the bathroom, on the northern wall, is an alternate entrance to the B&B, featuring a wooden ramp for wheelchair access.

Although this floor is often referred to as the "first floor", there is actually a floor below it. (The basement, which is not entirely a basement, as two of its walls are exposed at ground level. The floor plan for the basement lies a few pages ahead.) Because the B&B is built into the side of a hill, the main entrance to the main floor, on the south side of the B&B, is only a few steps up from ground level. But the gently sloping lawn outside flows downward so that the north and west walls of the B&B become exposed, and the main floor on those sides is actually one full story up above ground level.

SECOND FLOOR

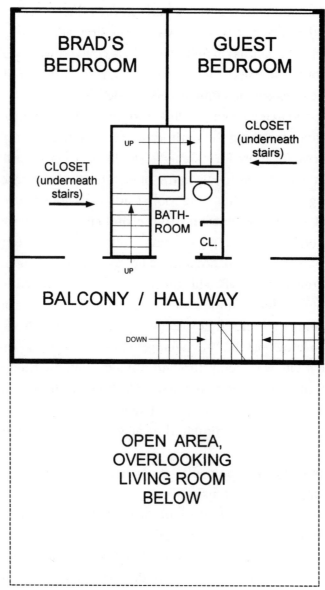

BRAD'S BEDROOM

GUEST BEDROOM

CLOSET (underneath stairs)

UP

CLOSET (underneath stairs)

UP

BATH-ROOM

CL.

BALCONY / HALLWAY

DOWN

OPEN AREA, OVERLOOKING LIVING ROOM BELOW

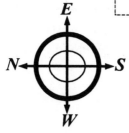

E
N · S
W

SECOND FLOOR

This floor consists of Brad's bedroom, another guest bedroom, and the second bathroom, (which, unlike the main floor bathroom, has *no shower*, much to the dismay of many of the long-term residents). There is also a balcony at the top of the stairs, overlooking the main floor living room and kitchen areas, as well as providing a glorious view out the front windows towards Northport harbor. Because of the sloping-roofed, A-frame structure of the house, the width of the house becomes considerably narrower on this floor, only allowing for the two-bedroom width. Also, because of the exposed cathedral-like A-frame ceiling that rises above the living room/kitchen areas, there is far less square footage of floor space on this level than on the main floor. However, the bedrooms are spacious on this floor and, like the ones facing east on the main floor, feature full-length floor-to-ceiling windows looking out on the densely wooded hills behind the B&B.

A narrow stairway winds upward to the right of Brad's bedroom door, leading to the third floor and directly into Kyle's bedroom.

THIRD FLOOR

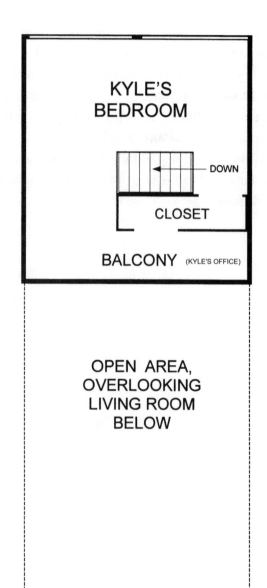

KYLE'S
BEDROOM

DOWN

CLOSET

BALCONY (KYLE'S OFFICE)

OPEN AREA,
OVERLOOKING
LIVING ROOM
BELOW

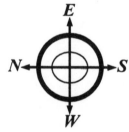

THIRD FLOOR

This floor consists almost entirely of Kyle's loft-style bedroom. The stairway that winds upward from the second floor leads directly into Kyle's bedroom. (There is a door at the bottom of the stairs, to allow for privacy.) Because this is the top floor, the ceiling reaches its peak on this level, allowing only for the relatively small width of the one bedroom. Like the bedrooms with eastern exposure on the floors below, Kyle's bedroom has full-length floor-to-ceiling windows looking out on the densely wooded hills behind the B&B. Directly to the west of Kyle's bedroom is a balcony, much like the one on the second floor, overlooking the main floor living room and kitchen areas, as well as providing that spectacular view out the front windows towards Northport harbor. Also, like the second floor, a large chunk of floor space is missing due to the overlook above the living room and kitchen areas, giving this the smallest square footage of any of the B&B's floors. On the balcony, Kyle has a little office space set up, with a computer, desk and file cabinets, where he keeps the business-side of **Kyle's B&B** in order, (as well as keeping a watchful eye on all the comings-and-goings below).

BASEMENT

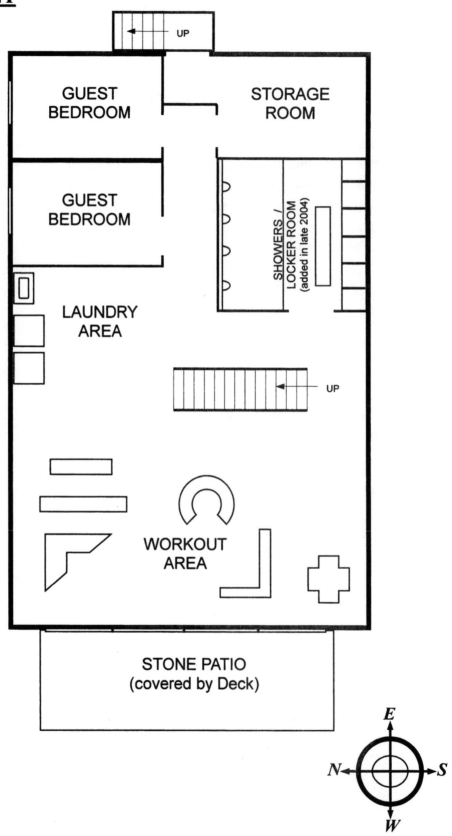

UP

GUEST BEDROOM

STORAGE ROOM

GUEST BEDROOM

SHOWERS / LOCKER ROOM
(added in late 2004)

LAUNDRY AREA

UP

WORKOUT AREA

STONE PATIO
(covered by Deck)

E

N — S

W

BASEMENT

This floor has seen the most change of all the floors in the years since Kyle first opened the B&B. More airy than a typical cellar, the basement is actually above ground on the north and western walls and features sliding glass doors in the front which lead out to a stone patio, (covered overhead by the main floor's deck), from which you can step directly onto the driveway. There are two guest bedrooms on this level, although they get used only when needed, after all other available rooms have been filled. Which isn't to say they aren't nice rooms; being that they face north, they aren't "underground", and both have large, full-size windows. They're also away from the main hubbub of the B&B, which allows for a little more privacy and quiet. However, there's something about being located in the basement, near the laundry area, which somehow makes the rooms a bit less desirable than the other guest bedrooms in the B&B.

That may change, however, with the revamping of the basement scheduled for late 2004/early 2005. The floor plan you are seeing here shows the basement *after* the revamping, which will add a deluxe workout area and a whole locker room shower area, (as was discussed in Episode # 96, when Brad and Richard both pointed out to Kyle how a locker room shower would reduce the stress caused by having only one shower available to the entire B&B). With easy access to the weights and exercise machines, as well as the showers, the basement guest bedrooms might yet become the rooms of choice for future guests at Kyle's B&B! (What fitness club can allow you to work out while you're doing your laundry?)

That concludes our tour of **Kyle's Bed & Breakfast**. . . . but be sure to visit the website, for more info and latest news about Northport's own gay B&B by the harbor at:

www.kylecomics.com

Thanks for stopping by!

ACKNOWLEDGMENTS

"Love is **all**. . . ."

There are so many people to thank, I could probably write an entire chapter of thank yous, and it wouldn't be enough. Let me at least break this down to manageable groups; to everyone listed below, I'd like to say a big **THANK YOU**:

The publishers, editors, and staff of all the publications that run **Kyle's Bed & Breakfast** . . . thank you for taking a chance on a new comic strip that didn't fit conveniently into three or four panels, and for bringing the comic strip to a vast audience, the devotion of whom I could only have dreamed of. I am so very grateful for your support and enthusiasm.

My many mentors within the comic book industry, too many to mention, but you have inspired me beyond words.

John Talbot, for your immediate enthusiasm for **Kyle's Bed & Breakfast** and for taking the ball and running with it, (and scoring!).

John Scognamiglio, for all of your patient efforts on my behalf over the past year, and to everyone at Kensington for your support in this project.

Larry Matheson, my college editor and still one of my biggest supporters.

Steven Rosenblum, for his wonderful photos on a very cold October day!

Book Revue bookstore in Huntington, New York. The coolest bookstore in the world, due to the amazing staff and owners. My second home.

My friends over the years who have always encouraged and supported my work . . . from Geneseo, from Spize, from Sam Ash, from the comics world, from Book Revue, from the Long Island gay community. . . . from everywhere.

Howard Cruse, for being so wonderfully helpful and friendly to me through the years, as well as being, like, the comics **icon** that he is. You inspire us all!

Ivan Velez, Jr., for showing up at just the right time and quietly letting me know I was on the right path. Now, finish that tenth chapter of **Tales of the Closet,** *please*!!!

Prism Comics and the **GLA,** for all of your hardworking efforts to honor and promote GLBT contributions to the comics industry.

Arlette and Nick, for all of your technical assistance over the years.

Marianne Williamson, for being a warm voice in the night and a glorious teacher.

The readers of **Kyle's Bed & Breakfast**, for your steadfast devotion and for constantly making me smile and making this a magnificent, mystical, glowing experience for me!

My family, for all of your love and support, and for always being there for me.

St. Jude

Jesus Christ

And, of course, God!